THE BIRTH OF PHILOSOPHIC CHRISTIANITY

ERNEST FORTIN: COLLECTED ESSAYS
Edited by J. Brian Benestad

Volume 1
The Birth of Philosophic Christianity: Studies
in Early Christian and Medieval Thought

Foreword by Ernest L. Fortin

Volume 2
Classical Christianity and the Political Order:
Reflections on the Theologico-Political Problem

Foreword by Dan Mahoney

Volume 3
Human Rights, Virtue, and the Common Good:
Untimely Meditations on Religion and Politics

Foreword by J. Brian Benestad

THE BIRTH OF PHILOSOPHIC CHRISTIANITY

Studies in Early Christian and Medieval Thought

ERNEST L. FORTIN

Edited by
J. Brian Benestad

ROWMAN & LITTLEFIELD PUBLISHERS, INC.
Lanham • Boulder • New York • London

ROWMAN & LITTLEFIELD PUBLISHERS, INC.

Published in the United States of America
by Rowman & Littlefield Publishers, Inc.
4720 Boston Way, Lanham, Maryland 20706

3 Henrietta Street
London WC2E 8LU, England

Copyright © 1996 by Rowman & Littlefield Publishers, Inc.

British Cataloging in Publication Information Available

Library of Congress Cataloging-in-Publication Data

Fortin, Ernest L.
The birth of philosophic Christianity : studies in early Christian and
medieval thought / Ernest L. Fortin ; edited by J. Brian Benestad.
p.   cm. — (Ernest Fortin, collected essays ; v. 1)
Includes bibliographical references and index.
1. Philosophy and religion—History of doctrines—Early church,
ca. 30–600. 2. Theology—History—Early church, ca. 30–600.
3. Philosophy and religion—History of doctrines—Middle Ages,
600–1500. 4. Theology—History—Middle Ages, 600–1500.
5. Christianity—Philosophy. I. Benestad, J. Brian. II. Title.
III. Series: Fortin, Ernest L. Essays ; v. 1.
BR100.F6714   1996   261.5'1'09015—dc20   96–19847   CIP

ISBN 0–8476–8274–9 (cloth : alk. paper)
ISBN 0–8476–8275–7 (pbk. : alk. paper)

Printed in the United States of America

⊖™ The paper used in this publication meets the minimum requirements of
American National Standard for Information Sciences—Permanence of
Paper for Printed Library Materials, ANSI Z39.48–1984.

CONTENTS

Contents

III. THE MEDIEVAL ROOTS of CHRISTIAN EDUCATION

IV. DANTE and the POLITICS of CHRISTENDOM

V. SELECTED REVIEWS

Contents

FOREWORD

Although originally written over a period of more than three decades, the essays in this volume and its companion volumes, *Classical Christianity and the Political Order* and *Human Rights, Social Justice, and the Common Good*, are informed by similar principles and guided by the same general concerns. All of them were born of a desire to know more about the world in which we live, the philosophic, religious, and political forces that shaped it, and the type of human being it tends to produce. As such, they are more preoccupied with achieving a measure of clarity about the ends of human existence than with offering made-to-order solutions to the problems to which the pursuit of those ends gives rise. Their goal is that of any genuinely liberal education, namely, self-knowledge, here taken to mean knowledge that does not lose sight of its native human context and seeks to overcome the knower's enslavement to the prejudices of the historical cave to which he happens to belong. St. Augustine and the intellectual tradition to which he was heir were convinced that anybody who wishes to learn has to start by "unlearning"—*dediscere*. Socrates spoke in the same vein of the awareness of one's ignorance— "wonder"—as the beginning of wisdom. True freedom of mind is not the precondition of this kind of endeavor, but its fruit. Even the essays devoted specifically to ancient and medieval thought, remote as they may appear to be from the items that dominate the intellectual agenda of our day, serve the same overall purpose.

Self-knowledge thus understood is arrived at, not by autistically or solipsistically peering into oneself, but by listening attentively to what thoughtful people of different times and places had to say about the good life—ultimately, the best life—a topic that has become all but taboo in polite academic company because of its alleged "elitist" connotations. To paraphrase a familiar saying, he knows not his time who only his time knows.

Citizens of modern liberal regimes, as most Westerners are nowadays, have a special motive for inquiring into their past. Since the modern world emerged by way of a profound transformation of the premodern world, and since the significance of that transformation cannot be properly assessed without some grasp of the original form, an effort to understand the premodern world appears to be in order. For this, a good deal of historical investigation is now required. Our medieval forebears could dispense with this type of investigation because their modes of thought stood in unbroken continuity with those of the ancients. No new tradition, such as the one that arose from a philosophic project in the course of the sixteenth and seventeenth centuries, had yet managed to interpose itself between them and their classical mentors. Averroes and Thomas Aquinas approached Aristotle as if he were a contemporary, as indeed in a crucial respect he was. Neither one experienced anything like the bewilderment or sense of alienation that overwhelms us when, without any preparation, we moderns turn to the works of classical or Christian antiquity. Multiple layers of sedimentation have to be peeled off one by one before a dialogue with these philosophers can begin in earnest. This is why any serious study of the past inevitably ends up taking the form of an archaeological expedition inspired, not by an atavistic attachment to the old for its own sake or a romantic longing for a return to it, but by the desire to gain a fresh insight into our own problems.

Two formidable intellectual obstacles stand in the way of a dialectical retrieval of premodern thought. One is the "idea of progress," with which we are still imbued despite its having been repeatedly challenged by some of the best minds and belied by some of the most painful events of our century. According to the Hegelian version of that idea, the development of human thought leads from lower to ever higher stages until the perfection of knowledge is attained. As latecomers in this process, we instinctively think of ourselves as wiser than our predecessors and hence as being in a position to understand them *better* than they understood themselves. Anything of lasting worth in their writings has been "assimilated" and survives as part of our own, presumably larger, synthesis. We can learn *about* them if we so desire, but we have nothing of importance to learn *from* them. Needless to say, anyone sharing this view will not be motivated to devote to the works of the past the time and energy needed to penetrate to the core of their teaching. The modern-day Christopher Columbus who sets out on what was once a perilous but exhilarating journey knows ahead of time that he will never discover anything but

Genoa.

The second major impediment to a fruitful engagement with pre-modern thought is the currently fashionable theory variously designated by such names as radical historicism, hermeneutical consciousness, or postmodernism, which traces its origin to Nietzsche and Heidegger and stipulates that the whole of human thought is essentially a function of its time, that human beings are "historical" through and through. Nothing is true or false in itself but only by reason of its being "held" so by the people of a given period. There are no permanent problems of any kind in the universe, and hence no transcendent or eternally valid principles of thought and action by means of which they could be elucidated. All our principles are rooted in certain "absolute presuppositions" (R. G. Colling-wood), in the light of which we understand everything else, but which are not themselves in the light. These presuppositions are the products of a mysterious historical dispensation with which they vary from one age to the next. What our predecessors took for objective and unchanging truths are nothing but social constructs or unconscious expressions of each period's secret interests or desires. Human beings do not have a "glassy nature," as Shakespeare called it. Their minds do not reflect the world around them—they create it. Stated in more traditional terms, the intellect is in the service of the will and is totally conditioned by it. Books invariably tell us more about their authors than about the world they purport to describe, and interpreters more about themselves than about the works they claim to interpret. This would explain the amazing variety of conflicting accounts that competent critics have offered, and continue to offer, of the classics of our tradition. One cannot understand the authors of the past better than they understood themselves; one can only understand them *differently*. From these authors we learn nothing that might be relevant to our own situation, save perhaps by accident. But that assumption too, like the preceding one, leaves us with little incentive to read older books with the utmost care, this time not because their intellectual content is already part of our substance, but because it can never become part of it.

This is not the place to enter into a lengthy discussion of the problems inherent in both of these positions. I, for one, have yet to be convinced that the subtle arguments adduced in support of them are entirely free of internal contradiction. The "experience of history" to which appeal is usually made in this connection shows only that the authors of the past have been interpreted differently by different people in different ages. It does not exclude the possibility that one or the other of these interpretations, or perhaps some as yet unknown interpretation, might be in substantial agreement with what the author himself had in mind. Whether it is or not is unfortunately not something of which we can have any direct knowledge, for one cannot make a judgment of this sort without comparing in one's own mind the author's understanding and that of his interpreter, and thus without presupposing that the author's understanding is at once both known and unknown. For this and similar reasons, I have found it safer to abide by the old rule of thumb according to which the historian's first duty is to understand the authors of the past *as* they understood themselves, that is to say, on their own terms and within their own frame of reference. Only once it has become reasonably clear that this frame of reference is inadequate can one profitably criticize them on the basis of premises that are foreign to their thought. Otherwise one runs the risk of substituting one's folly for their wisdom.

It might be added that the interpreter who adopts this maxim does not thereby condemn himself merely to repeating, slavishly and verbatim, what the author has already said. His job is to render his predecessor's thought intelligible to a new generation of readers and hence to restate it against a background of theories and opinions different from the ones that could be assumed on the part of the original readers. This often obliges him to raise questions that the author himself did not raise explicitly, but would undoubtedly have raised, had he been cognizant of them. All of this he can do without going beyond the parameters of the author's thought. One does not part company with an author by introducing necessary changes that do not betray his intention or contradict his fundamental premises.

A number of interlocking themes, all of them controversial, form the warp and woof of these collected essays and demand a few words of explanation at this point, if only to forestall possible misunderstandings. The first is the unique encounter between revealed religion and philosophy or perfected reason—"Jerusalem and Athens," for short—and the fruitful tension that marked their relationship, particularly during the early Christian centuries and the Middle Ages. In broadest terms, the problem has to do with the rank order of faith and reason considered not as parallel sets of doctrines, where an accommodation of sorts can often be reached, but as the grounds of two irreducibly different and mutually exclusive ways of life, one characterized by devout submission to the revealed word of God, and the other by a suspension of judgment in regard to any statement whose certitude is not vouched for by autonomous reason. By definition, the highest truths of divine revelation exceed the capacity of human reason and are destined to remain shrouded in mystery; and philosophy itself, lacking the ability to provide an adequate account of the universe or the whole in terms of its intrinsic causes, cannot reject apodictically the possibility of a miraculous intervention on God's part in the affairs of this world. Neither side being in a position to substantiate its claim to truth or refute that of its rival, the choice between them will always be based at least in part on extratheoretical considerations.

It is true that, almost from the start, Christianity showed itself more hospitable to philosophy than either Judaism or Islam, the two other great monotheistic religions of the West. As primarily a "faith" or a "life-giving doctrine"—*sana doctrina* (1 Tim. 1:10), rather than a "law" (*Torah*), Christianity was more or less forced to turn to philosophy for the dialectical tools and weapons it needed to formulate its teachings, refute heretics within its own ranks, and respond in kind to the philosophical attacks mounted against it by its pagan adversaries. In the process, theology, the "science" of God, acquired a formal precision that it had not previously known, and Christianity evolved into a learned religion. Yet the arrangement did not serve both partners equally well. It stripped philosophy of its pre-eminent status as an activity devoted to the unhindered pursuit of the truth and used it for purposes originally alien to it. In the eyes of many, the noblest accomplishment of human reason would henceforth be to show that the arguments adduced against the Faith on philosophic grounds are never such as to compel the assent of the unaided human reason. Not only is reason by itself unable prove the truth of divine revelation; it cannot even prove its possibility, for to do so would be to destroy its strictly supernatural character and rob the act of faith of its merit. At most, reason can show that neither the rationality nor the irrationality of divine revelation can be demonstrated by means of an argument whose premises do not presuppose the truth of the conclusion at which it claims to arrive.

Thomas Aquinas, who perhaps went as far as one can go in safeguarding the prerogatives of both Faith and reason, notes that on its own the human mind can produce no more than plausible arguments—"reasons of convenience"—to shed a modicum of light on the mysteries that the believer seeks to contemplate. Theology and philosophy live as it were on separate planets. They differ from each other not just in species but in "kind" (*genus*), that is to say, in the most radical way possible. The truths of theology are at the same time speculative and practical, something that cannot be said of any purely human science. The knowledge of these truths represents the good, not of the mind alone, but of the whole person. One cannot grasp them as "truths" unless one undergoes a root-and-branch change or a genuine "conversion." Differently stated, some things cannot be known without being willed (although they may exist without being willed). As applied to theology and philosophy, "science" is strictly an analogous term. No two disciplines could be less alike. That there should be an abiding tension between them is therefore not surprising. But neither is it something to be simply lamented; for, as has often been suggested, it may be in great part responsible for the extraordinary vitality that Western civilization has demonstrated over the centuries.

A second common feature of these essays is the prominence (and in some sense, the primacy) accorded to political philosophy, the master science that coordinates all of the city's important activities and orders them to their proper ends. Human beings are happy when they are well governed, and they are well governed when their rulers are both aware of the true ends of human existence and able to promote them within the societies for which they are responsible. To the extent that the practical order is rooted in the speculative order, rulers are ultimately dependent on natural science and metaphysics for the knowledge of those ends. Yet there is a point at which this natural order is reversed and philosophers themselves come under the de facto control of the city. Rulers qua rulers have nothing to say about the conclusions to be arrived at by the philosopher, but they have a lot to say about his role in the city, which is his natural habitat and the only place where he is likely to thrive; for there are no philosophers in the wilderness, or in the land of the lotus-eaters. Rulers can encourage philosophers and open their borders to them; but they can also restrict their activities, silence them, jail them, ostracize them, or, as sometimes happens, put them to death. In truth, the philosopher's position in society has never been altogether secure. Toward the beginning of Aristophanes's *Clouds*, Socrates is shown dangling precariously in a basket, at the total mercy of the poet, on whom he depends for his defense.

Political philosophy is that part of the philosophical enterprise in which philosophy comes to its own defense and, instead of taking itself for granted, makes a concerted effort to justify itself before the tribunal of the city. By situating itself within the context of human life as a whole, it discloses the full range of human possibilities and thus reveals human beings to themselves as no other science is capable of doing. In it, philosophy, politics, and theology come together to thresh out all of the fundamental problems of human life.

In spite of its centrality, or perhaps because of it, political philosophy has traditionally been the most neglected of the philosophical disciplines. Maimonides observes that in the religious community the study of the Torah, or the divine law, replaces political philosophy as the highest discipline. This is especially true of Judaism and Islam, both of which present themselves as political religions or divinely revealed laws; but it is also true to a large extent of the Christian tradition, where politics never achieved the same high standing as speculative theology or even natural philosophy. It is no accident that the *Politics* was the last of Aristotle's major treatises to be translated into Latin and the only one on which no commentary was written until after the middle of the thirteenth century. Even then, relatively little was done with it, save for the purpose of resolving the disputes that had arisen between the spiritual and the temporal powers. Those who seem to have derived the greatest benefit from the *Politics* are the anticlerical writers of the fourteenth and fifteenth centuries. With a few notable exceptions, even the prominent Neo-Thomists of the late nineteenth and early twentieth centuries failed to distinguish themselves by their work in this domain.

The spectacular rebirth that political philosophy has undergone in the last fifty years or so is a hopeful sign that the situation has at last begun to be redressed; but there is no guarantee that the trend will continue and will contribute to the revitalization of the other humanistic disciplines, as to a limited extent it already has. In a majority of our colleges and universities, political philosophy is either not taught at all or taught under some misleading rubric, such as "applied ethics."

Closely associated with political philosophy—and more offensive to reigning academic taste—is the notorious issue of esoteric writing or "noble lies," which played a crucial role in the Western tradition until roughly the end of the eighteenth century. Augustine called it the "art and method of concealing the truth"—*ars et ratio occultandi veri*—and, while cautioning against its abuses, credited it with having kept philosophy alive at a time when its very existence was threatened in the pagan world. To modern scholars, the method in question smacks of Averroism and is often identified with the "double-truth" theory imputed to the authors of the 219 Propositions condemned by the bishop of Paris, Etienne Tempier, in 1277. This is the theory which states that the same proposition can simultaneously be true in philosophy but false in theology, and vice versa. I know of no serious writer, Averroist or otherwise, who ever subscribed to this kind of nonsense.

True esotericism, if one insists on keeping that term, is something less ominous and more rational. It was an ingenious means of fulfilling one's social responsibilities toward everyone, those capable of benefitting from a more advanced education as well as those who would only be confused and possibly hurt by it. In essence, it consists in observing a prudent reserve in the public expression of truths that could easily be misunderstood and thus prove harmful to the speaker, the listener, or the truth itself if they should fall on the wrong ears. How this could be done was left in large part to the resourcefulness of each individual and varied greatly from one writer to another. Among the common literary devices were such things as elliptical speech, deliberate omissions, incomplete enumerations, distorted or truncated quotations, unexplained lapses of memory, double-entendres, and telltale contradictions in the text. By means of these stylistic anomalies one was alerted to the presence in the text of a more subtle teaching that could be uncovered and appreciated only by thinking through the author's explicit statements and repeating within oneself the genesis of his ideas. At the beginning of the *Stromata,* Clement of Alexandria speaks of this hidden teaching as an *engraphôs agraphon,* an oral teaching "inscribed *in* the text," and thus discoverable by competent and diligent readers. Origen spoke in the same sense of "listening with the third ear," just as we today speak of reading between the lines.

The source of this peculiar form of writing and the rationale behind it is to be sought, not, as is often said, in the hermetic, gnostic, or mystical divagations of late antiquity, but in such Platonic texts as the *Republic*, the *Seventh Letter*, and especially the *Phaedrus*, where it is presented as a means of preserving in the medium of the written word the advantages of oral communication, deemed superior on the ground that it allows the speaker to adapt himself more perfectly to the intellectual needs of his hearers. The method served not just one but several laudable purposes. It helped to maintain the private character of philosophy and shielded the philosopher from the reprisals of a society whose preexisting standards he could be accused of violating. It served as a reminder that anyone in search of the truth has to make a personal effort to arrive at a proper understanding of it. It was likewise an effective means of staving off the passivity to which students are often prone and of preventing an almost inevitable shift on their part from an interest in the questions debated to an interest in the answers already provided by others.

Since the beginning of the nineteenth century, it has been practically impossible to make a case for the use of such a method. In the introduction to his German translation of the Platonic dialogues, Schleiermacher tried to demonstrate its impossibility by means of a subtle argument that many of his readers found persuasive. John Henry Newman, who referred to it by its old name, the "economy of truth," rediscovered it while writing his book on the *Arians of the Fourth Century*, but seems to have succeeded mainly in arousing the indignation of his former co-religionists, against whom he defends himself vigorously in his *Apologia pro Vita Sua*. Added to the mix was the liberal demand for ever greater freedom of speech in the name of sincerity, intellectual probity, authenticity, progress, or truth itself. In retrospect, however, one wonders how much has been accomplished by this enormous change in perspective, particularly when one considers the frequency with which the present-day rhetoric of freedom of speech goes hand in hand with such powerful social forces as intellectual conformism, the tyranny of the majority, political correctness, and an increasingly vigilant thought police. Our predecessors preferred self-censorship, which they thought more compatible with human dignity and more beneficial to society.

The fourth recurrent theme concerns the distinction between Ancients and Moderns and its significance for the development of Western thought down to our time. Implied in that distinction is the break with the combined classical and Christian tradition that was inaugurated by Machiavelli in the sixteenth century and consummated by Machiavelli's (often unavowed) followers, beginning with Francis Bacon, Hobbes, and Descartes, in the course of the century that followed. The debate that ensued, the so-called "Quarrel of the Ancients and the Moderns," immortalized by Jonathan Swift in *Gulliver's Travels* and the *Battle of the Books,* has been going on with varying degrees of intensity ever since. The battle involved much more than the somewhat narrow, though by no means insignificant, issue over which it erupted, namely, the relative merits of classical Greek and seventeenth-century French tragedy. It was a battle about first principles: the first principles of classical philosophy or science versus those of an ascendant modern philosophy or science. Premodern morality was denounced for its impracticality—it supposedly made impossibly high demands on people—and an attempt was made to replace it with a more realistic approach to moral matters, one that was based on the low but solid foundation of utility or self-interest.

The controversy took a new turn toward the middle of the eighteenth century with Rousseau's blistering attack on the Enlightenment in his *Discourse on the Arts and Sciences,* and his "modern" defense of classical or premodern virtue, as opposed to the utilitarian or mercenary virtue promoted by early modern liberalism. Since then, the tendency has been to downplay the significance of the rift between the two camps by attributing it to a simple lack of perspective on both sides and to stress the continuity rather than the discontinuity between them. To do this, one could appeal to the Hegelian and romantic notion that the modern world is nothing but a secularized version of medieval Christianity. Instead of being dismissed as a time of unrelieved obscurantism, the Middle Ages began to be seen as the fountainhead of all that is valuable in the modern age, of modern science no less than of modern freedom. "We are indebted to them for everything," as Chateaubriand proudly announced in the *Genius of Christianity,* the most widely read religious book of the nineteenth century.

The flaw in that argument was pointed out by Nietzsche, who saw with blinding clarity that such a compromise was doomed to failure—that classical speculative philosophy and classical morality were inextricably bound up with each other. Getting rid of the one while keeping the other was like firing the architect and keeping the building, or doing away with the lawgiver while claiming the protection of the law. The West was in trouble, not because it was being threatened from without by hordes of invading barbarians, as it had been in the fifth century, but because it no longer believed in the justice of its principles. These principles were manifestly deprived of any independent support. They were mere constructs, grounded in nothing but free acts of the individual will. A crisis of major proportions was impending, one that involved the future not just of our civilization but of civilization *tout court.* It was, Nietzsche said, a "total" crisis, signalling the demise of the very principles that made civilization possible, the cataclysmic collapse of all horizons of meaning and value.

The name used by Nietzsche to designate this catastrophe is "nihilism," an older term that had now acquired a new and more pregnant meaning. Heidegger referred ominously to the same phenomenon as the "night of the world" and, following Nietzsche's lead, traced its origin to the particular understanding of reason that prevailed in classical Greek philosophy. This prompted him to study Aristotle with a meticulous care the like of which had not been seen since the heyday of Scholasticism. His purpose was to "uproot" the tradition of theoretical reason for which Aristotle stood and which he blamed for the predicament in which the West found itself. The result was a view of Aristotle that was not mediated by a long tradition of scholastic commentary and free of the limitations of that tradition. An alternative had been discovered to the interpretations that had hitherto long dominated the field of Aristotelian scholarship.

As it turned out, some of Heidegger's students were more impressed by Aristotle himself than by Heidegger's critique of him. There developed a renewed interest in and greater appreciation for classical thought as a whole. Whereas fifty years ago, the liveliest philosophical debates were between schools of modern thought—Kantians, Hegelians, and Utilitarians—or, more recently, between liberals and communitarians, today they are just as likely to be between Ancients and Moderns. At its best, the new debate is not a mere reprise of the old eighteenth-century dispute, or between Knockers and Boosters of modernity, to borrow Charles Taylor's terminology. A more discriminating approach to the problem at hand has emerged, along with a greater willingness on the part of a growing number of our contemporaries to face squarely the basic and still unresolved issues with which that problem confronts us.

Ernest L. Fortin, A.A.
Boston College
August 15, 1996

ACKNOWLEDGMENTS

The author and editor wish to take this opportunity to thank all those who had a direct hand in the launching and the realization of this project, among them: Stephen F. Brown, Matthew Lamb, and Patrick J. C. Powers. Daniel J. Mahoney found the right publisher and graciously contributed the Foreword to the second volume. The idea of publishing the three volumes simultaneously and as a set belongs to Jonathan Sisk, the editor-in-chief of Rowman and Littlefield, without whose encouragement and active support the project would probably never have seen the light of day.

Invaluable assistance was provided by the editorial staff of Rowman and Littlefield and, in particular, by Julie Kirsch and Dorothy Bradley, whose expertise and endless patience won both our gratitude and our admiration. We are also grateful to Phillip Wodzinski, a doctoral student in political science at Boston College, whose research talents and proof-reading skills, hitherto unknown to the world, revealed themselves to superb advantage on this occasion. Ann King, the retired secretary of the Department of Theology and Religious Studies at the University of Scranton, toiled endlessly and in a completely selfless way on virtually every page of the manuscript, at the risk of being driven out of her mind by its innumerable references to works in at least six different foreign languages, including Greek and Latin. Her dedication was paralleled by that of Shirley Gee, the omnicompetent administrative assistant of the Institute of Medieval Philosophy and Theology at Boston College. Further secretarial help was provided by Marie Gaughan, Patricia Macedon, and Barbara Quinn, of the University of Scranton. The staff of the Thomas O'Neill Library, Boston College was always there to help whenever necessary and also deserves special mention. The author is immensely grateful for generous financial help in the form of research fellowships received from the John M. Olin Foundation, the Lynde and Harry Bradley Foundation, the National Endowment for the Humanities, and the Boston College Graduate School.

None of the articles in these three volumes could have been written without constant input from the author's colleagues and daily conversation partners in the departments of Theology, Political Science, and Philosophy at Boston College, along with friends and long-time associates in other colleges and universities here and abroad. They shall not be listed individually for fear that too many names should inadvertently be left out. If they are ever tempted to peruse these books, they will have no trouble identifying their respective contributions.

The editor is especially indebted to his colleagues at the University of Scranton, Father Richard Rousseau, S.J., and Dr. Edward Matthews, as well as to Betsy Moylan, a librarian at the University, for their expert assistance. He thanks his wife, Janet Benestad, and their daughter Katherine, for help with various aspects of the project. He also expresses his appreciation to the University of Scranton for grants to support the writing of his foreword and the typing of numerous articles, and to Dr. Thomas Hogan and Dr. Richard Passon for their support of the whole endeavor.

Chapter 1. "Augustine and the Hermeneutics of Love" is reprinted from *Augustine Today*, Encounter Series, no. 16, ed. R. J. Neuhaus, Grand Rapids: 1993. By permission of William B. Eerdmans Publishing Co.

Chapter 2. "Augustine and the Problem of Human Goodness" is reprinted from the *University of Dayton Review* 22, no. 3 (1994): 177-92. By permission of the *University of Dayton Review*.

Chapter 3. "Augustine's *De quantitate animae* or the Spiritual Dimensions of Human Existence" is reprinted from *Lectio Augustini*: *Settimana Agostiniana Pavese VII*: (Palermo: Edizioni "Augustinus," 1991) 131-69. By permission of Edizioni "Augustinus."

Chapter 4. "The Patristic Sense of Community" is reprinted from *Augustinian Studies* 4 (1973): 179-97. By permission of *Augustinian Studies*.

Chapter 5. "Augustine and the Problem of Christian Rhetoric" is reprinted from *Augustinian Studies* 5 (1974): 85-100. By permission of *Augustinian Studies*.

Chapter 6. "Reflections on the Proper Way to Read Augustine the Theologian" is reprinted from *Augustinian Studies* 2 (1971): 253-72. By permission of *Augustinian Studies*.

Chapter 7. "A Note on Dawson and St. Augustine" is reprinted from *The Dawson Newsletter* IV/4 (1985-86): 12-14. By permission of *The Dawson Newsletter*.

Chapter 8. "Clement of Alexandria and the Esoteric Tradition" is reprinted from *Studia Patristica* 9 (Berlin: Akadamie Verlag, 1966), 41-56. By permission of Peeters Publishers.

Chapter 9. "Christianity and Hellenism in Basil the Great's Address *Ad adulescentes*" is reprinted from *Neoplatonism and Early Christian Thought: Essays in Honour of A. H. Armstrong*, ed. H. J. Blumenthal & R. A. Markus (London: Variorum Publications, 1981), 189-203. By permission of Variorum Publications.

Chapter 10. "Basil the Great and the Choice of Hercules: A Note on the Christianization of a Pagan Myth" is reprinted from *Graduate Faculty Philosophy Journal*, New School For Social Research, XI, 2 (1986): 65-81. By permission of *Graduate Faculty Philosophy Journal*.

Chapter 11. "The *Viri novi* of Arnobius and the Conflict Between Faith and Reason in the Early Christian Centuries" is reprinted from *The Heritage of the Early Church: Biblical and Patristic Studies in Honor of George F. Florovski*, ed. M. Schatkin and D. Neiman (Rome: Edizioni Orientalia Christiana, 1973), 289-318. By permission of Edizioni Orientalia Christiana.

Chapter 12. "The *Definitio Fidei* of Chalcedon and its Philosophical Sources" is reprinted from *Studia Patristica* 5 (Berlin: Akadamie Verlag, 1962), 489-98. By permission of Peeters Publishers.

Chapter 13. "The Paradoxes of Aristotle's Theory of Education in the Light of Recent Controversies" is reprinted from *Laval Théologique et Philosophique* 13 (1957): 248-60. By permission of *Laval Théologique et Philosophique*.

Chapter 14. "Gladly to Learn and Gladly to Teach: Why Christians Invented the University" is reprinted from *Crisis* 11, no. 4 (April 1993): 33-37. By permission of *Crisis*.

Chapter 15. "Thomas Aquinas and the Reform of Christian Education" is reprinted from *Interpretation* 17, no. 1 (Winter 1990): 3-17. By permission of *Interpretation*.

Chapter 16. "Dante and the Rediscovery of Political Philosophy" is reprinted from *Natural Right and Political Right. Essays in Honor of H. V. Jaffa*, ed. T. B. Silver and P. W. Schramm, (Durham: Carolina Academic Press, 1984), 9-26. By permission of Carolina Academic Press.

Chapter 17. "Dante and the Structure of Philosophical Allegory" is reprinted from *Miscellanea Mediaevalia* 13, no. 1, *Spache und Erkenntnis im Mittelalter* (Berlin and New York: Walter DeGruyter, 1981) 434-40. By permission of Walter DeGruyter.

Chapter 18. "Dante's *Comedy* as Utopia" not previously published.

Chapter 19. "Dante and the Politics of Neutrality" not previously published.

SELECTED REVIEWS

Peter Brown, *Augustine of Hippo: A Biography*, is reprinted from *Theological Studies* 29 (1968): 328-31. By permission of *Theological Studies*.

Robert J. O'Connell, *Augustine's Early Theory of Man* is reprinted from *Theological Studies* 30 (1969): 341-43. By permission of *Theological Studies*.

Oliver O'Donovan, *The Problem of Self-Love in St. Augustine* is reprinted from the *Review of Metaphysics* 34 (1981): 148-50. By permission of the *Review of Metaphysics*.

Ronald H. Nash, *The Light of the Mind: St. Augustine's Theory of Knowledge* is reprinted from *The Thomist* 34 (1970): 692-95. By permission of *The Thomist*.

Robert J. O'Connell, *Art and the Christian Intelligence in St. Augustine* is reprinted from the *Review of Metaphysics* 32 (1979): 561-63. By permission of *Review of Metaphysics*.

Dom C. Baur, *John Chrysostom and His Time*, vol. I, *Antioch* is reprinted from *Cross Currents* 12, no. 1 (1962): 106-07. By permission of *Cross Currents*.

Gerhart B. Ladner, *The Idea of Reform* is reprinted from *Cross Currents* 11, no. 1 (1961): 97-99. By permission of *Cross Currents*.

Paul Aubin, *Le Probléme de la "conversion": étude sur un thème commun à l'hellenisme et au christianisme des trois premiers siécles* is reprinted from *Cross Currents* 14, no. 4 (1964): 481-82. By permission of *Cross Currents*.

Hugo Rahner, *Greek Myth and Christian Mystery* is reprinted from *Cross Currents* 14, no. 4 (1964): 478-80. By permission of *Cross Currents*.

I

ST. AUGUSTINE AND THE
REFOUNDING OF CHRISTIANITY

AUGUSTINE AND THE HERMENEUTICS OF LOVE: SOME PRELIMINARY CONSIDERATIONS

"Theology is that part of religion which requires brains."
—G. K. Chesterton

In a letter written at the height of the bitter Pelagian controversy, St. Jerome pays tribute to Augustine's "world-wide fame" and hails him as a man whom "Catholics revere as the second founder of the ancient faith": *In orbe celebraris, Catholici te conditorem antiquae rursum fidei venerantur.*[1] The compliment, which is by no means unique—it would soon be echoed by others, including Possidius, Augustine's friend and biographer[2]—is all the more striking as in this instance it comes from someone whose relations with Augustine were often less than cordial. To speak of Augustine as a second founder is not to imply that his sole achievement was to restore the Christian faith to its pristine integrity at a time when it was being threatened by its absorption into Roman political life on the one hand and the spread of heresy on the other. Scholars have long been divided over the issue of whether or not the new founding was faithful to the spirit of the original founding, but no one ever claimed it was a simple return to that first one. How, then, do the two differ?

If one were to venture an answer to that complex question, one might be tempted to say that what primitive Christianity lacked and did not yet need was what now goes under the name of "theology," by which I mean nothing more than the concerted attempt to arrive at a clearer grasp of the teachings of the faith through the use of perfected reason or philosophy. It is a sign of Augustine's genius that he was the first Latin writer to develop and carry to a high degree of perfection—some would say to its highest degree of perfection—this new approach to the study of the divinely revealed truth, even if he himself never called it theology.[3] Others in his entourage, Ambrose and Marius Victorinus among them, had begun to move in the same direction, but their accomplishments are meager by comparison.

The feat was not a mean one, especially since philosophy was never taught as a formal discipline in the schools of the Latin West. Any knowledge of it that one might acquire had to come from books and an astonishingly small number of important ones at that: those of Cicero to begin with, Cicero's version of the *Timaeus*, Aristotle's *Categories* (for which Augustine had little use),[4] and, beyond that, a handful of Neo-platonic texts that had recently been translated into Latin.[5] Few authors in our tradition have managed to do so much with so little. To this curious state of affairs can be traced the unmistakable originality but also the peculiar limitations of Augustine's thought. One thing is certain: thanks to him, a new mode of knowledge, based on love and incommensurable with anything to which the philosophic tradition was accustomed, would dominate the intellectual scene for the next thousand years or more. My intention is to take a closer look at the nature of this knowledge and then turn briefly to three problems that are more directly related to the situation that we face at the present moment. For the sake of convenience, I shall concentrate on two of Augustine's most influential works, which happen to complement each other on this point, the *Confessions* and the treatise *On Christian Doctrine*.

I

It is interesting but not at all surprising that the passion for the truth that we associate with Augustine's intellectual activity was first kindled in his soul, not by the Bible, but by his reading of Cicero's *Hortensius* at the age of nineteen. No doubt, the Bible occasionally speaks of the truth in the sense in which we normally use that term (less often perhaps than we like to think), but it cannot be said to have any real interest in it. It clearly has no use for speculation, never indulges in it, and hardly shows any awareness of it. Philosophy, the science in which the quest for speculative truth culminates, is not mentioned at all in the Hebrew Scriptures and only once in the New Testament, where it is all but equated with "empty deceit" (Col. 2:8).

Indeed, unlike other, more or less contemporary literary texts, such as the *Iliad* and the *Odyssey*, the Bible in all of its parts comes across as not only nonphilosophical but downrightly antiphilosophical. It tells stories, recounts facts, and issues commands or recommendations about the way human beings ought to live, but it does not buttress its assertions with rational arguments and frowns on anyone who would demand such arguments. It has been pointed out, not entirely in jest, that the only character to give a reason for anything in the Bible is the serpent in Genesis. The very first chapter of that book contains an implicit criticism of any and all attempts to arrive at an independent knowledge of the whole that philosophy (not the Bible) calls the "world."[6] Of all the things created by God, the sky, the traditional symbol of that "whole," is the only one along with the human couple that is not specifically pronounced good.[7] As for the New Testament writers, whom Celsus, the first philosophic critic of Christianity, saw fit to mock as "theologizing fishermen," it is doubtful whether any of them would have made much sense of, say, the *definitio fidei* of Chalcedon, all of whose terms, with the single exception of "Jesus Christ," can be traced to a definite philosophic source.[8]

As employed by the sacred writers, "truth" is more apt to mean something like fidelity or trustworthiness.[9] To say that God is true is to proclaim that he is utterly reliable, that he does not renege on his promises, or, as we still say, that he is "true" to his word, as opposed to Satan, the "father of lies" (John 8:44) or the most untrustworthy of beings. The constant teaching of the Bible is that one "knows" God to the extent that one places one's trust in him and does his will. Christ's prayer, "This is eternal life, that they know thee, the only true God, and Jesus Christ whom thou hast sent" (John 17:3), is an invitation, not to develop a natural theology, but to love and obey God. In like manner, when Christ tells his disciples that "the truth will make (them) free" (John 8:32), he is not thinking primarily of freedom from error or from the opinions of the multitude, which is what philosophers strive for, but of freedom from sin. Granted, the Bible cannot help raising an implicit claim to truth insofar as it excludes every way of life other than its own, but it never engages in a rigorous discourse the aim of which would be to demonstrate by means of logical arguments the superiority of that way of life.

This is not to assert that the Christian tradition, as distinct from the New Testament, is indifferent to, or unconcerned with, the truth. Far from it. The biblical God may be short of "ideas" but theologians have usually been more than willing to supply what he lacks in this respect. The reason is that Christianity first comes to sight as a nonpolitical religion or as a "sound doctrine" (I Tim. 1:10; 3:3; Tit. 1:9; 2:1) rather than as a God-given law. In the absence of any divinely mandated legal and social system, unity was secured by a commonality of belief. Henceforth, one would be justified, not by the performance of lawful deeds, but by faith. Accordingly, no other religious tradition has ever placed a greater premium on purity of doctrine or been so much on its guard against heresy. It is no accident that the internal history of Christianity, in contrast to that of either Judaism or Islam, is dominated by theological rather than juridical disputes. Orthodoxy was thought to be more important than orthopraxy and what one held as a believer took precedence over any of the political or legal arrangements by which human beings are wont to order their temporal lives. There would thus appear to be something in the nature of the Christian revelation that renders theological speculation indispensable in the long run. My point is that this speculation is not indigenous to, or expressly demanded by, the New Testament itself.

The *Hortensius*, Cicero's protreptic or "exhortation" (*hortatio*) to philosophy, presented a startlingly different picture. It held up the theoretical life as the highest human possibility and the philosopher himself as the highest human type. It thereby made a young and avid Augustine, who had more than his share of riot and high summer in the blood and for whom the familiar *cursus honorum* was the mandatory road to success, aware of the fact that one's whole life could be actuated, not by the love of pleasure, honor, or any of the other worldly goods to which the vast majority of human beings are drawn, but by that most unusual of all passions—a passion so rare that few people recognize it when they come face to face with it—the passion for the truth. From that moment forward, Augustine would have no more pressing ambition. Even his early and, in retrospect, implausible nine-year flirtation with Manichaeanism is explained only by the fact that it promised a rational solution to his nagging intellectual perplexities.

The failed experiment with Manichaeanism was followed, as we know, by a period of skepticism during which, unable to conceive of an incorporeal being and hence in doubt about the very possibility of science, Augustine despaired of ever attaining his coveted goal. The last obstacle was removed when, having been introduced to the "works of the Platonists" by his friends in Milan, he discovered the world of ideas and learned of the existence of a spiritual substance on which all other substances depend.[10] The event, dramatic as it was, nevertheless turned out to be only the penultimate step in a process that reached its high point with his even more dramatic conversion to Christianity. The question is: What made this ultimate step necessary? Where exactly was Platonic philosophy at fault? Why is it that, having at last found what he was looking for, Augustine was dissatisfied with it and compelled to search for something else? What finally convinced him that happiness was not to be sought in philosophic contemplation but in the Christian ideal of the love of God and neighbor?

Augustine's works contain a variety of answers to that question but none more readily intelligible than his probing analysis of the internal difficulties besetting classical moral and political philosophy. Stated in simplest terms, the argument runs as follows. The pagan philosophers correctly define happiness in terms of virtue or excellence, that is to say, in terms of the highest goals to which human beings can aspire, but they are unable to show the way to those goals. People are happy when they are at one with themselves and with one another, and they achieve this harmony when justice prevails both within and among them. Yet experience demonstrates that few of them ever manage to live perfectly just lives. According to Aristotle, who speaks for the tradition in this regard, justice is the disposition that inclines us to seek the good of others and, if need be, to sacrifice ourselves for their benefit.[11] This means concretely that I must be prepared to give up what I have or can acquire so that someone else who also wants it may be able to enjoy it instead of me. It is unrealistic to think that people will comply with such a demand as a matter of course. By reason of their bodily nature, human beings are necessarily attached to what belongs to them as individuals and, when conflicts of interest arise, almost always prefer themselves to others. The love of their own cannot be eradicated from their souls and in virtually all cases proves stronger than their love of the true or the beautiful. To make matters worse, less than perfect laws combine with bad inclination and tyrannical habit to prevent them from becoming true lovers of justice. To this problem the pagan philosophers have no solution to offer. They are right in stressing the need for virtue but cannot secure its performance. They themselves are the first to admit that their model of the most desirable society cannot be translated into action. It exists in speech or "private discussion" only.[12] De facto, one is always faced with some sort of trade-off, that is to say, with a choice among a variety of regimes none of which is superior in every respect to any of the others. Even the mixed regime, which these philosophers present as the "practically" best solution to the problem, is nothing but an attempt to maximize the advantages and minimize the disadvantages of each individual regime.

Augustine's critique, which is all the more pertinent as it is based on his opponents' own principles, reminds us of the one that would later be developed by Machiavelli and his followers, who likewise took issue with classical thought on the ground of its impracticality. The difference is that Augustine never thought of lowering the standards of human behavior in order to enhance their effectiveness, as did the early modern philosophers when they boldly tried to root all moral principles in some powerful but selfish passion, such as the desire for self-preservation. If anything, his own standards are even more stringent than the most stringent standards of the classical tradition. As he saw it, pagan philosophy was bound to fail, not because it made unreasonable demands on human nature, but because its proponents did not know or were unwilling to apply the proper remedy to its congenital weakness. That remedy consists in following Christ, apart from whom one can do nothing (cf. John 15:5), for he alone both reveals the true goal of human existence and furnishes the means whereby it may be attained.

Underlying this whole argument is the view that the knowledge vouchsafed to us through divine revelation differs not only in degree of certitude but in kind from all other forms of knowledge. It is a salutary or beatifying knowledge—*rerum divinarum atque salubrium scientia*[13]—one that calls for a decision on the part of the knower and is inseparable from the love of God and neighbor. In and of itself it has the power to transform the individual who apprehends it. Its object is unique in that it cannot be known unless it is also loved. As such, it represents the good, not of the intellect alone, but of the whole person and thus carries with it the guarantee of happiness. As Augustine puts it elsewhere, anyone who is "taught of God" (Isaiah 54:13; John 6:45) has been given simultaneously both "to know what he ought to do and to do what he knows;[14] he not only has the power to come but does come;[15] he not only believes what ought to be loved but loves what he believes."[16] Of no other truth can it be said that it is intrinsically efficacious or, in one and the same act, both theoretical and practical. Between theory and practice there is in all ordinary cases a hiatus that can only be overcome by an act of the will, which philosophers are reluctant to make until such time as the necessary evidence is at hand. In classical philosophy, some disciplines—grammar, logic, or medicine, for example—were considered to be both sciences and arts, but only insofar as their practitioners were engaged in different acts at different moments. Not so in the present case, where the two formalities are bound together in such a way as to be inconceivable one without the other.

The foregoing remarks are corroborated in unexpected fashion by the discussion of the task of the Christian orator in Book IV of the *De doctrina christiana*. That task is said to comprise three parts, which are none other than the ones listed in Cicero's rhetorical treatises: to teach (*docere*), to please (*delectare*), and to move or persuade (*flectere*).[17] What scholars usually fail to note is that Augustine's treatment of this subject is anything but a simple rehash of the Ciceronian theory. We learn among other things that the Christian orator's preeminent function is not to persuade, as it is for Cicero's orator, but to teach. Moreover, the teaching in which he engages is not a matter of narrating in as plausible a way as possible the facts of the case, as any lawyer or political orator must begin by doing; it consists in imparting a "doctrine" in the strictest sense of the word, one whose truth cannot be called into question because it rests on the authority of God himself. Finally, the Christian orator does not have to use passion as a middle term in order to secure the assent of his listeners or resort to any of the adornments on which other orators rely for their success. There is, of course, nothing to prevent him from speaking persuasively and in a pleasing manner if he has the ability to do so, for he has nothing to gain by boring his audience. Indeed, it would be a shame if error were to be clothed in attractive garb by its proponents while truth is made to appear tedious for lack of proper embellishments. The fact remains that the divine truth is persuasive in its own right and does not owe its efficacy to the rhetorical prowess of the speaker.

It follows as a necessary consequence that, unlike his pagan counterpart, Augustine's orator must avoid lies at all costs, even the most harmless ones, lest by indulging in them he should be suspected of lying about the Christian message itself and undermine his own credibility. He may know vastly more than his less learned hearers and is thus often compelled to adapt himself to their limited intellectual capacities, but what he knows is not something other than what every Christian knows or should know. There is finally only one truth, "which all hear in the same measure when it is publicly spoken, but which each one appropriates in his own measure."[18] Never is there any question of persuading the hearer to accept a doctrine to which the speaker has not previously given his wholehearted assent. What one knows in one way "in the world at large" is not essentially different from what one knows "in the privacy of one's chambers."[19] The same cannot be said of Cicero's orator, who starts from the premise that human beings are vastly unequal in regard to intellectual capacity and will always prefer a plausible lie to an implausible truth.

It should be clear by now that the type of knowledge Augustine has in mind bears little resemblance to what he refers to as the "heartless doctrines"—*doctrinae sine corde*—of the philosophers, doctrines that he knew only too well since they are the ones in which, up to the time of their conversion, he and his friend Alypius had been entangled.[20] The problem with the philosopher is that he is too proud to acknowledge that his salvation could come from anyone but himself. This self-congratulatory or self-idolizing posture is at the root of his seeming condescension toward the multitude. Philosophers parade as lovers and teachers of moral virtue, but none of them appears to have been eager to place the service of his fellow human beings above his own good. Their model is Socrates, whose aloofness from the affairs of the city is a better index of his fundamental disposition than his public declarations of piety or his professed concern for the welfare of Athens.[21] If Socrates can boast of his ignorance, it is not because he is humble but because he has learned what true knowledge is and can distinguish it from its opposite. His would-be ignorance is the obverse of a deep-seated pride that causes him to distance himself from the rest of society. He speaks to his judges as one speaks to children, telling them only what is good for them, regardless of whether it is true or not.[22] His own public speeches were meant to be more "persuasive" than genuinely truthful. They were aimed as much at keeping the multitude away from the truth as they were at attracting to it the few who had proved themselves worthy of it by their ability to penetrate the disguise in which it is habitually cloaked. Philosophers follow their personal bent, associating with their own kind and mingling with others only as necessity dictates. A gulf separates their arrogance (*praesumptio*) from the humble "confession" of the believer.[23] Bridging that gulf is not any easy matter, as we know from the moving story of the philosopher Marius Victorinus, Augustine's older contemporary, who had converted to Christianity but, under pretense that walls do not make Christians, refused for a long time to be seen in church for fear of alienating his pagan friends.[24]

As was suggested earlier, the truth to which Augustine directs our attention is a truth whose object cannot be grasped unless it is also loved. This is not to be understood to mean that the object in question does not exist unless it is loved or that it is a simple projection of one's hopes and desires. It is nonetheless inevitable that sooner or later questions should be raised about its cognitive status. Augustine himself grounded his position in the biblical notion that human beings are created in the image of God. The argument assumes that the process by which a finite being attains its perfection takes the form of a return to its principle; hence, the familiar *a te-ad te* tandem that structures the whole of the *Confessions*.[25] Human beings come from God and their hearts are not at peace until they find their rest in him. But then one cannot love God without loving those whom God loves, and God loves all his creatures. This is what Augustine did not find in the books of the Platonists, however much he may have felt indebted to them for other reasons. By their pride, philosophers enshrine disunity among human beings. The knowledge in which they traffic is essentially divisive and forecloses any return to the unity and wholeness for which everyone consciously or unconsciously yearns.

II

Against the background of these remarks and in an effort to lend greater concreteness to them, it may be in our interest to glance at three specific issues in regard to which Augustine's concerns intersect in one way or another with those of our time. The first has to do with the Augustinian notion of love and friendship, particularly as it affects the life of society as a whole. As is well known, the model from which Augustine works is supplied by Acts 4:32, which extols the harmony that characterized the life of the earliest Christian community, all of whose members are said to have been "of one heart and soul." Until fairly recently, no one had noticed or paid much attention to the fact that Augustine frequently adds to that statement the words *in Deum*, "bent" or "intent on God." The addition, which is clearly deliberate (it occurs in thirty-one of the forty-two instances in which the verse is quoted[26]) tells us a great deal about Augustine's understanding of the relationship that binds people together as friends and fellow citizens. It makes it clear that human beings become one, not by looking at one another, but by looking together in the direction of something outside of and higher than themselves. Any deep and lasting relationship presupposes a common good of some sort in which the parties involved can communicate and which serves as the ground of their unity. It rests ultimately on God, the supreme good, the love of which is implied in the love of any lesser good that one may wish to pursue.

Our contemporaries usually have little patience with this line of inquiry and are more likely to think of friendship in terms of what is now called an "I-Thou" relationship. As the use of such unnatural nouns as the "I" and the "Thou" reveals, however, the new understanding is the product of a process whereby one prescinds from the actual end or ends to which individuals or communities are dedicated. It presumes that there are no preestablished, naturally knowable, or divinely ordained ends in the attainment of which human beings find their perfection, and it dismisses as meaningless any talk of such ends.

Little wonder that our modern sensibilities should be offended by the famous teaching of the *De doctrina christiana* which stipulates that God is to be "enjoyed" or loved for his own sake, whereas everything else, including all other human beings, is to be "used" or loved only as a means to that end;[27] for such a view would seem to reflect a purely instrumental conception of human love and friendship. Scholars have even asked whether Augustine himself, who omits any mention of this distinction in his later works, had not developed second thoughts about it, even though no such change of heart is recorded in the *Retractationes*.[28] There may be a simpler explanation, which is that, in accordance with a method of procedure inherited from the Platonic school, Augustine tends to study all things in the light of their highest principles and that this tendency is what leads to the extreme formulations for which he is notorious. Properly understood, the distinction between "enjoyment" (*frui*) and "use" (*uti*) directs our attention to one of the most problematic features of the New

Testament teaching on love, to say nothing of the modern account of love and friendship as "I-Thou" relationships. It is characteristic of the New Testament commandment of universal love that it ignores all the limitations that nature imposes on us as regards this matter. One is summoned to love others without discrimination and independently of their personal merits or qualities. But this could amount to little more than a tyranny of every individual over every other individual. The pitfall is avoided only if the love that unites human beings has its ground in the one good that can be shared by all of them without partition or diminution, namely, God himself.

It might be added, also in Augustine's defense, that his understanding of love has nothing of the sentimentality that attaches to this notion in the modern mind. No one who has reflected on the role of *disciplina* in Augustine's thought will have the slightest doubt about that. Augustine was all for persuasion when it could be used to good effect, but he knew its limits for having experienced them himself. Even his famous maxim, "Love and do what you will," seems to have had a much tougher meaning than the one that is now commonly attributed to it. It belongs to the context of the Donatist controversy and refers to the harsh treatment to which Augustine's disciples were compelled to resort in order to bring the adversary to his senses. The message was clear: one could deal with the intractable Donatists as the necessities of the case required, so long as one remembered to love them.[29]

My second set of remarks concerns the familiar charge that Augustine inherited from his Neoplatonic mentors: a tendency to deprecate human values, a negative view of the body and everything connected with it, an otherworldly or escapist outlook that is at odds with the spirit of the gospel, and a severity in moral matters that has justifiably earned him a place among the great rigorists of all times.[30] There are any number of statements in the Augustian corpus from which such an impression might be gained, but here again one wonders whether the complaints are not due less to any flaw in Augustine's thought than to our present inability to penetrate beneath the surface of his writings to the substance of that thought.[31]

The difference between Augustine and most present-day philosophers and theologians is not that the latter have a better grasp of the role of the body in human life or that they hold human and artistic values in higher esteem; it lies rather in the fact that Augustine was intent on preserving or restoring human wholeness by directing all of the individual's activities to the goal or goals to which they are intrinsically ordered. There are few more vivid accounts anywhere in Christian literature of the manner in which the soul rises "step by step" from the delights afforded by the bodily senses to the inner contemplation of the Wisdom from which these and all other delights derive than the celebrated "vision of Ostia" in Book IX of the *Confessions*. As a follower of those philosophers who, in his words, had come closest to Christianity, Augustine knew not only that love takes many forms but that there is gradual progression from the lower of these to the higher and that in life as we know it the latter continue to be supported by the former. Never is there any question of repressing the lower forms so that the higher ones might emerge through what has since been reinterpreted as a process of sublimation. To quote Augustine himself, "Cupidity must not be removed but transformed": *non auferatur cupiditas sed mutetur*. Love must be given the opportunity to "migrate" from the creature, by which it is held bound, to the creator: *Amor tuus migret: rumpe funes a creatura, alliga ad creatorem.*[32] The experience of the inadequacy of the objects to which it is first attracted, rather than the forced abandonment of these objects as a result of the pressures that society brings to bear on us, is what causes the soul to redirect its energies toward more noble or more suitable objects. This accounts for the astonishingly erotic images used in *Soliloquies*, I.13,22, for example, to describe something as ethereal as the love of wisdom:

REASON: Now, we are trying to discover what kind of a lover of wisdom you are: that wisdom which you desire to behold and to possess with purest gaze and embrace, with no veil between and, as it were, naked, such as wisdom allows to very few and these the most chosen of its lovers. If you were inflamed with the love of some beautiful woman, would she not rightly refuse to give herself to you if she discovered that you loved anything but herself? And will the purest beauty of wisdom reveal itself to you unless you burn for it alone?

AUGUSTINE: Why, then, am I unhappily held back and why am I delayed by this wretched torture? Surely, I have shown that I have nothing else, since that which is not loved for itself is not really loved. I do love wisdom alone and for its own sake, and it is on account of wisdom that I want to have or fear to be without other things, such as life, tranquillity, and my friends. What limit can there be to my love of that Beauty, in which I do not only not begrudge it to others, but I even look for many who will long for it with me, sigh for it with me, possess it with me, enjoy it with me; they will be all the dearer to me the more we share that love in common.[33]

In all of this there is no Rousseauean or Freudian attempt to derive the higher from the lower, if only because Augustine did not have any doubts about the preexistence of the higher as an independent object of desire. Nothing was more foreign to his mind than the modern scientific view which denies that there is in the human soul a yearning for the eternal, looks upon love as an "artificial" and, down deep, selfish feeling born of the repression of the sexual appetite,[34] and rules out *a priori* any moral, intellectual, and religious conversion of the kind that he himself underwent. If, as Augustine thought, the soul has its own natural order, and if that order can be restored through the convergence of wisdom, intellect, and love, there is no point in trying to reconstruct it on the basis of some materialistic or deterministic conception of nature. The famous dichotomies about which one hears so much nowadays, such as the irreducible opposition between duty and inclination, or between the individual and society, or between the pursuit of one's own good and the good of others, belong to the context of modern thought, not to that of Augustine's thought. One can read the whole of Augustine and never have the impression of being in the presence of a man who only pretends to love what he really hates.

My last series of comments focuses on the so-called hermeneutical problem as it arises in the first three books of the *De doctrina christiana*, the only work in all of patristic literature devoted in its entirety to this topic. The matter is of considerable theoretical and practical interest, especially in view of the innumerable controversies to which we have lately been treated concerning the possibility of interpretation. The currently most fashionable theory is the one that denies that possibility. Texts have no meaning independently of the activity of the interpreter, who cannot help injecting his own perspective into them. In Morris Zapp's memorable words, "Every decoding is another encoding."[35] Everything is interpretation, which is as much as to say that nothing is interpretation, as Nietzsche, the grandfather of our present-day deconstructionists, taught us more than a century ago; for all interpretation is necessarily interpretation in the light of something that is not itself subject to interpretation.

Faced with the task of explaining a text, the interpreter cannot be content with merely repeating the author's own words since in that case we should never know whether he has understood anything or not. This leaves him with no other choice but to explain the text in his own words, a perilous enterprise that inevitably leads to a subtle distortion of the author's meaning. To restate the problem in terms of the narrower hermeneutic circle in which every interpreter is supposedly trapped: one can only understand the part in relation to the whole, which is known to us only through its individual parts. There is, in short, no such thing as a presuppositionless interpretation. This implies that there is no preexisting text, either, not even for the author himself, whose work is always fraught with a variety of meanings of which he is not himself aware. In consequence, the old rule of thumb according to which the first task of the interpreter is to try to understand the author as he understood himself loses its *raison d'être*, based as it is on the naive assumption that there is "text" to begin with.

The same observations would apply to the Bible, whose meaning is not one but indefinitely many and which can thus be said to lack any determinate or permanent meaning. Words and sentences can obviously be taken in a variety of senses—literal, allegorical, ironic, or whatever it may be—and any text can contain more than one meaning, all of them intended by the author for the same or for different audiences. But a text that has an indefinite number of meanings has no meaning at all. It can confirm us in our prejudices, inasmuch as what we find in it is barely more than what we bring to it, but it cannot liberate us from those prejudices. Instead of a new world, our new Christopher Columbus always ends up by discovering Genoa. What was intended by Nietzsche as an appeal to creativity, the purpose of which was to rescue the modern herd animal from the abyss of mediocrity into which he was about to sink, has instead become an instrument of liberalism. Since there are no authoritative interpretations anywhere and no authoritative texts to interpret, one is free to think and act as one sees fit, as long as one does not interfere with anyone else's freedom.

As might be expected, the *De doctrina christiana* takes a different tack. It begins with a synopsis of the rules of faith and conduct by which Christians are to be guided in their reading of the sacred text.[36] The rule of faith includes such doctrines as those pertaining to the triune God and his attributes, Christ and his redemptive work, the Church as the body of Christ, and the last things or life after death. As for Christianity's moral teaching, it is summed up in the dual precept of the love of God and neighbor, the alpha and the omega of divine revelation. The whole of the Bible is in fact geared to the inculcation of this supreme commandment, so much so that anyone who has grasped it can dispense with Scripture altogether.

The logical difficulty in the present case is that we are not told how one arrives at a knowledge of the truths that are then called into play as rules of faith or of conduct. It does not suffice to say that one depends on the church for this information, for the same problem arises in connection with the foundation of that authority: one knows that the church can be trusted because its authority is vouched for by the Bible, and, conversely, one knows that the Bible can be trusted because its authority is vouched for by the church. The problem is alluded to by Augustine himself, who points out that there are two matters to be treated in his book, "things" and "signs."[37] By "things" he means in the first instance the basic truths that have just been presented in capsule form, and by "signs" the words used to express them. But he also says that "things are learned by signs" —*res per signa discuntur* (I.2.2)—at which point the argument again appears to beg the question: signs are interpreted in the light of things, which are themselves known only by means of these signs. Nothing, it seems, has been accomplished. A vicious circle similar to the one that plagues modern hermeneutics is apparently at work in the Augustinian scheme as well.

One might reply, first of all, that Augustine was not acquainted with the problem of interpretation in the precise form in which it would pose itself in our century and hence cannot be faulted for not dealing with it thematically; and, secondly, that the *De doctrina christiana* is an emphatically Christian book, that is, a book written by a Christian for other Christians—above all for Christian preachers, who were presumed to be familiar with the teachings of the faith, to be wholly committed to them, and to require no further proof of their truth. Does this mean that his treatment of this subject is inadequate and that he has less to teach us about it than any of those who have since written on it? Not necessarily.

It is significant that Augustine broaches the question of interpretation proper only in Book II, which is limited to a discussion of such external aids to the understanding of the Scriptures as may be provided by the study of grammar, history, the natural and mathematical sciences, and dialectic. It is only in Book III, which tackles the thornier issue of how one goes about making sense of the obscure passages of Scripture, that actual rules of interpretation, some of them borrowed from the Donatist Tyconius, are offered. We are given to understand that, contrary to what is often taken for granted today, there is no such thing as a universal hermeneutics and no necessity for it. Specific rules of interpretation are required only when the text is not clear and needs to be deciphered. I do not have to be well versed in hermeneutical theory to read the local newspaper, however slanted its reporting may be, and I can be reasonably certain that its unintelligible passages, if there are any, are due to some editorial lapse or typesetting error, in which case rules of interpretation would be useless anyway.

The tacit premise of modern biblical hermeneutics as it developed in the seventeenth century is that the Bible is unintelligible on its own terms and therefore in need of a complex exegetical method that allows us to understand its individual parts in terms of their genesis or the personal agenda of their respective authors. Spinoza, the first great philosophic exponent of that method,[38] denied that there is any speculative teaching to be extracted from the sacred text and reduced its moral teaching to two virtues, justice and charity, redefined and simplified in such a way as to support his own political program. Both are rooted in the desire for self-preservation and neither one bears any relationship to the various other moral virtues by which human beings are perfected in themselves. The argument in a nutshell is that the Bible is not the work of a single divine author, that its various parts do not cohere with one another, and that one ought to read it as one would read any other book, that is, in the light of such information as is accessible to the unaided human reason.

Augustine starts from the opposite premise. He assumes that, as a divinely inspired book, the Bible is in principle intelligible from beginning to end. To be sure, some of its parts are obscure, but the obscurities are deliberate. God has willed them as a means of arousing the curiosity of the reader, of sustaining his interest, and of keeping him humble. On this score, Augustine is in full agreement with Tyconius, although unlike Tyconius he is not at all confident that the application of the proper rules will eventually dispose of all the obscurities. The matter is of little practical consequence since we know beforehand that the teaching of the clear passages cannot be contradicted by that of the obscure passages, whatever it may be, the reason being that a benevolent God would never lead his followers astray or deprive them of any necessary aid to their salvation.

Few contemporary biblical scholars are inclined to pay much attention to Augustine's hermeneutical theory. Still, it is permissible to ask whether, as practitioners of a discipline that is not known for its propensity to reflect on its own presuppositions, they might not find it to their advantage to give more serious thought to it. Nobody denies the very significant contribution that modern scholarship has made to our understanding of the Bible. The only question concerns the level of that contribution and the criteria in the light of which its worth is best assessed. The question is not an easy one to answer, but the fact that it is again being raised is a sign that a few of our contemporaries are no longer as sure as they once were of the adequacy, let alone the ultimate superiority, of the modern hermeneutical framework.

I began by suggesting, somewhat timidly, that Augustine's thought suffers from certain liabilities that are attributable at least in part to the scarcity or the incompleteness of the philosophic materials with which he had to work. What the mystical Platonism with which he came into contact lacked most conspicuously was a fully developed notion of nature. When asked by his interlocutor, personified Reason, to state in a single sentence all that he wants to know, the Augustine of the *Soliloquies* replies: "God and the soul," nothing else![39] Nowhere in the tradition within which Augustine works does one find a *bona fide* science of nature or, unless I am mistaken, a single treatise *Peri phuseos*. The matter proved to be of some consequence for the evolution of Christian theology. On the basis of the distinction between "things" and "signs," Augustine's medieval disciples were inclined to view the world, not as something that had its own internal consistency and intelligibility, but rather as an elaborate system of symbols, an enchanted forest as it were, in which every tree, flower, or other natural object functions as a reminder of an invisible reality far more beautiful than anything the eye has ever seen.

The problem—and it is not unlike the one we ran into when we examined Augustine's theory of interpretation—is that in order to recognize a sign for what it is, one has to have some knowledge, however vague, of the reality that it signifies. In the Augustinian tradition, that knowledge was thought to come to us through divine illumination. Yet anyone acquainted with the debates surrounding this doctrine in the Middle Ages knows how elusive the arguments in favor of it can be. This explains in part the enthusiasm generated in the course of the thirteenth century by the recovery of Aristotelian natural philosophy, with all of the new possibilities that it afforded, as well as all of the subtle dangers that it conjured up. For this eventuality Augustine had left his disciples ill-prepared. In any case, the rediscovery of an independent realm of nature brought the age of medieval innocence to an abrupt end. The issue was stated most sharply by one of Augustine's disciples, who explicitly equates the tree of the knowledge of good and evil with philosophy and, by implication, the serpent of Genesis with the Aristotelian philosopher.[40] In his desire to achieve the greatest possible clarity about the truth of the Christian faith, Augustine had gone further than any previous Latin writer in attributing to God the ideas that the Bible seems to deny him. The turning point came when it dawned on some of the new Aristotelians that if one already knows what God thinks, one might be spared the necessity of listening to what he has to say.

NOTES

1.   Jerome, *Letter* 141 to Augustine (Migne, *Patrologia, Series Latina* or *PL*) 22. col. 1180.

2.   Cf. Possidius, *Vita Augustini* 7 (*PL* 32. col. 39), where Augustine is credited with having single-handedly brought Christianity back to life in Africa.

3.   Augustine appears to use the word only in connection with Varro's distinction between three kinds of theology: poetic, civil, and natural; cf. *De civitate Dei* (*City of God*) VI.5. Throughout the patristic period, "theology," the "discourse on God," is most often used in contradistinction to "economy," the account of God's operations in the world.

4.   Cf. *Confessiones* (*Confessions*) IV.16.

5.   *Conf.* VII.9.

6.   The Bible speaks not of the *kosmos* but of "heaven and earth," without any intimation that the two form a unity. It goes without saying that there is no "cosmology" as such in the Bible.

7.   See on this subject the penetrating remarks by Leo Strauss, "Jerusalem and Athens: Some Introductory Reflections," *Commentary* 43 (1967): 45-57, and "On the Interpretation of Genesis," *L'Homme* 21/1 (1981): 5-20. That man or "Adam" is not

called "good" save implicitly through his inclusion in the whole of creation is not surprising in view of what we learn about him in chapter 2 of Genesis.

8. For further details, cf. E. L. Fortin, "The *Definitio Fidei* of Chalcedon and Its Philosophical Sources," in chapter 12 of this volume.

9. The Old Testament term for "truth," *emet*, which is frequently translated by *aletheia* in the New Testament, is derived from a root conveying the notion of firmness. For the biblical uses of these two words, cf. G. Kittel, ed., *Theological Dictionary of the New Testament*, vol. 1 (Grand Rapids: Eerdmans, 1964), 232-47.

10. *Conf.* VII.9.

11. Aristotle, *Nicomachean Ethics* V.1134b6, 10.

12. Augustine, *Letter* 91.4. The allusion is to Plato, *Republic* 592b, which Augustine knew indirectly through Cicero's *De re publica*. The same argument is developed at considerable length in *De vera religione* (*On the True Religion*) I.1-VI.11, and in the *City of God* II.21, and XIX.21, apropos of Cicero's definition of the city, which in Augustine's view applies to Rome only on condition that the reference to justice be deleted from it.

13. *De doctrina christiana* (*On Christian Doctrine*) V.5.7.

14. Augustine, *De gratia Christi* (*On the Grace of Christ*) 13.14 (*PL* 44. col. 367).

15. *De gratia Christi* 14.15. col. 368.

16. *De gratia Christi* 12.13. col. 367. It is precisely because the word of God is spoken with power (cf. I Cor. 2:4-5) that anyone who resists it is guilty of sin.

17. *De doctrina christiana* IV.12. See, for a fuller treatment, chapter 5, "Augustine and the Problem of Christian Rhetoric."

18. Augustine, *Tractatus in Joannis evangelium* (*Tracts on the Gospel of St. John*) 98.2 (*PL* 25. col. 1881).

19. *Tractatus in Joan. Ev.* 98.6.

20. Cf. *Conf.* VIII.8. The expression *doctrinae sine corde* (*heartless doctrines*) is found in the Latin text edited by M. Skutella in 1934 for Teubner of Leipzig. "*Sine corde*" is not found in the C.S.E.L. or the Loeb edition of the *Confessions*. Ryan and Chadwick use the Skutella text for their translations.

21. See especially the subtle analysis of Socrates's relationship to Athens in Plato's *Apology of Socrates* which makes it clear that the philosopher lives in the city as someone who is not at home in it and does not really belong to it. For an interpretation of the *Apology* along the lines suggested here, cf. L. Strauss, "On Plato's *Apology of Socrates* and *Crito*," in T. L. Pangle, ed., *Studies in Platonic Political Philosophy* (Chicago and London: University of Chicago Press, 1983), 38-66; G. Anastaplo, "Human Being and Citizen: A Beginning to the Study of Plato's *Apology of Socrates*," in J. Cropsey, ed., *Ancients and Moderns* (New York and London: Basic Books, 1964), 16-49.

22. Cf. *Apology of Socrates* 39cff.

23. *Conf.* VII.20.

24. *Conf.* VIII.2.

25. This explains, among other things, the peculiar structure of the *Confessions*, which begin with an account of Augustine's spiritual odyssey (Bks. I-IX), end with a commentary on the first chapter of Genesis (Bks. XI-XIII), and unite the two apparently disparate parts by means of Book X, devoted to an analysis of memory, the intellectual faculty by means of which one uncovers the presence of God within oneself and begins one's ascent toward him.

26. Cf. T. J. van Bavel, *"Ante omnia et in Deum dans la Regula Sancti Augustini," Vigiliae Christianae* 12 (1958): 157-65.

27. *De doctrina christiana* I.22.

28. Cf. O. O'Donovan, *The Problem of Self-Love in St. Augustine* (New Haven and London: Yale University Press 1980), who calls Augustine's discussion of this matter in Bk. I of the *De doctrina christiana* a "false step" and notes that "there is not a single instance in any later writing of the verb *uti* being used of the love of men for other men," 29.

29. See on this subject J. Gallay, *"Dilige et quod vis fac*: notes d'exégèse augustinienne," *Recherches de science religieuse* 43 (1955): 545-55.

30. See the discussion of Plato and the Platonic tradition on the body in chapter 3.

31. Cf. G. Madec, "Le spiritualisme augustinien à la lumière du *De immortalitate animae," L'Opera letteraria di Agostino tra Cassiciacum e Milano* (Palermo: Edizioni "Augustinus," 1987), 179-90.

32. Augustine, *Sermo Denis* XIV, in *Miscellanea Agostiniana*, vol. I, (Rome: Tipografia Poliglotta Vaticana, 1930- 1931), 66-67.

33. *Writings of St. Augustine*, vol. 1, trans. Thomas Gilligan (Washington: The Fathers of the Church, 1948), 372-73.

34. Cf. J. J. Rousseau, *Emile*, Bk. IV, trans. A. Bloom (New York: Basic Books, 1979), esp. p. 329: "And what is true love itself if it is not chimera, lie, and illusion? We love the image we make for ourselves far more than we love the object to which we apply it. If we saw what we love exactly, there would be no more love on earth." Cf. *Discourse on the Origin and Foundations of Inequality*, ed. R. Masters, J. J. Rousseau, *The First and Second Discourses* (New York: St. Martin's Press, 1964), 135. Also Kant, *Conjectural Beginning of Human History*, who, pursuing Rousseau's line of thought, writes:

> Next to the instinct for food, by means of which nature preserves the individual, the greatest prominence belongs to the sexual instinct, by means of which she preserves the species. Reason, once aroused, did not delay in demonstrating its influence here as well. In the case of animals, sexual attraction is merely a matter of transient, mostly episodic impulse. But man soon discovered that for him this attraction can be prolonged and even increased by means of the imagination—a power that carries on its business, to be sure, the more moderately, but at once also the more constantly and uniformly, the more its object is removed from the senses. By means of the imagination, he discovered, the surfeit was avoided

which goes with the satisfaction of mere animal desire. The fig leaf, then, was a far greater manifestation of reason than that shown in the earlier stage of development. . . . *Refusal* was the feat that brought about the passage from the merely sensual to spiritual attractions, from mere animal desire gradually to love, and along with this from the feeling of the merely agreeable to a taste for beauty, at first only for beauty in man but at length for beauty in nature as well. In addition, there came a first hint of the development of man as a moral creature. This came from the sense of decency, which is an inclination to inspire others to respect by proper manners, i.e., by concealing all that which might arouse low esteem. Here, incidentally, lies, the real basis of all true sociability." Kant, *On History*, ed. L. W. Beck, (Indianapolis: Bobbs-Merrill, 1963), 56-57.

35. This reference is to David Lodge's scintillating novel, *Small World* (New York: Warner Books, 1984), 28.

36. Similar synopses are to be found at the beginning of the *De agone christiano* (*On Christian Combat*) and the *Enchiridion*.

37. *De doctrina christiana* I.2.2.

38. The crucial text is that of the *Theologico-Political Treatise*, ch.7: "On the Interpretation of Scripture."

39. Augustine, *Soliloquia* (*Soliloquies*) I.2.7.

40. St. Bonaventure, *Third Sunday of Advent*, Sermon 2, *Opera Omnia*, vol IX (Quaracchi), 62-63. Cf. J. G. Bougerol, *Introduction to the Works of St. Bonaventure* (Patterson, NJ: St. Anthony Guild Press, 1964), 150-51.

2

AUGUSTINE AND THE PROBLEM OF HUMAN GOODNESS

To mention Augustine's name is to evoke one of a handful of towering geniuses in the history of the Christian West. Even in an age that has repudiated much of what he stands for, he is still acknowledged as a giant among giants, a phenomenon of sorts, a thinker of surpassing depth and subtlety. His weakness, if he has one, is that he tried to be all things to all people; his greatness, that he mostly succeeded.

A quick glance at his life reveals that he was simultaneously or by turns: a professor of rhetoric who could not collect his fees or maintain discipline in his classroom (*"un professeur chahuté,"* P. Courcelle); a simple priest occasionally invited to address synods of bishops, something unheard of in those days; a prominent bishop who actually worked, and this in the heyday of parasitic Byzantine court bishops (his diocese, Hippo Regius, on the coast of present-day eastern Algeria, over which he presided for thirty-four years, was second only to Carthage in North Africa); a spiritual writer of the first rank and the true originator of African monasticism (his *Confessions* became *the* classic of the religious life in the West and retained that position until, for better or for worse, it was replaced by the less theologically-oriented *Imitation of Christ* in the sixteenth century); a preacher so good that circus owners had to avoid conflicts with his sermons lest they should lose a substantial portion of their attendance—another rarity, especially if one agrees with Paul Claudel that the greatest proof of the divinity of the Church is the fact that it spread through preaching (these sermons were frequently stolen before they could be published and so many copies of them were made that no scholar has yet been found to undertake a critical edition of them); an advisor to popes; a defender of the weak; a consultant to the rich and the powerful; and with that the enumeration has barely begun.

Always a busy man and, to hear him talk, not a well man (but then, most of the work in this life seems to be done by people who do not feel too well), Augustine managed in his spare time to become the most prolific writer of the ancient world. Possidius, his friend and biographer, who compiled a list of his works, notes that no one could possibly read them all,[1] and Isidore of Seville, echoing him a century and a half later, adds that anybody who claims to have done so is surely a liar.[2] His only rivals in that department are Aristotle, Epicurus, and Pliny the Elder. Except for Aristotle's major treatises, however, most of their works have perished. His have survived, nourishing the piety of Christians across the ages and accidentally giving rise to a thriving if at times tedious industry known as Augustinian scholarship.

For more than a thousand years he dominated the intellectual scene, establishing the positions from which others would start and forcing, if not the abandonment, at least a reconsideration of the entire legacy of classical thought. His was the arch under which philosophers and theologians had to pass, the standard by which they could expect to be judged or against which they sought to measure their achievements. His *City of God,* perhaps the most famous book (I do not say the most widely read book) in all Christendom, is a monumental celebration of the recent death of the pagan gods, a first-class funeral or, better still, a massive tombstone destined to insure that they would never come back to life. And they never did. So successful was it that fifteen centuries later Nietzsche could complain that the Western world had yet to invent a single new god.[3] Even the late Paul Tillich once said, "If you want to call me anything, call me an Augustinian." Augustine could have dispensed with the compliment, but that it should have been uttered says something about his reputation.

Nor was any author quoted or misquoted more often. There are no fewer than two thousand references to him in Thomas Aquinas's two *Summae* alone, and no fewer than three thousand references in Calvin's *Institutes of the Christian Religion.* As the same Paul Tillich observes, when you cite someone that often with approval, you are more than a friend; you are a disciple. Some of his most famous sayings have not been found anywhere in his works and were presumably invented by later admirers. With apologies to the great Adolph Harnack, the late nineteenth-

and early twentieth-century historian of dogma, Augustine never called the pagan virtues "splendid vices," although he might have, and he never explicitly stated that "everything contributes to the good of those who love God, even their sins—*etiam peccata*," although he certainly thought so.

Unfortunately or, as others prefer to think, fortunately, it is not possible to recall the lofty esteem in which Augustine was held for so long without at the same time alluding to the disfavor into which he has lately fallen in some scholarly circles. One would have to look far and wide for a single Church Father whose fame has suffered so much at the hands of modern critics or about whom it has become fashionable to speak with such condescension. I do not wish to imply that in reading Augustine one should simply allow one's critical faculties to slip into remission but only that, given his accomplishments, a measure of modesty is in order. Such at any rate was the frame of mind of a previous generation of scholars. Not anymore.

In a recent book entitled *Eunuchs for the Kingdom of Heaven,* one such critic, Uta Ranke-Heinemann, who speaks for a large segment of the academic community, has denounced Augustine as "the father of a fifteen-hundred-year-long anxiety about sex and an enduring hostility to it";[4] a misogynist and a hater of pleasure; a derailed Neoplatonist with an unbridled "urge to break away from anything earthly and beloved on this earth";[5] a "neurotic who took his sexual phobia with him to the grave";[6] a Christian who frowned on postmenopausal sexual relations and only reluctantly gave up the notion that intercourse between married people even for the sake of begetting children was at least mildly sinful; a one-time Manichee who in converting to Christianity did little more than replace the goal of pleasure without children with that of children without pleasure and went on to persuade the world that, once marriage is separated from procreation, husbands are nothing but shameful lovers, wives nothing but "harlots," marriage beds nothing but "bordellos," and fathers-in-law nothing but "pimps."[7]

Others have been quick to add that this melancholy appraisal of human behavior is by no means restricted to the domain of sexuality. It is part of a broad syndrome encompassing the whole realm of material and aesthetic values. One of our best known specialists, Robert J. O'Connell, S.J., has spent much of his professional life taking Augustine to task for his world-denying tendencies, his negative valuation of the body and everything connected with it, an escapist mentality that stands in sharp contradiction to the spirit of the Gospel, and a severity in moral matters that has justifiably earned him a place of choice among the great rigorists of our tradition. This severity, coupled with a disembodied conception of human existence, is what O'Connell refers to as Augustine's "angelism," a strange aberration that supposedly underlies his "bleak judgment" of the corporeal world and his understanding of death as the soul's longed-for release from the shackles of the body.

The barrage is all the more unexpected as it is belied by any number of statements to the contrary in Augustine's works. Augustine did, after all, spend an inordinate amount of time and energy defending the goodness of nature against the Manichees, the quintessential world-haters of his time, as well as against the Platonists, whom he accused, falsely in my opinion, of a similar animosity toward the body and worldly goods.[8] Nor as a Christian could he have done otherwise, for, as he says pointedly, "by blaming the nature of the flesh we wrong the creator."[9]

It is hardly necessary to mention if only parenthetically that Ranke-Heinemann's and O'Connell's critiques proceed on the basis of noticeably different premises. Ranke-Heinemann objects to Augustine's insistence on the subordination of bodily pleasure to man's spiritual activities. O'Connell's preoccupations appear to be closer to those of modern aestheticism, which severs the link between beauty on the one hand and truth and moral goodness on the other. The important point is that in both cases the frame of reference is supplied not by Augustine himself but ultimately by Nietzsche, the most powerful exponent of the view that Christianity bears the chief responsibility for the nihilistic depreciation of all that is good and pleasant in life.[10] Implicit in this adoption of an alien frame of reference to interpret Augustine's works is the claim that one can understand him *better than* he understood himself without first making the necessary effort to understand him *as* he understood himself. The claim is a dangerous one inasmuch as it prevents us from achieving a genuine appreciation of the power of Augustine's thought and thus deprives us of the opportunity either of learning something of importance from him or of engaging in a serious criticism of him if such criticism should prove necessary.

Be that as it may, it is barely conceivable that Augustine, who did more than anyone else to shape the moral sensibilities of the West, should have been so egregiously mistaken on an issue as central to the Christian life as one's relationship to and proper use of material or private goods. Either Augustine was wrong and his modern critics are right, or Augustine was right and his critics are wrong, or else his critics have misunderstood him and only think they disagree with him. If, as seems likely, this last supposition is the correct one, what could possibly have given these critics the impression that Augustine was an incurable pessimist who poisoned the whole of human existence by categorizing as evil any enjoyment that might accrue to us from the use of the earthly goods that a tender loving God has placed at our disposal? The answer, I submit, lies in part with Augustine's peculiar treatment of moral matters, a treatment characterized by a *prima facie* radicalism that led him to paint a picture of human life that comes across to many readers as excessively gloomy and uncompromising.

Take, to begin with, the discussion of the early Roman republic and its heroes, for whom Augustine professes sincere admiration but whose moral qualities he finally dismisses as vices rather than virtues, the reason being that the pagans had no knowledge of the true God and that without this knowledge virtuous behavior is impossible.[11] Simply put, there is for Augustine no such thing as moral virtue properly so called, by which I mean moral virtue unaccompanied by the dianoetic or intellectual virtues. Among the writers of classical antiquity, Aristotle and his followers are the only ones to speak of the nonphilosophic virtues as genuine virtues apart from their connection with theoretical wisdom, and Augustine was no Aristotelian. His position is that in order to be morally good one must be rightly ordered to the ultimate end of human existence and that one cannot be so ordered if one is ignorant of that end. It follows that the noble pagans who lacked this knowledge and worshipped false gods were not truly virtuous. Yet Augustine is the first to admit that such knowledge is inaccessible to all but a small intellectual elite, together with those to whom it has been vouchsafed by God himself through divine revelation. His blanket condemnation of pagan virtue would thus seem to be grossly unfair to its practitioners, many of whom were presumably acting in good faith and had no choice in the matter anyway. Moreover, it was on the face of it highly impolitic since by berating pagan virtue Augustine could not help casting discredit on the very practices on which Rome had always depended for its political well-being.

Another notorious case in point is Augustine's definition of civil society, the *republica* or commonwealth, which has frequently been taken to mean that the state is an amoral entity with no stake in the character of its citizens, that politics has nothing whatever to do with ethics, and that Augustine is best read as a champion of value neutrality or a social science positivist before the letter.[12] In the *City of God* (XIX.21), Augustine, quoting Scipio, Cicero's mouthpiece in the *Republic,* calls civil society an "assemblage of people held together by a common acknowledgment of right and a community of interests." Reverting to the same theme later on, in XIX.24, he is compelled by the facts to amend that statement by striking from it any reference to the key notion of right or justice, the "bond of men in cities," according to Aristotle,[13] on the ground that it is not to be found in any of them. Civil society, he says, is an assemblage of human beings held together, not by an acknowledgment of right, but by "a common agreement as to the objects of their love," regardless of the moral quality of these objects. Only in this attenuated or truncated sense can Rome be said to have been a commonwealth. When all is said and done, cities are mere compacts of wickedness entered into not for the sake of virtue or the good life but for the sole purpose of preserving a modicum of peace among their members and keeping them from constantly being at one another's throats.

The thrust of Augustine's remarks on this subject becomes clearer when we turn to another well-known chapter of the *City of God* (IV.4) where kingdoms are proclaimed to be nothing but "gigantic larcenies" (*magna latrocinia*) and larcenies nothing but "small kingdoms" (*parva regna*)—that, save for the magnitude of the crimes committed, what Alexander does on a grand scale and with a huge fleet is not essentially different from what a pirate does on his own and with a single ship. The passage of Cicero's *Republic* from which Augustine borrows this story has regrettably come down to us in a mutilated state, but we at least know that it belonged to the section of the dialogue in which for the sake of argument Philus, one of the interlocutors, defends the thesis that justice is merely the right of the stronger, that is to say, of the rulers, and hence a matter of convention rather than of nature. People abide by it not because it is intrinsically desirable but for reasons of necessity or self-interest. Down deep, the brightest among them know that it is but a pretense. Even though hardly anyone cares to admit it publicly, every political group is organized for the benefit of those who run it. This is obviously true of the corrupt regimes, but it is also true, in a less conspicuous way, of the good regimes, whether they be monarchies, aristocracies, democracies, or some mixture of the three; for even the best of cities is governed by laws that cannot but favor the particular interests of its dominant class and thus benefit some of its members at the expense of the others. Differently stated, the perfectly just regime has never existed in practice and never will.[14] The choice of one regime over another always involves a trade-off of some sort in which the gains registered on one front are offset by the losses incurred on another. There is no such thing as a genuine common-weal or a truly common good. The sad but inevitable conclusion to be drawn from this observation is that every citizen is willy-nilly complicit in the systemic inequities of the society whose life he shares and contributes to their perpetuation. From this loftiest of perspectives as distinguished from that of the ordinary political life, the distance between the conqueror and the thief is in fact negligible. Both are in it for themselves and neither one can claim any moral superiority over the other.

The best commentary that I know of on the story of Alexander and the pirate is the following exchange between the pirate Menas and Antony's lieutenant Enobarbus in Shakespeare's *Antony and Cleopatra*, II.6.83-95:

Menas: You and I have known, sir.
Enobarbus: At sea, I think.

Menas: We have, sir.

Enobarbus: You have done well by water.

Menas: And you by land.

Enobarbus: I will praise any man that will praise me:
  though it cannot be denied what I have done by land.

Menas: Nor what I have done by water.

Enobarbus: Yes, something you can deny for your own safety:
  you have been a great thief by sea.

Menas: And you by land.

Enobarbus: There I deny my land service.

Menas and Enobarbus are no strangers to each other. They have fought side by side in the past but have since gone their separate ways, one to become a pirate, the other a soldier in Antony's army. Menas, for one, is not about to grant the higher moral standing of his rival. As far as he is concerned, nothing important sets them apart. What one does by sea, the other does by land; the thievery is the same on both sides. Nor can Enobarbus appeal to his "service" or the justice of his cause. For a man like Menas, justice is a sham and a pretense, a mere cover lending a kind of spurious dignity to his selfish pursuits. The only thing that distinguishes him from Enobarbus is that, having nothing to lose by flaunting his selfishness, he can be up front about it.

The question is whether Menas can dismiss as irrelevant the distinction between the private enterprise in which he is engaged and the public character of the legitimate soldier's service. As a "soldier" of the sea, the pirate is literally a man without a country. Having renounced all allegiance to a common cause, he lives for himself alone. His pretext is that the common cause that the soldier serves is unworthy of such dedication; and he is convinced that in his heart of hearts the soldier knows it, too, even though he is unwilling to admit it. In his eyes, the soldier's justice is a form of hypocrisy, a mere show, with which he himself can dispense.

Menas can speak this way only because he abstracts from a crucial consideration, which is that pirates, who bear no public responsibilities, are condemned to living inglorious lives, whereas conquerors, who have the possibility of establishing the conditions of relative safety and prosperity from which countless others will profit for a long time to come, are often glorious, even if the glory they seek is first and foremost their own. To be sure, their conquests are rarely just, but this does not preclude their later being used for nobler purposes.

Weak as it may be, however, Menas's position is not without a grain of unpleasant truth. A man is only as good as the cause he serves, and there are moments when questions are bound to arise about the worthiness of the cause to which the dedicated soldier has pledged his loyalty. Surveying the problem from the vantage point of the philosophic life, Cicero was able to point in a roundabout way to a deeper kinship between the conqueror and the pirate than between the conqueror and the truly just individual. Augustine could do no less. With or without the benefit of philosophy, the Christian finds in his religious faith a means of transcending the distinctions that dominate the political life and of acceding to a higher sphere from which the deeds of the pagan hero are barely distinguishable from acts of outright piracy. Just as for Plato the only virtue is philosophic virtue, so for Augustine the only virtue is Christian virtue. Everything else merits the common reprobation in which it is engulfed.

Given our own modern habits of thought, Augustine's method of procedure in regard to pagan virtue and the moral possibilities of the political life may seem strange; yet there is nothing farfetched about it. It merely conforms to the familiar principle that the unqualified noun designates the perfected object. A thing is good to the extent that it has all that belongs to it by reason of its nature—*bonum ex integra causa,* as the old scholastic adage had it. To speak of a chair *tout court* is the same thing as to speak of a good chair, inasmuch a defective chair is not a chair in the full sense of the word. If I walk into a furniture store and ask for a chair, I do not have to specify that I want a good chair and would sound ridiculous if I did, for the adjective "good" adds nothing to what I mean when I use the word "chair" without qualification.

The same remarks apply to Augustine's treatment of virtue and of the city, which he ultimately understands as perfect virtue and the perfect city. As its etymology implies, the term "perfection," from the Latin *perficere,* "to bring to completion," is synonymous with wholeness. To the extent to which anything that belongs to them is lacking, the virtue or the city in question falls short of its definition and is less than what its name indicates. Aristotle intimated as much when he stated that "what a thing is when fully developed," whether it be a human being, a horse, or a city, "we call its nature" (*Politics* 1252b33). That is why, toward the end of Shakespeare's *Julius Caesar,* Antony cannot praise the slain Brutus more highly than by calling him simply "a man":

> This was the noblest Roman of them all.
> All the conspirators save only he
> Did that they did in envy of great Caesar;
> He only, in a general honest thought
> and common good to all, made one of them.
> His life was gentle, and the elements
> So mix'd in him, that Nature might stand up
> And say to all the world: "This was a man!" (V.1.68-75)

What renders Augustine's approach to these matters problematic at first sight is that it prescinds from an all-important practical consideration, namely, the various degrees of goodness or badness of which moral virtue and cities are susceptible. This is the issue that is dealt with in a round-about way under the heading of "fuzzy logic" by modern philosophers. The example often used for purposes of illustration is that of a chariot that is falling apart and will eventually be reduced to a heap of broken wheels, shafts, and panels in a corner of the yard. The question is, at what point did the chariot cease to be a chariot? To which the answer can only be: when it first began to disintegrate, however slightly. No matter how one looks at it, a chariot with a missing spoke, let alone a missing wheel, is less of a chariot than one that is whole. If my chariot is not too badly damaged, I may continue to call it by that name, but only to indicate that the time has not yet come to discard it, either because it is still serviceable or because it can be repaired.

A more commonsensical approach to the problems of ethics and politics will generally shun outrageous statements of the kind that Augustine relishes but that are of little use to statesmen, whose first task is not to speculate on the nature of civil society but to try to improve the lives of the mostly imperfect societies they are called upon to rule. This is not to say that Augustine was incapable of offering sound practical advice when required to do so but only that his more extreme statements were intended to serve a different purpose, that of bringing to light the limits of the political life. Augustine himself is the first to admit that according to other, "more plausible" (*probabiliores*) definitions of the city "Rome was indeed a republic, albeit one that was much better administered by the ancient Romans than by their descendants."[15] Why he preferred his own less flattering definition is a question to which we shall return in due course.

Another way of formulating the same problem is to say that, instead of taking moral phenomena on their own level or as they appear to decent nonphilosophers, Augustine tends to study them in the light of their highest metaphysical principles or, as one might say, in the light of the Platonic ideas. Viewed in that light, all human endeavors invariably fall short of the mark. This, more than anything else, is what lends credence to the charge that Augustine had a grievance against them and little of a positive nature to say about them. Fortunately, there is another side to his thought which, though often overlooked by scholars, evinces a much greater sensitivity to the quandaries in which we typically find ourselves than what we have seen thus far might lead us to believe. For all his seeming intransigence, Augustine is anything but an enemy of moderation, a blind idealist, or a fanatic who would let the world perish rather than make a single exception to his moral principles. It was not his way to sever *à la* Kant the link between "rightness" and "goodness" or between ethics and politics.

An intriguing dilemma in regard to which Augustine may have been more flexible than would seem from some rather blunt statements is the one posed by his teaching regarding self-defense. According to that teaching, killing an assailant to save the life of a third party for whose welfare one is responsible is a morally good act, whereas killing an assailant to save one's own life in similar circumstances is a sinful act.[17] Not a very realistic view, to say the least, for we all know how people tend to react when threatened by dangers of this sort.[18] Laying down rules of conduct for extreme situations and especially for situations that allow us virtually no time to think anyway is a luxury with which, as a rule, the ancient moralists felt they could dispense. What we would have here is just another example of Augustine's reluctance to make any concessions whatever to human nature. It may be, however, that the burden of the argument lies elsewhere. His main concern is not so much with whether killing in self-defense is morally permissible as with what the taking of a human life even in legally sanctioned self-defense does to the soul of the killer. Socrates was right: it is better to suffer evil than to commit evil.

Thus enunciated, however, such a principle is still only a "common" principle. It is a principle to be borne in mind at all times, for no decent person takes pleasure at the thought of being responsible for the death of another human being, even if that human being deserves to be put to death; but it says nothing about the modalities of its application to concrete situations. In the *Crito,* the seventy-year old Socrates invokes it to justify his refusal to escape from jail with the help of powerful friends. He does not tell us what he would have done had he been thirty years younger at the time of his trial. The same preoccupation with the effect of certain unpleasant though legitimate actions on the soul of the doer shows up again in Augustine's treatment of capital punishment, where the carrying out of the justly pronounced death sentence is entrusted, not to the judge or some other dignitary, but to the hangman, that is to say, to some bloodthirsty individual whose inhumane cruelty might otherwise be vented on innocent people.[19]

Equally vexing questions come to the fore when one turns to another celebrated Augustinian contribution to Western ethics, namely, the just war theory, the grandfather of the great sixteenth- and seventeenth-century treatises on the subject, which are often barely more than a series of attempts to systematize Augustine's insights into this problem and adapt them to a new set of circumstances. According to that theory, a war is just when it is waged to repel an unjust aggressor, defend an ally, secure a legitimate right of passage, rescue the victims of oppression in countries other than one's own whenever feasible, and the like. The theory stipulates that all other means of redress shall first have been exhausted, that the war shall be undertaken only out of necessity and for the sake of peace, and that it shall be carried on without undue harshness or violence. The assumption in all such cases is that a war can only be just on one side. As Augustine puts it with admirable succinctness, "when we wage a just war, our adversaries must be sinning."[20] If Rome's wars were just, those of the invading barbarians were unjust.

But were the barbarians behaving unjustly toward Rome? The picture is far from clear. There is plenty of evidence to show that in many if not most cases they were themselves acting out of necessity and under pressure from powerful hordes to the east from whom they had little choice but to flee. Besides, in the course of the negotiations, Rome had few scruples about breaking faith with them, to the point of indulging in unspeakable treacheries. Thousands of barbarians serving in the Roman army were mercilessly butchered once the reaction against them had set in, and others, after having been promised asylum, were reduced to the most abject slavery upon their arrival.[21] Rome, too, bore its share of the responsibility for the evils that were befalling it. Augustine all but says it was only getting what it deserved.

Beyond that was the nasty question of the justice of Rome's own borders, often hinted at but rarely broached explicitly in the literature of the period. It was no secret that these borders had been acquired through conquest or unjust aggression. But how can a war undertaken for the defense of unjust borders be considered just? The problem is not unlike the one that came up over a thousand years later in the wake of the Spanish conquest of the New World. Even if one grants the legitimacy of wars of civilization and agrees that according to natural justice the European invaders had some right to vast tracts of land that were not being put to good use,[22] one can hardly hold it against the native Americans for taking up arms in their own defense.

All in all, Augustine's just war theory left much unsaid, although not unnoticed. If anything can be thought to have motivated it, it is the conviction, not that wars can ever be completely just, but that under more or less favorable circumstances they might become a trifle less unjust. There are limits to how far one can go in establishing a nation's right to the territory over which it rules or in laying down rules for the defense of that territory. For Augustine, the choice was between civilization and barbarism, and it was in the light of that choice that the decision to support one side or the other had to be made. No one had fewer illusions than Augustine about the justice of the Roman Empire. If his heart was still with it, it is because he thought that the prospects for justice, slim as they always are, were greater within it than outside of it.

Save for the ban on apostasy,[23] the one moral principle to which according to all appearances Augustine refused to allow any exception whatever is the one that prohibits lies, a lifelong preoccupation of his that found expression not only in numerous discussions here and there in his works but in two whole books, the *De mendacio* (originally published against his will and later found by him to be "unbearable," *molestus*),[24] and the *Contra mendacium,* published some twenty-five years later, in 420. It is ever permissible to lie? Augustine admits that this question, too, is fraught with obscurity—*latebrosa.*[25] This time, the matter is complicated by the fact that the Old Testament patriarchs had few qualms about lying. In a desperate effort to explain away Jacob's whopper (Gen. 27:5f.), Augustine could think of nothing better to say than that the statement was meant to be interpreted mystically rather than literally. It was not a lie but a mystery: *non mendacium sed mysterium,*[26] an explanation that does not convince too many people nowadays, or so I gather. Frankly, I am not sure that it ever did. In any event, the bottom line is that, by the witness of the sacred Scriptures themselves, lying in any of its forms is absolutely forbidden: *nihil aliud illa testimonia Scripturarum monere nisi numquam esse omnino mentiendum.*[27]

Augustine's position on this score is highly original. As far as I know, he is the first major author to rule out all lies, including the noble or salutary lies that the entire classical tradition, both pagan and Christian, had hitherto condoned, a well-known fact that caused Oscar Wilde to speak, a bit exaggeratedly perhaps, of the aura of mendacity that adorns the pale brow of antiquity.[28] The prohibition extends even to such lies as one might resort to in emergency situations and for any number of commendable purposes.[29] Accordingly, the *De mendacio* is at pains to catalogue all the different kinds of lies that people tell and all the different situations, real as well as hypothetical, in which they might be tempted to tell them or consider it their duty to do so.

One can easily understand Augustine's unflinching opposition to lies told for the sake of gaining an unfair advantage over others, but what about lying when, say, a decent human being's life is at stake? If Augustine was ready to let a woman commit adultery in order to save her husband, why would he have been so unbending when it comes to telling an innocuous lie for a similar purpose? Augustine raises the issue briefly, but only to call attention to the disparity between the two cases.[30] The reason alleged for the greater severity in the case of lies is that the liar's soul is necessarily corrupted by the fact that he tells a lie, whereas only the woman's body is affected by a sexual act performed under duress—a lame argument at best, for one fails to see how a falsehood uttered on those rare occasions on which justice cannot be served in any other way would corrupt anybody's soul. What makes the two cases so different? Very little, it seems.

There may, in fact, have been a more profound reason for Augustine's adamant stand against lies, to wit, the need to avoid any statement that could cast the slightest doubt on the veracity of the Bible or the credibility of those entrusted with the task of preaching it to others. Make a single exception to the rule against lies and there is no telling how many more will follow. One could end up interpreting the Bible the way the classical philosophers and their disciples had been interpreting the pagan myths for centuries, namely, as beautiful (and sometimes not so beautiful) lies. The problem was rendered particularly acute by the fact that, unlike the other great monotheistic religions, Judaism and Islam, Christianity first comes to sight as a "faith" or a "doctrine" rather than as a divine law. It was thus forced to place an exceptionally high premium on truthfulness. As Augustine sees it, there are no more pernicious lies than the ones pertaining to the doctrines of religion.[31] Under no conditions can such lies be permitted, and the best way to prevent them is to banish lies altogether.

Still, to bring Augustine's examples up to date, one cannot help asking whether he himself would have given away the whereabouts of a Jew who was being pursued by the Gestapo had he been pressed to do so. It is a bit facile to say that one can always avoid an outright lie by resorting to a circumlocution of some sort, a clumsy subterfuge for which few thugs are apt to fall. There is the further argument that lying destroys the trust on which the entire social order rests and should be forbidden on those grounds, but it is not entirely convincing either, for the social order is just as likely to be undermined by its inability to protect the lives of innocent citizens. Although I have not seen it invoked explicitly in this context, Augustine's "third-party principle," which states that one is sometimes obliged to do for others what one is not allowed to do for oneself, would seem to come into play in this instance as well.

Augustine's overall approach as I have been presenting it is neatly summed up in his natural law theory, which has yet to receive the attention it deserves from modern scholars and where Augustine's radicalism reveals itself in its purest form. This is obviously not the place to enter into a full-blown discussion of this topic, great as its importance may be for the Western world (and, I might add, only for the Western world, for the natural law has never played a significant role anywhere else). The only aspect of the doctrine that concerns us is the definition of the natural law, which, for Augustine, is the law requiring that "all things be properly ordered in the highest degree," or that at all times the lower be subordinated to the higher both within the individual and in society at large.[32] Human beings are properly ordered when what is most noble in them, reason, controls the spirited part of the soul, when both reason and spiritedness combine to rule the desiring part, and when reason itself is ruled by God. Thus understood, the natural law is nothing other than the "divine reason or will prescribing the conservation of the natural order and prohibiting any breach of it."[33] It extends to all of one's activities and is coextensive with the whole of virtue. As such, it is inseparable from wisdom or properly cultivated reason. What it imposes on everyone as a moral duty is nothing short of the perfection of human nature.

It goes without saying that such an ideal is one that is rarely if ever encountered in real life. It exists only in discussions that take place behind closed doors—*domesticae disputationes*[34]—or in the heavenly city in which the community of the redeemed in Christ finds or will find its permanent home. Augustine knew very well that for the most part his exalted moral principles were not directly applicable to the conditions of daily life and had to be diluted in order to become effective. Innumerable obstacles, stemming from our bodily and fallen nature, stand in the way of our becoming perfect lovers of justice. Book III of *On Free Choice of the Will* traces them back to two general roots: the "ignorance" that so often clouds our judgment and the "difficulties" that so often hinder the exercise of our free will. Clearly, there are limits to what can reasonably be expected of human beings. To make matters worse, the complexity of the situations in the midst of which one is compelled to act is often such as to make it virtually impossible to satisfy some of the demands of the moral law without violating others.

But if, as I have been arguing, Augustine's theory makes unfulfillable and hence unreasonable demands on us, why would he have bothered to propose it? Two possible answers suggest themselves, one general and the other specific. The general answer is that human beings usually accomplish more when they are encouraged to raise rather than to lower their sights. This combination of high ideals and moderate expectations is by no means proper to Augustine. It is typical of the whole of premodern thought and stands in sharp contrast to the combination of modest ideals and absolute expectations that characterizes the thought of the great theorists of the modern period, beginning with Machiavelli, who have taught us to go to "the effectual truth of the matter"—*la verità effettuale della cosa*[35]—instead of its imagined truth or to study human beings as they are rather than as they ought to be.

This cannot be the whole story, however, for it does not explain why, at the risk of sounding irresponsible, Augustine found it necessary to heap so much scorn on the political life. There is a more specific answer to that question, although it is not an answer that we, as products of a liberal democratic tradition that lacks any notion of the regime as a *total* way of life, are in a good position to appreciate. We may recall that in the *City of God* and the writings related to it Augustine set two goals for himself. The first was to counter the charge that Christianity was responsible for the Empire's recent setbacks and in particular for the fall of the city of

Rome itself at the hands of Alaric and the Goths in the year 410, a dramatic if largely symbolic event—the barbarians retreated after two weeks—that made Rome's vulnerability evident to everyone with eyes to see. The second was to entice the pagan elite of his time to embrace the new faith, something that a number of them were reluctant to do on the ground that Christian morality was incompatible with the duties of citizenship. It frowned on war, preached the love of one's enemies, urged everyone to requite evil with good, and in general taught people to be more concerned with the good of their souls than with that of the fatherland. The problem was brought home to Augustine in a poignant way by one of his friends, the aged Nectarius of Calama, a pagan whose heart, as Augustine says, "still glowed with patriotic fire," who had imbibed from Cicero's *Republic* "the loyal citizen's sentiment that there is no limit either in measure or in time to the claim that their country has upon the care and service of right-hearted men," and who could not countenance a religion that was liable to weaken that sentiment.[36]

The trouble is that the means by which these two goals might be achieved were in obvious tension with each other. One consisted in moderating the "patriotic zeal" of Augustine's pagan friends so as to enlist them in the service of a "higher and nobler country"; the other, in reinforcing the patriotic zeal of his own coreligionists so as to attach them more firmly to the service of their earthly country. The critique of Roman political life and Roman religion that permeates so much of the *City of God* was calculated precisely to make the pagan nobility aware of the problematic character of its devotion to Rome, admirable as it may have been from another point of view. Hence the critique's manifest one-sidedness—"Rome was never a commonwealth," "the pagan virtues are nothing but vices"—for only by means of this kind of exaggeration could Rome's inherent shortcomings be made visible to the naked eye. There was no more effective way of persuading the pagan "holdouts" of his day that the time had come to embrace the new faith.

It is interesting to note in this connection that much of Augustine's argument is inspired by Cicero's account of Roman history in Book II of the *Republic*. The difference is that Scipio, who tells that story in the dialogue and is faced with the problem of restoring his fellow country-men's badly shaken faith in Rome, deftly conceals her defects (but not without letting the informed reader know that he is well aware of them) whereas Augustine lets the cat out of the bag and lays these defects out for everyone to see. His is an attempt not to promote Rome but to demythologize Cicero's account of it by stripping that account of its "embellishments."[37]

Augustine could afford to be more outspoken than his pagan prede-cessor about such matters because he could fall back on the Christian faith in an effort to rekindle a measure of public-spiritedness among his fellow countrymen. The gist of his argument is that, far from destroying patriotism, Christianity strengthens it by making of it a religious duty. It thereby serves the city more effectively than the moribund pagan religion that his adversaries were trying to reinstate could ever do. True, Christianity makes a much stronger claim on the allegiance of its followers than does the temporal society to which they belong, but, as a transcendent or transpolitical religion, it does not take them out of that society or abrogate their membership in it. What characterizes the Christian life on this level is a dual citizenship of a kind that had never been seen before. In order to be at one and the same time a good Christian and a good citizen, one had only to render to Caesar what is Caesar's and to God what is God's. Fine, except that to anyone who was convinced that everything was Caesar's the new arrangement was less than satisfactory, especially since what was left of one's attachment to one's fatherland was supported less by a powerful natural inclination than by the detour of the love of an unseen and mysterious God.

That Augustine's approach to such matters should have been frequently challenged by theocrats, Erastians, and virtually everyone in between during the centuries that followed is not surprising in view of the fact that the problem (later baptized the "theologico-political problem" by Spinoza) does not admit of any neat theoretical solution. Whether the approach of Augustine can still be recommended as a means of implanting or reimplanting the Christian faith in a world in which it is again more often than not on the defensive is a question that is best kept for another day. Whatever the answer to that question, the strategy seems to have worked remarkably well in Augustine's own time, as can be seen from the praise bestowed on him by some of his illustrious contemporaries, among them St. Jerome, who, as mentioned in chapter one, refers to him as the "second founder of the ancient faith," and Possidius, who credits him with having single-handedly brought Christianity back to life in Africa.[38]

NOTES

1. *Vita Augustini* 18.9.
2. Migne, *Patrologia, Series Latina* (or *PL*) 83.1109.
3. F. Nietzsche, *Antichrist* 19.
4. Uta Ranke-Heinemann, *Eunuchs for the Kingdom of Heaven: Women, Sexuality and the Catholic Church*, trans. Peter Heinegg (New York: Doubleday, 1990), 78. The text goes on as follows: "He (Augustine) dramatizes the fear of sexual pleasure, equating pleasure with perdition in such a way that anyone who tries to follow his train of thought will have the sense of being trapped in a nightmare. He

laid such a heavy moral burden on marriage that we cannot be surprised if people unnaturally oppressed by it were stung into rejecting Christian sexual morality lock, stock, and barrel."

5. Ibid., 81.

6. Ibid., 92.

7. Ibid., 83.

8. I say "falsely" because the allegation seems to be based on a literal inter-pretation of the Platonic myth of the pre-existence and fall of the soul. For what I consider to be a more adequate understanding of the nature of Plato's myths, cf. J. Klein, *A Commentary on Plato's Meno* (Chapel Hill: University of North Carolina Press, 1965).

9. Augustine, *De civitate Dei* (*City of God*) XIV.5. The remark is aimed at both the Manichees and the Platonists. See also, for Augustine's critique of Porphyry's dictum that the soul must escape from every kind of body—*omne corpus fugiendum*—*De civ. Dei* X.29.2 and XII.27. In the first of these two references, Augustine alludes to the peculiarly Neoplatonic doctrine of the hypostatic union of body and soul in the human being, which the Council of Chalcedon later used as an analogy to explain the union of the divine and human natures in the one person of Christ: "Our nature itself testifies that a human being is incomplete unless a body be united with the soul. This certainly would be more incredible were it not of all things the most common; for we should more easily believe in a union between spirit and spirit or, to use your own terminology, between the incorporeal and the incorporeal, even though the one were human, the other divine, the one changeable, the other unchangeable, than in a union between the corporeal and the incorporeal." Cf. E. L. Fortin, *Christianisme et culture philosophique au cinquième siècle* (Paris: Etudes Augustinennes, 1959), 111-123.

10. See, among numerous other places, the important Preface to the second edition of *The Birth of Tragedy*, 5, where Nietzsche writes:

> Christianity was from the beginning, essentially and fundamentally, life's nausea and disgust with life, merely concealed behind, masked by, dressed up as, faith in "another" or "better" life. Hatred of "the world," condemnations of the passions, fear of beauty and sensuality, a beyond invented the better to slander this life, at bottom a craving for the nothing, for the end, for respite, for the "sabbaths of sabbaths"— all this always struck me . . . at the very least (as) a sign of abysmal sickness, weariness, discouragement, exhaustion, and the impoverishment of life.

Elsewhere, in *Ecce Homo*, "Why I Am a Destiny," 8, we read:

> The concept of "God" invented as a counterconcept of life— everything harmful, poisonous, slanderous, the whole hostility unto death against life synthesized in this concept in a gruesome unity! The concept of the "beyond," the "true world" invented in order to devaluate the only world there is—in order to retain no goal, no

reason, no task for our earthly reality! The concept of the "soul,"
the "spirit," finally even "*immortal* soul" invented in order to
despise the body, to make it sick, "holy"; to oppose with a ghastly
levity everything that deserves to be taken seriously in life . . . .

11. Cf. *De civ. Dei* V.19: ". . . no one without true piety, that is, true worship
of the true God, can have true virtue." *De civ. Dei* XIX.25: "It is for this reason that
the virtues which the mind seems to itself to possess and by which it restrains the
body and the vices . . . are vices rather than virtues so long as there is no reference
to God in the matter."

12. For further information cf. H. A. Deane, *The Political and Social Ideas of
St. Augustine* (NY: Columbia University Press, 1963), 118f. J. D. Adams, *The
Populus of Augustine and Jerome* (New Haven and London: Yale University Press,
1971), 123f.

13. *Politics* I.1253a37. For an extensive discussion of Augustine's definition of
civil society, see chapter four of this volume.

14. As a Christian, Augustine was bound to attribute this state of affairs to
man's sinful condition rather than to nature itself.

15. *De civ. Dei* XIX.21.4.

16. *De sermo Domini in Monte* (*The Lord's Sermon on the Mount*) I.16.50 (*PL*
34.1254).

17. Cf. *De libero arbitrio* (*On Free Choice of the Will*) I.5.13; *Epist.* 47.5.

18. Augustine's position stands in sharp contrast to that of Thomas Aquinas,
who grants to everyone the right to kill in self-defense. That right is grounded in the
natural inclination that impels all beings to seek their own preservation within the
limits of possibility. One is under a greater obligation to provide oneself than to
provide for others. As for Augustine's opinion to the contrary, it is rejected with the
polite remark that Augustine proscribes as unjust only that act which has as its direct
object, not the defense of one's own life, but the taking of the aggressor's life. Cf.
Summa Theologiae II-II qu. 64, a. 7. From this text was later derived the famous
"double-effect" principle in moral theology.

19. *De diversis questionibus LXXXIII* (*On Eighty-three Different Questions*)
53.2. Cf. *De ordine* (*On Order*) II.12: "What is more hideous than a hangman? Is any
spirit fiercer and more cruel than his? Yet he is assigned a necessary place by the
laws and is a proper part of any well ordered city. In himself he is evil; from the
point of view of the city he is the terror of evildoers."

20. *De civ. Dei* XIX.15.

21. R. Bainton, *Christian Attitudes toward War and Peace* (New York and
Nashville: Abingdon Press, 1960), 99-100.

22. In classical political theory, property belongs in the strictest sense to the one
who knows best how to use it and is disposed to act in accordance with that
knowledge. Everyone nevertheless recognized that this was not a principle that cities
could adopt as a matter of course, for any attempt to do so would result in chaos.

23. It bears noting, however, that in certain unusual contexts even apostasy can

raise some interesting questions, as we can surmise from Shusaku Endo's powerful novel, *Silence*, trans. William Johnston (Tokyo: Sophia University Press, 1969), concerning the persecution of Christians in seventeenth-century Japan.

24. Augustine, *Retractationes* (*Retractions*) I.27.

25. Augustine, *De mendacio* (*On Lying*) I.1.

26. Augustine, *Contra mendacium* (*Against Lying*) IX.24.

27. Augustine, *De mendacio* XXI.42. Not all instances of biblical lying could be explained away that easily. Most notable among these are the lies told by the Hebrew midwives in Exodus 1:15-21, and by Rahab in Joshua 2:1-7. In both cases, the problem is compounded by the fact that the liars were rewarded by God for what they did. Unable to condemn what God himself had approved, Augustine did the next best thing: he attributed the lies in question to the fact that the persons involved had not yet achieved the moral perfection for which they were nevertheless striving and which would become available only in Christian times.

28. Cf. O. Wilde, "The Decay of Lying," in *Intentions*, 17th ed. (London: Methuen, 1934), 49. See on the problem of noble lies in patristic literature John Henry Newman, *Apologia pro Vita Sua*, chap. 5 and note F, where Newman defends himself against the attacks provoked by his discussion of the "reserve" or "economy" practiced by the Church Fathers in his book on *The Arians of the Fourth Century*, and, in addition, Newman's "Answer in Detail to Mr. Kingsley's Accusations" in the Appendix to his *Apologia*.

29. Cf. Augustine, *De mendacio* XIII.23, where Bishop Firmus of Thagaste, "firm in name and even firmer in will," is applauded for having braved death rather than disclose to the imperial emissaries the hiding place of a fugitive whom he was sheltering.

30. Augustine, *De mendacio* VII.10. See Augustine's reflections on the case of a woman committing adultery to save the life of her husband in E. L. Fortin, *Classical Christianity and the Political Order: Reflections on the Theologico-Political Problem*, edited by J. Brian Benestad (Lanham, MD: Rowman and Littlefield Publishers, 1996), ch 7.

31. Cf. Augustine, *De mendacio* IV.25; *Contra mendacium*, XI.25; XXI.41.

32. Augustine, *De libero arbitrio* I.6.15.

33. Augustine, *Contra Faustum manichaeum* (*Against Faustus, the Manichean*) XXII.27.

34. Augustine, *Epistula* (*Letter*) 91.4.

35. Machiavelli, *The Prince*, chap. 15.

36. Augustine, *Epist.* 91.1.

37. Further details cf. E. L. Fortin, "The Patristic Sense of Community," in chapter 4 of this volume.

38. Jerome, *Epist.* 141 (to Augustine) (*PL* 22. col. 1180). Possidius, *Vita Augustini* 7 (*PL* 32. col. 39).

3

AUGUSTINE'S *DE QUANTITATE ANIMAE* OR THE SPIRITUAL DIMENSIONS OF HUMAN EXISTENCE

The *De quantitate animae* is the longest of the three works that the newly converted Augustine devoted to the study of the human soul, the other two being the *Soliloquies* and its unfinished complement, the short treatise *On the Immortality of the Soul*.[1] It also happens to be the least studied of his early works. If I am not mistaken, the remarkably complete *Bulletin Augustinien* published each year since 1955 by the *Revue des Etudes Augustiniennes* lists only one article dealing thematically with it, in contrast to dozens of articles dealing with the other dialogues.[2]

To be sure, the same period witnessed the publication of English, French, German, Italian, Polish, Russian, and Spanish translations of the *De quantitate animae*, but always as part of larger collections involving several if not all of Augustine's works. John H. S. Burleigh did not see fit to include it in his edition of Augustine's earlier writings for the *Library of Christian Classics*, probably because it is less openly religious in tone than the other dialogues. While the *De quantitate* is not infrequently mentioned in essays devoted to Augustine's thought in general or some particular aspect thereof, here as elsewhere the harvest is not nearly as plentiful as one might expect. Even R. J. O'Connell, who has scrutinized Augustine's early works more diligently than perhaps anyone else in our time, usually cites it for the sole purpose of buttressing conclusions arrived at from other sources. It is almost as if this dialogue had become the object of a conspiracy of silence on the part of modern scholars. People have gone to it for information concerning problems in which they themselves had a special interest; no one, as far as I can tell, has tried to understand it on its own terms or from the perspective of its author.

The phenomenon is all the more curious as the *De quantitate animae* is a work to which Augustine attached a good deal of importance. Twenty-five years after its publication, he was still recommending it to his interlocutor in the dialogue, Evodius, now bishop of Uzalis, who had apparently forgotten some of the lessons once learned from his master.[3] The *Retractationes* stress the fact that its subject is treated "with great care and subtlety"—*diligentissime ac subtilissime* (I.7.1). Scholars have occasionally detected a tone of reproach in the use of the adverb *subtilissime* and suggested that Augustine was later dissatisfied with himself for having indulged in excessive or superfluous refinements.[4] The suspicion seems unwarranted, for it is unlikely that *subtilissime* would have been coupled with the laudatory *diligentissime* if it were meant to be taken in a pejorative sense.

Nor is there any indication that Augustine had since changed his mind about any of the points developed in the dialogue. The *Retractationes* make only two further comments neither of which touches upon the substance of the argument. Their aim is merely to clarify the meaning of certain statements that could be misinterpreted by careless readers. One is a fleeting allusion to the Platonic notion of recollection, which, we are told, should not be construed as a tacit admission that Augustine subscribed to the doctrine of the preexistence of the soul, a difficult topic on which, at the time, he was not prepared to take a stand. The other is a remark in which he voices his desire to refrain from any unnecessary entanglement in external activities and return to himself, he being the one to whom "above all," *maxime*, he owes himself. His intention, he says, was not to exclude God, to whom we owe all of ourselves and everything we have; it was to point out that no one is obliged to prefer other human beings to himself. Scripture commands us to love our neighbor as ourselves, not *more* than ourselves.

We hardly need to recall that the human soul was a fundamental theme of the classical and specifically Platonic tradition to which Augustine was so profoundly indebted. In *Enneads* IV.3, Plotinus insists on the centrality of this issue for the whole of the philosophic enterprise. It is no accident that the references to the soul (*psychē*) in the *Enneads* are two and a half times as numerous as the references to either the One (*eis*) or the intellect (*nous*), the next two most frequently used terms. The reason is simple. Anyone who would seek the truth must know something about the instrument with which he seeks. The goal of philosophy is self-knowledge, which the divine oracle enjoins upon us and without which the philosopher cannot give an adequate account of his own doings. Unlike Theodorus, the mathematician in Plato's *Theaetetus* whose science is unaccompanied by any awareness of his needs as a human being, the philosopher cannot remain blind to the reasons that motivate his quest for knowledge. He owes it to himself to gain an insight into the nature of the soul and therewith an understanding of its place within the whole, its relationship to the other beings in the universe, both above and below it, and the many factors which, unless one is aware of them, are liable to interfere with its operations, such as inveterate habits, unexamined opinions, and the promptings of a disordered appetite.

Augustine was of the same opinion. He too makes it clear that knowledge of the soul ought to be an object of primary concern to us. In Letter 166.3, addressed to St. Jerome and dated from the year 414, he confesses to being among those who are obsessed by that question: *Quaestio de anima multos movet, in quibus et me esse confiteor.* The preoccupation was not a recent one. In one of his earliest works, the *De ordine*, he informs us that philosophy "treats of two questions, one regarding the soul and the other regarding God," and that the two are inseparable. One "enables us to know ourselves and the other to know our origin." The former, which is "sweeter" (*dulcior*), makes us worthy of the happy life and is for "those who are still learning"; the latter is "for those who are already well-instructed" and "brings us happiness" (II.18.47).

The same thought, as we saw in Chapter One, is echoed in the famous passage of the *Soliloquies*, where Augustine states flatly, "I desire to know God and the soul . . . ., nothing else": *Deum et animam scire cupio. Nihilne plus? Nihil omnino* (I.2.7). Not surprisingly, it reappears in the *De quantitate animae*, which opens with a remark by Evodius to the effect that, since Augustine has forbidden him to inquire into the "things above us," he might be permitted to investigate "what we ourselves are"—*quid simus nos* (1.1). He, too, will be reminded that in the end truth consists in knowing two things, God and oneself, and furthermore that this knowledge is always granted to those who pursue it with pure and sincere hearts: "By virtue of a certain divine Providence it cannot happen that religious souls who piously, chastely, and diligently seek to know themselves and to know God—that is, to know the truth—will be denied the possibility of finding it" (14.24).

These texts and others like them are sufficient evidence that, in tune with his Platonic or Neoplatonic masters, Augustine held the study of the soul to be the pivot on which the whole of the intellectual life turns and the key to our understanding of everything else. This alone should encourage us to take the *De quantitate animae* more seriously than has hitherto been the case and try to ascertain its specific contribution to the project undertaken in the dialogues.

THE PHILOSOPHIC DIALOGUE AND ITS USES

This said, one has to admit that, for all the care with which it was supposedly written, the *De quantitate animae* is not an easy book to decipher. Toward the end of the dialogue, Augustine acknowledges that the discussion has not only been long but fertile in twists and turns, in detours and circumvolutions: *ambages* and *anfracta* (31.63). All kinds of false starts have been made and the conversation has kept veering into paths that turned out to be dead ends. Augustine is not entirely pleased with the result. He apologizes to Evodius for his failure to shed as much light as would have been necessary on a number of crucial points, such as the origin of the soul, the number of souls, and the world soul (32.69), and he graciously offers to return to them at a later date should the opportunity present itself (36.81).

Such being the case, one wonders why Augustine chose to write a dialogue rather than a treatise, which would have allowed for a more orderly treatment of the subject matter. No direct answer to the question is offered either in the *De quantitate* or in any of the other dialogues. It is nevertheless safe to assume that Augustine, who had read Cicero's dialogues and was acquainted with at least some of Plato's dialogues or parts of them, had a good idea of the reasons that had prompted his pagan predecessors to adopt this highly original literary genre. In the *Tusculan Disputations*, V.4.11, Cicero, who claims to be following the method used by Socrates, the first man to "bring philosophy down from heaven and into the city," tells us that he employed the dialogue form because it allowed him to do three things: (a) to conceal his private opinions—*ut nostram ipsi sententiam tegeremus*, (b) to lead others out of error, and (c) in every discussion to look for the solution that comes closest to the truth.

The observation is illuminating insofar as it condenses in three lines one of the great themes of classical thought, to wit, the essential difference between a written teaching and an oral teaching, as well as the superiority of the latter over the former.[5] Books have a certain advantage in that they enable the writer to reach a wider audience and to do so over a much longer period of time. The trouble with them is that, once published, they can fall into anybody's hands and are liable to be misused by unwise or unfriendly readers.[6] In the absence of their authors, they cannot defend themselves and always reply with the same words to the questions that are put to them. In this decisive respect, the master who converses with his students is in a more enviable position. He can assess their moral character, adapt himself to their intellectual needs and capacities, and determine what they can most profitably be taught at any given moment. Strange as it may seem to most of us, not all truths were thought to be salutary. Origen, who has a lot to say on this subject, was of the opinion that it is always dangerous to speak about God. He was not the only one to think so. None of the great writers of the past believed in the possibility of popular enlightenment and most of them cautioned against it. We forget too easily that, throughout most of history, freedom of speech was an unknown commodity, not only because governments did not tolerate it, but because of the restraints that, out of a sense of responsibility, serious writers saw fit to impose upon themselves in regard to such matters.

What rendered the dialogue form appealing to so many of them—Xenophon, Plato, Aristotle, and Cicero are only the most famous—is that it combines the advantages of both types of communication, oral and written. It enables the writer to reach out to distant places and future generations, and, by recreating the natural setting within which the master's teaching is imparted to a group of students, it permits him whenever necessary to "conceal" his own opinion either through silence or through the use of noble lies. At that point, the burden of interpretation shifts to the reader who becomes, as it were, an active participant in the discussion and must figure out in each case whether the statements made by the various characters represent their real thought or just an effort at accommodation to the demands of the situation.

Augustine appears to have been attracted to the dialogue form for similar if not altogether identical reasons. Unlike Plato and Cicero, he never condoned the use of lies, against which he would soon be writing the first of two books, the *De mendacio*, in 395—Christianity, he thought, had done away with the need for them—but he knew as well as anyone else that the whole truth in matters of supreme moment can be safeguarded only if its investigation is accompanied by a prudent reserve in the expression of that truth. As he observes in the *De ordine*, anyone who "dares to embark rashly and without order upon the study of such questions will become not studious but curious, not learned but credulous, not prudent but unbelieving" (II.5.17; cf. I.11.31). The same advice is given in the *De quantitate animae*, where Evodius is "warned and warned again not to run headlong and heedlessly to the writings or discussions of spellbinders," lest his studies and efforts "divert him more readily than would sloth or inertia from that peaceful sanctum of the mind to which the soul in its present life is a stranger" (31.63). In the *Contra academicos*, Augustine even goes so far as to contend that one "commits a grave sin," *graviter peccat*, by teaching certain truths to any chance comer (III.17.38). All of the dialogues, one could say, are attempts to achieve a rational understanding of what he and his young friends already accept on faith or the authority of the Scriptures. At the same time, he was well aware of the fact that this kind of understanding is the preserve of a small group of naturally gifted and well trained individuals.

The first question that the reader of the *De quantitate animae* needs to ask is whether Evodius, the only character in the dialogue besides Augustine, fits into that category. It is significant that the dialogues never show us Augustine conversing with anyone who is as old as he is or might otherwise be considered his intellectual equal, unless one takes the personification of Reason in the *Soliloquies* to be such a person. Evodius is certainly no exception. Nothing that he says or that is said about him reveals a man of exceptionally high intellectual achievement or promise. We know from the *Confessions* that he had been a member of the secret police, which by that time he had left, presumably for moral reasons.[7] His desire for the truth is ardent and sincere, but this does not make him any less impetuous, argumentative, and impatient with Augustine's probing analyses and picayune questions—*interrogatiuncula*, as he calls them disparagingly (29.57). His knowledge of logic is deficient and he is as yet unacquainted with natural philosophy. Augustine implies as much when he tells him that without this kind of knowledge he himself would have been at a loss to solve any of the problems with which they are concerned (31.63). As the dialogue is about to end, he again reminds Evodius that before he can arrive at the clarity that he seeks, he has a lot to learn: *multa alia . . . . tibi desunt* (32.68).

All of this would tend to make of Evodius a typical rather than an ideal addressee of Augustine's discourses. The chances of his getting to the bottom of things are virtually nil. Little wonder that twenty-five years later he was still raising some of the same questions. One can only conclude that on a superficial level the *De quantitate animae* does not try to teach more than what a man of undeniable good will but less than outstanding intellectual merit or preparation can suitably absorb. Anything that might be needed for a fuller understanding of its subject will have to be sought beneath the surface of the text or outside of it.

THE SUBJECT OF THE DIALOGUE

Evodius, who initiates the discussion, lists six questions to which he would like to have answers. He wants to know (1) where the soul comes from; (2) what its "quality" or essential characteristic is; (3) what is meant by its "quantity"; (4) why it was united to a body; (5) what happens to it as a result of this union; and finally (6) what becomes of it once it leaves the body. This heavy agenda will remain largely unfulfilled. The first two questions are treated summarily in Chapters One and Two respectively, and the last three, although mentioned again at the very end of the book, are dropped at least as questions to be dealt with separately. This leaves us with the third question, that of the quantity or greatness of the soul, with which the bulk of the text—more than 95% of it—is taken up.

It should be pointed out, to begin with, that the expression *quantitas animae*, from which the dialogue takes its title, is by no means common in Latin and does not occur in any of Augustine's other works save for the references to the *De quantitate* in the *Retractationes* and *Letter* 162. Why Augustine chose to speak of the soul in this manner becomes clear when we reflect on the content of the dialogue. Philosophically, quantity is defined as that which can be divided into homogeneous parts. It applies properly to bodies or tridimensional substances and, by extension, to mathematical entities, such as lines and figures, which cannot be defined without reference to their spatial dimensions. These and only these are, strictly speaking, capable of being measured or numbered. The application of the term "quantity" to a nonquantifiable substance is Augustine's way of directing our minds to the true subject of the dialogue, namely, the incorporeality of the soul or, as is more commonly said today, its spirituality. In this new acceptation, which survives in such terms as "magnanimity" and "longanimity," "quantity" refers, not to the corporeal dimensions of the soul—it does not have any—but to its power and capacity to act, its *virtus* and its *potentia* (3.4). In Augustine's phrase, to call Hercules great is to allude, not to the size of his body, but to the magnitude of his accomplishments. Human beings have no choice but to describe spiritual realities by means of terms borrowed from the realm of sense experience. We name things as we know them, and corporeal realities are the only ones of which we have any direct perception. This means no more than that a new meaning has been imposed on the term "quantity" so as to make it signify something to which it did not originally extend (cf. 17.30).

This is not to imply that Augustine is the first to speak of the soul in this manner. The expression *quantitas animae*, while rare in Latin (not even his disciple, Claudianus Mamertus, whose *De statu animae* borrows so much from the *De quantitate*, uses it) has its equivalent in the Greek *megethos psychēs*, which already appears in Aristotle's *De anima*, 407a4 and 10, where Plato's account of the creation of the soul in the *Timaeus* is criticized on the ground that it seemingly attributes to the soul the same physical dimensions as the body. But Augustine did not have to go all the way back to Aristotle in order to find it. It is frequently encountered in the *Enneads*, as is the distinction between physical and spiritual greatness —between things that are great *en ogkō*, or by reason of their bulk, and things that are great *en dynamei*, or by reason of what they are capable of doing.[8] In *Enneads* II.9.17, for example, the Gnostics (assuming that they are the ones of whom Plotinus wishes to speak) are chided precisely for their inability to distinguish between these two vastly different forms of greatness. The point is worth noting if only because Christians, many of whom held the soul to be a corporeal substance, are sometimes thought to be included among those whom Plotinus is attacking.

This whole question of the incorporeality of the soul was not for Augustine a matter of curiosity or idle speculation. Books III to VII of the *Confessions* show him wrestling desperately with it for a period of some nine years. We do well to remember that the *De quantitate animae*, which could serve as a commentary before the letter on those five books, was written during the year that he spent in Rome prior to his return to Africa in 388. It is roughly contemporaneous with the first draft of the *De moribus ecclesiae catholicae et Manichaeorum* and Book I of the *De libero arbitrio* and is sandwiched between them in the *Retractationes*. Since both the *De moribus* and the *De libero arbitrio* were directed against the Manichees, as is clear from their content and from the *Retractationes*, it is not unreasonable to suppose that in writing the *De quantitate*, Augustine likewise had the Manichees in mind. The supposition is confirmed by the fact that certain themes or expressions, such as "free will" (*liberum arbitirum*, 36.80), "true religion" (*vera religio* 34.78), the sensitivity of plants (33.71), and the notion of the soul as a parcel of the divinity (34.77), at least the first two of which make their appearance for the first time in this dialogue, originally belong to the anti-Manichaean polemic. The difference is that Manichaeanism is not expressly mentioned either in the text of the *De quantitate animae* or the notice devoted to it in the *Retractationes*. For this reason, it is probably more accurate to say that the immediate target in the present case is not Manichaeanism itself but the Manichee within Augustine's soul, or Augustine himself to the extent to which he had succumbed to Manichaean materialism and had then become engaged in a heroic struggle against it. What the dialogue gives us, it seems, is a re-enactment, for Evodius's benefit and ours, of the process by which, under the influence of Neoplatonism, he was finally able to break out of this mold.

Accordingly, the dialogue is divided into three parts. The first is an attempt to prove by means of philosophic arguments that the soul is indeed an incorporeal substance. The second is a refutation of the most obvious objections to that thesis. The third is an account of the true greatness of the soul through an examination of its various operations. Given the limited amount of time at our disposal, we cannot possibly go into all the details of the discussion, but neither is it indispensable that we do so. Our purpose will have been achieved if we succeed in grasping Augustine's mode of procedure and the conclusions to which it leads.

THE PROOF OF THE SOUL'S INCORPOREALITY
AND THE OBJECTIONS TO IT

The basic argument may be stated simply as follows: Bodies or corporeal substances are characterized by the fact that they are extended in three directions: length, breadth, and depth. If it can be shown that some entities lack spatial dimensions altogether without being any less real for that reason, the existence of incorporeal substances will have been established and one can go on from there to prove that the soul is such a substance.

Evodius readily grants that some things—justice, for example—exist even though they are incorporeal but denies that the soul is one of them (4.5). He still thinks of it as a material substance, "something akin to the wind," which both contains the body and is contained by it (4.6). The remark says more about his moral character—he is a lover of justice—than it does about his intelligence. He has not yet learned to distinguish between the soul, which is a substance, and justice, which is the quality of a substance. More importantly, he fails to see that if the soul is corporeal, both the justice that he loves and, as he will later discover, the science that he seeks have no foundation. Hence the need for a new argument which, this time, will focus on memory, the faculty by which we retain within ourselves images of things that are absent, such as past events and distant places. Some of these places—Milan, say, which Augustine and Evodius had left only a few months before—are obviously much larger than we are. This alone would seem to suggest that body and soul are not only different substances but different kinds of substances, even though we still do not know how precisely they differ.

At this point, Augustine turns to mathematics, which, because of the intermediary position that it occupies between the world of material and that of immaterial substances, serves as a bridge from one to the other. Shorn of one of its dimensions, a tridimensional object such as a cube becomes a plane figure, possessed of only two dimensions. By suppressing a second dimension, one arrives at the notion of a line, which has only one dimension. And by reducing the line to its principle, the point, one is left with an entity that has no corporeal dimensions whatever and is intelligible to the mind alone. But the mind would not be capable of understanding such an entity if it were not itself incorporeal. No faculty can exceed the limits of the object that specifies it.

Throughout all of this, Evodius's interest in justice has not been neglected. The different geometrical figures referred to in the argument are ranked with a view to their conformity with the principle of equality, the very essence of justice (9.15). An equilateral triangle is more perfect than a scalene triangle because of the perfect equality of its sides and angles.

A square is more perfect than a triangle because, being more symmetrical—its angles face one another, as do its lines—it exhibits an even higher degree of equality. A circle is more perfect than a square because all the points along its circumference are equidistant from the center.

I leave it to others to judge the appropriateness of this strange mixture of mathematics and morals and decide whether the argument is convincing in every respect. One obvious difficulty is that it looks upon the point as a purely intelligible reality rather than as the culmination of a process that remains entirely within the realm of the imagination. There may be better ways of proving the incorporeality of the soul, although it is by no means certain that they would be equally effective with someone like Evodius. Besides, this particular mode of arguing has other advantages. It gives Augustine the opportunity to subject Evodius to an *exercitatio mentis* or mental gymnastic by which, if all goes well, his intellect will gradually be freed from the shackles of the senses (cf. 15.25). The method was well known to the ancients. Augustine was familiar with it from Varro, who advocated the use of the liberal arts for this very purpose. These arts were not to be cultivated for their own sakes. They were an essential ingredient of the moral formation of the future citizen and thus pointed in the direction of moral and political virtue; and they functioned as tools with which to sharpen the mind for the exercise of the dianoetic virtues or the pursuit of contemplation. They would soon be designated by the terms *quadrivium* (invented by Boethius) and *trivium*, from the Latin *via*, meaning "road" or "way," in this case the way that leads by degrees from less perfect to more perfect forms of knowledge.

That Augustine should have opted for this approach is further evidence that Evodius was not ready for more solid food. After all that has been said, he is still not convinced that the soul is an immaterial substance. Two main considerations prevent him from accepting Augustine's argument. The first is that the soul's development seems to be linked to that of the body. Babies are manifestly incapable of certain functions which adults perform as a matter of course. If so, it seems reasonable to believe that the soul grows with the body and shares its tridimensional character. Secondly, Evodius is troubled by the fact that the soul experiences pleasure and pain in different parts of the body—another indication, he thinks, that the soul is spread throughout the body and thus spatially extended like it (15.26).

With the answers to these questions we come to what is undoubtedly the most difficult part of the dialogue and the one where Evodius comes closest to being given a *bona fide* lesson in philosophy. In reply to his first objection, Augustine will argue that the growth of the soul is not to be conceived on the model of physical growth. It is not related to the changes that the body undergoes but comes about through the exercise of its own faculties. As for the second objection, it can be countered by observing that the phenomenon of sensation to which Evodius adverts proves the exact opposite of what he thinks it proves: not that the soul is corporeal but that it must be incorporeal. What is peculiar about it is that it is indivisibly present in all parts of the body without being circumscribed by any of them. Otherwise it, too, would feel pleasure or pain, not according to the whole of itself, as it unmistakably does, but only in one or the other of its parts.

The argument is, to say the least, a subtle one. To appreciate its force, one would have to be acquainted with a number of complex philosophical issues: the distinction between sense knowledge and intellectual knowledge, the manner in which the latter is acquired, the properties of a good definition, the difference between reason and science as well as between reason, which is a faculty, and reasoning, which is an act, the nature of vision and its medium, and a variety of other more or less subtle notions with which Evodius is only vaguely familiar. Whether he will ever be able to master them is an open question. The prospects are not very good. Some things have nevertheless been accomplished. The stage has been set for the last section of the dialogue, the one dealing with the true greatness of the soul, which Augustine introduces with the following words: "Now let me tell you, if you will—rather, let me assist you to an appreciation of how great the soul is, not in regard to extension in space and time, but in regard to its power (*vis*) and capacity (*potentia*)." Evodius, who by this time has been taught more than one lesson in humility and has had about as much as he can take, gladly acquiesces in the proposal: "I yield to you completely," he replies, "and am eager that you give me an explanation, one that I can follow—*quod tibi congruenter mecum videtur agi posse*—of what greatness there is in the soul" (32.69).

THE SOUL AND ITS OPERATIONS

The explanation will be given in terms of the various operations of the soul and their proper rank (33.70ff). We know the nature of a thing when we know what it can do, and we know what it can do when we have seen it at work and observed all of its activities from lowest to highest. Seven operations or levels of activity—*gradus actionis* (33.75)—are listed in ascending order and divided into three categories. Three of them, animation, sensation, and art, have to do with the action of the soul on the body and bodily things. The next two, the moral purification of the soul and its maintenance in the state of purity, concern the action of the soul on itself. The last two, the turning toward God and the contemplation of the truth, concern the mind's action in relation to the divinity and constitutes its highest achievement. This, we now learn, is the soul's true home, *mansio,* and the goal of everything that precedes (33.76).

This is not the only such enumeration in Augustine—we find others in the *De ordine*, the *De musica*, the *De libero arbitrio*, the *De genesi contra Manichaeos*, the *De doctrina christiana*—but it appears to be the most complete. Since the publication of F. Cayré's classic work, *La contemplation augustinienne*,[9] the tendency among scholars has been to cite it as an example of Augustine's would-be mysticism, although the term is carefully avoided in the title of Cayré's book. This is not the place to reopen the lively debate that once pitted against one another the defenders and opponents of Augustinian mysticism, a mysticism which, if it exists, would have been inspired in large measure by .[10] I, for one, see no reason to deny that the religious experi-ences occasionally described in Augustine's works bear some resem-blance to the ones that would one day be called mystical. On the other hand, there is little to be gained by applying to Augustine a term that is foreign to his vocabulary and laden with overtones that often take us in a quite different direction.

In classical and Christian antiquity, "mystical"—"pertaining to the mysteries," from the Greek *myein*, "to initiate into the mysteries"—was first and foremost an attribute of things rather than of persons. Texts, doctrines, numbers, chants, rites, cultic ornaments or implements, and, in the Christian tradition, the sacraments and the days of the sacred season of Lent were labeled "mystical" insofar as their deeper meaning was accessible only to the initiated or to believers.[11] Never was the word used to characterize the states of mind or internal dispositions with which it came to be associated from the late Middle Ages onward. In the few instances where it is applied to human beings, its connotations are objective rather than psychological or subjective. It merely designates someone who is initiated or initiates others into the mysteries.[12] The word appears only once in all of Plotinus, in its adverbial form—*mystikōs*—with reference to the hidden meaning of a pagan myth, and not a very edifying one at that.[13] Augustine uses the term more frequently but still not very often and always in connection with things rather than persons.[14] As has often been remarked, his approach to religious matters is highly rational, some would even say intellectualist. "I am so constituted," he says in the *Contra academicos*, "that I impatiently desire to apprehend the truth not by belief alone but by understanding" (III.20.43). In the *De ordine*, he thanks his mother for having taught him to place the knowledge of the truth above everything else—to desire, hope for, and love nothing else (cf. II.20.52). This is not the kind of language that is most typical of the mystical tradition.

For similar reasons, there is a serious question as to whether one can talk of Plotinian Neoplatonism as being essentially mystical or leaning toward mysticism. No doubt, its claim that the highest principle in the universe is beyond *logos* and *ousia* and the vocabulary that it uses in speaking about the intelligible world is reminiscent of the nondiscursive modes of thought that tend to predominate in mystical literature. Yet a closer look at the evidence suggests that, intensely spiritual as it may have been, Plotinian thought is not nearly so nonrational or suprarational—the distinction between the two terms is easily lost—as it is sometimes painted. We have it on the authority of Macrobius that the representatives of this school were famous, not for their attempt to transcend reason, but for their unswerving dedication to it.[15] The same point is made by Olympiodorus, who notes that Plotinus, Porphyry, and their disciples honored philosophy above all else, while others, such as Iamblichus, Syrianus, and Proclus, deferred to theurgy—*hieratikē*.[16] As for the emphasis on the supraessential quality of the One, which became the hallmark of later Neoplatonism, it may be no more than a way of intimating that the highest principle in the universe is not a particular being. Plotinus himself uses the term "supraessential" only once, again in its adverbial form, *hyperontōs*.[17] One thing is certain: the impersonal God of the *Enneads* is not exactly the kind of being whose presence Christian mystics claim to experience within themselves.

Neoplatonic "mysticism," it would seem, is just another name for the school's two most salient features: (a) its conspicuous apoliticism, as evidenced by its general lack of interest in Plato's great political dialogues, the *Republic* and the *Laws*, and its focus on the *Phaedrus*, the *Phaedo*, and the *Parmenides*—it is in this sense that Plotinus has been called a *Plato dimidiatus*—and (b) the religious imagery in which it is wont to express itself. Both features reflect the conditions of the period in which it developed, a period marked by the decline or the depersonalization of political life and an accompanying surge of religiosity among people for whom the ideal of personal salvation was the only one capable of satisfying the longings of the human heart.

Augustine's own term for the highest human experience is *contemplatio*, the Latin equivalent of the Greek *theōria*, now redefined in accordance with the New Testament command of the love of God and neighbor. This contemplation was the fulfillment of the ideal that began to take shape in his mind when, at the age of nineteen, he read Cicero's *Hortensius*.

This new ambition was thwarted precisely by his inability to conceive of a nonmaterial substance.[18] Bodies do not think and without thought there is no disinterested quest for the truth or any other properly human good. The point was made with the utmost clarity by Plotinus, who states that "if the soul is a body, there will be neither sensation, nor thought, nor science, nor virtue, nor nobility."[19] In this regard, the restoration of the world of ideas by Neoplatonism was an event of the utmost importance not only for Augustine but for the whole of the Western tradition. Throughout the hellenistic and the early Christian periods, that is to say, for five hundred years or more, the most influential schools of philosophy, Stoicism and Epicureansim, denied that the human soul was a spiritual substance. Even Aristotle, to the extent to which he was known, was assumed to be a materialist because he taught that the soul was the form of the body and hence inseparable from it.

The irony is that this emphasis on the spirituality of the soul and its implications for the whole of human life is the very point on which Augustine, the mediator of Platonic philosophy to the Latin West, has been most vehemently attacked in our time. As indicated in Chapter One, contemporary scholars allege that Augustine put forth "a negative view of the body" under the influence of Neoplatonic mentors.

Foremost among the recent proponents of this view is R. J. O'Connell, S. J., who sees the *De quantitate animae* as the "high-water mark" of this disembodied view of human existence or what he is fond of calling Augustine's "angelism," taking his cue from a passage in which the soul's nature is said to be equal to that of the angel, *par angeli* (34.78).[20] This would account, among other things, for Augustine's "bleak judgment" of the corporeal world and of death as the soul's "complete escape and acquittal from the body."[21] The world in which we live is not our God-intended home but a penal condition into which we "fell."[22] The term is revealing, for behind it lies the Platonic doctrine of the preexistence of the soul and its subsequent fall, which Augustine supposedly accepted uncritically and without any awareness of its profoundly anti-Christian implications.

O'Connell readily grants that some of the statements made in the *De quantitate animae* run counter to that view. At one point in the text, Augustine alludes to the future resurrection of the body, thereby implying that soul's union with it is not a wholly undesirable condition (33.76). Similarly, he stresses the fact that Christians have to be concerned with the welfare of human society—*societatem humanam magni pendere* (33. 73)—another concern that is alien to Neoplatonic philosophy. But these would have been for Augustine minor inconsistencies, a source of mild embarrassment but hardly a sufficient reason to rethink the whole of his philosophic position. We are left with a sincere but naive Christian whose mentality at that early date was still half pagan. One wonders how a man of Augustine's stature could have been so thoughtless. Is O'Connell possibly mistaken either about the true character of Platonic philosophy, or about Augustine's understanding of it, or about the nature of Christianity itself? The problem calls for a much closer examination than any that can be undertaken here, but a few cursory remarks may be in order.

First of all, it is too easy to attribute to either Plato or Plotinus the blend of disembodied spiritualism and dire pessimism in regard to the material world for which they are so often blamed. Even the *Phaedo*, the Platonic dialogue most open to this kind of criticism, conveys a markedly different teaching. It sets forth two views that are in obvious tension with each other: one that perceives the body as a prison from which the soul must escape if it is to regain its freedom, and one that stresses the positive contribution that the bodily senses make to the life of the soul by making possible its ascent to the suprasensible world of ideas. In so doing, it does not present a distorted picture of human life; it merely respects its complexity by showing how human beings are constantly being pulled in opposite directions by a dual nature whose conflicting needs are reconcilable only with the greatest difficulty.

Besides, by the time of Plotinus and Porphyry, the old body-prison analogy had been largely discarded in favor of a novel theory that might be described as that of the hypostatic union of body and soul and that emphasizes to a far greater extent than Plato had done the essential unity of the human being. The body was no longer thought of as a simple instrument of the soul, united to it accidentally like the hammer to the hand. But neither was it defined, like the soul itself, as a co-substantial principle out of which the human being was compounded. On that score the Neoplatonists remained solidly opposed to Aristotle's hylomorphic theory. Rather, body and soul were seen as two complete substances that mysteriously came together, like sunlight and air or fire and iron, so as to form a single substance without merging into each other or forfeiting their respective identities. The new theory, which by an interesting historical accident is best known to us from one of Augustine's letters, proved valuable in other ways as well. Via Leo the Great's Tome, it provided the model for the account that the Council of Chalcedon would soon be giving of the "unconfused union" of the divine and human natures in the single person of Christ.[23] Recent studies have shown that this is the conception with which Augustine was already working in the dialogues.[24] The *De quantitate animae* bears witness to it through its use of the expression *neque discrete, neque confuse*—"with neither separation nor confusion" (34.77)—in which it is characteristically summed up.

To accuse Neoplatonism of otherworldliness and blame Augustine for having succumbed to it is to negate the significance of this unique moment in our history. Moreover, it is to take the Platonic myths not as myths but as statements of fact and thus misinterpret them. The account of the soul as a noncorporeal being fallen from its heavenly abode into the world of matter is nothing but a figurative way of accounting for the personal dispositions or character traits that human beings exhibit and that frequently constitute a hindrance to the life of reason. The same goes the theory of reminiscence, which does not imply that to learn is literally to recall the knowledge acquired in a previous existence. The myth of the *Meno* is a paradigmatic myth, a myth whose purpose is to explain myth by demonstrating how all Platonic myths function.[25] Part of its teaching is that any new knowledge is necessarily based on preexisting knowledge and hence that certain things are somehow known by nature.

For all his ignorance of Plato's dialogues, Augustine appears to have understood Platonic philosophy remarkably well. He was able to divine that all learning is in some way a matter of remembering and that the obstacles to be overcome are precisely the opinions or hidden prejudices with which the process starts.[26] In order to learn, he once suggested, one must begin by unlearning.[27] Like everyone else, Evodius has first to purge himself of these prejudices, and this means in the first instance becoming aware of the tyranny that they exert over him. He must not only recognize that, as a spiritual substance, the soul is endowed with a life of its own, distinct from that of the body; he must reflect on the practical consequences of that doctrine and its bearing on the kind of life one is called upon to lead. The difficulties are enormous and the *De quantitate animae* is there to remind us of them.

For all of this, Augustine remained indebted to the Neoplatonists, whom he would soon enlist as allies in his battle against Manichaeanism and its enslavement to materialistic modes of thought. Like the rest of the dialogues, the *De quantitate animae* belongs to the so-called Neoplatonic phase of his intellectual evolution, a phase in which the reconciliation between Platonic philosophy and the teachings of the Christian faith may have seemed easier than proved to be the case. The later Augustine will be less lavish in his praise of Neoplatonism. These philosophers, he says in the *City of God*, "speak as they have a mind to, and in the most difficult matters do not scruple to offend religious ears; we on the other hand are bound to speak according to a certain rule, lest freedom of speech beget impiety of opinion regarding the matters about which we speak" (X.23). He will likewise reproach himself with having once laid too much stress on the liberal arts. Although there is a sense in which it is true to say that "without the good arts," the soul is "famished" or that without scientific training, nobody reasons accurately, one does well to remember that some souls are thoroughly ignorant of these arts, though none the less pious for it, and others thoroughly grounded in them, though not pious at all.[28]

What he eventually found most troubling was the Neoplatonic teaching concerning the divinity of the soul, a teaching that is writ large across the pages of the *Enneads* but of which at this early date he may not have been fully apprized.[29] He began by criticizing the Manichees for holding that the soul is divine. He would have been equally critical of the

Neoplatonists had he realized that they shared the same opinion and may even have been the source of the Manichaean teaching.[30] Still, one should probably not underestimate his shrewdness when it comes to such matters. In accordance with the goal pursued in the dialogues, he may simply have thought it opportune to tone down his disagreement with Neoplatonic thought, to which there was already enough opposition on the part of Christians, until such time as he had been able to extract from it all that could be used to support the truth of the Catholic faith.[31]

NOTES

1. In *Retractationes* (*Retractions*) I.5.1, Augustine notes that the *De immortalitate animae* (*On the Immortality of the Soul*) was written as an aide-memoire for what was to be the third book of the *Soliloquia* (*Soliloquies*). He never returned to it. The text began to circulate against his will and, without having been revised, was finally counted among his works.

2. The article in question, A. Benito y Duran, "El dialogo de la cuantivalencia del alma de San Agustín," *Augustinus* 7 (1962): 175-202, while substantial, can hardly be regarded as the last word on the subject.

3. Cf. Augustine, *Epistula* (*Letter*) 162.2 (Evodius to Augustine), Migne *Patrologia, Series Latina* (or *PL*) 33.705.

4. See G. Bardy's introduction to his edition of the *Retractationes, Bibliothèque Augustinienne*, vol. 12, Paris, 1950, 68 and 233. In the dialogue, Augustine keeps insisting that a question as "subtle" as this one calls for a subtle treatment; cf. 4.6; 15.25.

5. The classic statement of the problem is Plato, *Phaedrus* 74b-278b, which was well known to the Greek Fathers and which is paraphrased by Clement of Alexandria in the first chapter of the *Stromata*. Cf. E. L. Fortin, "Alexandria and the Esoteric Tradition," in chapter 8 of this volume.

6. On the need for readers who are both intelligent and friendly toward the writer, cf. Plato, *Gorgias* 487a, and *Republic* 450e. Unintelligent readers will misunderstand you; unfriendly ones will find a way of using your own words against you.

7. Cf. Augustine, *Confessiones* (*Confessions*) IX.8.17. Peter Brown suggests that Evodius had "made a cult of human frailty," that he regarded himself as "worthless," as "dust and ashes," and as "having been 'predestined' by God alone." According to Brown, these expressions of impotence "lacked a philosophical basis" and "belonged more to the world of ascetic sensibility than to theology." *Augustine of Hippo: A Biography* (Berkeley and Los Angeles: University of California Press, 1967), 152-53.

8. Cf. Plotinus, *Enneads* I.6.5; III.6.1; V.2.1; 3.2; 7.5, *et passim*.

9. F. Cayré, *La Contemplation augustinienne* (nouvelle édition), (Paris: Desclée de Brouwer, 1954), esp. 52-76. Cf. Id., "Notion de la mystique d'après les grands

traités de saint Augustin," *Augustinus Magister*, vol. 2 (Paris, 1954), 609-22.

10. For an overview of the debate, cf. A. Mandouze, "Où en est la question de la mystique augustinienne," *Augustinus Magister*, vol. 3 (Paris: Etudes Augustiniennes, 1955), 103-63. Id., Saint Augustin: *L'aventure de la raison et de la grâce* (Paris, 1968), esp. chapters 9-12, where an abundant documentation on the subject is gathered and analyzed.

11. Cf. Tertullian, *Adversus Marcionem* V.9; Irenaeus, *Adversus Haereses* I.16.1; St. Jerome, *Commentarium in Isaiam* IV.11.10; VI.16.14; St. Ambrose, *Espositio in Lucam* 6; 7.9; Leo the Great, *Sermo* 32.4; 42.2.

12. E.g. Ovid, *Fasti* IV.536; Ausonius, *Idyllia* I.2; Hegesippus, *De bello Iudaico* V.34.2.

13. Cf. Plotinus, *Enneads* III.6.19.

14. E.g., *De civitate Dei* (*City of God*) II.8; *Tractatus in Joannis evangelium* (*Homilies on the Gospel according to St. John*) 9.2; *Sermo* (*Sermon*) 51.22.32.

15. Macrobius, *In somnium Scipionis* I.11.11.

16. Olympiodorus, *In phaedonem* 123.3 Novins.

17. Plotinus, *Enneads* VI.8.14.

18. Cf. Augustine, *Conf.* III.7.12; V.10.19; 14.25; VII.1.1; 20.26.

19. Plotinus, *Enneads* IV.7.6.

20. Robert J. O'Connell, *St. Augustine's Early Theory of Man, A.D. 386-391*, (Cambridge, MA: Harvard University Press, 1968), 159. *St. Augustine's Confessions: The Odyssey of Soul* (Cambridge, MA: Harvard University Press, 1969), 16. *Art and the Christian Intelligence in St. Augustine* (Cambridge, MA: Harvard University Press, 1978), 52 and 61.

21. Robert J. O'Connell, *St. Augustine's Early Theory of Man*, 204; *Art and the Christian Intelligence*, 62.

22. Robert J. O'Connell, *St. Augustine's Platonism* (Villanova, PA: Augustinian Institute, Villanova University 1984), 3.

23. Augustine, *Epist.* 137.11.

> Some insist upon being furnished with an explanation of the manner in which the Godhead was so united with a human soul and body as to constitute the one person of Christ, when it was necessary that this should be done once in the world's history, with as much boldness as if they were themselves able to furnish an explanation of the manner in which the soul is so united to the body as to constitute the one person of man, an event which is occurring every day. For just as the soul is united to the body in one person so as to constitute a man, in the same way is God united to man so as to constitute Christ. In the former personality there is a combination of soul and body; in the latter there is a combination of the Godhead and man. Let my reader, however, guard against borrowing his idea from the properties of material bodies, by which two fluids when combined are so mixed that

neither preserves its original character; although even among material bodies there are exceptions, such as light, which sustains no change when combined with the atmosphere . . .

Cf. E. L. Fortin, "The *Definitio Fidei* of Chalcedon and Its Philosophical Sources," in chapter 12 of this volume.

24. Cf. J. Pépin, "Une nouvelle source de saint Augustin: le *Zêtêma* de Porphyre 'Sur l'union de l'âme et du corps'" *Revue des études anciennes* 66 (1964): 53-107. G. Madec, "Le spiritualisme augustinien à la lumière du *De immortalitate animae*," *Augustiniana testi e studi* II (Palermo: Edizioni "Augustinus," 1988), 179-90.

25. See, for a penetrating analysis of this theme, J. Klein, *A Commentary on Plato's Meno* (Chapel Hill: University of North Carolina Press, 1965).

26. For Augustine's final assessment of this matter, cf. *De trinitate* (*On the Trinity*) XII.15.24; *Retractationes* (*Retractions*) I.4.4; 8.2.

27. Cf. Augustine, *Contra academicos* (*Against the Academicians*) III.17.38. This may well have been a key element of the maieutical art attributed to Socrates. The student must be "delivered of" his false opinions before he can give birth to the truth. Cf. J. Klein, *A Commentary on Plato's Meno*, 165.

28. Cf. Augustine, *De beata vita* (*On the Blessed Life*) I.8; *De immortalitate animae* (*On the Immortality of the Soul*) I.4; *Retractationes* I.3.2.

29. Cf. Plotinus, *Enneads* IV.2.1; 7.10; 8.5; 8.7, et passim.

30. The suggestion is made by Plotinus, *Enneads* II.9.6. Plotinus's remarks are generally thought to be aimed at the Gnostics, who are not mentioned by name in the text. It should be noted that the connection between Gnosticism and Manichaeanism, which is often taken for granted today, does not appear to have been made by anyone in antiquity.

31. Cf. Augustine, *Contra acad.* III.20.43.

4

THE PATRISTIC SENSE
OF COMMUNITY

Jeremy Duquesnoy Adams's essay, *The Populus of Augustine and Jerome: A Study in the Patristic Sense of Community*,[1] recommends itself both by the importance and the timeliness of the subject with which it deals. The reader hardly needs to be reminded that the notion of community has once again come to occupy a prominent place in current philosophic and theological literature. Yet the many books and articles devoted to it are as much a symptom of its decay as they are of our renewed interest in it. It is probable that there would be less talk of community among us if we all had a better perception of what a community really is. One is therefore grateful for any guidance that he may be able to receive, especially from such giants as Augustine and Jerome, who had the advantage of writing at a time when the sense of community was still very much alive or at least much more alive than it tends to be in the minds and hearts of the men of our day.

The focal point of the investigation is supplied by the word *populus,* which refers unambiguously to the human community, as distinguished from some of its closest analogues, such as *civitas,* which is also used to designate the urban settlement in its purely physical aspect, and *gens,* which draws attention to the common ethnic origin of certain human groups. As for the choice of Augustine and Jerome, in whose works the concept of community bulks large, it requires no lengthy justification. Augustine's intellectual genius is unrivaled among the writers of late antiquity. Both Augustine and Jerome exerted an enormous influence on the millennium that followed. Both likewise lived in a time of crisis, witnessed the same dramatic events, and shared many of the same experiences, however different they may have been from each other in temperament and cast of mind. This is not to suggest that together they exhaust the mind of their literate generation on the subject at hand but only that one stands to learn more from them than from any of their less distinguished contemporaries.

Adams, needless to say, is not the first scholar to take up this issue in our time. But if the problem is an old one, the manner in which it is approached is not. Since considerations of method occupy a good deal of space in the book, it may be advisable to preface our critique with a few comments about the author's methodological presuppositions. For the sake of brevity, I shall limit myself to those parts of the book that treat of Augustine, who receives the lion's share of Adams's attention and is by and large the more important of the two writers on whom he has chosen to concentrate.

While recognizing that our own questions in regard to human society may differ at times from those of Augustine, Adams professes to be primarily interested in the questions that Augustine posed for himself (cf. p. 3). His work is, in the main, one of interpretation. Its purpose is to determine Augustine's thought on the issue before us, rather than to criticize him in the light of questions raised by later generations, including our own, or, one might add, in the light of questions that Augustine himself should have raised but failed to raise. The tool employed both in uncovering the questions and ascertaining the answers to them is that of semantic analysis, based on a close scrutiny of the various appearances of *populus* in its multiple contexts. A high degree of semantic consistency on Augustine's part has been assumed at the outset and is in turn borne out by the results of the inquiry (cf. p. 8 ff.).

Adams's study finds its closest parallels in the earlier studies of R. T. Marshall, José R. Rosada and Gabriel del Estal, Joseph Ratzinger, Wolfgang Seyfarth, and Herbert A. Deane, from which the author has benefited but which nevertheless fall short of his own ideal of thoroughness and methodological precision. Marshall's essay[2] and the long article by Rosada and del Estal on the political vocabulary of the *City of God* [3] are at once less exhaustive and more deductive in their method of procedure than Adams's analysis. Ratzinger and Seyfarth[4] both resort to terminological analysis on occasion but are less directly concerned with it than Adams. Finally, Deane's synthesis,[5] for which Adams expresses particular admiration, was unfortunately too broad in scope to allow for any in-depth study of the terms fundamental to its argument. Adams's own approach may thus be seen as a refinement of or an improvement upon that of his predecessors. Its chief claim to novelty lies in its ability to provide a "set of hard data" (p. vii; cf. p. 109) on the basis of which it hopefully becomes possible to determine inductively, and with great accuracy, the full range of meaning that *populus* assumes in Augustine's writings and to elucidate some of the more problematic aspects of his social and political thought. The hardness of the data is amply vouched for by a series of elegant content-analysis tables (easily translatable into computer language) which have been appended to the text and which make it possible to take in at a glance the diverse uses, both in regard to frequency and density, of *populus* for the whole of the *City of God,* and of *gens* for Books XV-XVIII of that work. The reader is informed toward the end of the essay that such a method is not only adapted to the study undertaken by the author but "designed for use by generations of scholars yet unformed, and for whole families of questions not yet conceived by their perverse professional fertility" (p. 121). The present work does not itself pretend to do more than assemble part of the materials needed for a broader study of the general theory of patristic "group identity" which Adams intends to make public in the near future (p. vii). Pending the results of that study, there is nothing to prevent us from trying to form at least a tentative opinion as to the merits of the new approach.

From a survey of all available data, it would seem that the noun *populus* "normally represented for Augustine a fairly definite, fairly coherent cluster of concepts" (p. 68). Although Augustine sometimes uses it to designate a particular segment of the population of the city, to wit, the multitude or the common people, as opposed to the rulers or the aristocrats, Adams's main concern is with its application to the social group in its totality. A descriptive analysis of *populus* in that broader sense reveals that the association to which it most often refers exhibits the following basic characteristics. In general it is made up of human beings, even if Augustine occasionally allows himself to conceive of a *populus* of angels. It implies rationality, inasmuch as men belong to it "by virtue of their thought or at least their structured emotions" (p. 109). In their reflective moments, one finds these men engaged in some action or line of action involving common consent and related to matters that can be gathered for the most part under the headings of politics and religion. Furthermore, the group that they constitute is a "comprehensive group," formed of rulers and subjects, adults and children, men and women, as well as of people belonging to different social classes. Such a group is, most typically, governed by a law or by "values subject to juridical review" (p. 110). While some of its members may be more active, articulate, or morally responsible than others, all of them are included in its total life, help to define its tastes, and share a common destiny. To these characteristics, which are common to Augustine and Jerome, may be added others that are proper to Augustine, who takes it for granted that the group in question must have reached an adequate (albeit unspecified) size and places greater stress on the degree of conscious unity that is achieved within it (p. 112).

Of the concrete objects to which the term *populus* is habitually applied, five deserve special mention: the local Christian community, the Church at large, the local civil community, the Roman people as a whole, and lastly, the Jewish people or People of Israel (cf. pp. 113-16). Redefined in twentieth-century phraseology, Augustine's *populus* appears to Adams as "a legitimate, unified polity, whether earthly or heavenly, temporal or eternal, formed and sustained by an associative consent belonging ultimately to the order of conscious ethics" (p. 68).

One immediately recognizes in the foregoing description a series of key concepts which Augustine has borrowed from classical political philosophy and whose meaning has been extended in such a way as to encompass the religious communities with which he was familiar. Upon examination, some of the elements of Adams's interpretation (or reinterpretation, as the case may be) are bound to strike the reader as slightly anomalous. Specifically, one may ask how much clarity has been achieved by defining *populus* as a "legitimate" polity. Unless the criteria of legitimacy are spelled out, the definition will prove to be of little practical value and may even be thought to beg the question; for there is a sense in which it is permissible to say that a polity which is not legitimate is not a polity at all. But since we shall have an opportunity to return to this question later on, nothing more needs to be said about it here.

The two elements of the presumed legitimate polity to which, as far as I can see, Adams attaches the greatest significance are those of "consent" and "law." Both notions obviously play a major role in Augustine's political scheme. Once a majority of the members of a given society have reached the point of disagreeing on all fundamentals, that society has to all intents and purposes ceased to exist and has been replaced by two or more societies bent on pursuing different and conflicting goals. There are indications, however, that Augustine was more deeply concerned with the nature of the goals themselves than with the agreement they were capable of eliciting. People have been known to agree on bad things as well as good ones. What distinguishes a civil society from other civil societies and determines its rank among them is ultimately the objects to which it looks up or the kind of excellence that it strives to actualize in its corporate life. If that is the case, the wisdom embodied or reflected in the goals toward which a particular society bends its efforts are at least as relevant to the issue as the consensus that prevails among its members with respect to those goals. Briefly stated, it may not be feasible to give an adequate account of Augustine's thought without some discussion of the relation of consent to wisdom in the life of human societies.

A possible clue to the direction which such a discussion might suitably take is provided by the second element that has been singled out for special consideration, that of law. One of the principal sources, if not the principal source, from which Adams's remarks pertaining to the role of law in society are drawn is the well-known definition of a people found in Books II and XIX of the *City of God*. The interpretation of that definition raises a problem which appears to have been missed altogether in the commentary devoted to it. It is surely no accident that the word "law" is absent from the definition that Augustine has taken over from Cicero. What Adams translates by "law" (p. 20) is in reality *ius* or "right," a term which has been preferred for good reasons and whose connotations differ in important respects from those of *lex*. One cannot speak of right without at the same time alluding to its connection with wisdom. Everyone knows what a law is, in that he has been taught to obey it, or has to be reminded periodically to do so, or has been punished for disobeying it. There are temporal laws, written or otherwise, in all societies, and Augustine himself could think of no better way of characterizing particular societies than by the laws under which they live.[6] But no one would dream of equating these laws with absolute or natural right. It takes another capacity, which has not been perfected and may not even exist in all men, to assess their reasonableness. What is at stake in Augustine's definition is precisely the principle in the light of which the laws obeyed (or disobeyed) by men within the framework of civil society are to be judged. Augustine prized law and order (or consent) as much as anyone else, but not to the point of making of them the be-all and end-all of the political life. He was too well-versed in classical political thought to have lost sight of the one factor on which the dignity and true human worth of all political arrangements, whether they be expressed in the form of laws or simply exemplified in the general way of life of a people, were dependent in the final analysis. Until the notion of wisdom implicit in Augustine's definition is taken into account, it is unlikely that the discussion will ever reach the level to which Augustine himself was intent on raising it. But lest someone should accuse us of being overly taken up with Adams's would-be omissions, let us look instead to other parts of the book from which further enlightenment concerning these and related matters may be anticipated.

Turning to Adams's statistics, we learn, among other things, that Chapters 21, 22, and 23 of Book XIX of the *City of God*, to which we have just referred and in which Augustine discusses *ex professo* Cicero's definition of a people, have the highest incidence of *populus* occurrences of any three-chapter set in all of the *City of God*, and that the statistically comparable four-chapter set of Book II, 19-22 has the second highest frequency ratio (p. 142). This, in Adams's view, should prove "heartening" to Augustinian scholars, who are accustomed to paying much heed to these two series of texts. Why Adams's discovery should produce such a heartening effect is not completely clear, especially since the reader is warned elsewhere that the frequency factor could mean little by itself. Moreover, the discovery in this instance merely confirms what sensitive critics have always regarded as obvious about the importance of these two units of composition as well as their relationship to each other. If that were the only advantage to accrue to us from the use of the statistical approach, we should have every reason to complain.

The real gains presumably lie elsewhere, in the method's ability to direct our attention to other, less well-known parts of the work which exhibit a similar frequency of *populus* uses. Such are Books XVII, XVIII, and XVI of the *City of God* in that order. The implication is that one would be well advised to concentrate on these books rather than on certain more picturesque but perhaps less informative passages which seem to have caught the fancy of McIlwain and a host of other modern scholars. One such widely publicized passage is the episode of Alexander and the pirate in Book IV, Chapter 4, where *populus* occurs only once, and in the plural besides, to designate the nations subdued by the emperor (cf. p. 142). It may be that a thorough analysis of Books XVI-XVIII will eventually prove more rewarding than the brief account of the legendary pirate's curt reply to the effect that what the conqueror does on a world-wide scale and with total impunity is not substantially different from what he himself does with a lone vessel and at much greater risk to his life. For the time being, however, we seem to learn little more from those three books than that Augustine exploited coherently the distinction between *populus* and *gens* to describe Israel's prophetic destiny, especially from the periods of the Exodus and the monarchy onward (cf. pp. 48-51). Israel, in other words, could not be thought of as a people in the most proper sense prior to its emergence and consolidation as a politically unified nation under Moses and, later, under Saul.

Notwithstanding Adams's strictures, one hesitates to fault McIlwain and his followers for making an issue of the short chapter on Alexander and the pirate, whatever else one may wish to think of the inferences that McIlwain himself draws from it concerning the general character of Augustine's political views.[7] It is difficult, first of all, to remain insensitive to the famous opening line of that chapter, in which Augustine asks point-blank: "Without justice, what are kingdoms but great robberies?" One can always object that the reaction of most critics to Augustine's challenging question is based on a purely subjective impression which is of little interest to the serious or statistically-minded scholar. Yet impressions of this sort constitute a moral fact that cannot easily be discounted in any discussion of political matters. There are also other reasons for thinking that the chapter fully merits the attention that it has traditionally commanded. Augustine's source for the Alexander episode, one may suppose, is again Cicero's *Republic.*[8] Regrettably, the text of the *Republic* has come down to us in a mutilated state at this point; but we at least know that the story belonged to that section of the dialogue in which Philus, for the sake of argument, defends the cause of injustice and outlines the conventionalist thesis regarding the origin and nature of civil society. If justice is only a sham or a pretense, that is to say, if there is no such thing as the common good, the difference between an emperor and a pirate may indeed be negligible. The fact, however, that Philus's case for injustice is made in a purely provisional way suggests that from another point of view the relevance of that distinction cannot be prematurely disregarded.[9] Recall for a moment our discussion of the brief but illuminating exchange between the pirate Menas and Antony's lieutenant, Enobarbus, in Shakespeare's *Antony and Cleopatra.*

It is to Adams's credit that he has himself foreseen the objection that Books XVI-XVIII, to which his statistics point as being of unusual interest, may not be as instructive as we had originally been led to believe. He therefore proposes that, if the reader is not satisfied with what he has learned, he should take notice of Chapters 8 and 13 of Book X, two chapters which are coterminous on his chart and which together contain no fewer than thirteen *populus* appearances. We are immediately informed that Chapter 8 may be conveniently left aside, since its eight appearances have, in fact, little to offer. The five appearances of Chapter 13, on the other hand, are remarkable in that they exhibit "a spread of attributes quite similar to that of the definition passages," i.e., II.19-22 and XIX.21-24. This chapter deserves careful consideration because it includes "most (if not all) of the elements of the two great definitions, enriched and extended by literary and historical dimensions which they lack" (p. 143). The historical examples alluded to are those of the Israelites and the Spartans. The case of the Israelites poses no new problem, inasmuch as Israel is constantly referred to as a people in the Bible. It would appear at first sight that the model of the Spartans is equally uninteresting, since it teaches us only that Augustine knew what every reader of the political literature of antiquity knows, namely, that Sparta was always regarded as the prime example of a well-ordered polity. If we were to leave it at that, it might be a bit farfetched to claim that our knowledge of Augustine is greatly enhanced by the passing reference to Lycurgus and his Spartans. Adams clearly has something else in mind, however. The specific argument developed from the information supplied by chapter 13 is that it includes the startling admission that the Spartans were truer to their laws than the Israelites to the law of Moses. From this observation we may be tempted to infer that the Spartans were a people in a fuller sense of the word than the people of God itself. It is significant, according to Adams, that the text in which this juicy tidbit occurs is situated midway between the definition passage of Book II and the parallel passage of Book XIX; in which case one notices a neat progression from the early condemnation of all earthly societies (Book II), to the paradoxical instance of an earthly polity whose excellence surpasses that of the old Hebrew polity (Book X), and, finally, to what Adams takes to be a complete rehabilitation of civil society (Book XIX). This same Chapter 13 is considered most revealing for the further reason that it lends direct and unexpected support to the thesis that Augustine took a far less negative view of political society than is generally recognized by a large segment of modern scholarship.

It is entirely possible, of course, that some Gentile communities were truer to their false gods than the wayward Israelites were to God himself, at least at certain moments in their history. Augustine may have thought so himself; but that is emphatically not the point that he makes in the chapter under scrutiny. As nearly as I can make out, Adams's interpretation is based on a pure and simple misreading of Augustine's text. In comparing the behavior of the Spartans to that of the Israelites, Augustine states: *non enim populus Israel sic Moysi credidit quem ad modum suo Lycurgo Laecemaemonii, quod a Iove seu Apolline leges, quas condidit, accepisset* (Book X.13). The sentence may be translated as follows: "For the people of Israel believed Moses, but not in the way in which the Spartans believed their Lycurgus (when he stated) that he had received from Jupiter or Apollo the laws which he gave them." Adams has taken the text to mean that the Spartans were receptive and faithful to the laws of Lycurgus, whereas the Israelites were unfaithful to the Mosaic law. The remainder of the chapter makes it abundantly clear, however, that that is not at all the meaning intended by Augustine. chapter 13 forms part of a general treatment of miracles which begins with chapter 7 of Book X. Against Porphyry, Augustine argues that miracles are not only possible but that there was a definite reason for their having occurred at certain moments rather than at other moments in Israel's history. The divine law, he tells us, was given, not to "a single man or even a select group of wise men," but to the people as a whole. It was therefore imperative that its promulgation, unlike that of Lycurgus's laws, be attended by "marvelous signs and earthquakes," which everyone could witness and which proved that, in handing down that law, Moses acted, not on his own initiative, but as an instrument of God. The question in all of this is not whether the Israelites were either more or less faithful to the law of Moses but whether they had a valid motive for accepting that law in the first place. Within this context the somewhat cryptic allusion to the wise Lycurgus takes on its full significance.

Augustine's argument is corroborated by evidence derived from other sources, of which the most readily accessible is undoubtedly Plutarch's *Lycurgus*, 6. According to Plutarch's account, Lycurgus had conceived the ambitious project of reforming the old Spartan regime. To further his designs he journeyed to Delphi, from which he returned with an oracle stating that he had been proclaimed a god by Apollo, that his laws were superior to all other laws, and that the city which observed them would become famous throughout the world. Since the revelation of Delphi was neither witnessed by anyone nor confirmed by miracles of any kind, we have only Lycurgus's word for its divine sanction. Anticipating some resistance to his proposed reform, Lycurgus proceeded to organize a conspiracy which soon permitted him to oust the king and take over the government of the city. Given the ambiguous circumstances surrounding these events, Augustine was certainly justified in contrasting the Israelites' trust in Moses with the Spartans' "trust" in Lycurgus. He himself, one surmises, was as skeptical about the divine origin of Lycurgus's mission as were the old Spartans who were done in by the reformer. The contrast that he draws is not between the belief of the Spartans and the unbelief of the Israelites but rather between the private and, hence, highly dubious character of the Delphic oracle and the public and eminently credible character of the Mosaic legislation. The matter is of some importance to Augustine, and the more so as it is directly related to one of the fundamental themes of Book X, namely, the universality of the new religion whose beginnings could be traced back to the Chosen People and which Augustine was forced to defend against the attacks of Porphyry, for whom philosophy and philosophy alone represented the true way of salvation.

By far the most important substantive issue discussed in Adams's book has to do with the classic problem of Augustine's modification of Cicero's (or more precisely Scipio's) definition of a people in Books II and XIX of the *City of God*. The problem is taken up on three separate occasions, once in the chapter on Augustine, a second time, more briefly, in the general conclusion, and again at greater length in Appendix A, which presents, in addition to Adams's own solution, an up-to-date account of the debate that has raged on and off for upwards of seventy-five years on this point. The issue is one of considerable practical as well as theoretical interest, as it is intimately bound up with Augustine's over-all appraisal of civil society. The solution to the problem depends to a very large extent on the stance and posture that the Christian will be inclined to adopt in regard to the political life and his involvement in it. If civil society is possessed of an inner consistency and an ethical substance of its own, one need have no qualms about devoting himself wholeheartedly to the pursuit of its goals. If, on the other hand, civil society is held to be irretrievably vicious and devoid of all justice, it becomes virtually impossible to reconcile its demands with those of the Christian life.

Oddly enough, the question is said by Adams to pertain to the category of questions which we have to raise but which Augustine did not pose for himself. True, the terms in which many of the more recent discussions of this *crux interpretum* are couched evince preoccupations that were totally foreign to Augustine. One should nevertheless bear in mind that Augustine was very much concerned with the nature and, hence, the limitations of civil society and went so far as to premise his apology for Christianity on a detailed and searching analysis of those limitations. But one cannot probe the limitations of civil society without at the same time pronouncing himself on the issue of its intrinsic worth.

To come immediately to the heart of the matter, the question in a nutshell is whether or not justice is of the essence of civil society. In the *Republic*, Scipio had defined a people, not as any group "brought together in any sort of way" (*quoquo modo congregatus*), but as a reasonably large assemblage of human beings "bound into one by a common acknowledgment of right and a community of interests" (*iuris consensu et utilitatis communione sociatus*).[10] Augustine first objects to that definition on the ground that the justice or right demanded by Scipio is rarely if ever found to exist in actual cities. Reverting to the same problem some seventeen books later, he suggests that if the definition is to be maintained, it can only be on condition that the reference to justice be deleted from it. Accordingly, it is not necessary that the men who come together to form a people be united in a common acknowledgment of right but only that they agree as to the "objects of their love" (*rerum quas diligit concordi communione sociatus*).[11] Ever since the end of the nineteenth century, scholars have voiced surprise and even astonishment at the fact that a man as passionately dedicated to the pursuit of justice as was Augustine should have propounded a definition of civil society that not only overlooks justice but excludes it positively from the compass of the political life. What is one to make of Augustine's emendation of Scipio's definition?

According to Adams's survey of the literature on the subject, the critics who have sought an answer to this question in recent years fall into two broad camps: those who detect an opposition between Scipio's definition and Augustine's reworking of it and hold that Augustine actually intended to divorce ethics from politics, and those who stress the compatibility and mutual inclusiveness of the two definitions. Among the representatives of the first group one finds Figgis, Baynes, Cotta, Carlyle, and McIlwain. To the second group belong such equally distinguished scholars as Troeltsch, Arquillière, Bardy, Gilson, and Deane. Adams's own sympathies are clearly with the second group. Like them, he is persuaded that Augustine was not a political immoralist and that he had no desire to extrude justice from the realm of politics. His own proposal is that the key to the problem lies in Augustine's use of the word "love," which both substitutes for "justice" in the revised definition and enlarges its scope. Since, for Augustine, justice is already included in the notion of love, it is pointless to contend that the second definition nullifies the first. "The two definitions are not only reconcilable, but end up by being one, in the sense that the second absorbs the first" (p. 131). The argument is summed up in the form of a syllogism which reads as follows: "*Major proposition*: no civil society is valid unless it is a *populus* (i.e., has justice). *Minor proposition*: but most (or normal) civil societies are *populi* (because they are unified by love). *Conclusion*: therefore most (or normal) civil societies are valid" (pp. 132-33).

Adams's attempt at syllogizing may leave his readers more perplexed than ever. A good number of them will probably have their doubts about the proper distribution of the terms of his argument or its general agreement with the rules of Aristotelian logic. However that may be, one can certainly question the validity of the distinction implied in the major premise between *populus* and civil society. In terms of Augustine's problematic, is there such a thing as a civil society which is not a *populus* and vice versa? It would seem not, since civil society (literally, the "commonwealth" or *res publica*) is precisely, as the name indicates, the "thing of the people." The supposition that the connection between the two might be severed is not only unwarranted; as we shall see, it hopelessly blurs the point that Augustine is trying to make. But rather than spend more time trying to unravel the confusions under which Adams's syllogism labors—a task that would involve us in a host of considerations pertaining to the nature of the political regime (Cicero's *forma rei publicae*), the relation of the regime to the city, and eventually the question of the best regime, of which no account is taken in Adams's essay—it may be preferable to make a fresh start and pursue the argument along somewhat different lines.

One can readily agree with Adams that, if the object of the "love" to which Augustine refers in the second definition conforms to the requirements of divine revelation, the problem is automatically solved and the seeming discrepancy between the two definitions vanishes altogether. It suffices, however, to reread the pertinent passages of the *City of God*, and of such parallel texts as *Letters* 91 and 138, to realize that this is not what Augustine is talking about. Augustine had no interest in demonstrating that the cities and nations of the earth were true *populi*. His basic purpose is rather to show that they did not have everything that a *populus* could and should have. They were deficient precisely as regards justice; and without justice, no society can rightfully claim the title of *populus* or *res publica*.

Justice is indeed of the essence of civil society, as Cicero and the great political philosophers of antiquity had asserted; for it is justice which establishes the proper relations among citizens by seeing to it that everyone receives his due or is treated exactly as he deserves to be treated. Ideally, all human societies should be governed by just principles; unfortunately, they are not, as the experience of the past and our own experience teach us. The most that can be said is that some of them are more just than others; but this is merely to affirm that they draw nearer to the ideal of perfect justice toward which all of them should strive. None has ever attained that ideal or has come even reasonably close to it. If one seeks justice, as one must if he wishes to fulfill his longing for wholeness, he will have to look for it elsewhere, in a new kind of society which differs radically from political society as men have known it, not only by the loftiness of its principles but by the power that it grants to all men of living in accordance with them. To put it bluntly, perfect justice is the prerogative of that city alone whose founder and ruler is Christ, the city of God.[12]

In the light of these remarks, one begins to glimpse what is meant by the assertion that unjust cities are not to be called cities, or, if one insists on calling them by that name, that justice is not to be included in their definition. The familiar principle invoked by Augustine, though never expressly stated, is that the unqualified noun applies only to the perfected object. To illustrate by means of a trivial example: if I speak of a table without further qualification, I have in mind the kind of object that fulfills the definition of a table. A table is a table to the extent that it possesses all the attributes indispensable to its function. If a leg is missing, I can still call it a table; but a table with three legs is surely less of a table than one with the usual four. I may be more reluctant to use that name if all four legs have been broken, even though I may continue to do so because I perceive in its scattered remnants the intention of the craftsman. A stage is sooner or later reached, however, at which it no longer makes any sense whatever to speak of it as a table, since it has become indistinguishable from any other heap of wood of comparable size. By reason of the known or remembered origin of that heap, I can point to it and say: See what has happened to my table! Yet it is evident that by this time what was once a table is not such any more. One may also ask—and we come here to the interesting question: When did the table whose disintegration is now complete cease to be a table? To which the answer can only be: from the moment when it first began to disintegrate. For if it had not lost some of its "tableness" at that moment, it could never have lost it altogether. For purposes of emphasis, I occasionally use the expression, a *good* table; but even in that case the qualifying epithet really adds nothing to what is already implied in the noun. If it suggests anything, it is simply that all or most of the tables that I am attempting to salvage from the chaos of my attic or the wreckage of a burnt-down office building are not particularly good and that I must be careful to select only the ones that can still be of some use. "Good," joined to the noun, merely indicates preeminence, with the implication perhaps that preeminence is rare.[13] Thus, to speak of the goodness of a table means no more than to say that it lacks none of the essential features of a table. As the Scholastics, who knew their Augustine, as well as their Aristotle, used to say: *bonum ex integra causa*.

It should not be too difficult to apply the analogy to the problem under consideration. Are the cities and nations of the world "peoples" and was Rome itself such a "people"? Absolutely speaking, they are not, since they failed in a crucial respect to measure up to the definition of a people. In all of them the element of justice, which in the *Republic* had previously been demonstrated to be an integral part of the commonwealth, has been judged to be mostly wanting. The justice of which Scipio had spoken does not exist in deeds; it exists only in speech and in private speech at that, as Augustine, who was aware of the innumerable restrictions imposed on public speech, was careful to point out.[14]

There is nothing paradoxical or in any way baffling, therefore, about the fact that, from the standpoint of strict justice, Augustine should have refused to actual cities the title of "cities" or "commonwealths." After all, where on earth does one come across a perfect city? To be sure, one can always take a more commonsensical view of the matter and use the word, as most people do, in connection with any and all cities, good or bad. Augustine was not above doing so himself (as Adams's statistics reveal), especially when the justice or the "quality of life" of these societies was not at issue.

What is even more serious, however, is that one actually takes the heart out of Augustine's argument when one subsumes purely and simply the "justice" of the first definition under the "love" of the second. The beauty of Augustine's argument, properly understood, is that it exploits the essential limitation of civil society in favor of the more perfect life which Christianity proffers and makes readily available to all men. In order to be compelling, the argument could not be predicated exclusively on Christian premises. Its effectiveness derives from the fact that it is explicitly founded on premises indigenous to the thought of the philosophers with whom Augustine was forced to contend. A quick glance at Cicero's *Republic* will show us how this is so.

Book II of the *Republic* extols the glories of republican Rome, which the interlocutors have agreed to take as the model of the most perfect city.[15] The memorable events of early Roman history are reviewed for the purpose of illustrating Rome's superiority over all other cities. It has previously been granted on all hands that justice is the soul of the political life and that its choicest fruits are nowhere more conspicuous than in the exploits of the old Roman heroes. The conversation is carried on by a group of decent and in some cases eminent Roman citizens, all of them united in their patriotic zeal for the welfare of the city. It requires little ingenuity, however, to sense that the lavish praise bestowed on Rome by Scipio and his fellow Romans is accompanied by an undercurrent of barely disguised criticism which extends from beginning to end of the book. Only a few salient details need to retain our attention.

The catalogue of Rome's crimes starts with Romulus, the founder and first ruler of the new city, who acceded to power by doing away with his brother, Remus, and maintained that power by treacherously murdering the Sabine king, Titus Tatius, with whom he had offered to share his throne after the notorious incident of the abduction of the Sabine women.[16] Against the background of these incidents, Romulus's later innovations can easily be seen as a series of unreasonable concessions made to the senatorial faction whose enmity had been aroused by his misdeeds.[17] Nor does the situation improve as time goes on. The pattern of injustice set by Romulus is perpetuated in a variety of ways during the reigns of his successors. We may pass over the episode of Tarquinius Superbus, admittedly a bad king, whose excesses were responsible for the downfall of the monarchy and the hatred which the Romans harbored toward it from that moment on. If the events of those years suggest anything, it is that all was far from well in the state of Rome's affairs. Lucretia is forced to commit suicide in order to vindicate her honor.[18] Her husband, Collatinus, is exiled even though he was innocent.[19] As the story unfolds, we find Rome embarking upon a series of military campaigns which in time were to make of her the mistress of the civilized world. Rome's wars were supposedly "just" wars, in the sense that they had been "declared" and were waged solely for the defense of her allies.[20] This does not alter the fact that before many centuries had elapsed, Romulus's village had grown into a world empire. One can only assume that Rome was not all that eager to return her allies to independent status upon successful completion of their defense. We had been given to understand at the outset that all these undertakings were the result of careful planning on the part of a long succession of sagacious rulers. Yet Scipio's hearers finally have to own that most of what happened was due to accident or necessity much more than to design.[21]

Little wonder, then, that by the end of Book II, the participants in the dialogue are prepared to return to the question of justice and its relation to civil society with a renewed sense of urgency.[22] Their patriotism remains unshaken; but now that they have been properly "edified," it has become easier to wrest from them the admission that they should perhaps look to nature herself rather than to the Rome of old for an exemplar of the best city.[23] What the reader of the *Republic* has, in fact, been treated to is a vastly idealized panorama of Roman life in the heyday of the republic. For all his manifest caution and the pains that he has taken to invest Roman history with an aura of unimpeachable decency, Cicero may have been as radical in his approach to the problem of civil society as was his predecessor and model, Plato. At any rate, he, too, seems to have despaired of ever finding perfect justice on the level of politics. But in order to arrive at that conclusion, one has to take seriously certain aspects of the text with which the methodological innovations of modern scholarship are ill at ease. Let us confess in all candor that the "data" on which it rests are generally poor grist for the statistical mill.

Augustine was spared the trouble of searching far and wide for the materials of his critique of Rome. All he had to do was to rely on Cicero's remarkably astute assessment of the fundamental imperfections of the political life even at its best. Are we to infer from what has been said that he had no use for civil society and was prepared to reject it out of hand? Hardly so. Even if civil society needs to be complemented by membership in a "higher city,"[24] it can and must, within the limits of human possibility, continue to perform the difficult but all-important task of preserving peace in a world whose affairs are forever being disrupted by the recurrent manifestations of human greed or selfishness. His final verdict concerning the worth of civil society reminds us in a strange way of Freud's famous (or infamous) quip about women: it is still the best thing of its kind that we have. Given the odds that are stacked against it, it needs all the help we can give it. The situation, I gather, has not changed that much since Cicero's or Augustine's day.

The concluding chapter of the essay endeavors to broaden the scope of the inquiry by pointing summarily to a cluster of subsidiary problems pictured as revolving in concentric orbits around the nucleus of "core results." To the "rings of synthetic relevance" that stand to be illuminated by Adams's solid data pertain such matters as the prudence of Constantine's attempt to identify the Christian Church with the Roman Empire, assuming that that is what Constantine was trying to do (pp. 117-18); the once much debated issue as to whether the Roman Empire died a natural death or simply succumbed to a blow inflicted from without by increasingly powerful barbarian invaders;[25] Hildebrand's allegedly Augustinian view of Christian society; and, finally, the theme of progress in Augustine's works. The link between the new set of problems and the information yielded by Adams's study becomes understandably more tenuous as one moves away from the center toward the outer rim of his fictional universe. On the last point mentioned, the findings amount to little more than a rather trite assertion to the effect that Augustine thought mankind had progressed in military competence and general education since the time of the Flood (p. 120). It is doubtful whether there is much mileage to be got from Augustine's text on education (*De civ. Dei* XXII. 7), which hardly does more than reiterate and flesh out what Cicero had said on the subject of intellectual progress from earlier to more recent times.[26] For the record, it may be worth noting that Cicero's statement is made apropos of the story of Romulus's ascension and subsequent deification, which took place in an age that would have already been "so well educated that it rejected with scorn every impossible tale."[27] It so happens that that momentous event occurred during a sudden eclipse of the sun and had as its sole witness a "rustic" (*homo agrestis*) by the name of Proculus Julius, whose tale was promptly accepted by everyone. Augustine was apparently not the first to have had doubts about the truth of Romulus's translation to the gods!

The book ends with the curious remark that the peripheral issues just listed may exert a more powerful attraction on most readers than the central theme of the essay (p. 121). If that is so, one wonders whether these side issues would not have provided a more appropriate starting point than the one for which the author has opted. Having conceded the primacy of method, Adams had to resist the temptation of allowing himself to be guided by the natural questions by which the curiosity of the researcher is normally aroused. In any event, he himself is the first to grant that the vast amount of energy expended in pursuit of Augustine's theory of community has finally led to a "spare, rather bland conclusion" (p. 69). It is unlikely that the majority of his readers will disagree with him. Moreover, as I have tried to suggest, one cannot be sure that the meager results at which he was able to arrive are entirely reliable in all cases. But even if the mountainous laboring appears to have given birth to a fairly small mouse, it is not to be disdained on that account. Adams's book is not so much a gastronomical feast to which the reader has been invited as it is an attempt to involve him in the preparation of the promised meal, for which the author has graciously provided the basic ingredients. What we learn from such an exercise is that Augustine's notion of community may be more subtle and complex than is commonly assumed. Neither is it evident that it can be grasped adequately by the sole use of the method so cleverly displayed in the essay. That method could still prove useful, but one suspects that it will have to be complemented by other tools, less amenable perhaps to statistical treatment, but better adapted to the nature of the subject matter. We should nevertheless be thankful for the new insight that has been afforded us into the extraordinary difficulties that the modern scholar encounters when he takes on a thinker of Augustine's stature. From such a lesson in moderation—or humility, to use a term that is more germane to Augustine's frame of mind—only good things can come.

NOTES

1. Jeremy Duquesnoy Adams, *The Populus of Augustine and Jerome: A Study in the Patristic Sense of Community* (New Haven and London: Yale University Press, 1971).

2. R. T. Marshall, *Studies in the Political and Socio-Religious Terminology of the De civitate Dei*, Patristic Studies 86 (Washington, D. C.: Catholic University of America Press, 1952).

3. G. del Estal and J. J. R. Rosada, "Equivalencia de 'civitas' en el 'De civitate Dei'," *La Ciudad de Dios* 167 (1954): 367-454.

4. J. Ratzinger, "Herkunft und Sinn der Civitas-Lehre Augustins," *Augustinus Magister* (Paris: Etudes Augustiniennes, 1954), 965-79. Id., *Volk und Haus Gottes in Augustins Lehre von der Kirche* (Munich: K. Zink, 1954). W. Seyfarth, *Soziale Fragen der spätrömischen Kaiserzeit im Spiegel des Theodosianus* (Berlin: K. Zink, 1953).

5. H. A. Deane, *The Political and Social Ideas of St. Augustine* (New York: Columbia University Press, 1963).

6. Cf. *De libero arbitrio (On Free Choice of the Will)* I.7.16.

7. Cf. C. H. McIlwain, *The Growth of Political Thought in the West* (New York: Macmillan, 1932), 154 ff., and, most recently, Rex Martin, "The Two Cities in Augustine's Political Philosophy," *Journal of the History of Ideas* 38 (1972): 195 ff.

8. Cicero, *De re publica* III.14.24.

9. *Antony and Cleopatra*, Act II, scene 6, lines 83-95. The discussion of this passage is in chapter 2, p. 27.

10. Cicero, *De re pub.* I.25.39; cf. *De civ. Dei* II.21.

11. *De civ. Dei* XIX.24.

12. *De civ. Dei* II. 21.

13. Cf. Aristotle, *Nicomachean Ethics* I.7.1098a7ff.

14. Augustine, *Epistula (Letter)* 91.1.

15. Cicero, *De re pub.* I.46.70.

16. *De re pub.* II.8.14.

17. *De re pub.* II.9.15-16.

18. *De re pub.* II.25.46.

19. *De re pub.* II.31.53.

20. *De re pub.* II.17.31; cf. III.23.35.

21. *De re pub.* II.33.57; cf. II.11.22.

22. *De re pub.* II.44.70.

23. *De re pub.* II.39.66.

24. Cf. Augustine, *Epistula (Letter)* 91.1.

25. Recall, for example, A. Piganiol's famous closing line, *L'Empire chrétien*, (Paris: Presses universitaire de France, 1947), 422: "La civilisation romaine n'est pas morte de sa belle mort . . . . Elle a été assassinée."

26. *De re pub.* II.10.19.

5

AUGUSTINE AND THE PROBLEM OF CHRISTIAN RHETORIC

It is surprising, particularly when one considers the importance which the Church Fathers attached to the transmission of the word of God, that so little should have been written on the art of preaching during the early Christian centuries. The one notable exception is, of course, Book IV of Augustine's *De doctrina christiana,* which has long been acclaimed as the first handbook of Christian rhetoric.[1] While no one to my knowledge has ever questioned the uniqueness of Augustine's treatise, the novelty of the views contained therein has been the subject of a good deal of discussion in recent years. With few dissenting voices, the trend among scholars has been to minimize Augustine's originality in favor of the once commonly held opinion that the core of his teaching is simply derived from Cicero's rhetorical works.

There are, to be sure, a number of features that set Augustine's treatise apart from those of his illustrious predecessor, not the least obvious of which is that the content of Christian rhetoric, which is drawn for the most part from sacred Scripture, differs significantly from that of pagan rhetoric. It is also true that Augustine regards the rules of the rhetorical art as being less important to the Christian orator than to the statesman or the lawyer in a civil court and even goes so far as to propose that they may be dispensed with altogether if the preacher has reached the age beyond which they can no longer be profitably acquired.[2] A greater simplicity would likewise seem to be required of the Christian orator than would normally be the case with his pagan counterpart, although it is not clear in this instance whether Augustine is taking issue with Cicero himself or merely reacting against the excessive formalism of the rhetors of his own time.[3]

All of these points nevertheless leave untouched the central issue of the nature and principles of the rhetorical art, and scholars are virtually unanimous in asserting that Augustine remains by and large faithful to the Ciceronian tradition. Thus, in his monumental study of the influence of the Latin classics on Augustine, Professor Harald Hagendahl is able to state that he has "followed the course of Augustine's exposition with a view to showing how much it tallies with Cicero's rhetorical treatises in the general conception of rhetoric and even in words: in the division, terminology and other technicalities, whether rendered literally or by paraphrase."[4] The conclusion at which he arrives is clear and peremptory: Augustine's teaching is based on the system of rhetoric introduced into the Roman world by Cicero. That teaching "follows . . . Cicero's views so closely, often even in the minutest particulars, that it cannot make a substantial claim to novelty and originality in the doctrinal system, at most to a slight modification on this or that point."[5]

Even Professor H.-I. Marrou, who has gone further than anyone else in defending the revolutionary character of the *De doctrina christiana,* concedes that as regards the fundamentals of rhetoric Augustine has been content to repeat the views developed by Cicero, the chief theorist as well as the greatest master of Roman eloquence.[6] The same basic position is adopted by J. Oroz, who agrees with Marrou that the themes of Christian and pagan rhetoric are worlds apart but finds that on all other important points the *De doctrina christiana* remains well within the boundaries defined by the Ciceronian tradition.[7] The new wine of the Gospel has simply been poured into the old pagan cask without in any way causing it to be altered in the process.

Yet, when all the evidence is sifted out, one wonders to what degree full justice has been done to the subtlety of Augustine's thought; for it is still conceivable that the cribbings from Cicero have been used to formulate a notion of rhetoric which resembles that of Cicero in outward appearance more than in inner substance. With the help newly provided by A. Hus's study of *docere* and its cognates in Cicero's rhetorical works,[8] one may be in a better position to review the merits of the case and determine more accurately the extent of Augustine's originality. That originality, as far as I can tell, is much greater than anyone has yet dared to maintain.

Like the *Orator* and the *De oratore,* the *De doctrina christiana* assigns to the orator the threefold duty of "teaching" (*docere*), of "pleasing" (*delectare*), and of "persuading" (*flectere*). To teach, Augustine adds, again quoting Cicero, is a matter of necessity: *docere necessitatis est*. To speak in a pleasing manner adds an element of charm to the orator's words: *delectare suavitatis*. Finally, to persuade pertains to the triumph that the orator seeks for his client or his cause: *flectere victoriae*.[9] The question is whether the "teaching" to which the *De doctrina christiana* refers has anything at all in common with what Cicero originally intended by that term. A fresh look at the relevant texts suggests that Augustine has in fact profoundly modified the Ciceronian doctrine on two major points at least: first, by asserting the priority of the teaching function of the orator over the two other functions, and, secondly, by investing the terms *docere* and *doctrina,* which best express that function, with a meaning that could never have been ascribed to them by Cicero. We shall gain a new insight into the matter if we begin by examining that "teaching" to which in Cicero's view a substantial portion of the orator's efforts must be devoted.

Cicero's remarks occur within the broad context of a discussion of the two leading forms of oratory, namely, deliberative or political and judicial oratory.[10] Before reaching any important decision in matters of public policy or rendering a verdict in a court of law, the assembly or the judges must be supplied with all of the necessary information pertaining to the issue before them. A judge, for example, should not only know what crime has been committed but, as much as possible, why and how it was committed, what the provisions of the law in regard to such a crime might be, and a host of other relevant data. The lawyer is thus faced with the initial task of apprizing his hearers of the facts of the case, or, if the facts are not contested, of establishing the validity of his case on the basis of commonly accepted principles of justice.[11] To that extent he may be said to teach. But the teaching with which he is concerned is clearly in the service of something else, which is to persuade the judge of the innocence of his client.[12] This and nothing else is the end to which all of his energies are directed. The criminal lawyer will not spare any effort to obtain a favorable verdict; the political orator, if he can help it, will not settle for anything less than a vote resulting in the adoption of the measure that he advocates. In either case, whatever teaching they may be called upon to do remains subordinate to the one goal on the attainment of which the success or failure of their respective endeavors hinges. Neither of them will have accomplished anything if the accused is convicted or if the proposal in behalf of which he pleads is defeated.

This is not to deny that the orator's teaching function is as much a part of the rhetorical art as either of the other two functions; for the outcome of the legal or juridical proceedings in which he is involved will be affected to a very large extent by the manner in which the case is presented in the first place. Not any kind of presentation will do. The speaker must see to it that his narration of the facts is not only clear but "credible."[13] This alone requires considerable skill on his part, and all the more so as the art which he brings to that "narration" must remain imperceptible to the listener.[14] The same rule applies to the *loci communes* or general principles which the orator has at his disposal and which are not all equally suitable to his needs. Attention must be drawn to those principles which support his case and away from those which could conceivably weaken it. One may argue, for example, that the particular law which the accused has violated needs to be reinterpreted in the light of a higher principle which it contravenes, or, inversely, that the higher principle in the light of which the accused would appear to stand convicted is itself in need of correction by some more precise law justifying its transgression in specific instances.

One gathers therefore that the "teaching" which the orator dispenses cannot be construed as a universal teaching in the strict sense, since it has to do either with the particulars of the issue at hand or with a series of more general arguments whose usefulness depends less on their intrinsic worth than on the opinion that people commonly entertain in regard to them. What is most important in all such cases is not that the argument be defensible on rational grounds but that it seem plausible to the hearer. The orator is of necessity less concerned with the truth than with its appearance. A plausible falsehood is infinitely more valuable to him than an unlikely truth.

It should not be inferred from these remarks that Cicero had no regard for the truth in political or judicial matters but only that he was aware of the frequent impossibility of arriving at any completely objective solution to the problems that they raise. The questions to which the orator addresses himself can rarely be decided on the basis of knowledge alone. If he speaks about them, it is less for the purpose of instructing his hearers than of persuading them, and passion rather than reason is the instrument par excellence of persuasion, the middle term as it were by which the orator seeks to win the assent of his audience and gain acceptance for such courses of action as practical wisdom may dictate given the nature of the case and the circumstances that surround it.[15] Hence the confidence that he inspires is as much a function of the opinion that others have formed of him as a man as it is of his competence or his ability to speak well. People will trust him if they are convinced that he is a good man and that he has their common good at heart.[16] In that regard, his own person is a better witness to the "truth" of his assertions than any of the arguments that he may be able to muster in support of them.

The deeper point of Cicero's observations could easily be missed, however, if one were to leave it at saying that opinion rather than true knowledge is the stuff of rhetoric or that the complexity of human affairs precludes any attempt to approach them with the detachment that characterizes rational or scientific discourse. One cannot point to the limitations of any rhetorical argument without at the same time raising the larger issue of the relation of rhetoric to philosophy and, more generally, of the political life to the philosophic life. What distinguishes Cicero's works from the common run of rhetorical treatises is precisely that they are guided by an awareness of philosophy and its ambiguous relationship to the city. For the orator that Cicero has in mind is not just the man who combines a natural talent for public speaking with a knowledge of the rules of rhetoric but a new type of orator in whose person the accomplishments of the statesman and the philosopher coalesce and are brought to a higher level of perfection.[17] The consequences of this important fact will come to light if we glance briefly at the attributes of the perfect orator as they are outlined in the *Orator* and the *De oratore*.

The highest form of oratory is political oratory, and political oratory deals with the greatest and best of human affairs: religion, death, piety, patriotism, right and wrong, the virtues and vices of men, the duties of citizens, their pleasures and pains, the passions by which they are moved, and the evils to which they succumb.[18] One cannot begin to speak wisely about such matters until one has achieved a true understanding of human nature; for only the man who has a thorough knowledge of the whole is the proper judge of the ends of human existence and of the means by which they are best attained. It follows that the orator must have mastered not only the art of persuasion but all of the theoretical sciences as well.[19]

Needless to say, few men have either the capacity, or the opportunity, or for that matter the desire to engage in such pursuits. Even the greatest orators of the past—Pericles, Demosthenes—did not conform to the proposed ideal and it is doubtful whether anyone could.[20] The crucial point, however, is not whether the perfect orator has ever existed or ever will but, assuming that the quest for theoretical wisdom has uncovered a dimension of reality that transcends the horizon of the political life, whether there is any common measure between the knowledge that is ideally demanded of him and the notions of justice by which most men are guided. If by justice one understands, as Cicero did, not simply the rules governing the distribution or the exchange of goods among fellow citizens but the perfect order of the soul or the perfectly just way of life, one may come to the conclusion that the degree of justice of which a particular society is capable at any given moment will fall considerably short of what a wise man would regard as truly just. To say nothing of other matters, it is doubtful whether Cicero seriously thought that belief in the gods of the Roman Pantheon was compatible with justice in this loftier sense. Yet any orator speaking in behalf of Rome would necessarily have to defer to such beliefs. Viewed in that perspective, the question is not only how much injustice a society can tolerate but how much justice it can bear without endangering its own existence.[21] Granted that all societies should strive for justice, a point is sooner or later reached at which it becomes impossible, without injustice, to enforce such measures as would be in perfect accord with the demands of theoretical reason. The counsels of the wise man will represent at best a compromise between what reason is capable of knowing about justice and the needs of the society for which they are intended.

But this can only mean that in addressing his fellow citizens, the orator is compelled to adopt an ironic posture. Although his teaching does not correspond fully to what he himself knows to be true, it is essential that it be perceived as a true teaching by his hearers. He will be successful to the extent to which others remain ignorant of the fact that what he does is the one thing that he cannot claim to be doing.[22] There is an element of high comedy in the highest form of oratory. Cicero's perfect orator is a liar, not because he wants to be, but because he has no choice in the matter. Between thought and speech or between theory and practice there is a necessary cleavage, of which Cicero himself, whose aim it was to bring about a fusion between Greek philosophy and Roman virtue,[23] seems to have been uniquely aware.

It is hardly surprising therefore that Cicero should have refrained from using the word *doctrina* to characterize the content of the orator's speech. As opposed to the older and more neutral *docere,* which designates the act by which knowledge or information of any kind is imparted to another person, *doctrina* refers specifically to the object of philosophic inquiry and functions most often as the equivalent of the Greek *epistêmê* in Cicero's own dialogues and treatises.[24] Philosophers qua philosophers speak to the educated for the purpose of instructing them and not for the purpose of swaying them: *docendi non capiendi causa.*[25] The proper mode of their discourses is dialectical rather than rhetorical. These discourses may have an eloquence all their own, but of a kind that is only remotely akin to that to which the typical orator is accustomed.

A vastly different picture emerges the moment we turn to Augustine's Christian adaptation of the Ciceronian doctrine. Augustine's preacher must also begin by instructing his audience, and this he does by laying before them the truths of the faith and, whenever necessary, by using arguments based on the proper authorities to clarify any difficulties that they may have in regard to them.[26] But, as might be expected, the kind of teaching in which he engages is no longer the object of the subtle depreciation that we encountered in Cicero. The substance of that teaching is the "sound doctrine" of which St. Paul had spoken and in which the preacher has steeped himself through the assiduous reading and study of the Scriptures.[27] Its cognitive status is therefore totally different from that of the pagan orator. Augustine's preacher teaches in a way in which even Cicero's perfect orator could never be said to teach. It is above all the superior dignity of that "teaching" which accounts for Augustine's inversion of the order of rank of the three functions performed by the orator. The duty to teach is not merely the Christian orator's first duty; it is his highest and in a sense his only duty.[28] The preacher will have accomplished all that is essentially required of him if what he teaches is the truth. If he is to be judged at all, it is on his ability to discharge that function rather than on any natural endowments or oratorical talents that he may or may not possess. He has no other title to be heard. Hence, departing from the canon of Ciceronian orthodoxy, Augustine takes it for granted that, regardless of the style in which the preacher expresses himself, whether it be the simple, the moderate, or the grand, his primary goal is still to instruct his audience. The *munus docendi* is no longer restricted to the simple style and vice versa; it pervades all three styles and is itself the end to which they are universally ordered.[29]

The same concern for the primacy of the truth is evinced by another less conspicuous but equally significant alteration that Augustine has introduced into the Ciceronian scheme. Contrary to what Hagendahl suggests, one observes that, in paraphrasing the text of the *De oratore,* Augustine has tacitly deleted all reference to what Cicero regarded as the chief merit of any rhetorical argument, namely, its plausibility. The word *verisimiliter* does appear in the *De doctrina christiana,* but only in connection with the teachers of false doctrines.[30] The suggestion is not that, for Augustine, the truths (*vera*) of the faith are implausible but only that it would be misleading to describe them as plausible truths. The contrast on which the whole discussion plays is precisely between the eminently truthful character of the Christian faith and the apparent truths or merely plausible teachings of the promoters of erroneous doctrines.

This does not mean that it is not to the preacher's advantage to cultivate the other qualities of a good orator if he has the ability to do so. There is surely no reason why the divine truth should not be rendered as appealing as possible to the hearer. Even a preacher has nothing to gain by boring his audience. It would be strange, to say the least, if error were to be clothed in an attractive garb by its proponents while truth is made to appear tedious and dull for lack of proper adornments.[31] Furthermore, it sometimes happens that the hearer is already familiar with the truths of the faith but cannot bring himself to act in accordance with them; in which case the preacher may be summoned to use whatever powers of persuasion he has at his command to induce him to reform his life.[32] For all of these reasons, then, one should not underestimate the benefits of eloquence. In general, the man who speaks both "wisely" and "well" will accomplish more than the one who speaks only wisely.[33]

Here again, however, the classic formula, *sapiens et eloquens,* which Augustine inherits this time from the *De inventione,*[34] partially masks a more profound disagreement with Cicero on the relation of teaching to persuading in rhetorical discourse. The truth which the Christian is "persuaded" to accept is not a truth in any ordinary sense of the word but, as we saw in chapter one, a beatifying or saving truth,[35] which is fully appropriated only when it issues in those deeds to which it points as its fulfillment.

It is hardly necessary to point out that such a doctrine is incommensurable with the "heartless doctrines"—*doctrinae sine corde*—of the philosophers.[36] The precise manner in which the two modes of thought are related is more complex than one might be tempted to assume on the basis of some of Augustine's well-known pronouncements on the subject.[37] The objection to philosophy from a religious point of view is not so much that its teachings are sometimes at odds with those of the faith, for in that case a measure of agreement could still be reached between the philosopher and the Christian, if not always on the solutions to the common problems with which they both deal, at least on the nature of those problems and the terms in which they might suitably be posed. The more serious difficulty arises from the philosopher's own inability to arrive at any firm conclusion concerning matters of the utmost interest for the whole of human life. The philosopher is compelled by his love of the truth to suspend his judgment about all such matters until the theoretical issues to which they give rise have been fully examined. The question is whether one can ever be satisfied that the necessary clarity about any of these fundamental issues has been reached. If the object of the investigation should prove to be more elusive than had been anticipated or the problems more readily accessible than the solutions to them, the philosopher may find it difficult to commit himself heart and soul to any position whatever. What had begun as an attempt on his part to set forth the truth about the good life has, it seems, transformed itself into an endless and hence unfulfilled quest for the nature of the good life.

It is precisely this radical character of philosophy, which refuses to take knowledge itself for granted, that constitutes the ultimate challenge to the Christian faith. The opposition in the final analysis is not so much between one set of doctrines and another but between the self-proclaimed ignorance of the philosopher and the firmly held beliefs of the religious thinker. The touchstone of one's attachment to the truth is one's willingness to die for it. But, even though philosophers have often been persecuted across the centuries, few of them have ever demonstrated any real appetite for martyrdom. It may be objected that Socrates was willing to sacrifice himself for the truth. Even this example, however, is not decisive; for there is no guarantee that what Socrates did at the age of seventy is exactly what he would have done had his trial taken place thirty years earlier.[38] The lesson that later philosophers learned from Socrates is not that they should be ready to lay down their lives for the truth but that, for their own protection, they would be well-advised to accommodate themselves to the prejudices of the society in which they happen to live. Philosophers may parade as lovers and teachers of moral virtue, but none of them seems to have been eager to place the service of his fellow men above the good of the mind.[39] Socrates's own "coldness" and aloofness from the affairs of the city is no doubt a better index of his fundamental disposition than his public declarations of piety or his professed concern for the welfare of his fellow Athenians.[40] The philosopher poses a threat to religion and society not because he knows too much but because he knows too little. By questioning all things, he undermines the consensus on which both religion and society depend for their well-being.

But even this is only half the story. If Socrates can boast of his ignorance, it is because he has learned what true knowledge is and is able to distinguish it from its opposite. His would-be ignorance is merely the obverse of a deep-seated pride which causes him to place himself above the rest of society. He speaks to his judges or to the citizens of Athens as one speaks to children, telling them only what is good for them, regardless of whether it is true or not.[41] His own speeches were more "persuasive" than genuinely truthful.[42] They were aimed as much at keeping the multitude away from the truth as they were at attracting to it the few who had proved themselves worthy of it by their ability to penetrate the disguise in which it is habitually cloaked. Between his arrogance (*praesumptio*) and the humble "confession" of the believer, it is difficult to see how any reconciliation could be effected.[43]

Even though Augustine could not accept Plato's and Cicero's views concerning the essential disproportion between theoretical reason and political reason, he was nevertheless very much aware of the need to speak differently to different audiences. It would obviously be foolish to think that everyone is capable of the same degree of understanding of the divine truth. The Scriptures themselves are often written in a manner that makes it hard for most people to grasp them without the aid of an interpreter.[44] Anyone who undertakes to explain them to the general public must first learn to express himself in a language that all men can understand and not in a language that is intelligible only to the learned.[45] Moreover, it is reasonable to suppose that there are depths of understanding to which the untrained multitude is incapable of acceding. One would perform a disservice to the simple faithful by burdening them with subtleties that exceed their powers of comprehension. Accordingly, the *De doctrina christiana* makes it clear that there are questions which "by their very nature are not understood or are barely understood no matter how much, how often, how clearly, or how well they are expounded, and these either should never be brought up before a popular audience or only rarely, when there is a special reason to do so."[46] By maintaining a prudent reserve on all such questions, the preacher does not commit an injustice toward anyone, since the doctrines that he passes over in silence would only be misunderstood and possibly misused by the majority of his hearers. The situation is different if one has the opportunity to deal in private conversation with individuals whose intelligence, degree of preparation, and willingness to learn can be assessed more easily and more accurately.[47]

But if the mode of presentation of the divine truth varies with each audience, its substance does not, and on this level all Christians are united in the knowledge of the same basic truth. There is only one truth, "which all men hear in the same measure when it is publicly spoken, but which each one appropriates in his own measure."[48] The wise preacher undoubtedly knows *more* than his less learned fellows, but what he knows is not something *other* than what every Christian knows.[49] To the extent to which he has achieved a more profound grasp of the divine mysteries, he can add to the knowledge that others already have of them, but the foundation on which he builds is the same in all cases. There can be no question of persuading the hearer to accept any doctrine to which the speaker has not previously given his own wholehearted assent. What one knows in one way "in the world at large" is not essentially different from what one knows "in the privacy of his chambers."[50] Embroidering on the metaphor that St. Paul had used in the First Letter to the Corinthians, Augustine explains that the milk with which the mother nourishes her suckling is the very food from which her own sustenance is derived and which has merely been transformed into a substance that is more easily absorbed by the child. It therefore makes no sense to speak, as others had done, of an "opposition" between the simple fare that is provided for beginners and the wisdom reserved for those who have attained a higher level of spiritual advancement.[51] The latter simply perceive more perfectly what the former strive to assimilate according to their own capacity.

What is even more important, however, is the conclusion regarding the need for absolute truthfulness which Augustine draws from these premises. The Christian's commitment to the truth is such that he can never publicly or privately betray it in speech even for the noblest of causes. There may be valid reasons for not revealing to others all of one's thoughts on some subjects; but it is one thing to withhold the truth from someone and quite another to lie to him.[52] The sacred writers themselves deliberately concealed certain doctrines from the multitude, but without ever lying about anything: *nonnulla obtegunt, sed nulla mentiuntur.*[53] The Christian orator can do no less. One can say without exaggeration that there is no moral principle which Augustine defended with greater vehemence and on which he was least willing to compromise. Never, even under the most extreme circumstances, is one allowed to speak an untruth. The question is, Why? For it is surely not self-evident that the true interests of one's fellow men are better served by the determination to speak the truth at all times than by an occasional breach of truthfulness. To take a simple example, one has a hard time imagining that a man who perpetrates a white lie in order to save, not indeed his own life, but the life of a loved one or perhaps some other innocent person is guilty of any sin whatever. Christian charity, to say nothing of plain common sense, would seem to prescribe as much. Yet Augustine, who was prepared to make allowances for what would appear to be the much more grievous crime of adultery,[54] is adamant in his refusal to make even the slightest concession on that point.

The reason, we discover, is not unrelated to the central task of preaching the word of God which has been entrusted to the Christian orator. That reason is best illustrated by Augustine's reaction to Jerome's commentary on Chapter Two of the Letter to the Galatians, in which Paul gives an account of his famous altercation with Peter at Antioch.[55] It may be recalled that on that occasion Paul publicly upbraided Peter for refusing to eat with the Gentiles in order to placate the circumcision party, headed by James. Following Origen's interpretation, Jerome had attempted to remove any trace of dissension among the apostles by contending that Peter was not guilty of wrongdoing but had merely sought to accommodate himself to the prejudices of the Judaizers. Had not Paul himself done as much by circumcising Timothy and, on James's advice, by providing for the offering of sacrifices in accordance with the prescriptions of the old law, thereby giving credence to the belief that Christian salvation was linked to these observances?[56] It is hardly likely, then, that he should have quarreled with Peter over a similar issue. Far from finding fault with Peter, Paul actually sided with him but feigned to rebuke him lest others should interpret his conduct as signifying that the Gentiles were to be subjected to the Jewish law.[57]

Augustine expresses utter astonishment at the fact that Jerome had chosen to endorse what would really amount to an *officiosum mendacium* on Paul's part.[53] For if what Peter did is what he was supposed to do, then Paul lied when he accused him of not being straightforward about the truth of the Gospel. That he should have done so for a good cause is beside the point. Nor does it matter that the enemies of the faith should seize upon the disagreement of which Paul speaks as a pretext for discrediting the New Testament. Nothing can justify the imputation of lies to the Bible. To suggest for one moment that the sacred writers indulged in falsehood is to jeopardize the authority of the whole of Scripture and open the door to every kind of malice. "If one were to admit in that supreme authority even one polite lie, nothing at all would be left of these books, because whenever anyone finds something difficult to practice or hard to achieve, he will follow this most dangerous precedent and explain it as the thought or practice of a lying author."[59] As long as the *veritas doctrinae* remains intact, one can always turn to it to rectify any error into which he may have fallen; but if that standard is itself subject to doubt, the very possibility of a return to the truth is destroyed forever.[60] It is therefore preferable to believe that, out of weakness, "Peter did so act as to compel the Gentiles to live like Jews."[61] Better a thousand times a cowardly Peter than a lying Paul. No immediate advantage could ever compensate for the unlimited harm that is done by calling into question even a single passage of Scripture.

What is said of the sacred writers applies, *mutatis mutandis,* to all Christian teachers as well; for what confidence could one have in a person who is of the opinion that it is sometimes permissible to lie? Could not he, too, by any chance be lying when he speaks to others about the mysteries of the faith?[62] Like everyone else, the Christian orator may unwittingly err in his interpretation of the sacred text; but if what he says is conducive to the love of God and neighbor, which is the principle in the light of which all of Scripture is to be interpreted, he leads no one astray and is not himself guilty of any wicked deed.[63] What is intolerable is to think that anyone could arrogate to himself the prerogative of using evil in order to bring about a greater good among men. One puts it mildly when one says that Cicero's ideal orator had no such qualms about lying to his hearers. The road leading from the *De oratore* to the *De doctrina christiana* may indeed be longer and more tortuous than the casual reader would ever have suspected.

It would be futile to deny that, in elaborating his views on Christian oratory, Augustine has relied extensively on the tradition of Roman rhetoric in which he had been trained. He himself certainly made no great effort to conceal his indebtedness to that tradition and to its foremost representative, Cicero. But it would be a grave misconception to think that one can give an adequate account of his thought merely by listing the numerous parallels between the two authors. One is reminded in this connection of Lord Acton's remark (to Mary Gladstone) that a disposition to detect resemblances is one of the greatest sources of error. The paradox of Book IV of the *De doctrina christiana* is that it is precisely when Augustine sounds most like Cicero, to the point of reproducing his own words, that he stands at the furthest remove from him. There are good reasons to believe that Augustine quoted Cicero the way Shakespeare's devil quotes the Bible—for his own purposes. The success with which he was able to do so is amply demonstrated by the difficulty that one experiences in trying to assess the originality of his thought.

Modern scholars have been guilty not so much of misreading Augustine as of rashly ascribing to Cicero what is in fact a profound albeit silent transformation of Cicero's basic teaching. The pitfall might have been avoided if, before attempting to second-guess Augustine, greater pains had been taken to arrive at a satisfactory interpretation of the original Ciceronian doctrine. It should probably be added that anyone embarking upon such an endeavor would have received little direct encouragement from Augustine himself. In defending what he considered to be the cause of truth, Augustine had much to gain and little to lose by stressing the similarity rather than the dissimilarity between his position and that of Cicero. Nor was there any "special reason" for calling attention to that strategy. To discuss openly the points on which at a deeper level the divergences between the Christian and the classical views of truth become truly significant would have necessitated the public disclosure of a whole gamut of problems that are of no interest to most Christians or, as far as that goes, to most preachers.

Like all the great books on rhetoric written in antiquity, whether it be the *Gorgias,* the *Phaedrus,* the *Orator,* or the *De oratore,* the *De doctrina christiana* is rhetorical in mode as well as in content. In this respect at least it remains remarkably faithful to the spirit of the classical tradition. The moderation in speech that it both advocates and displays may well be the most important lesson that Augustine learned from his revered pagan masters.

NOTES

1. Cf. Harald Hagendahl, *Augustine and the Latin Classics* (Göteborg: Universitetet, 1967), 558.

2. Augustine, *De doctrina christiana* (*On Christian Doctrine*) IV.3.4.

3. Cf. H.-I. Marrou, *Saint Augustin et la fin de la culture antique* (Paris: E. de Boccard, 1938), 524ff. C. Morhmann, *Études sur le latin des chrétiens* I (Rome: Edizioni Di Storia E Letteratura, 1958), 359.

4. H. Hagendahl, *Augustine and the Latin Classes,* 565.

5. Ibid., 567. For a somewhat more balanced view, cf. M. Testard, *Saint Augustin et Cicéron I* (Paris: Etudes Augustiniennes, 1958), 235-6, 261, 268-9, 279, 330. Also, among the older studies, C. S. Baldwin, *Medieval Rhetoric and Poetic* (New York: Macmillan, 1928), 52: ". . . and now scarcely an edition or translation of Augustine's works is published which, by cross references and footnotes, does not so stress the 'classical elements' in Augustine's rhetoric that the reader is led to believe that only minor differences distinguish the rhetorical doctrines of Cicero and Augustine." M. Comeau, *La rhétorique de saint Augustin d'après les Tractatus in*

Joannem (Paris: Beauchesne, 1930), 21: "Ainsi le livre du *De doctrina christiana,* en dépit de quelques vues personnelles à son auteur, se place-t-il naturellement dans la longue série de rhétoriques que les écrivains latins publièrent à l'envi jusqu'aux invasions barbares. La théorie du style et de l'éloquence n'y présente aucune nouveauté." Further references in H. Hagendahl, *Augustin and the Latin Classics,* 565, n. 1. A stronger emphasis on the newness of Augustine's position is to be found in L. D. McNew, "The Relation of Cicero's Rhetoric to Augustine," *Research Studies of the State College of Washington* 25, 1 (March, 1957): 5-13.

6. H.-I. Marrou, *Saint Augustin et la fin de la culture antique* (Paris: E. de Boccard, 1938), 520. See also Marrou's review of Hagendahl's book in *Gnomon* 41 (1969): 282-85.

7. J. Oroz, "El *De doctrina christiana* o la retorica cristiana," *Estudios Clasicos* 3 (1956): 452-59. Id., "La retorica augustiniana: Clasicismo y Cristianismo," *Studia Patristica* 6 (1962): 490: "Por lo dicho hasta ahora, podemos affirmar que la obra de san Augustin sobre la retorica es notamente clasicista, es decir sigue la linea ortodoxa de los autores clasicos, y sobre todo de Ciceron."

8. A. Hus, *Docere et les mots de la famille de docere: Étude de sémantique latine* (Paris: Presses Universitaires de France, 1965).

9. Augustine, *De doctr. christ.* IV.12.27. Cf. Cicero, *Orator* 69; *De oratore* II.310; also *Brutus* 185; *De optimo genere Or.* 3.

10. On the lesser importance of epideictic rhetoric, cf. Cicero, *Orator* 207; *De oratore* II, 43ff.

11. Cf. Cicero, *Orator* 120ff; *De oratore* II.307ff.

12. On persuasion as the goal of rhetoric, cf. Cicero, *Orator* 128; Cicero, *De oratore* I.60; II.214; Cicero, *Brutus* 279.

13. *Narrationes credibiles: Orator* 124. Cf. Aristotle, *Rhetoric* III.16.1417a.

14. Cf. *Orator* 78.208-9; *De oratore* II.153,156,177; *De doctr. christ.* IV.6.10.

15. Cf. *Orator* 15; *De oratore* II.185 ff, 201 ff.; *Tuscalanae disputationes* (*Tusculan Disputations*) IV.55.

16. On the orator as *vir bonus dicendi peritus,* cf. A. S. Wilkins's introduction to the *De oratore* (Oxford, 1888), 47.

17. Cf. *De oratore* I.48.60; II.337.

18. *Orator* 118.

19. *Orator* 14ff.

20. *Orator* 3,7,19,101.

21. On the whole question of the necessity and feasibility of justice, see esp. Cicero, *De re publica* Bk. III.

22. *De oratore* II.310-11.

23. *De oratore* III.137.

24. Cf. A. Hus, op. cit., 283ff.

25. *Orator* 63

26. *De doctr. christ.* IV.4.6.

27. *De doctr. christ.* IV.21.45; 27.59; 31.64.

28. *De doctr. christ.* IV.12.28.

29. *De doctr. christ.* IV.17.34; 25.55. Cicero, *Orator* 69 and 101.

30. Compare *De doctr. christ.* IV.2.3 with *De oratore* II.80. *Probabiliter* is substituted for *verisimilis* in *Orator* 122.

31. *De doctr. christ.* IV.2.3; 14.30.

32. *De doctr. christ.* IV.12.28.

33. *De doctr. christ.* IV.5.7; cf. IV.5.8; 6.9; 25.55; 26.56; 27.59. See Augustine's defense of his own use of rhetoric in *Contra Cresconium* (*Against Cresconius*) 1.1.

34. *De doctr. christ.* IV.5.7. Cicero, *De inventione* I.1.

35. *De doctr. christ.* IV.21.35: *rerum divinarum atque salubrium scientia.*

36. *Confessiones* (*Confessions*) VIII.8.19. See chapter one, pp. 7-8.

37. E. g., *De doctr. christ.* II.40.60.

38. Cf. *Crito* 53d.

39. Cf. *Apology of Socrates* 31b.

40. *Apol. of Socrates* 31d.

41. Cf. *Gorgias* 521e.

42. *Apol. of Socrates* 17a-b, 20d-e, 22b *et passim.*

43. Cf. *Confessions* VII.20.26.

44. *De doctr. christ.* IV.21.45.

45. Ibid., IV.8.22; cf. *De Genesi contra Manichaeos* (*On Genesis against the Manichaeans*) I.1.1; *De moribus ecclesiae catholicae et de moribus Manichaeorum* (*On the Way of Life of the Catholic Church*) I.1.

46. *De doctr. christ.* IV.9.23.

47. *De doctr. christ.* IV.9.23.

48. *Tractatus in Joannis evangelium* (*Tracts on the Gospel of John*) 98, 2 (Migne *Patrologia, Series Latina* or *PL* 35.1881).

49. *Tractatus in Joan. Ev.* 98.7 (*PL* 35.1884).

50. *Tractatus in Joan. Ev.* 98.2 (*PL* 35.1881).

51. *Tractatus in Joan. Ev.* 98.6 (*PL* 35.1883).

52. Cf. *Contra mendacium* (*Against Lying*) 10.23; *De mendacio* (*On Lying*) 10.17.

53. *De vera religione* (*On True Religion*) 28.51.

54. Cf. *De sermone Domini in monte* (*The Lord's Sermon on the Mount*) 1.16.

55. See especially Augustine, *Epistula* (*Letter*) 28.40, and 82.

56. Cf. Acts 16:3 and 21:17-26.

57. See Jerome's letter to Augustine in Augustine, *Epist.* 75.3.4 (*PL* 33.252).

58. *Officiosum mendacium: Epist.* 28.3.4; 40.3.3; 82.2.21.

59. *Epistula* (*Letter*) 28.3.3.

60. Cf. *De mendacio* 19.40.

61. *Epist.* 82.2.8.

62. Cf. *De mendacio* 8.11.

63. *De doctr. christ.* I.36.40.

6

REFLECTIONS ON THE PROPER WAY TO READ AUGUSTINE THE THEOLOGIAN

I

It is perhaps an indirect tribute to the greatness and complexity of Augustine's genius that, despite the proliferation of patristic studies in our century, few important books have been devoted to a comprehensive and critical examination of his theological thought. Eugene TeSelle's recent essay, *Augustine the Theologian,*[1] fills this conspicuous lacuna with a commendable blend of daring and modesty. As the latest and in some ways the most successful attempt of its kind, it bids fair to become the work to which scholars and students will turn in the first instance for a synthetic and up-to-date account of Augustine's position on many of the leading problems of Christian theology. The book is all the more welcome as Augustine, who occupies a place of honor as one of the greatest seminal thinkers of the Western tradition, has once again become the focus of a major controversy pitting the embattled defenders of hellenized Christianity against its energetic and increasingly vociferous opponents.

Aside from the fact that it was able to incorporate many of the significant findings of contemporary scholarship, TeSelle's *Augustine* is happily free from the defects that occasionally mar Portalié's otherwise admirable book-length article,[2] originally published in 1902 and long regarded by experts as "the indispensable introduction to the study of Augustine."[3] It is not visibly disfigured by any confessional bias, as was Portalié's; it shows a greater sympathy for the theology of the Greek Fathers and a sharper awareness of Augustine's indebtedness to them, thanks in part to Altaner's pioneering incursions into what until a few years ago had been mostly unexplored territory; it is more sensitive to the dynamic and pulsating quality of Augustine's thought, as opposed to Portalié's study, in which Augustine's insights are often made to conform to the pattern and rubrics of later (specifically scholastic) theology; and it exhibits a timely interest in the possible affinities that link Augustine across the centuries to some of the most influential thinkers of our age.

The book as a whole presents itself as a contribution to historical theology or doctrinal history and concentrates on the strictly theological side of Augustine's achievement. It is not directly concerned with the problem of Augustine's sources or the chronology of his works, except to the extent to which they have some bearing on his intellectual development. Nor does it purport to dwell on the externals of his career. For a general outline of Augustine's life and thought, the character of his day-to-day life as a churchman, and the particulars of his involvement in the wider life of his times, the reader is referred to the excellent studies of Bonner, Van der Meer, and Brown.[4] Even as regards Augustine's theological views, the author generally confines himself to those issues which lie at the heart of Augustine's vision—God, man, the cosmos—to the virtual exclusion of such topics as the theology of history, society and politics, or the Church and its sacraments, which, although falling well within the purview of Augustine's theology, are considered to be less fundamental to it and more closely allied to its practical dimension. The book comprises two main parts, the first of which is devoted to Augustine's formative years ("The Apprentice") and the second to the period of his maturity ("The Master"). The chronological dividing line is 396, the year of Augustine's accession to the episcopal see of Hippo, at which time a major change is alleged to have taken place in his orientation. These two parts are preceded by an introduction, which includes a brief account of Augustine's life up to his conversion as well as a general discussion of his sources, and followed by a conclusion, which attempts to assess Augustine's strength and weaknesses as a theologian in the light of the book's findings.

TeSelle readily acknowledged Augustine's importance not only in himself but for the whole of Western theology, both Protestant and Catholic, which in many ways appears to him as hardly more than a series of annotations to Augustine's work (p. 19). His stated aim is to learn from Augustine "something about the way in which he, in his situation, approached the problem of theology." Accordingly, he is less preoccupied with reporting what Augustine said than with uncovering what he meant or, as he puts it, with construing his statements properly (p. 24). From such a study one may hope to gain a new insight into the nature of the theological enterprise and thus find himself in a better position to "think through the problem again with some measure of the breadth and originality exemplified in him" (p. 19). It is not clear from the outset whether the author regards Augustine's problems as our problems, that is to say, as permanent problems to which he may or may not have given adequate answers, or, more simply stated, whether the substance of Augustine's thought, as distinguished from the form in which it is cast or the modalities of its presentation, is still immediately relevant to our time. The ambiguity is not removed by the observation with which the book ends, to the effect that "as we enter a new era, it may well be that we will find Augustine a reliable guide" (p. 350). There is little doubt, on the other hand, that TeSelle is not simply hiding behind Augustine to expound views which do not always coincide with those of the master. Notwithstanding his respect for much of what Augustine wrote, he does not hesitate to part company with him whenever he finds that there are good reasons to do so. The criteria to which he appeals in accepting or rejecting specific Augustinian doctrines are not discussed *ex professo* in any one place and must be gleaned from a series of remarks that have been scattered throughout the book. A sampling of these remarks would seem to indicate that his own thought is bounded at one end by Augustine and at the other by a variety of modern thinkers the most famous of whom are undoubtedly Whitehead and Heidegger.

The method used is at once genetic or historical and structural phenomenological and bears some similarity to that employed, in TeSelle's opinion with considerable success, by O. du Roy in his study of Augustine's early Trinitarian speculation.[5] By deftly combining both approaches, TeSelle is able to follow the meanderings of Augustine's thought without destroying its inner coherence, and to intuit its essential unity without prying it from the historical context to which it is presumed to be wedded. The final product is a "inematic" (originally du Roy's expression) rather than a synoptic or panoramic account of Augustine's intellectual evolution, covering a span of close to fifty years of more or less intense literary activity.

Such a method would appear to be especially appropriate in Augustine's case, inasmuch as more is known about the development of his thought and the chronology of his works than about those of any other ancient writer. Yet its application can prove cumbersome and perilous at times. Having set his sights on a series of moving targets, the historian is often compelled to revert to the same topic several times in the course of the book. The question of the Trinity, for example, is discussed in chapter 2 and again in chapters 4 and 5, as new elements are introduced into the Augustinian scheme. The same is true of the problem of sin, grace, and predestination, which is likewise taken up once in chapter 2 and a second time in chapter 6, within the more definitive framework of the Pelagian controversy. Whereas in these instances the treatment tends to be slightly redundant, in other instances it suffers from the opposite though less easily discernible defect of incompleteness. A case in point is Augustine's Christology. The subject is broached at some length in chapter 3 on the basis of the data supplied by Augustine's early works; but little is said about the later formulations of the same problem, which may be thought to represent a more advanced stage of reflection and which anticipated, if they did not actually prepare, the dogmatic definition of Chalcedon on the union of the two natures in Christ.

It is also a fact that, although the chronology of Augustine's works is generally well established, there are embarrassing gaps in our information concerning the individual parts of composite works, such as the *Letters* and the *Sermons,* or of those major works which are known to have been written over relatively long periods of time. TeSelle is sensitive to the difficulty and has himself felt the need to engage in a good deal of speculation about the actual date of composition of some of the earlier books of the *De Trinitate* (pp. 223-37).

A similar problem exists in relation to Augustine's sources, many of which are either lost altogether or survive only in the form of fragments. In the absence of any native context, it is frequently impossible to determine with certitude whether the author of the isolated fragment is speaking in his own name, reporting someone else's opinion, or merely accommodating himself to the beliefs and prejudices of his hearer. Thus, from some of Augustine's quotations, one might easily conclude that Porphyry was a devotee of theurgy (cf. p. 249); but Augustine himself was reluctant to do so and leans rather toward the view that Porphyry was a devotee of reason, whose interest in the phenomenon of theurgy was more philosophic than genuinely religious.[6] It is hardly necessary to add that Augustine's failure to mention an author in a particular work is not by itself sufficient proof that he had not yet read him or did not have him in mind as he wrote. By moving the date of Augustine's initial encounter with Porphyry downward, TeSelle is able to strengthen his argument for a noticeable evolution in Augustine's thinking some time after 400 (cf. pp. 71, 110, 125, 237ff., 251). The evidence remains circumstantial, however, and the conclusions drawn from it are at best plausible.[7]

Finally, the method is not the one that Augustine himself advocated and ostensibly used in reading other authors. Although this alone may not be an adequate reason for casting doubts on its validity, it does raise a question as to the kind of understanding that it is capable of giving us of Augustine's works. But on this score the results should perhaps be allowed to speak for themselves. A method, after all, is only a tool, whose merits, like those of the proverbial pudding, are best demonstrated in its employment. The remarks that follow will hopefully shed further light on the matter.

II

Much of the appeal that Augustine holds for the modern reader stems from the fact that he was continually engaged in dialogue not only with his coreligionists but with the pagan world and above all with the great intellectual tradition of antiquity. Since Alfaric, scholarly discussions of this topic have tended to focus on Augustine's peculiar relationship to classical philosophy at the time of his conversion. TeSelle's opinion, briefly summarized, is that the early Augustine was firmly convinced of the substantial harmony between Platonism and Christianity, that he was unaware of the extent to which he was reading the doctrines of the philosophers into the text of the Bible, and that he unwittingly adhered to a teaching which he later found to be at odds with the faith (cf. pp. 35, 73, 124, 146, 188, 198, etc.). That thesis agrees on the whole with the one recently advanced by Robert J. O'Connell in his brilliant essay on *St. Augustine's Early Theory of Man*[8] and may be regarded as a modification of Alfaric's position, according to which Augustine, while feigning to embrace the Christian faith, was really converted to Neoplatonism. What the new interpretation questions is not so much Augustine's sincerity, about which there can no longer be any serious doubt, as his understanding of the essentials of Christian dogma at that critical juncture in his life. It does full justice, against Alfaric, to the quality of Augustine's moral character, but it contributes little to the enhancement of his stature as a thinker. When all is said and done, one finds it difficult to accept that the young Augustine was naive to the point of mistaking Platonic philosophy for the truth of Revelation. There is ample evidence that the Augustine of the dialogues had already faced squarely and resolved in his own mind the issue of their fundamental differences, even if, in the peaceful atmosphere of Cassiciacum and for reasons which were more obvious to him than they are to his modern critics, he was intent on stressing the points on which they agree rather than those on which they disagree. Any final unraveling of this persistent enigma may be contingent on one's ability and willingness to read the dialogues as Augustine wanted them to be read. Such a reading demands that one take into account not only the words spoken by the characters but the characters themselves, their individual reactions to what is being said by others, their occasional silences, and a host of other apparently insignificant but nonetheless revealing details.

The case of Monica and her role in a series of playful and delightfully ironic episodes is particularly instructive in this regard. Monica and Augustine both share the same faith but not in the same way. Monica has nothing but contempt for the sciences whose study is recommended by Augustine in the *De ordine*. Her simple piety is of the kind that does not need to be buttressed by long speeches. She is first and last a lover of the Scriptures, who is unacquainted with the teachings of philosophy and has to be persuaded that St. Paul did not mean to condemn all philosophers indiscriminately.[9] But if she is not a theologian, she is not a fool either. She sees through Augustine's evasive answer to the question as to whether women are suitable candidates for the philosophic life,[10] and when Augustine lightheartedly declares himself ready to become her disciple, she tells him politely that she has never heard him fib so well.[11] At one moment in the dialogue Augustine sees her headed for what promises to be a brilliant philosophic career.[12] But given her age, the tyranny of custom over the minds of most people, the small number of truly philosophic natures, the enormous difficulties inherent in the philosophic quest, the long cycle of studies by which the mind must be exercised from its early years,[13] and the inordinate amount of time and leisure required to reach the threshold of wisdom, one is not surprised to find that the hopes that Augustine holds out for her philosophic salvation were not as high as his tongue-in-cheek statement had first led us to believe. Throughout the discussion she is mostly silent and the closing scene makes it plain that she is better at praying than at intellectual debate.[14] If philosophy is a preparation for death, a *meletê thanatou* in the Platonic sense, then Monica, who can face death courageously, is indeed a true philosopher;[15] but her strength obviously comes from a source other than the disinterested contemplation of the eternal order of the universe.

The *De beata vita,* where she plays a somewhat more glamourous role, does not paint an essentially different picture of her. It shows us a Monica who is more concerned with the integrity of Augustine's faith than with adjusting its claims to those of philosophy. If it were up to her, many a stone would be left unturned. She is only interested in the conclusion of the argument and cares not a whit for the meticulous examination of the premises on which it is made to rest.[16] Her tone becomes more conciliatory as the dialogue progresses, but her theology is not visibly improved by it. When she speaks again, it is for the sole purpose of seeing to it that everyone is treated courteously.[17] By that time her intervention is more apt to put an end to the discussion than to advance it. Insead of trying to refute the adversary, as she is urged to do, she summarily dismisses him as an epileptic and rushes off, possibly to prepare the meal which the group will enjoy before they reconvene for the next round. Having failed to nourish their minds, she at least has the satisfaction of feeding their bodies.

What has just been said of Monica applies in varying degrees to the other participants in the dialogues, who as a body are characterized by their inequality[18] and have presumably been selected to epitomize the gamut of possible responses or types of responses to the problems treated. Seen in that perspective, both dialogues inculcate a lesson in taste. They teach among other things how one discusses the arcana of Christian theology in the presence of a devout but intelligent mother to whom the privilege of a higher education has unfortunately been denied, or of a small but typical assembly of Christians whose ability to live the Christian life is unquestionably superior to their theoretical understanding of it.

If such is the case, the immediate addressees of Augustine's discourses are as much of a key to their correct interpretation as is their content. The dialogues merely conform to Augustine's own principles by speaking safely about the most important and hence most dangerous matters. In general, they serve the dual purpose of producing agreement among a group of people who at the outset appear to be hopelessly divided on the issues at hand, and of satisfying the legitimate curiosity of the inquisitive student whose mind has been previously exercised and alerted to the existence of problems of which their less learned fellows barely have any inkling. If these dialogues prove anything, it is not that at the time of their writing, Augustine was still ignorant of some of the most important divergences between the biblical and the philosophic understandings of man and the universe, but that he did not deem it appropriate to make a complete and open disclosure of the abstruse theological difficulties implied in their correlation before an audience made up largely of people the majority of whom could not reasonably be expected to derive much benefit from such a disclosure. On that premise, the discovery that "revelation upset many of the precipitate judgments of the philosophers" (p. 198) cannot be said to belong to Augustine's so-called mature period. It dates from the time of his conversion, even if his full thought on the matter is more likely to be found in the interstices of his works than in any of their explicit utterances. A close reading of the dialogues suggests that Augustine was not only using philosophy to gain a better understanding of his newfound faith—an understanding to which Monica, for all her deep seated and admirable piety, would never have access—but had already set out to reformulate the teachings of classical philosophy to suit the requirements of Christianity. It is true of course that he eventually felt the need to revise some of the philosophic opinions to which for a while he had uncritically assented; but the few strictures recorded in the *Retractationes* and elsewhere do not total up to anything like a rejection of the basic position adopted at the beginning of his career. It is scarcely conceivable that he would have taken the pains to re-edit the dialogues for posterity if their overall teaching were one which he had come to repudiate in later life. As they stand, these dialogues present us with what may still be his most detailed and searching investigation of the problem of the relation of faith to reason in all of its essential dimensions.

III

A few of the more striking consequences of Augustine's reinterpretation of Platonic philosophy come to the fore in his exegesis of the first chapters of Genesis and particularly in his treatment of the problem of creation, to which he returned on many different occasions, not only in his commentaries on Genesis (*De genesi contra Manichaeos, De genesi liber imperfectus, De genesi ad litteram*), but in the *Confessions* and the *City of God.* TeSelle bestows some of his highest praise on this aspect of Augustine's work; he finds Augustine's exegesis superior to that of his Greek predecessors, Philo, Origen, and Basil. He pronounces it basically sound in the light of modern biblical scholarship and goes so far as to submit that Augustine may have "succeeded in giving (probably for the only time in the entire history of exegesis, for what it is worth) a satisfactory interpretation of the opening chapters of Genesis, with all their perplexities" (p. 198). He further insists that Augustine's views owe much of their value to the scientific questions that he brings to the text, his willingness to take seriously the problems that it raises, and his ability to use philosophic arguments in wrestling with them. The bulk of that section (pp. 197-223) is given over to a careful scrutiny of the manner in which Augustine went about his task. The impression conveyed is that Augustine does a masterful job of harmonizing the text of the Bible with the doctrines of the philosophers, or of articulating a view of the whole of creation which is both philosophically defensible and consonant with the teaching of revelation.

The only regret that one might wish to express is that the analysis limits itself, for the most part, to showing how Augustine resolved the apparent inconsistencies of the biblical account, thereby neutralizing the arguments by which his opponents sought to discredit its authority. Augustine's own thought seems to have moved within a broader horizon. He saw the labyrinthine complexity of the sacred text as forming a "nest" in which the faith is nurtured; but, as TeSelle points out (without, however, making a concerted effort to follow his own lead), he also compares it to a "leafy orchard"[19] filled with hidden and, one suspects, forbidden fruit. There are reasons to think that Augustine's text is likewise "multidimensional." To construe it properly, one must be attentive not only to the plethora of haggadic statements and edifying discourses encountered in it but to the questions which it raises only obliquely, to wit, the cognitive status of the creative narratives, the notion of God which they presuppose, and the doctrine of creation itself, which stands in such sharp contrast to the philosophic view of the eternity of the world and which may be seen as the issue on which the quarrel between biblical faith and philosophic reason hinges in the last analysis. In that respect, the *City of God,* which invokes divine omnipotence and the authority of Scripture,[20] goes to the heart of the matter more directly than most of the other texts. TeSelle's remark that this was done "in part, perhaps, because the tide was now running against Origen" (p. 199), accords well with his thesis that Augustine's thinking had taken a new turn between the earlier works and the parallel discussion of the *City of God.* But the discrepancy, if there is one, could just as easily and perhaps more naturally be explained by the different intentions pursued in each of these writings or sets of writings. The commentaries on Genesis and the *Confessions* are clearly addressed to Christians, and not even primarily to theologically-minded Christians but to all Christians who can read. The nature of these works did not call for a thematic discussion of the philosophic implications of the problem, whereas the *City of God,* which explicitly takes up the issue of the Christian versus the pagan interpretations of the *archai* or origins, could hardly avoid such a discussion. One cannot infer from the silence of the earlier works that Augustine had not yet thought the problem through, or from the slant that the argument takes in the later works that he had arrived at a new understanding of it. In all of these texts there is elaborated a theology which is at variance with anything that Augustine could have discovered in his pagan sources. The God to which they consistently refer is an acting God, who is to be accepted by men as much as he is to be apprehended by them. He is the God of Monica no less than of the literate Christian involved in subtle philosophic and theological disquisitions about the nature of his relations with man. He is a God to whom one prays, whose providence extends to all creatures, and who presides in a special way over the destinies of those creatures who have been endowed by him with reason and free will. He is a God of infinite power, on whose "will" the universe depends for its existence and in whom it finds its fulfillment, as opposed to the God of reason, governed only by the intelligible necessity of an eternal world. He is also the God who promulgates and sanctions the moral law under which men live and to which they owe an unflinching obedience at all times. An examination of Augustine's views on the moral life, which does not fall within the compass of the book, would disclose the far-reaching practical implications with which, in Augustine's mind, the *fiat* of Genesis was laden. It would also lead by a direct route to the question of the perfect beginning, which forms an integral part of Augustine's anthropology and which is again diametrically opposed to the philosophic view according to which the origins of human history, assuming that one can even speak of them, are essentially barbaric, inasmuch as they are marked by the absence of philosophy, on which the attainment of human perfection was regarded as intrinsically dependent.

Through such considerations, we are brought face to face once more with the fundamental option between divine authority and human reason against the backdrop of which Augustine's theological speculation consciously unfolds. That option is perhaps nowhere more concisely stated than in the passage of the *Confessions* which opposes the *confessio* of the Christian to the *praesumptio* of the philosopher.[21] The distinction not only illumines from within the title and the general tenor of Augustine's book, but establishes the unity of its two separate and at first glance unrelated parts, the first describing his spiritual odyssey (Books I-X) and the second dealing with those chapters of Genesis from which the new vision of human life to which he had attained draws its intelligibility. It may be that Augustine anticipated "no incompatibility between Christianity and authentic philosophy" (p. 73), but in that event, what he understood by philosophy is a far cry from what his pagan masters meant by it; and he, more than anyone else, knew it.

IV

The same basic problem may be approached from a slightly different angle by considering Augustine's teaching concerning the existence of eternal and immutable ideas or essences,[22] which appears to have been the object of innumerable discussions in the philosophic schools of late antiquity. TeSelle rightly points out, as others before him had done, that for Augustine, the Platonic "ideas" become practical ideas in the mind of the divine artist, and that these ideas are the causes of all that occurs, even if they are not the sole determinant of the process (p. 214). The source of Augustine's doctrine is said to be Varro and ultimately Varro's teacher, Antiochus of Ascalon, the first philosopher to have broken with the skepticism of the New Academy and to have undertaken to restore the teaching of the Old Academy, now blended with Stoic and Peripatetic elements (p. 46). The significance of that doctrine lies in the fact that for Augustine the world is an intelligible whole, not in its own being, to be sure, but in the divine intellect, and that it is rightly construed only when seen as a "universe," organized by a single unifying principle. Hence the human mind, "which naturally seeks to unify all that it finds, will not be satisfied in its quest until it comes to know what is in the mind of God" (p. 78), that is to say, until it comes to know the divine ideas. Since created things never conform perfectly to the divine exemplar, there exists "a certain tension" between their being and that of the divine ideas, the latter remaining inevitably superior to the former. That tension is not to be resolved by foresaking the temporal and fleeing to the eternal but by seeing created things in their proper light or setting them in their intended relationship (cf. p. 213). The rest of the discussion abounds with enlightening remarks about the way in which Augustine, who was unfamiliar with the Hebrew mentality, creatively misinterprets the text of Genesis in accordance with the philosophic and scientific notions of the time. It also contains a lucid explanation of the curious Augustinian distinction between the "daytime" and "evening" knowledge of angels, the one referring to their uninterrupted contemplation of created beings as they preexist in the mind of God, and the other to their knowledge of these same beings as they are in themselves (pp. 210-11).

While one may be grateful for the wealth of information thus brought to light, one would have appreciated a more thorough discussion of Augustine's tacit modification of the original and at the time still widely accepted Platonic doctrine. It is possible, as TeSelle proposes, that some of Augustine's concepts were inspired by or borrowed from Varro. But since Varro's text has not come down to us, one can only guess what its precise intention was. We know from Augustine that Varro's treatment of theological problems was cautious or political in the sense that it deliberately eschewed any statement that might have offended traditional piety;[23] and we also know that Varro identified the soul or its rational part with the divine nature.[24] Both observations open up the possibility that, in spite of appearances, the Varronian doctrine may have been more truly Platonic than Augustinian or pre-Augustinian. Its subtle antireligious thrust becomes apparent when we examine a dialogue like Plato's *Euthyphro,* which may be cited for purposes of illustration, even though it is never mentioned by Augustine. The famous question explored by that impious dialogue on piety is simply whether a thing is right because it is willed by God or the gods, or whether it is willed by the gods because it is right. If the first alternative is the correct one, the gods are the ultimate source of truth, and piety consists in doing what they command, that is to say, in abiding by the prescriptions of revealed or established religion. If, on the other hand, God's will is itself dictated by what God knows to be right, the eternal ideas in the light of which he makes his will known to men are necessarily superior to him, and true piety consists in the pursuit of such knowledge as one may be able to acquire of them. The possession of that knowledge, assuming its possibility, renders superfluous any further attempt to discover God's will. Human perfection or the imitation of God is to be found in doing what God himself does rather than in doing what he orders. Since the two positions do not seem to admit of a middle ground, one is again confronted with a choice between the rival claims to supremacy of revealed religion on the one hand and autonomous reason on the other. Needless to say, the problem is not proper to the *Euthyphro*. It occurs in various guises in any number of other Platonic dialogues and it is central to the action of the *Republic,* where the teaching concerning the gods, so vital to the early education of the guardians,[25] is quietly dropped in favor of the "greatest and most fitting"[26] of all studies (though not necessarily for everyone), the *idea* of the Good.[27]

One gathers that Augustine's interest in this whole question was anything but academic. It was prompted by the highly problematic character which the Platonic doctrine was bound to assume in the eyes of the believer. By placing the "ideas" in the mind of God, Augustine was not just annexing an old philosophic teaching to Christian theology, he was subjecting it to a transformation which enabled him to reinstate the religious notion of divine possession—the "enthusiasm" demoted by the philosophers—without prejudice to man's rationality, and thus fuse or compose two traditionally antagonistic and supposedly irreconcilable views. Monica's unsophisticated faith was vindicated, however much it may have differed from Augustine's in regard to its apprehension of the Christian mystery. The dovelike innocence of the simple Christian had at last found an ally in the serpentine wisdom of the worldly philosophers.[28]

V

Much of what has been said thus far points to the fact that Augustine's theology, like Varro's, albeit for different reasons, was "political" in its manner of treatment or couched, with rare exceptions, in what might be called a political context. Before going on to other matters, however, it may be worth our while to glance rapidly at TeSelle's remarks concerning Augustine's views on civil society or his political theology in the more usual sense of the term. By the author's own admission the pages devoted to this subject (pp. 268-78) are sketchy and inadequate. Their inclusion is justified on the ground that the *City of God* merits a place of its own in any survey of Augustine's thought. As it turns out, TeSelle's harshest judgments are reserved for this phase of Augustine's intellectual activity. The deference ordinarily shown for the master even when his teaching is being criticized has practically disappeared. Augustine, the politician *malgrè lui*, is suspected of being a coward, given to compromise with the established order, and unable to stand his ground against the recurrent pressures of worldly society (pp. 273-74). Granted that there is something to be said for his theory, he still misused it "to give ideological support to oppression and shortsighted policies" (p. 277). In Augustine, Christianity has sold out to Nabuchednezzar. The surrender was fatal not only because of the harm that it wrought at the time but because of the precedent that it set for future generations.

Were it not for TeSelle's integrity—an integrity demonstrated on virtually every page of the book—the reader might wonder at this point whether the initial decision to refrain from a more complete treatment of Augustine's political theory was not secretly motivated by his lack of sympathy for it. It could simply be, however, that in tackling this problem, he found himself at a disadvantage, due to the relative scarcity of first-rate materials on which to rely, or perhaps the general climate of the times in which we live. Ours is, as we have recently discovered, a politically untutored age. Its greatest masters—Husserl, Heidegger, Whitehead—differ from the philosophic giants of former ages by the all but total absence of any political dimension from their thought. The lessons that we have learned from them have furnished us with few of the tools needed to analyze the political crises of our predecessors or, for that matter, to cope with our own. This does not mean of course that our contemporaries are not interested in politics, but only that their eagerness to become involved in it, to say nothing of an often irrepressible desire to manipulate it, is at times matched only by an artificially induced and deadening incapacity to understand it.

Be that as it may, the present reviewer cannot help thinking that for all its possible shortcomings, Augustine's political thought deserved a better fate. Augustine is, after all, the first Christian writer to have grappled on a grand scale with the perennially vexing question of the relation of Christianity to civil society. His theory is admittedly incomplete, inasmuch as it seldom goes into any concrete details concerning the structure of the *polis* or the business of its administration. Its virtues lie elsewhere, in the unusually penetrating grasp of the issues implied in the conflict between Christianity as a universal religion, or a universal way of salvation, as Augustine called it,[29] and the classical notion of man as a naturally political animal. Regardless of whether one agrees with it or not, it still represents one of the few intellectually respectable solutions to have been proposed in the course of the centuries. As for Augustine's own personal behavior, any final judgment of it is best left to God, even to a God as severe as Augustine's God is sometimes made out to be. It is doubtful whether the circumstances of that behavior are any easier to evaluate at a distance of close to sixteen hundred years than they were in Augustine's own time. But rather than dwell on the matter, which remains peripheral to the central theme of the book, one could perhaps leave it at saying that, in retrospect, and by comparison with the fanaticism or the intransigence of such a political movement as Donatism and Pelagianism (in this they are at one), Augustine's political theology may have more to recommend it than has met TeSelle's usually discriminating eye.[30] As we shall see, the failure to appreciate it at its true value may be nothing more than the obverse of a gradual dimming of the eschatological conscience in modern times.

VI

With these observations in mind, we turn to the larger issue of the parallel between Augustine and the marching wing of contemporary philosophic and theological thought to which the book draws our attention from time to time. The author's comments on this subject, although they are generally made only in passing, are all the more important as they reveal an interest in Augustine that is not merely archaeological but relevant to the preoccupations of twentieth-century man, and as they often clash with those of other scholars, such as Dietrich Ritschl and Robert J. O'Connell, who would lay at Augustine's doorstep the responsibility for many of the woes that continue to beset present-day Christian theology.[31]

TeSelle's interpretation stresses the continuity rather than the discontinuity between Augustine and modern thought or at least that segment of modern thought represented chiefly by Whitehead and to a lesser degree Heidegger, as well as by those theologians whose thinking has been shaped or influenced by them. We are told, for example, that the "similarity of Augustine's views to many currents in modern philosophy and theology is striking" (p. 222), and, in connection with the problem of grace and the whole complex of ideas which make up Augustine's *Glaubenslehrer,* that "what Augustine was doing has many similarities with, indeed, is in many respects the primogenitor of the spirit of much of nineteenth- and twentieth-century theology as seen in Schleiermacher and Barth, Scheeben and Rahner" (p. 312). Like Kierkegaard and Nietzsche, Augustine is assigned to that category of writers who, in Jaspers's phrase, "thought with their blood" (p. 190).[32] His metaphysical schema, "which is centered on dynamic processes rather than permanent substance," which is applied analogously "to both the physical world and man's inward life," and which never loses sight of the human experiences and activities from which it takes its departure, reflects in TeSelle's view "something of the same concern that animated Whitehead, Teilhard, and before them, Leibnitz" (p. 145). An unmistakable Augustinian strain is likewise detected in the theory of knowledge propounded by such Neo-Thomists or transcendental Thomists, as they are now called, as Maréchal, Rahner, and Lonergan, whose Thomism is said to be in a crucial respect "far more Augustinian or Bonaventuran than it is Thomist" (p. 106). Even Augustine's ancient cosmology of spiritual powers may not be as foreign to our own way of thinking as one might be tempted to believe. It, too, has its present-day analogue, which "is to be found in what many heralds of 'secularity,' theistic and non-theistic, are saying today about man: that he has awesome and god-like powers for the transformation of the world and ought not to await direct divine intervention but must accept his own responsibility and act decisively to change the world for the better" (p. 216).

Needless to say, TeSelle is not proposing that Augustine's theology could be restored *en bloc* or that the possibility of a pure and simple return to it should be seriously entertained. Although less critical of Augustine's overall stance and posture than either Ritschl or O'Connell, he makes no bones about the fact that it needs to be complemented by or emended in the light of the insights of more recent thought. The points which he finds least palatable and on which a corrective is most sorely needed, besides the ones alluded to earlier, have to do with such notorious issues as infant baptism, original sin, and predestination. Like many of our contemporaries, TeSelle finds it difficult to accept that the evils from which we suffer are incurable (to paraphrase a famous modern thinker), or that God could be as selective in his offer of salvation as Augustine apparently thought he was. Thus, starting from the Christian life as the paradigm, "it would be possible to develop an understanding of grace and predestination quite different from that associated with Augustine—*if* his doctrine of infant baptism were dropped and *if* the biblical view that God wills all men to be saved were taken seriously" (p. 330; TeSelle's emphasis). This, TeSelle claims, is precisely the task which the Church undertook not long after Augustine's time and with which theologians are still attempting to come to grips. What is more, there are hints in Augustine's own works which suggest that he himself was already beginning to move in the same direction (p. 332).

In any event, Augustine cannot reasonably be held to account for all the limitations of his theology. He lived in what the book describes as "an historically unsophisticated age" (p. 188); the theology which he inherited from his predecessors was still on many points in a "relatively undeveloped state" (p. 227); and he can hardly be faulted for having accepted, especially at the start, the picture of the world presented by the historians, the scientists, and the philosophers of antiquity, "which was, after all, the best that was available, however poorly the information had been gathered and however uncritically it had been sifted" (p. 343). We, on the other hand, are more fortunate, having at our disposal "a far greater supply of information about the cosmos and the history of the human race and the vicissitudes of the people of God, together with a far more critical way of assessing it and bringing it into a unified picture" (ibid.).

TeSelle's remarks on these and related questions will undoubtedly please his readers, the majority of whom have been trained to think, consciously or unconsciously, in categories that are different from, if not totally alien to, those of Augustine. The *prima facie* evidence that they have acquired for most of us is such that any demurrer is bound to be drowned out by a loud and spontaneous chorus of dissenting voices. It would be pointless to deny that the development of modern science has greatly added to our knowledge about man and the universe of which he is now seen to be an infinitesimal part, and that it has greatly expanded our ability to understand and control the forces of nature. Interestingly enough, Augustine seems to have anticipated this progress, more clearly perhaps than most of his contemporaries, when he spoke of the "wonderful and stupefying advances" of which the human mind was capable.[33] Nor can anyone doubt that the Augustinian influence is still very much at work in current theology. Like the vestiges of God in creation, Augustine's stamp is everywhere present in modern thought, openly or in disguise, from Schleiermacher to Tillich and from Kant to Whitehead. But the objective historian owes it to himself to be equally alert to those elements of Augustine's thought which have been stricken from the roster of defensible ideas and which may be more indispensable to the inner coherence of his theology than some of his more recent interpreters are willing to own.

Specifically, one cannot help wondering, in the light of the events of recent history and of our own increasingly precarious situation, how much has been gained by substituting emergent structures and dynamic processes for Augustine's eternal forms or ideas, or by replacing Augustine's sophisticated political theology with modern scientific, evolutionary, and futuristic apoliticism. The least that can be said is that the present state of Western society is not likely to generate any undue enthusiasm in some circles concerning the ultimate success of the modern scientific enterprise. Having seen with our own eyes what the conquest of nature is capable of doing to the conqueror, we may still find Augustine's views on these matters wiser and more to the point than the ones to which we have lately become accustomed. For, if Augustine foresaw the virtually unlimited possibilities of human art and industry, he was more alive than most of his latter-day followers or would-be followers to the potential destructiveness of scientific inventions and, in general, to the nagging ambivalence of human progress.[34] More than those of either Whitehead or Teilhard, to name two authors for whom TeSelle professes high regard, his works testify to what a true representative of the great Augustinian tradition once described as the experience of the abyss.

All of this amounts to asking whether, on the level of the highest principles, Augustine's thought is as easily harmonizable with the prevalent and currently most powerful modes of theological thought as TeSelle seems to suggest. To phrase the question in slightly different terms, does the tradition of modern theology inaugurated, let us say, by Schleiermacher represent a necessary and desirable development or prolongation of Augustine's position, or does it rather rest on a choice or decision made at the beginning of that tradition, tacitly repeated in the course of its evolution, and therefore as much in need of critical examination as are the premises underlying Augustine's own view of the whole?

A possible clue to the manner in which the problem might suitably be posed, though by no means definitively solved, is furnished by Schleiermacher. Schleiermacher, the legitimate father of the "new theology" and the first man to have undertaken to bridge the gulf between traditional Christianity and the Enlightenment, was himself to a large extent a product of the Enlightenment. He also happens to be the first writer to have questioned the existence of a secret or hidden teaching in the works of the ancient authors.[35] He shared with his enlightened contemporaries the belief in the fundamental harmony between science and society and hence in the possibility of a perfectly rational society brought into being by the unrestricted diffusion of scientific knowledge. His implicit and typically modern faith in the necessarily beneficent character of science dispensed him from reflecting with utmost seriousness on the problem as such and its ambiguous relationship to human society, and it made it all but impossible for him to conceive that the greatest minds of the past could have withheld, not for reasons of self-interest but of simple prudence, certain truths which might have been misunderstood or misused by an unwise or unfriendly reader.[36] In this, however, he can hardly be said to have innovated. His originality consisted not so much in restating the Enlightenment thesis concerning the final reconciliation between science and civil society as in assuming that a similar pre-established harmony existed between the basic tenets of the Christian faith and the deepest intentions of modern philosophic thought. He was able to make a plausible case for that harmony only by postulating the identification of man with religious man and by assimilating the Kingdom of God to the heavenly city of the eighteenth-century philosophers.

Augustine was surely less sanguine about the capabilities of human science and human nature generally. But the results that he obtained by demanding more and expecting less of most men are not demonstrably inferior to those which his modern critics have thus far been able to achieve by deliberately lowering the goals of human activity in an effort to increase their chances of realization. The science or philosophy that he learned from his pagan mentors, however "uncritical" it may have been, displayed what may yet prove to be a more sober understanding of the human condition. It at least preserved him both from Schleiermacher's naive optimism and from the disillusionment to which the collapse of Schleiermacher's unfounded hopes eventually led. If so, the cleavage between Augustine and his twentieth-century disciples may be wider than is generally assumed.

There is nevertheless one point on which Augustine, as the principal architect of Western theology, seems to have profoundly influenced the development of modern thought and in some remote way laid the groundwork for its newest and most extreme manifestations, and that is the emphasis on God's free will, as reflected particularly in his teaching on creation, divine providence, and natural law. But that influence was exerted on a level that is seldom attained in the current discussions of the problem.

The foregoing remarks are intended less as a criticism of TeSelle's rich and well-informed essay than as a modest sample of the kind of reflection that it is capable of stimulating. What the book shows beyond the shadow of a doubt is that after more than fifteen centuries Augustine's theology continues to present a challenge that is unmatched in the history of Christian thought. The success with which the challenge has been met in the present case must be measured in terms not only of the agreement that the book will elicit but of the disagreements that it will provoke. Its overall value, which is great by any standard, will not be diminished by the realization that there are other, less popular but not necessarily less valid, ways of reading Augustine and of demonstrating his relevance to the modern scene.

NOTES

1. Eugene TeSelle, *Augustine the Theologian* (New York: Herder and Herder, 1970), 381. While generally well edited and elegantly presented, the book contains a few minor *lapsus* which could easily be corrected in a subsequent edition. Section 2 of chapter 6 begins on page 319 and not 389 as indicated in the Table of Contents (p. 6). On p. 34 Pierre Hadot is referred to, perhaps unfortunately, as "Père" Hadot. Footnote 12 on p. 196 should read, "Introduction, Section 2" instead of "chapter 1, Section 2." Augustine's *De doctrina christiana* is cited on p. 249 as the treatise *On Christian Teaching* and elsewhere as the treatise *On Christian Instruction.* On p. 271 the *latrocinia* mentioned by Augustine in a famous chapter of the *City of God* came out as "rubber bands" and not "robber bands," which I presume is what was intended. Footnote 7 on p. 316 belongs on p. 315.

2. "Augustin, Saint," *Dictionnaire de théologie catholique*, Tome 1 (Paris, 1902) col. 22682472.

3. E. Gilson, *Introduction à l'étude de saint Augustin* (Paris: Vrin, 1949), 329. Id., *History of Christian Philosophy in the Middle Ages* (New York: Random House, 1955), 591. V. J. Bourke, Introduction to the English translation of E. Portalié, *A Guide to the Thought of St. Augustine* (Chicago: H. Regnery Co., 1960), xxi.

4. G. Bonner, *St. Augustine of Hippo: Life and Controversies* (Philadelphia,

1963). F. Van der Meer, *Augustine the Bishop* (London and New York, 1961). P. Brown, *Augustine of Hippo, A Biography* (Berkeley, 1967).

5. Augustine, *L'inteligence de la foi en la Trinité selon saint Augustin* (Paris: Etudes augustiniennes, 1966).

6. Augustine, *De civitate Dei* (*City of God*) X.11.

7. Cf. the recent discussions of this problem by J. J. O'Meara, "Porphyry's *Philosophy from Oracles* in Eusebius's *Praeparatio evangelica* and Augustine's *Dialogues* of Cassiciacum," *Recherches Augustiniennes* 6 (Paris, 1969), 103-139, and "Studies Preparatory to an Understanding of the Mysticism of St. Augustine and His Doctrine on the Trinity," *Augustinian Studies* 1 (Villanova, 1970), 268f.

8. Robert J. O'Connell, *St. Augustine's Early Theory of Man* (Cambridge, MA: Harvard University Press, 1968). Also, by the same author, *St. Augustine's Confessions: The Odyssey of Soul* (Cambridge MA: Harvard University Press, 1969).

9. *De ordine* (*On Order*) 2.17.46.

10. *De ordine* 1.11.31.

11. *De ordine* 1.11.32-33.

12. *De ordine* 2.1.1.

13. *De ordine* 2.16.44.

14. *De ordine* 2.20.52.

15. *De ordine* 1.11.32.

16. Augustine, *De beata vita* (*On the Happy Life*) 6 and 10.

17. *De beata vita* II.16.

18. *De beata vita* II.16.

19. *Confessiones* (*Confessions*) XII.28.38. Similar comparison in Clement of Alexandria, *Stromata* VII.18.111 and VI.1.2. For a brief commentary on Clement's texts, cf. E. L. Fortin, chapter 8, "Clement of Alexandria and the Esoteric Tradition."

20. *De civ. Dei* XI.4f.

21. *Conf.* VII.20.26.

22. Cf. *De diversis questionibus LXXXIII* (*On Eighty-three Diverse Questions*) qu. 46; *De civ. Dei* VII.28 and XIX.3, etc.

23. *De civ. Dei* III.4; VI.2; VII.17; VII.23.

24. Cf. *De civ. Dei* IV.31; VII.5; VIII.1; VIII.5.

25. Plato, *Republic* II.377ef.

26. Ibid., VI.504d.

27. The teaching of both the *Euthyphro* and the *Republic* is corroborated by the creation myth of the *Timaeus* (27df.), in which the demiurge who fashions the visible universe looks back to an eternal model which is clearly outside of him and above him. There is much to be said for TeSelle's suggestion that Porphyry may have "supplied to Augustine precisely that element which is most akin to biblical thought and which is found in the *Timaeus*," (p. 254). Under the circumstances, however, the Platonic myth could prove helpful only once it had been fumigated and purged of its antireligious overtones.

28. The same Augustinian doctrine is discussed from a different point of view

by Theodore Kondoleon, "Divine Exemplarism in Augustine," *Augustinian Studies* 1 (Villanova, 1970), 181-195. For further details on the antecedents to that doctrine, cf. in addition to the references cited by TeSelle, A. H. Armstrong, "The Background of the Doctrine 'That the Intelligibles Are Not Outside the Intellect'," E. R. Dodds et al., *Les Sources de Plotin* (Genève: Fondation Hardt, 1957), 393-413; P. Hadot, *Porphyre et Victorinus* 1 (Paris: Etudes Augustiniennes, 1968), 382f.

29. E.g., *De civ. Dei* X.32.

30. For a new and generally more sympathetic appraisal of Augustine's political views, see R. A. Markus, *Saeculum: History and Society in the Theology of St. Augustine* (Cambridge, England: Cambridge University Press, 1970).

31. D. Ritschl, *Memory and Hope: An Inquiry Concerning the Presence of Christ* (New York: Macmillan, 1967). R. J. O'Connell, *St Augustine's Early Theory of Man, A.D. 386-391* (Cambridge, MA: Harvard University Press, 1968), 285f., and *St. Augustine's Confessions: The Odyssey of Soul* (Cambridge, MA: Harvard University Press, 1969) 186f.

32. The expression is really Nietzsche's in *Zarathustra*, I.7. Nietzsche's injunction, "Write with blood, and you will experience that blood is spirit," becomes fully intelligible only when the soul is replaced by the "self" and when the self is identified with the body; cf. *Zarathustra*, I.4. If there is a kinship between Augustine and Nietzsche on this point, it is certainly not one which Augustine would have readily acknowledged. One might prefer to forget the fate of the "blood-spirit" mystique in Nietzsche's own country less than forty years after his death.

33. *De civ. Dei* XXII.24.

34. On this subject see especially H.-I. Marrou, *L'ambivalence du temps de l'histoire chez saint Augustin* (Montreal: Institut d'études médiévales, 1950). T. E. Mommsen, "Orosius and Augustine," *Medieval and Renaissance Studies* (Ithaca, NY: Cornell University Press, 1959), 325-48; "St. Augustine and the Christian Idea of Progress," *Journal of the History of Ideas* 12 (1951), reprinted in *Medieval and Renaissance Studies*, 265-98.

35. F. Schleiermacher, *Platons Werke* 1 (Berlin: G. Reimer, 1804), 11f.

36. Cf. Plato, *Republic* V.450d.

7

A NOTE ON DAWSON AND ST. AUGUSTINE

Christopher Dawson's memorable essay on "St. Augustine and His Age," first published in 1930 as part of a collection of articles commemorating the fifteenth centenary of Augustine's death,[1] is anything but an archaeological expedition or an exercise in antiquarianism. It belongs to the existential context of the period between the two world wars and was motivated by what was then widely perceived to be a crisis of major proportions, one that threatened to engulf the whole of Western civilization. That crisis was brought forcefully to the attention of the European intelligentsia as far back as 1919 by Paul Valéry in a famous article that began with the ominous words, "We civilizations, we know now that we are mortal," and went on to compare the finest civilizations of the past to the "phantom shapes of great vessels once laden with riches and knowledge" but later swallowed up by the chasm of history, which, as we now realize, is "big enough to hold everybody."[2]

Valéry's piece, written almost entirely under the aegis of Nietzsche, rightly diagnosed the crisis as first and foremost an intellectual crisis. The West was in trouble, not because its economy was in shambles or because its existence was menaced by powerful enemies on its borders, as it had been at other moments in the past, but because it had repudiated virtually everything that it stood for. It was critically wounded, finished perhaps, because it no longer believed in itself or in the justice of its principles. Of the three elements of which it was compounded—Christianity, Greek philosophy, and Roman law—none was likely to survive the catastrophe in recognizable form. The blow was all the more cruel as it was self-inflicted. Westerners were unable to defend the superiority of their civilization for the simple reason that they had renounced the standards by which that superiority could be established. They were at a loss to demonstrate that truth should prevail over error because they had finally concluded that the distinction between them was unclear. Nothing was true or false, everything was relative.

The main concern was not that the human species might be annihilated. The bomb was still twenty-five years away and modern science had not yet come up with the means of blowing up the planet. No, life would go on, but it was in danger of becoming a diminished and impoverished life, dedicated only to the satisfaction of one's bodily needs, the pursuit of equality rather than excellence, and, lest boredom should set in, the cultivation of an indefinite variety of decadent art forms. Spengler was even more pessimistic. By the time the final version of the *Decline of the West* was written, he had come to the conclusion that what Valéry regarded as still only a possibility was an absolute certainty. The future belonged to Nietzsche's "last man," whose hegemony could no longer be averted. More than ever before, human beings would be in touch with one another, but, having replaced the morning prayer with the morning paper, they would cease to be in touch with anything higher than themselves. Moreover, insofar as Western "culture" was the only universal "culture," that is to say, the only one capable of understanding all the others, its demise heralded the twilight of human creativity or "culture" *tout court.* A global "fellahinism" was in store for all of us.

One of the side effects of the new climate of opinion was to stimulate interest in a hitherto much neglected period of history, that of the tail end of ancient civilization and the fall of the Roman Empire. Prior to World War I, historians had focused almost exclusively on the birth and rise to prominence of the great civilizations of the past. With the sudden realization that, like all of its predecessors, the West, too, might be doomed, the question of the manner in which civilizations begin to fall apart and eventually die became an object of passionate inquiry, indeed, history's most fascinating problem. Not surprisingly, scholarly attention was drawn to the waning years of the Roman Empire and the upheavals that precipitated its downfall. Here was a renowned civilization that had not only gone under but in the process had bequeathed to posterity a well-documented record of its breakdown, the only corpse sufficiently well preserved to lend itself to a dissection (E. F. Gaus).

Among the ancient writers to whom one might turn for information about this critical period none was better suited than Augustine, who had been prompted by the dramatic events of his day to meditate on the fate of empires and the destiny of the human race. From him one could learn something about what conceivably lay in store for us: whether the dislocations of our troubled times were the necessary prelude to a larger and more powerful synthesis, or whether they portended a return to the barbarism that had once plunged Europe into darkness for centuries; whether our future was "that of the generations of Caesar and Augustus or that of the generations of Diocletian and Constantine," as Guglielmo Ferrero put it famously in his *Words to the Deaf,* a book that was promptly translated into a dozen different languages.

This somber theme is taken up over and over again by Dawson not only in books and articles that date from the twenties and thirties but in numerous others as well. A *Dublin Review* article of October, 1927, notes that

> Of all the changes that the twentieth century has brought, none goes deeper than the loss of unquestioning faith in the future and in the absolute value of our civilization, which was the dominant note of the nineteenth century.[3]

In a similar vein, Dawson writes elsewhere:

> Western civilization is passing through one of the most critical moments in its history. In every department of life traditional principles have been shaken and discredited, and we do not know what is going to take their place.[4]

In tones reminiscent of Ferrero's gloomy diagnosis, a 1933 essay published in *The Catholic Mind* warns us that

> Today the world is on the move again, and no one can tell where it is going or what will happen next: whether our civilization is going to recover its stability or whether it will collapse in ruins.[5]

Another *Dublin Review* article that appeared in January, 1927, laments the shaking of our foundation and notes wistfully that "we are growing accustomed to the idea that our civilization is but one civilization among many, with no greater claim to permanence than those of the past ages." Finally, so as not to prolong the list, a passage from an important book that belongs to the same general period asserts, with reference to Spengler, that

> *The Decline of the West* is only an extreme statement of the new

relativist attitude to history which has become almost universal. During the last ten or twenty years there has been a general reaction against the unquestioning faith in the transcendent value of our own Western culture which marked the nineteenth century. There are civilizations but not *Civilization;* and the standards and achievements of each culture are valid only within the limits of the culture; they possess no absolute significance.[6]

Unlike so many others, however, Dawson never succumbed to the unremitting pessimism that pervades the European literature of those years. The reason is not that he was blind to the magnitude of the threat that weighed upon us, but rather that he found in the resources of the Catholic faith, to which he had converted in 1914, an element of hope that is conspicuously absent from the works of the secular theorists of his generation. Religion, he was convinced, was the key to history and the source of the vitality of any civilization. Just as the Christian religion had instilled new life into a moribund Roman Empire, so it could revitalize our own ailing civilization if only we opened our eyes to the predicament we were in and learned to appreciate the significance of our loss of faith in a transcendent God. What Augustine had done for his time, Dawson would try to do for ours.

The theme that runs through Dawson's essay on Augustine and holds it together is that Augustine is not only "the founder of the Christian philosophy of history but . . . . the first man in the world to discover the meaning of time" (p. 69). The abrupt appearance of the expression "philosophy of history," which is not part of Augustine's vocabulary, may come as something of a surprise, but one does well to remember that Augustine had recently come in for some harsh criticisms on the part of scholars such as H. Scholz who compared him to Hegel and found him wanting insofar as he had left God's children with empty heads, i.e., insofar as he was unable to demonstrate the inherent rationality of the historical process.[7] Scholz's views, it might be added, were part of a program initiated by Jacob Burckhardt the object of which was to contrast modern "thisworldliness" with medieval or Augustinian "otherworldliness." This, as I understand it, is the tendency against which Dawson felt the need to react. In so doing, however, he was careful to avoid the oversimplifications into which earlier Augustinian scholarship had fallen.

The essay reminds us among other things that Augustine is the one who finally laid to rest the old cyclical conception of history, which was still powerful in his day and threatened to deprive human life of its true significance by involving it in a process of meaningless repetition (p. 69). The result was a new and deeper understanding of moral freedom and responsibility. With Augustine, history becomes "a creative process," the new is allowed to emerge, and progress is seen as a real possibility. It is interesting to note that at about the same time Hannah Arendt had reached a similar conclusion, arguing in her dissertation on Augustine's notion of *caritas* as both a personal and a social force, that Augustine was the first philosopher of freedom and, indeed, "the only philosopher Rome ever had."

The emphasis on history also provided Dawson with a new insight into the difference that separates Augustine from Origen, whose views on this subject dominated the thinking of the Greek fathers. Origen, Dawson thought, was too much under the spell of Neoplatonism. His notion of the kingdom of God is still too close to the world of Platonic ideas. Not enough weight is given to human activity and no attempt is made to indicate how the temporal order can be informed by Christian principles (p. 68). In a word, Origen's speculations are incapable of grounding "a true Christian culture." Augustine's do have that capacity inasmuch as they lend solid support to the Christian's engagement in the task of building a better society.

This is especially apparent in Augustine's notorious discussion of Cicero's definition of civil society as "an assemblage of human beings bound together by a common acknowledgment of right and by a community of interests" (*City of God*, II.21), a definition that Augustine himself, as we saw in chapter 2, later proposes to amend by removing from it any reference to the notion of justice (ibid., XIX.24). Dawson is on the right track when he insists that, by so doing, Augustine had no intention of divorcing ethics from politics, something of which he had been accused by the brothers Carlyle in their mammoth and enormously influential *History of Medieval Political Theory in the West*. Augustine did not find anything wrong with Cicero's definition. His point is rather that the classical philosophers knew perfectly well what a good society is like, but that, knowing nothing about divine grace, which alone enables human beings to overcome their propensity to evil, they were incapable of providing for its realization.

More recent scholarship has not invalidated Dawson's analysis; it has merely corrected it on minor points and added a few refinements to it. We now see more clearly that the *City of God* was written not only to defend the Christian faith against its pagan detractors but to refute the position taken by some of Augustine's own coreligionists—Origen, Eusebius, Orosius, and their followers—who sought to rejudaize Christianity, as it were, by presenting the Christian Empire as the embodiment of the Kingdom of God on earth. For Augustine, there is strictly speaking no such thing as a Christian polity. No doubt, Christians must work for the improvement of civil society and have much to contribute to it. Society can become more Christian and will be the better for it if it does.

Still, there is no inner correlation between temporal progress and the coming of the Kingdom. The two belong to different orders altogether and do not necessarily develop *pari passu*. To interpret the messianic prophecies of the Old Testament in a temporal sense, as the Byzantine theologians had done, is both misleading and dangerous. Dawson saw this very well, although his remarks concerning Augustine's relationship either to Orosius or to the political ideals of the Middle Ages would probably have to be revised in the light of the work that has since been done on this subject by T. E. Mommsen, R. A. Markus, and others.

This said, a number of questions remain concerning Dawson's account of modernity and therewith the nature of the crisis in which it is caught up. Dawson is inclined to trace the origins of modernity to the Protestant Reformation's endeavor to drive a wedge between culture and spirituality, the unity or harmony of which Dawson was eager to restore. As he puts it somewhat bluntly in a *Dublin Review* article of January, 1933: "The attempt of the Reformers to spiritualize religion ended in the secularization of society and civilization. The Reformation is a classical example of the blunder of emptying the baby with the bath."

While not wholly indefensible, this thesis nevertheless calls for certain qualifications to which Dawson himself would probably not have objected. The Reformation was essentially a transformation of the theological tradition. At the same time, and quite independently of the Protestant movement, there occurred a transformation of the philosophical tradition, spearheaded by Machiavelli and brought to completion by the great thinkers of the seventeenth century, some of whom had a profound impact on contemporary Protestant divines. Viewed in this light, Protestantism, particularly in its more extreme forms, seems to have functioned less as the originator of modernity than as its carrier or the agent of its propagation. Without a clear grasp of the modern development as a whole, it is doubtful whether one will ever be able to make complete sense of the problem with which it confronts us.

In fairness to Dawson, it should be added that few scholars at the time were fully apprized of the crucial role played by Machiavelli in the break with premodernity that occurred toward the beginning of the sixteenth century. For reasons that are not hard to appreciate, none of Machiavelli's early disciples, and they are much more numerous than is usually realized, cared to be publicly associated with the man whom Shakespeare would soon be calling the "murdrous Machiavel." It would be almost a hundred years before anybody dared to proclaim, as does Francis Bacon in Book Two of the *Advancement of Learning,* that "we are much beholden to Machiavel and others that write what men do and not what they ought to do." In retrospect, one suspects that Machiavellian "realism" may have had a lot more to do with the breakdown of the synthesis between culture and spirituality lamented by Dawson than the "two kingdoms" theory of the great Reformers.

A further question arises concerning Dawson's thesis that religion is the key to history and its prime mover. Not that Dawson wishes to scant the importance of reason in human affairs, but his statements often leave us with the impression that its role is at best a secondary one. In the end, the foundations of everything are religious, or so Dawson would have us believe. A devout Christian may well be inclined to think that ultimately such is indeed the case. Yet a close study of Dawson's treatment of this matter might reveal a tinge of irrationalism that is more redolent of certain forms of late modernity than it is of the great tradition of Christian thought that Dawson is trying to reaccredit.

Thirdly, Dawson is certainly to be applauded for his forceful denunciation of the once popular view that the Christian religion was hostile to culture and his suggestions as to how the two might be brought into harmony with each other. Valuable as it may be, however, his argument leaves untouched some of the thornier problems involved in the reconciliation of faith and reason as the grounds of two distinct and irreducibly different ways of life. The question here is whether the extraordinary vitality that Western civilization has demonstrated across the centuries is attributable to the influence of Christianity alone or whether, as others have suggested, it does not have a good deal to do with the persistent and, in the long run, eminently salutary tension between the Christian faith and the Greek philosophic tradition which it fertilized and by which it was in turn fertilized across the centuries.

My final query is related to the focus on the notion of a Christian culture and the preoccupation with the embodiment of Christian principles in society at large. This explains Dawson's interest in such massive historical units as "cultures," "civilizations," and "societies." There is something refreshing about this approach, which, instead of subjecting Christianity to the tyranny of dialectics and abstract ideas, sees it as a force capable of informing all of our personal and societal activities. The difficulty is that these macrocategories are themselves abstractions invented by Rousseau, Kant, and Hegel as counterpoises to the dehumanizing effects of modern science. As such, they exhibit a certain remoteness from the vital concerns of most people, who, as citizens of this or that particular regime, are more likely to think in terms of the principles of that regime or the issues raised by its confrontation with other regimes. Simply put, a person may sacrifice himself and be willing to die for his country or his faith, but I have never heard of anyone doing the same for his "culture" or his "civilization." This is not to imply that Dawson was totally unaware of the importance of politics but only that as a rule his arguments are not developed along political lines. The fault, if it is a fault, is not his alone. By the beginning of the twentieth century, political philosophy had virtually disappeared from the scene and was no longer taken seriously by even the greatest philosophical minds of the time, whether it be Husserl, William James, Bergson, Whitehead, or Heidegger. Its rediscovery, and with it the new possibilities that it offers for a concrete study of human phenomena, came only later, toward the middle of the century. My guess is that Dawson would have welcomed it and perhaps made greater use of it had he had more time to rethink his own project in terms of it.

NOTES

1. Martin C. d'Arcy et al., *St. Augustine* (London: Sheed and Ward, 1930). The volume was reissued in 1945 under the title, *A Monument to St. Augustine,* and reprinted under its original title as a Meridien Book by the World Publishing Co. of New York in 1957. My references are to the 1957 edition.

2. Paul Valéry, "La crise de l'esprit," *Variété*, in *Oeuvres*, Bibliothèque de la Pléiade, vol. I (Paris: Gallimard, 1957) 988. Valéry did not claim to know how many great civilizations had existed: "Count them we could not. But these shipwrecks, after all, were none of our business." Toynbee, who read Valéry's article in England, where it was first published, later attempted to enumerate them and came up with a total of twenty-one. Thirteen had perished and seven others were in the process of being absorbed into the final one, our own Western civilization.

3. C. Dawson, "The Crisis of the West," *Dublin Review* (Oct. 1927): 261.

4. C. Dawson and J. F. Burns, eds., *Essays in Order* (New York: Macmillan, 1931), v.

5. C. Dawson, "Man and Civilization," *The Catholic Mind* (1933): 435.

6. C. Dawson, *Progress and Religion* (London, 1929), 38.

7. H. Scholz, *Glaube und Unglaube in der Weltgeschichte* (Leipzig: J. C. Henrichs, 1911), along with J. Ratzinger's critique of Scholz, *Volk und Haus Gottes in Augustins Lehre von der Kirche* (Munich: K. Zink, 1955).

II

THE ENCOUNTER BETWEEN
ATHENS AND JERUSALEM

8

CLEMENT OF ALEXANDRIA AND THE ESOTERIC TRADITION

It is generally agreed that Clement of Alexandria is the first of the orthodox Fathers, and indeed the only one among them, who lays claim to a secret, oral tradition, independent of sacred Scripture and ultimately derived from the Apostles. His clearest statement to this effect occurs in the first chapter of Book I of the *Stromata*.[1] This famous chapter is a lengthy justification of Clement's decision to write his book. Such a justification is necessitated by the inherent and inescapable dangers of written works. Books have their fate in more ways than one. Even if they are not intended for the general public, once published they are liable to fall into anybody's hands. They cannot answer all the questions that are put to them and, when they do, it is only to repeat what they have already said. Furthermore, there is no guarantee that these answers will be understood properly. Books cannot defend themselves. They are constantly in need of their author or of someone imbued with his teachings and thus qualified to interpret these teachings to others.[2] For this reason, Clement argues, the greatest care should be taken not to reveal to the unwise multitude the divine mysteries that he alleges to have received from his predecessors and teachers in the faith. This caution is motivated not by avarice but by a sincere desire to protect both the hearer and the truth. One does not hand a sword to a child or poison to a maniac.[3] Anyone rash or nearsighted enough to set down in writing doctrines or opinions that could give scandal to the common reader, if only because he is not ready for them, is not a teacher but a traitor.

Both the authenticity and the origin of Clement's claim to this secret tradition have been disputed by modern scholars. In his recent book on *Tradition in the Early Church*, Professor R. P. C. Hanson, reiterating the views of Van den Eynde, Mondésert and Daniélou, refuses categorically to take Clement's remarks at face value and dismisses the idea of a hidden or esoteric teaching as mere affectation on his part.[4] Aside from the fact that the modern reader finds it difficult to imagine the content of this secret teaching, it seems hardly possible that there should have existed in the early Church an important store of dogmatic truths distinct from those contained in sacred Scripture and known only to a small group of initiates or superior Christians. Any pretense to such knowledge smacks at first glance of Gnosticism rather than of orthodox Christianity. Under these conditions, one is tempted to look upon Clement's would-be secret teaching as an April Fools' purse in the path of the reader, promising much and containing nothing.

Hanson's position, which enjoys the support of most contemporary critics, stands at the opposite extreme from that of an older generation of scholars who not only accepted the idea of an oral tradition but transformed this oral tradition into a kind of catchall and conveniently appealed to it to establish the antiquity and, by implication, the authenticity of certain doctrines or practices not attested or not clearly attested in the early Christian writings.[5]

Upon reflection, it may be legitimate to ask whether these two conflicting solutions do not suffer from the same defect in that they both attempt to dispose of an admittedly delicate problem by slicing the knot instead of unraveling it. In its crudest form the dilemma with which they confront us may be stated as follows. Either the secret teaching exists or it does not. If it exists and if it represents Clement's best thinking on the most important theological matters, the present-day reader, having no access to this tradition, is doomed to remain forever in the dark as to its content. If, on the other hand, as the vast majority of recent scholars are inclined to think, no such oral tradition exists, the Fathers lead us astray by adverting to it and what they have to say about it is just arrant nonsense. The first alternative may be prettier and more flattering to Clement than the other; but neither one, it must be avowed, is particularly attractive. A fresh look at the evidence supplied by the *Stromata* and by a number of other ancient texts, however, suggests an interpretation which differs somewhat from both of these radical solutions and which, while doing justice to the element of truth they contain, has the added advantage of being more consonant with Clement's own explicit assertions on the subject.[6]

Contrary to what both groups of scholars have assumed, Clement does not state or otherwise imply that there existed two distinct and parallel traditions, one handed down by word of mouth from teacher to student and known only to a small elite within the Church, and another contained in writings that are the property of all. What he does say is that the content of the oral teaching or tradition should find its way into the written text, but in such a way that its presence will be missed by the casual or unprepared reader and sniffed, as it were, by the student who has somehow been made aware of the deeper issues and who needs only a minimum of guidance in order to arrive at the truth by himself.[7] Never at any moment does he insinuate that one should look for his most profound teaching anywhere except in his published works and more specifically in the *Stromata*; and he always insists that the resourceful and perspicacious reader will find in that work all the elements or clues that are necessary for an adequate understanding of it.

The crucial point that the remarkable first chapter of the *Stromata* makes is precisely that the unwritten teaching is revealed "through writing" and not in a purely oral manner. There would obviously be no point in alerting the reader to the dangers of the undertaking upon which he is about to embark if Clement had systematically avoided any discussion of the highest and hence most dangerous matters. This simple observation is corroborated by what he himself tells us regarding the nature of the *Stromata*. The mysterious truths in question are, to quote an expression that appears to be proper to him, *engraphōs agrapha*,[8] or unwritten teachings inscribed in the text itself, albeit in a peculiar way. The *Stromata* do "contain the truth," but "covered over or hidden, as the edible part of the nut in the shell."[9] These truths have been "purposely scattered" like seeds throughout the book "so that they might escape the notice of those who peck like jackdaws, but germinate and produce fruit whenever they find a good husbandman."[10] The same thought occurs, not insignificantly, in the description given of the work as a whole in the opening chapters of Book IV. As the name itself indicates, the *Stromata* are "a series of notes patched together in a motley way, continually dropping one subject for another, suggesting one thing in the course of discussion and declaring something else."[11] In much the same manner, Clement goes on to compare his book to a thickly wooded mountain where vegetation of every sort, growing promiscuously, by its very abundance conceals from the plunderer the fruit trees that are intended for the rightful owner.[12]

On the basis of these and similar admissions, then, it would be erroneous to assert that Clement has refrained altogether from expressing his most profound teaching in his written work. This is not to say that the greatest mysteries are fully explained by the author[13] or that their discovery is within reach of any chance comer. The very sublimity of the mysteries involved precludes their being revealed clearly in writing and made available to all indiscriminately.[14] Like the Apostles, for whose absence he makes up,[15] the Christian teacher must become all things to all men. His writings must be adapted to the needs and capacities of every category of reader; they must be capable of exerting an improving and christianizing influence on all of them.[16] This universal responsibility notwithstanding, he cannot speak in the same manner to everyone.[17] Clement's work was obviously not intended for the wholly uneducated, who do not read books; nor was it written exclusively or primarily for persons who are thoroughly versed in these matters and who may be presumed to be informed of the private teaching of the book or at any rate immune to its dangers. Between these two extremes, however, there is still a wide range of possibilities. The typical, if not the only, addressee of Clement's book, one may say, is not the beginner but the more advanced student, who has already received some instruction, but who is not yet in possession of the highest knowledge and is both desirous of acquiring this knowledge and capable of benefiting from it; in which case the essential duty of the teacher is to point out the direction in which such a student should walk, leaving it to him to discover the rest for himself.[18] "All these notes," Clement tells us, "work together for the recollection and declaration of the truth for those who can rationally inquire. Some students dig much and find little gold; but those who are really of golden stock, mining for what is akin to them, will find a great deal in the few hints that have been scattered for their benefit from beginning to end."[19] In all these texts once again, there is not the slightest hint that Clement's secret teaching has been relegated entirely to the private sphere of oral transmission in such a way that it would remain inaccessible to the reader whose sole source of information is the author's written works.

Just how Clement can refer to this higher teaching as an "unwritten" teaching (*agrapha*), even though it is actually included in the book, will become clearer if we reflect for a moment on his discussion of the superiority of oral teaching over written teaching. This superiority arises from the fact that the teacher who addresses an individual or a group is in a unique position to gauge the effect of his words on the hearer. Thanks to the direct contact with his audience, he can usually diagnose with a fair measure of accuracy their native intellectual ability, their moral character, and their degree of preparation.[20] He is thus able to determine what is best suited for them at any given moment and in so doing lead them by the hand to the perception of the most difficult truths. Written works are in the best sense reminders of a teaching that has been imparted orally and for which no adequate substitute exists.[21] In the absence of this oral teaching, the clever writer can at best transpose the procedures that are proper to it on the plane of the written word and, by camouflaging his thoughts, obviate within the limits of possibility the inconveniences to which written teaching is exposed. In terms that are practically identical to those used by Clement, one could describe this method as the art of being nonchalant while saying important things, of showing under the veil, of revealing without letting on that one is doing so.[22] The manner in which this tour de force is realized may be expected to vary a great deal from one work to another and will depend in large measure on the judgment and ingenuity of each writer. Among the devices most commonly used, Clement mentions elliptical or allusive speech, the judicious selection of words and symbols, apparent contradictions, and deliberate omissions,[23] all of which may serve the twofold purpose of awakening the discerning reader to the presence of a momentous teaching and of keeping the whole truth from the hurried or heedless one. Even the outward disorder of the *Stromata,* we are told, is calculated to render the truth more difficult of access but also more lovable and profitable to those who are not repelled by the uncommonly high demands in time and effort that it makes upon them.[24] It is hardly necessary to add that the significant omissions to which Clement alludes are themselves an integral part of the teaching of the book and are not to be construed as belonging to a separate teaching. An author's silence, concerning a topic about which he has promised to speak or is normally expected to say something, may reveal as much if not more about his real thought than many words spoken lightly.[25]

This ability to speak to two or more essentially (and not only accidentally) different audiences at the same time is a prerogative that the *Stromata* claim to share with sacred Scripture. For sacred Scripture too, as Clement boldly asserts, "gives birth to the truth while remaining virgin in the concealment of the truth."[26] Precisely because the truth does not belong in the same fashion to everyone, the Spirit who spoke through the prophets was not concerned with being easily understood.[27] Prophecy (i.e. Revelation) ceases to be perfectly clear the moment one attempts to go beyond the mere rudiments of the faith.[28] Whatever one may think of the way in which Clement accounts for the mysterious character of the Bible, one cannot disregard the information that his remarks supply concerning the manner of composition of his own work. This work belongs to a special category of books which has all but disappeared in recent times and which the modern reader finds it all the harder to appreciate at its true value. To repeat what has been said, the great merit as well as the charm of such works is that they are meant to be read and understood in more than one way, a purpose achieved by deliberately setting forth the truth in a veiled manner.[29] The discourses contained in these books are thus susceptible of different though by no means arbitrary interpretations, or of different levels of understanding,[30] willed by the author and corresponding to the different classes of readers for whom they were written. They are designed to produce a teaching effect on competent and serious students and a persuasive effect on lesser minds who are either unsuited for such a teaching or unwilling to take the pains to acquire it. In this manner they may be said to reflect the qualities of the "gnostic," who possesses the full truth and is thereby capable of imparting it to others, but who also knows how, when, and to whom this knowledge may be passed on.[31] To speak of an oral or unwritten teaching in cases such as these remains legitimate if only because the books in question presuppose an oral teaching, which they imitate, and can be properly understood only when read in the context of a living tradition which supplies the right perspective and guarantees the validity of the interpretation.

It goes without saying that the mode of expression endorsed and presumably employed by Clement requires more than an ordinary degree of refinement or sophistication on the part of the writer. One is thus led to ask whether this peculiar method was a creation of the Church Fathers themselves, designed to cope with the specific situation brought about by the emergence of Christianity within the Greco-Roman world, or whether it was simply an adaptation to their own needs of a practice evolved by their pagan or Jewish predecessors. On this question of the origin of Clement's esotericism, no less than on that of its nature, there has been considerable fluctuation among scholars. The few who have attempted to deal with it have pointed for the most part to the pagan mystery religions, Gnosticism, or contemporary Rabbinic literature as possible sources from which Clement's views may have been derived. Professor Hanson himself had originally proposed a Philonic origin, but he has recently abandoned this position in favor of Daniélou's thesis, according to which Clement's esotericism consists of speculations and midrash of the type that one finds in the so-called Judeo-Christian literature of that period.[32] Much evidence can be produced in support of each one of these hypotheses. There are overt references to the pagan mysteries in many passages of the *Stromata,* just as there are numerous and striking similarities between Clement and Philo or between Clement and Judeo-Christian literature. By the extensive use of the allegorical method, for example, Clement is able to draw an elaborate parallel between the various objects connected with the Temple and the New Testament realities. Père Daniélou has shown convincingly that his commentaries on this subject belong, not to any native Alexandrine tradition, as Bousset contended, but to an earlier exegetical tradition of Jewish or Palestinian origin.[33] It is difficult to conceive, however, how these somewhat free and at times fanciful interpretations, set forth with a great profusion of detail, could qualify as the silent teaching of the book. These efforts to harmonize the Old and New Testaments are meant for the readers who are interested in Scripture alone and who are apt to be puzzled by the discrepancies between its different parts, rather than for those who are more concerned with the discrepancies between the letter of the sacred text and the teachings of philosophy. They serve the express purpose of "charming" these "timid" or "untutored" minds by removing some of the obstacles that stand in the way of their faith.[34] However important these *rapprochements* between the two testaments may be in other respects, they do not provide us with an immediate clue to the esoteric teaching to which the opening chapter of the *Stromata* alludes. It is significant that the only source to which Clement himself refers us in the thematic discussion of that first chapter is not Philo or any other Jewish or Christian predecessor, but Plato.

If, following Clement's lead, we glance rapidly at a few representative texts from Plato's works, we shall have no trouble in identifying many of the ideas that we have already encountered in the *Stromata*. The whole matter is summed up most clearly and concisely in the famous passage of the *Seventh Epistle* in which Plato says: "I do not believe that arguing about these points is a good thing for men, save a small elite who are capable of discovering the truth for themselves with the help of a few intimations. As for the others, we would merely fill them with unjust contempt, which is unbecoming, or with a vain and foolish self-sufficiency by the very sublimity of the teachings imparted."[35] The authenticity of this *Seventh Epistle* is sometimes rejected by modern scholars; but whether or not one accepts the text as genuinely Platonic—and Clement certainly did—matters little in the present case, since the theory of writing that it propounds is identical with that of the dialogues.[36] Clement's observations concerning the superiority of oral teaching and the dangers of written works is hardly more than a restatement of the doctrine of the *Phaedrus*.[37] His remark that books are the intellectual progeny of the writer, that their function is to supplement and serve as reminders of a teaching dispensed orally, and that they are in constant need of being defended and interpreted by their authors, harks back to the same source.[38] His allusion to the disciples of "golden stock" echoes implicitly the myth of the *Republic* which explains the natural differences among men in terms of the varying proportions of gold, silver, and brass that have gone into their make-up.[39] The image of the "path to the truth," which the student is expected to discover with the help of a pathfinder until he is able to trace his own way, is likewise Platonic,[40] as is the theory of the medicinal or white lie by means of which the truth may be shielded from the incompetent or the merely curious.[41] Various other Platonic concepts reappear trussed up in biblical attire. Beneath the "trustworthy friends" of the Second Epistle to Timothy lurk in Clement's mind the "reasonable friends" of the *Republic*[42]; and in the "discourses inscribed in the soul" of which the *Phaedrus* speaks, the same author seems to have discerned the "knowledge written on the heart and foretold by the prophet (Jeremiah)."[43] Even the terms that originally belonged to the language of the mystery cults have in many cases been lifted directly from Plato, and more specifically from the *Banquet* and the *Phaedo*, both of which describe the ascent to the highest knowledge in terms of an *epopteia* or final initiation into the mysteries.[44]

Unfortunately, the typically Platonic character of Clement's views has been obscured for us by the reluctance on the part of most present-day scholars to take seriously the traditional position concerning the esotericism of the dialogues. The case against this esotericism has been stated in the most outspoken if not the best possible manner by Professor Harold Cherniss in his book, *The Riddle of the Early Academy*. According to Cherniss, the notion of a secret teaching in Plato is nothing but an expedient devised and industriously propagated by Zeller and his followers to explain the alleged discrepancy between the doctrine of idea-numbers as expressed in the dialogues and Aristotle's critique of that doctrine in the *Metaphysics*; no basis whatever can be found for it either in the dialogues themselves or in the Platonic tradition.[45] To the extent to which the existence of the secret teaching is deduced solely from this shaky premise, Cherniss can hardly be blamed for dismissing it. In his eagerness to "lay the ghost of esoteric Platonism" to rest,[46] however, he goes considerably beyond the simple rejection of Zeller's hypothesis when, referring to the section of the *Seventh Epistle* quoted above, he adds: "For myself, I do not believe that Plato wrote this *Epistle*; but if I did, I should recognize that he himself has borne witness beforehand against anything which I might write about the real purport of his thought, and I should account it the madness of stubborn insolence to seek to describe or even to discover the serious doctrine of a man who has condemned all those who ever have made the attempt or ever will."[47]

Pushed to its ultimate conclusion, Cherniss's interpretation confronts us with the paradox of a great philosopher who, in his love for his subject, has abolished once and for all the possibility of discovering his real thought or, what amounts to the same thing, of engaging in a genuinely philosophic pursuit. That such was Plato's intention is more than doubtful. Far from discouraging the study of philosophy, the *Seventh Epistle*, like the *Phaedrus*, merely denounces as illusory or dangerous any endeavor to convey the highest teachings to the unthinking multitude.[48] It claims, not without good reason, that the secure but unphilosophic possession of a philosophic truth is contrary to the essence of philosophy. It thus denies that such teachings, for which one becomes fitted only through a long period of instruction and arduous effort,[49] can be communicated publicly without losing their philosophic character and degenerating into mere opinion or prejudice. In the light of this fact, it is quite conceivable that Plato should have repudiated in advance any attempt to publicize a teaching that, by its very nature and not through any caprice on the part of the author, is reserved to a few wellborn and well-bred natures.[50] But one cannot infer from these remarks that a writer is in no way able to present an essentially private teaching in written form for the benefit of a privileged few who have withstood the "tests" to which they have been subjected through education[51] and have thus shown themselves to be both capable and worthy of it. A presentation of this kind is accomplished precisely by means of the "slight indications" of which Plato speaks and which are both necessary and sufficient for students such as these. Any genuine interpretation of a book written in this manner must of necessity be based on a minute scrutiny of the text and of all its peculiarities. The full meaning of that text will reveal itself only if one consents to read it with the "third eye," to adapt an expression from Origen,[52] that is to say, only if one pays the closest attention not only to what the characters say, but to everything they do and for that matter to all the other details of the narrative.

Perhaps the only effective way of establishing the existence of these hidden depths or *hyponoiai* would be to take a Platonic dialogue and read it in this manner. Such a demonstration would entail a much lengthier discussion than any that can be reasonably undertaken here; but for purposes of illustration, and at the risk of some oversimplification, we can at least suggest in a general or provisional way the lines according to which this demonstration would proceed. It is not irrelevant to a correct understanding of the *Republic,* for instance, that the dramatic setting of the dialogue is the Piraeus and not, as in the *Banquet* or the *Protagoras,* Athens; that the occasion which brings Socrates and his friends together is a festival in honor of one of the goddesses, which they plan to attend and which is completely forgotten in the course of the discussion;[53] that the discussion itself does not really get under way until old Cephalos, the head of the household, has retired; that Socrates accepts to remain only under compulsion—to say nothing of a host of other apparently trivial details. Only by pondering these facts and being attentive to the questions they silently raise, does the reader begin to realize that the quest for the gods has in effect been replaced by the quest for the nature of justice or, more generally stated, by philosophy. Only then does he gradually become aware of the revolutionary character of the book; of its veiled criticism of the traditional gods of the city; of its daring proposal of an entirely new approach to the problems of human living; of the reasons why the conversation in which the characters are about to engage could not decently have taken place in the presence of a venerable representative of the old and established order; of the role of the philosopher in the city; of the conditions under which he may be induced to take an interest in its affairs, and of the manner in which he may be expected to exercise his activity. It goes without saying that these subtleties and implied meanings do not disclose themselves at a cursory reading and must be painstakingly dug out of the text if they are going to be perceived at all.

This repeated insistence on the necessity of concealing one's deepest thoughts, this stubborn refusal to dole out the truth promiscuously, is not just a second-century prejudice invented or shared by the Christian authors, as people have sometimes said, but a carefully considered position grounded above all in a keen awareness of the potentially destructive character of this type of knowledge.[54] The precise nature of this danger is outlined by Plato in the *Republic.*[55] It has its roots in the fact that any actual city, no matter how perfect it may be, relies for its existence and its stability on certain inherited and commonly accepted opinions or conventions that can never be justified on the basis of reason alone. These opinions and conventions are embodied in laws and institutions which define the way of life and specific nobility of that city, and they are transmitted through education under these laws to each new generation of citizens. Such *nomoi,* whether written or unwritten, were thought to owe their effectiveness to the respect they were able to command on the part of the citizen body—a respect ultimately founded on the belief in the hoary antiquity and divine origin of these laws. One could not openly question this traditional or ancestral morality, even in the name of an allegedly higher norm, without weakening the unconditional claim that the laws make on the allegiance of the citizens and thereby dissolving the sacred bond of the city. Any attempt to emancipate prematurely the minds of men by fostering the spirit of free inquiry, it was felt, would promote lawlessness and irreverence and lead in the end to the corrosion of the entire political order. As a Christian, Clement was less concerned with the welfare of the earthly city than with that of the City of God, as Augustine later called it. His own reasons for concealing his innovations, we may presume, were different from those of the pagan philosophers. What these reasons were is itself a vast question that can barely be touched upon here. For the moment, we can only leave it at saying that the perfect Christian or "gnostic's" choice of his way of life cannot in any final sense be predicated on an ignorance of, or a refusal to consider, what Clement appears to have regarded as the most noble alternative to the Christian Faith, namely, philosophy (represented for him by Plato), however attractive and hence perilous from the standpoint of the Faith this alternative may have been.

The foregoing interpretation of the first chapter of the *Stromata is* indirectly supported by a piece of evidence from a different though not altogether unrelated source whose importance seems not to have been recognized by patristic scholars. We find the notion of a living oral tradition not unlike the one described by Clement in a little known but valuable fragment of Farabi's treatise, *On the Origins of Greek Philosophy*.[56] The document informs us that shortly after the closing of the school of Athens certain restrictions were imposed on the teaching of philosophy in Alexandria by order of the Emperor and the bishops. Public instruction in logic was not permitted to extend beyond the first part of *Prior Analytics* (I.7), which meant that it was not to include a study of the categorical figures of the syllogism, for fear that Aristotle's theory of demonstration would prove detrimental to the Faith. The remainder of the treatise, as well as the other parts of logic, continued to be "read" (i. e., taught) privately, however, and assumed the character of an esoteric teaching that was kept alive by means of an unbroken chain of interpreters down to Farabi's own day. Even Farabi's Christian (Jacobite) teacher, we are told, was not allowed to lecture on any but the officially approved books of the *Organon*—a ban subsequently lifted in favor of the Muslim students.

This testimony, coupled with what we know of Farabi's philosophy, is of interest to us not only because it establishes a direct link between the philosophic tradition of antiquity and that of the great Arabic philosophers, of which Farabi himself was the originator, but especially because it sheds light in retrospect on Clement's distinctly Platonic approach to the problem of the communication of knowledge. It points characteristically to the school (or schools) of Alexandria as the center in which classical philosophy in its original political context had been preserved and from which it was transmitted (via Antioch) in the form of an esoteric tradition to the Islamic world, where it continued to play a major role throughout the Middle Ages. Of particular significance is the insight it provides into the basic issue with which Clement had to contend, by bringing to the fore the permanent tension, if not always the open conflict, between philosophy, conceived not just as a body of doctrines but as a way of life, and revealed religion. One could not express this issue more clearly than by saying that no final reconciliation is possible between the rival claims to supremacy of a knowledge based on the evidence of the senses or of discursive reason and acquired through instruction and human industry, on the one hand, and on the other hand an altogether different type of knowledge purporting to be higher than the highest knowledge accessible to the unaided human reason, but at the same time unverifiable by means of universally admissible canons of evidence. Viewed in this context, the classical notion of science as certain knowledge obtained by a process of reasoning from self-evident premises may be seen as preempting and implicitly casting discredit upon any other (specifically religious) form of scientific knowledge. The choice that on the highest level one must make finally reveals itself as a choice between heaven-sent madness and man-made sanity,[57] between a life lived on the basis of pious acquiescence in and wholehearted allegiance to a divinely inspired truth, or one that remains interiorly uncommitted, although it may conform in deed and in speech, to any option for which independent reason has not found adequate support.

Clement was fully aware of this fundamental choice even if, out of a noble regard for the weakness of lesser minds, he deliberately avoided any open discussion of it in his work. His strategy reminds us in a strange way of the one he ascribes to Moses in that it shrewdly combines wisdom with moderation in the expression of that wisdom.[58] Other writers could afford to be less restrained because they were less bold. Not so with Clement. It is not the least striking among the many irregularities of the *Stromata* that they demand the greatest veracity of the gnostic and in the same breath condone the use of salutary lies.[59] In his own eyes, Clement would not have been more exacting in the matter of truthfulness but naive or irresponsible if he had spoken and acted otherwise. What he feared above all else was the "lie in the soul"; for that reason he saw more clearly than any of his predecessors had done that utter dedication to the truth was not only compatible with, but impossible without, some form of concealment.

NOTES

1. Clement of Alexandria, *Stromata* I.1.11.

2. *Strom.* I.1.14.

3. *Strom.* I.1.14.

4. R. P. C. Hanson, *Tradition in the Early Church* (London: SCM Press, 1962), 26-27.

5. This view, which was widely accredited especially among Roman Catholic theologians during the eighteenth and nineteenth centuries, appears to have been propounded for the first time by E. Schelstrate, *De disciplina arcani*, Rome, 1685. It was still shared by Newman (*Arians of the Fourth Century*, 29ff., 42 et passim), who later discarded it in favor of his developmental theory of Christian doctrine. Cf. *Oxford Dictionary of the Christian Church*, s. v. "*Disciplina Arcani.*"

6. E. F. Osborn's article, "Teaching and Writing in the First Chapter of the *Stromateis* of Clement of Alexandria," *Journal of Theological Studies*, N. S. 10, (1959): 335-43, summarizes the contents of that first chapter and pleads intelligently, but not without oversimplification, for a reconsideration of the *Stromata* as the third book of Clement's projected trilogy. The author makes no attempt, however, to come to grips with the central issue of the nature of Clement's real or hypothetical secret teaching.

7. *Strom.* I.1.15.

8. *Strom.* I.1.10; VI.7. 61; VI.15.131.

9. *Strom.* I.1.18.

10. *Strom.* I.12.53; cf. VII.18.110: "The dogmas that are the seeds of true knowledge have been interspersed here and there, so that the discovery of the secret traditions may not be easy to anyone of the uninitiated."

11. *Strom.* IV.2.4; cf. VI.1.2.

12. *Strom.* VII.18.111; cf. VI.1.2.

13. *Strom.* I.1.4: "We do not profess to give a full explanation of the mysteries."

14. *Strom.* I.12.55.

15. *Strom.* VII.12.77.

16. *Strom.* I.1.15; I.1.16; II.1.2.

17. *Strom.* I.1.7.

18. *Strom.* IV.2.5.

19. *Strom.* IV.2.4.

20. *Strom.* I.1.9.

21. *Strom.* I.1.14; cf. I.1.11.

22. *Strom.* I.1.15.

23. *Brachylogy*: I.1.15; I.14.60. Omissions: I.1.14; VII.14.88. White lies or deliberate contradictions: VII.9.53. Symbols and allegories: II.1.1; V.4.21; V.9.58-9, etc.

24. Ibid., I.9.43; VI.15.132; VII.18.111.

25. Needless to say, one could find many instances of the same phenomenon both before and after Clement. Nietzsche tells us, for example, that one of the most distinctive features of his early essay on *The Birth of Tragedy* is the "profoundly hostile silence" that it maintains on the subject of Christianity; cf. *Ecce Homo*, "The Birth of Tragedy," 1.

26. *Strom.* VII.16.94.

27. *Strom.* I.9.45.

28. *Strom.* VI.15.131.

29. *Strom.* I.2.20: "It goes without saying that the *Stromata* strive artfully to conceal the seeds of knowledge."

30. *Strom.* VI.15.132: *polykeuthēs gar ho logos.*

31. *Strom.* VI.15.119.

32. Loc. cit., 26, n.4.

33. J. Daniélou, "Aux sources de l'ésotérisme judéo-chrétien," *Archivio di Filosofia*, No. 2-3 (1960): 39-46.

34. Cf. *Strom.* I.1.18, where these "timid" persons (*psophodeēs*, frightened at every noise) are described precisely as the ones whose sole preoccupation is with faith and who will therefore have nothing to do with philosophy. As far as I have been able to determine, there are no other instances of the use of *psophodeēs* in Clement.

35. Plato, *Epistula* VII 341d-e. Cf. *Strom.* V.11.77; V.12.78; Origen, *Contra Celsum* VI.6. Compare also Plato, *Epist.* II.312d and 314a-c with *Strom.* V.10.65; I.1.14.

36. Compare *Epist.* VII.340b—345a with *Phaedrus* 274b—278b.

37. *Strom.* I.1.9; I.1.14. Plato, *Phaedrus* 275e; *Epist.* II.314c.

38. Compare *Strom.* I.1.1 with *Phaedrus* 275a, 278a; *Strom.* I.1.11 and I.1.14 with *Phaedrus* 275a, 276d; *Strom.* I.1.14 with *Phaedrus* 275d-e, 276c.

39. *Strom.* IV.2.4; V.14.98. Plato, *Republic* III.415a; V.468e.

40. *Strom.* IV.2.5. Plato, *Epist.* VII.340c.

41. *Strom.* VII.9.53. Plato, *Republic* II.382c; III.389b-c; V.459c-d.

42. *Strom.* I.1.3. Plato, *Republic* V.450e.

43. *Strom.* VI.15.131. Plato, *Phaedrus* 276a, 278a.

44. *Strom.* I.19.92; I.28.176; V.3.17; VII.11.68. Plato, *Phaedo* 69c; *Symp.* 210a.

45. H. Cherniss, *The Riddle of the Early Academy* (Berkeley and Los Angeles: University of California Press, 1945), 9-13, 28-9.

46. Cf. H. Cherniss, *Aristotle's Criticism of Plato and the Academy* (Baltimore: Johns Hopkins Press, 1944), xii.

47. H. Cherniss, *The Riddle of the Early Academy*, 13.

48. Plato, *Epist.* VII.340b-e, 341d-e; cf. *Republic* VI.496a.

49. Plato, *Epist.* VII.340e—341a, 341c-d.

50. Ibid., 341b-c. 343a, 344c.

51. Ibid., 341a. Cf. *Strom.* I.1.9.

52. Origen, *C. Cels.* VI.8.

53. Cf. the brief but penetrating interpretation of this scene in Origen, *C. Cels.* VI.4, c. init.

54. Plato, *Republic* VI.497d.

55. Plato, *Republic* VII.536b-539d.

56. The text is published, with a German translation, in M. Steinschneider, *Al-Farabi (Alfarabius) des arabischen Philosophen Leben und Schriften* (St. Pétersbourg: Commissionaires de l'académie impériale des sciences, 1869), 85-89, 211-213. See also M. Meyerhof, *Von Alexandrien nach Baghdad: ein Beitrag zur Geschichte des philosophischen und medizinischen Unterrichts bei den Araben*, Sitzungsberichte der preussischen Akademie der Wissenschaften, Philosophisch-Historische Klasse (Berlin, 1931), 389-429. Id., "La fin de l'Ecole d'Alexandrie d'après quelques auteurs arabes," *Bulletin de l'Institut d'Egypte* 15 (1932-1933): 109-123. R. Walzer, "New Light on the Arabic Translations of Aristotle," *Oriens* 6 (1953): esp. 129. N. Rescher, "Al-Farabi on Logical Tradition," *Journal of the History of Ideas* 24 (1963): 127-132.

57. Cf. Plato, *Phaedrus* 244d.

58. *Strom.* I.24.160.

59. *Strom.* VII.8.60; VII.9.53.

9

CHRISTIANITY AND HELLENISM IN BASIL THE GREAT'S ADDRESS *AD ADULESCENTES*

In his remarkable but often neglected address *To Young Men on the Benefits to be Derived from the Reading of the Pagan Authors,* Basil the Great takes special issue with the pagan orators on the ground that they can never be trusted to tell the truth. Orators are all the more dangerous as they indulge in falsehood as a matter of deliberate purpose rather than of simple expediency. They not only make a habit of lying but have mastered its principles and reduced it to an art: *hē peri to pseudesthai technē.*[1] Such a practice is not to be condoned under any circumstances. In their dealings with their fellow human beings, Christians are expected to shun lies altogether. They have no reason to conceal the truth, especially since, if they heeded the injunctions of the New Testament, they would never wrangle or go to court in the first place.[2]

Basil's aversion to all manner of deception is demonstrated elsewhere by his indignant reaction to the pious fraud perpetrated by his brother, Gregory, the future bishop of Nyssa. In an attempt to bring about a reconciliation with one of their uncles who had sided with Basil's opponents at the time of his election as bishop of Caesarea, Gregory had forged at least two letters which were duly forwarded to Basil in the estranged uncle's name. The forgery was exposed when the pretended author disavowed any knowledge of the missives. Basil completely ignores the motive that prompted his brother's action and thinks only of rebuking him for his deviousness. The incident, he says, "has caused us to blush with shame; covered with disgrace by our involvement in fraud, falsehood, and deceit, we prayed that the earth might open and swallow us up."[3]

As one reads the address *To Young Men* with a measure of attention, however, one wonders to what extent Basil himself was always scrupulously faithful to the principle of absolute truthfulness that we have just heard him enunciate. His specific purpose in the present case is to explain how the works of the pagan authors can lead to a better understanding of the Christian faith. In keeping with its stated aim, his address contains an unusually large number of references to classical texts, rendered literally or more often in the form of a paraphrase, from a wide range of poets and prose writers. What is most striking is that virtually all of these texts have either been tacitly distorted or given a meaning that is different from and even diametrically opposed to that intended by the original authors. Two examples, to which Basil obviously attaches considerable importance, will suffice to illustrate the point.

The first has to do with the famous episode of Odysseus and the Sirens in Book XII of the *Odyssey*. The reference occurs within the context of a discussion of the choice to be made among the various subjects treated by the poets. The general principle proclaimed at the outset is that, since poets assume many guises, not all of which are equally commendable, one should not pay attention to everything they write but only to those works or parts of works that are conducive to virtue. Poets deserve to be listened to when they relate the words and deeds of good men, which Christians ought to cherish and emulate.[4] If, on the other hand, they should happen to engage in descriptions of immoral behavior, Basil's young students are urged to reject them, "stopping their ears, no less than Odysseus did when, according to what these same poets relate, he avoided the songs of the Sirens."[5]

Basil's recommendation is bound to leave the informed reader somewhat puzzled, for what he credits Homer's hero with doing is the very thing that he refused to do. Forewarned by the magician, Circe, about the grave peril that he would soon be facing, Odysseus dutifully poured wax into the ears of his companions but refrained from blocking his own ears, precisely so that he might hear the voice of the mysterious temptresses. Worse still, he is not completely honest with his crew when he claims to be following Circe's orders to the letter: "She bade us avoid the music of the wondrous Sirens . . . Me alone she bade listen."[6] Circe had given no such command but had merely proposed that if he was bent on listening to the deadly songs, he should at least take the precaution of having himself bound to the mast of the ship, lest, like everyone else, he should succumb to their powerful attraction.[7] On the matter of truthfulness, Odysseus hardly measures up to the rigid standard laid down earlier. If he was reputed for anything, as Basil undoubtedly knew, it was less for his veracity than for his ability to speak "safely" at all times.[8] Xenophon, to whose authority Basil appeals elsewhere in the address, tells us that he was especially clever at adapting his words to his audience, saying one thing when haranguing the soldiers and quite another when talking to his peers.[9] One can only conclude that Odysseus, too, like the professional orators against whom Basil inveighs, had mastered the dangerous art of lying. It is not easy to see how, in this particular instance at any rate, his example could be of much benefit to Basil's young hearers.

Of equally doubtful value from a moral standpoint is the use that is made of a second memorable episode from the same poem in the very next section of the address. Basil had begun by reminding his readers that it is through the exercise of the moral virtues that one gathers up a treasure for the next life. Since the Greek writers are given to celebrating virtue in their works, young students have much to gain by becoming familiar with them and by doing so at an early age, that is to say, at a time when virtuous habits are easily implanted and are more likely to take root in their souls.[10] As a result of the good dispositions acquired in youth, the burden of virtue grows lighter as time goes on. This, says Basil, is what Hesiod meant when he wrote that "the road leading to virtue is rough and hard to travel at first and full of abundant sweat and toil, and steep withal, only to become smooth and beautiful once the summit has been reached, and infinitely more pleasant than the road leading to vice."[11] In Basil's opinion, these words were written for no other reason than to exhort all men to moral goodness. Hesiod's real purpose, it may be noted in passing, seems to have been rather more down to earth. His remarks are not addressed to everyone indiscriminately, as Basil contends, but to his own brother, the "foolish Perses," by whom he had been cheated out of his inheritance.[12] One can scarcely blame him for claiming his due, but at the same time there is some question as to whether his concern for virtue was as noble and genuinely disinterested as Basil would have us believe.

Be that as it may, Basil has it from an unnamed but exceptionally gifted commentator that Homer's poetry, more than anyone else's, was in all of its essential parts an "encomium of virtue."[13] As proof of the validity of that assertation, the reader is referred to the description of Odysseus's arrival in the land of the Phaeacians. According to Basil, the shipwrecked Odysseus would have inspired nothing but "reverence" (*aidōs*) to Nausicaa and her companions as he emerged from the thicket under which he had been sleeping.[14] In spite of his nakedness, he had no reason to feel embarrassed since he was "cloaked with the virtue that the poet had given him in place of garments."[15] As if this were not enough, the address goes on to explain that the admiration which all of the Phaeacians eventually conceived for him was such as to cause them to abandon the proverbial softness of their ways and, indeed, that there was not a single person among them who would have loved anything more than "to become Odysseus, and Odysseus saved from a shipwreck."[16]

It takes little ingenuity to realize that Homer's charming tale has again been embellished to a very large extent. If we turn to the original text, we notice that the initial sentiment which Odysseus, covered with brine and looking for all the world like a desperate, hunger-driven lion, instills in the hearts of the Phaeacian maidens is not reverence, about which nothing is said in Homer, but terror or panic.[17] At the sight of him only the "bold" Nausicaa has the courage to stand her ground and resists the temptation to flee.[18] Odysseus's first speech is ably designed to reassure her and is less an encomium of virtue than a masterpiece of cunning and flattery.[19] The young princess, amusingly enough, is not fooled by it. What fascinates her is not the speaker's virtue but his "wit" and his "commanding appearance."[20] She herself hardly comes across as a paradigm of beguiling candor as she straightaway proceeds to devise a clever scheme of her own, the purpose of which is to conceal from the king and the queen the fact that her first encounter with this intriguing stranger had taken place without their knowledge and approval.[21] The truth will be discovered anyway, but even then Odysseus does not hesitate to lie about Nausicaa's behavior, lest her father should be inclined to find fault with her.[22] Nor is Odysseus as unmindful of his nakedness as Basil makes him out to be. His first gesture had been to break off a leafy branch with which to shield his male parts,[23] and when, a few moments later, Nausicaa bids her attendants to assist him with his bath, shame prompts him to decline the offer.[24] Odysseus, it seems, had less faith than Basil in the merits of his own virtue or that of the pleasant company in the midst of whom fortune had unexpectedly placed him.

After several days of conversation and merrymaking, Odysseus finally reveals himself to his gracious hosts, but only as a man who lives on everyone's lips with his "wiles" and not his virtuous deeds.[25] By this time the reader has come to understand that the whole interlude had no other object than to mark off the distance that separates Odysseus's rugged endurance from the gentle manners of this far-off land. Its significance is forcefully brought out by the songs of Demodocus, which alternate in dramatic fashion between war on the one hand and love or peace on the other.[26] No doubt the easygoing Phaeacians are impressed and not a little mystified by what they have learned about this chance visitor to their peaceful shores, but the idea that they were moved by his example to reform their lives is a piece of pure invention—whether it be that of Basil or of the unidentified commentator whom he professes to follow—and there is not a shred of evidence in the story that any one of them ever had the faintest desire to share his fate. As one perceptive critic puts it, "For all their charm and real helpfulness, the Phaeacians are inconsequential and a little ridiculous compared to the man who lives life whole."[27]

The same high-handed treatment of the classical authors is observable in a large number of other, more complex or more subtle cases that could not suitably be examined within the limited scope of the present essay.[28] The significant fact about all of them, however, is that Basil himself seems to have been perfectly aware of the liberties that he was taking with his sources. With few exceptions, his examples are derived from works that were widely circulated and easily available to him as well as to everyone else; for there would have been no point in explaining to his readers how to exegete a series of texts to which they did not have ready access or which were unlikely to fall into their hands. Moreover, Basil's own works attest his ability to quote his authors faithfully when he wanted to or to recognize an accurate citation when he saw one, as is shown by the pains that he sometimes took to restore to their primitive form certain texts which he knew to have been misquoted by others.[29] If one adds to that the obvious care with which the address *To Young Men* is written, it becomes still more difficult to blame the author's idiosyncrasies on slovenliness or to dismiss them as mere lapses on his part.[30]

One may be tempted to object, on the basis of certain scholarly hypotheses, that the bulk of Basil's information was simply inherited from an older tradition of tropological interpretation, represented prototypically by the *Problemata Homerica* of Heraclitus, or perhaps from one or more treatises, presumably of Cynic-Stoic origin, that have since perished.[31] There is no denying, of course, that such a tradition was widespread and had been in existence for a long time; but the supposition that Basil was indebted to it in any but the most general way would seem to be ruled out by the relative scarcity of precise parallels between the address and the few treatises of a roughly comparable nature, including the *Problemata Homerica,* that have come down to us from antiquity.[32] Besides, even if some of Basil's blunders could be traced back to a definite source, we should still be left, as usual, with the task of accounting for the peculiar combination of texts encountered in the address.

It is perhaps more to the point to observe that the address itself contains evidence of a positive sort to prove that the discussion of Homer is anything but a slavish or mindless imitation of some lost model. In two distinct but related passages, Basil chides those who think of happiness only in terms of "overloaded tables" and "dissolute songs" and who "range over every land and sea, as if compelled to pay tribute to some exacting master by their ceaseless activity."[33] Needless to say, the restless traveller who scours earth and sea in search of adventure but nonetheless politely agrees with his Phaeacian hosts that life is never more pleasant than when the houses are filled with music, the tables laden with bread and meats, and the cups overflowing with wine freshly drawn from the mixing bowls, is none other than the fabled Odysseus, who has just been presented to us as the epitome of every virtue.[34] It is barely imaginable that a writer of Basil's stature should have been so careless or doltish as unwittingly to advocate in one breath what he vehemently decries in another. The contradiction, one surmises, is deliberate and deftly calculated to bring out what, from a Christian point of view, had long been seen as the problematic character of the whole of classical literature. The pertinent question, then, is not whether Basil knew that he was falsifying his sources but why he should have consciously and repeatedly done so at the risk of misleading his readers as to his own intention or that of the authors to whom he refers.

We shall find it impossible to answer that question if we start out with the idea that the way of life of the pagan hero or the Greek sage was easily harmonizable with the moral teachings of Christianity. The fact of the matter is that the ideal of human excellence embodied in and glorified by the works of the most widely acclaimed of all Greek poets could not by any stretch of the imagination be thought to constitute a natural preparation for the gentle but austere morality of the Sermon on the Mount. Contrary to what is sometimes asserted, the Christian writers never canonized the real Homer and never underestimated the threat that he posed to the integrity of their faith.[35] That they should have quoted him profusely and made lavish use of him in their own works is not surprising since he continued to function as the major pivot of Greek education. All indications nevertheless point to the conclusion that they never ceased to look upon him as a purveyor of false values and were more intent on counteracting his influence than on holding him up as an exemplar of Christian or pre-Christian virtue. Some of them, as is well known, would have gladly prohibited the reading of his poems altogether; but such a measure would merely have compounded the problem, either by depriving Christians of the only humanistic education open to them at the time or by investing the ubiquitous Homer with the enticing aura of a new and forbidden pleasure. There was a wiser and more effective solution, which was to allow Christians to study Homer while taking other means to offset the danger to which they were thereby exposing themselves.

Just how this could be accomplished becomes evident if we reflect for a moment on the implications of Basil's curious recommendation that, in reading the works of the pagan authors, one should skip over the bad and retain only what is good.[36] The irony is that the young student for whom the recommendation is primarily intended is in no position to act upon it.

Since, as Basil admits, he still lacks a firm grasp of the criteria by which to make this kind of judgment, he cannot reasonably be trusted to edit the text as he goes along, excising all that is harmful and concentrating solely on what is beneficial to him. Even with the best of intentions, he will end up by taking in everything, the "poison" along with the "honey," oftentimes without any clear perception of the difference between them.[37]

Given this situation, the only viable course of action was to preempt in the mind of the reader any interpretation of the pagan authors that tended to place them at odds with the Christian faith. It is a matter of common experience that one's understanding of a given text is conditioned in the first instance by what one expects to find in it. Having been taught that classical literature was by and large devoted to the praise of virtue, the young student would be predisposed to look for a confirmation of that view in the poems that he chanced to come across. The risk involved in any contact with a pagan writer was neutralized by the superimposition of a Christian image which not only valorized certain elements at the expense of others but created the illusion of a greater kinship than actually existed between the poet's thought and the teaching of the Bible.

If the secret of Basil's success lay anywhere, it was, to use his own analogy, in his ability to fill the ears of his students with the metaphorical wax of Christian principles. The immediate impact of such a device was less to teach the student to discriminate between the objectionable and the non-objectionable parts of the works that he read than to blind him temporarily to the true nature of the objectionable parts and thus prevent him from seeing in the text at hand anything that might be construed as a serious alternative to his faith. The firmness of his principles, like the fastness of the colors that dyers apply to previously treated materials, was secured in advance by the careful preparation to which his trusting soul had been subjected.[38] If, later on, a number of hitherto undetected discrepancies came to light, nothing would be lost; for, once immunized against all dangers from without, his mind would tend to reject as a foreign substance any element that could not be integrated into the Christian scheme.

We know nothing unfortunately about the "nephews" for whom Basil's treatise is supposed to have been written.[39] From the few remarks that are made concerning them, however, one gathers that they were not particularly well-suited for the kind of higher learning to which the argument ultimately points. The opening section of the address calls attention, as Hesiod had done, to three types or categories of persons: those who are capable of arriving at the truth by themselves and can therefore dispense with the help of others; those who, lacking that ability, wisely seek the guidance of a prudent counselor; and those who are neither able to guide themselves nor willing to be guided by someone else.[40] We are given to understand that the nephews in question belong to the second category, but even this is uncertain. Basil's initial distinction is paralleled, toward the end of the address, by another threefold distinction, this time concerning the degrees of illness to which the soul, no less than the body, is prone: people afflicted with slight ailments normally take it upon themselves to consult a physician; those who suffer from more serious diseases find it necessary to summon the physician to their homes; while those who have abandoned all hope of recovery often refuse to admit the physician even if he should call on them.[41] Nothing is said directly about the condition of the would-be nephews, but the address ends with the urgent, almost wistful plea that the sound advice contained in it will not be utterly wasted on them. Basil can only pray that they will be docile to his admonitions. At best, they represent typical rather than the highest addressees of his work. The fine points of the discussion may not have been intended for them at all.

Happily, not everyone falls into the same category. The presumption is that at least some of Basil's readers will be shrewd enough to see through the rhetorical and partly specious character of the argument. On that basis it is fair to say that his poorly concealed blunders were meant to be discovered and were designed to serve the intellectual needs of the more gifted student. It was generally granted that, without prejudice to its unity, the Christian faith was susceptible of varying degrees of understanding and, moreover, that under the right conditions any effort to probe its depths would yield better results if it was guided by an awareness of the most compelling alternative to it. The task in that case was not only to point out the conflict between pagan and Christian morality but to encourage those who were capable of it to penetrate to the root of that conflict. There was a good chance that, by pondering Basil's mistakes and the reasons that prompted them, the reader would achieve a clearer grasp of the implications of his faith and convince himself of its superiority over all rival claims to his allegiance.

In that respect Basil's art of lying, if the term is appropriate, is identical with his art of teaching. Its real purpose is not to indoctrinate the student and even less to mislead him but to equip him with the weapons needed to defend himself and eventually mount his own assault on the "external wisdom"[42] of the ancients. It is no accident that the precedents adduced in support of Basil's thesis are those of Moses and Daniel, whom the Bible describes as having been well-versed in the learning and wisdom of the Egyptians or the Babylonians.[43] Humanly speaking, it makes sense to say that a man who is called upon to liberate his people from foreign oppression must have an intimate knowledge of the oppressor and be competent to deal with him on his own level.

The usual objection to such an interpretation is that one is not entitled to speak of an ongoing contest between the pagan elite and the representatives of the Christian faith for the simple reason that the Church had by then "fully accepted traditional education and teaching," thus putting an end to the "radical opposition" that had once existed between "Hellenism" and Christianity.[44] It is perhaps true that the signs of Christianity's impending triumph were already abroad,[45] but the fact remains that what the Church Fathers were prepared to take over from the cultural heritage of the pagan past was anything but its traditional content. One misses the subtle point of Basil's address altogether if one neglects to read it against the backdrop of a life and death struggle which may have abated as time went on but which could never be resolved by the external victory of one side over the other.

That, in attacking Homer, Basil was not merely tilting at shadows is demonstrated by a contemporary event of considerable symbolic significance, namely, the Emperor Julian's educational reform and, in particular, the famous Rescript of June 17, 362, stipulating that no one could be appointed to a teaching position within the empire without the sanction of the municipal council and that of the Emperor. What is interesting from our point of view is not the law itself—on the face of it, it demanded no more than that the nominee have the proper moral and professional qualifications—but Julian's intention in promulgating it, which was to debar Christians from all state-subsidized public schools by impugning their moral character.[46] Christians were unfit to hold such positions for the precise reason that, having repudiated the pagan gods, they could not, without "lying," explain to their students the true meaning of the works of Homer or any of the other Greek poets.[47] Any attempt on their part to do so necessarily put them in disagreement with themselves in that it forced them to teach outwardly what they professed to reject inwardly.[48] The only possible excuse for their strange behavior is that it enabled them to earn a living, but this only betrays their "shameless cupidity" and willingness "to do anything for the sake of a few drachmas."[49] Since their own law made it a sin to partake of food that had been sacrificed to idols, should they not be that much more eager to preserve their ears and tongues from the adulterous contamination of pagan writings? If they were consistent, they would either abjure their faith or renounce their loathsome profession altogether.[50] Now that freedom of religion has been granted to everyone, nothing prevents them from retiring into their own churches and exercising whatever literary talents they may have on the gospels of Matthew and Luke.[51]

Under the circumstances, it comes as no surprise that Julian should have been so strongly attracted to Neoplatonism, which by then had eclipsed or absorbed all of its philosophic rivals and which, in its popular forms, such as that found in Iamblichus, could more readily be transformed into an instrument of imperial policy.[52] By reason of its mystical flavor, Iamblichus's thought was well-adapted to the religious temper of the times, and by reason of its unabashed polytheism, it offered some chance for an eventual revival of the national gods.[53] Instead of demoting military valor precisely when it was most needed, it might be made to sanction less passive and more politically useful modes of conduct. The hope was that, properly controlled and supported, it would provide the empire with dedicated and public-spirited soldiers who were prepared to defend it, instead of a pious citizenry who were content to pray for it.[54] In an age afflicted with more problems than it could handle and which tended to blame Christianity for many of those problems, one could think of no better antidote to the unitary and somewhat apolitical tendency inherent in or fostered by the Christian faith.

Beneath the slanderous accusations of boorishness and duplicity to which we have just listened, one immediately senses Julian's more relevant objection to the presence of Christians in the schools. The despised "Galileans" constituted a major obstacle to the restoration of a Neoplatonic Hellenism not because they knew too little but because they knew too much. They had learned a great deal about pagan literature since the days of their unlettered forebears and, instead of condemning it outright, had noiselessly gone about reinterpreting it in a manner that lent greater credence to their faith. As Julian himself expressed it so vividly, "We are shot with shafts feathered from our own wings, for from our own books they take arms against us."[55]

The obvious flaw in the argument is that it was not without its own element of hypocrisy. Since the Greek intelligentsia had long since ceased to take the gods of pagan mythology seriously, one could not in fairness hold Christians to account for doing as much. Julian's point was nevertheless well taken. A pagan would normally have had no qualms about teaching Homer to his students, for what was at stake was not the existence of the gods themselves but the ideal of human greatness figuratively expressed in the stories that were told about them. Not so with Christians, whose monotheistic faith denounced as fleshly and diabolical everything that the pagan gods had traditionally stood for. By reserving his harshest invectives for his former co-religionists, Julian was merely taking a leaf from their book. As a one-time Christian, he, too, was privy to the art of impaling his adversaries on the butts of their own shafts.[56]

If there is anything to be learned from Basil's address, it is that the co-optation of the pagan classics as a kind of *praeparatio evangelica* or propaedeutic to the faith entailed not so much the appropriation of the old values as their transmutation in accordance with the demands of the Gospel. In the eyes of their pagan adversaries, Christians could not do justice to Homer and Hesiod because they had turned their backs once and for all on the particular type of nobility that is exemplified in their works. What was most troubling is that, having come to know them from within, they were able to empty them of much of their substance even while pretending to defend them. The Homer whom they pressed into service as a witness to their faith is mainly a figment of their pious and immensely fertile imaginations. He has little in common with the Homer whom their pagan ancestors had known and revered. The image that they created of him bears eloquent testimony to both the vitality of their religious convictions and the lengths to which they were prepared to go in order to propagate them. Whether or not the strategy of spiritual warfare that they invented for this purpose entangled them in a web of complicated lies is a question which they themselves were understandably loath to raise and which they managed to circumvent by giving to the old art of lying a new and more felicitous label. They called it the "economy of truth."[57] The expression dates from that period, but the unimpeachable Christian pedigree of the word *oikonomia*[58] was enough to remove from it any taint of opprobrium and guarantee its success for a long time to come.

NOTES

1. Basil the Great, *Ad adulescentes* IV.30-31, ed F. Boulenger, *Aux jeunes gens sur la manière de tirer profit des lettres helléniques* (Paris: Les Belles Lettres, 1935), 45. Although lies are often defended on grounds of necessity or utility by the ancient authors (e.g. Plato, *Republic* V.459c), I know of no other use of the expression, "the art of lying," in Greek literature. An analogous expression occurs in Augustine, *Epistula* (*Letter*) 1.1: *Contra huiusmodi homines opinor ego illam utiliter excogitatam tegendi veri artem atque rationem.*

2. *Ad adul.* IV.33-34. Cf. I Cor 6:1-7.

3. *Epistula* (*Letter*) 58, to his brother Gregory; see also *Epistula* 59 and 60, to Gregory, his uncle. Cf. Y. Courtonne, *Un témoin du IVe siècle oriental: saint Basile et son temps d'après sa correspondance* (Paris: Les Belles Lettres, 1973), 37-39. What Basil does not say is that he himself had tried to lure Gregory of Nazianzus to Caesarea under false pretenses in order to secure his support in the forthcoming election to the vacant see; cf. Gregory of Naz; *Ep.* 40.

4. *Ad adul.* IV.4; also VI.1-4.

5. *Ad adul.* IV. 9-10.

6. *Odyssey* XII.159-160.

7. *Odyssey* XII.49.

8. Cf. Xenophon, *Memorabilia* IV.6-15, with reference to *Odyssey* VII.171, where Odysseus is credited with being a "safe speaker."

9. *Mem.* I.2.58. The same principle is said to have been observed by Socrates in IV.1.3ff.

10. *Ad adul.* V.5-8.

11. *Ad adul.* V.11-13. Cf. Hesiod, *Opera et Dies* 285-90.

12. *Op. et Dies* 27-41.

13. *Ad adul.* V.25-27.

14. *Ad adul.* V.30.

15. *Ad adul.* V.32.

16. *Ad adul.* V.36-37.

17. *Odyssey* VI.130-137.

18. *Od.* VI.139-141.

19. *Od.* VI.145-185.

20. *Od.* VI.187.

21. *Od.* VI.251-315.

22. *Od.* VII.303-307.

23. *Od.* VI.128-129.

24. *Od.* VI.221-222.

25. *Od.* IX.19-20: "I am Odysseus, son of Laertes, known before all men for the study of crafty designs."

26. *Od.* VIII.72-82; 266-366; 499-520.

27. C. H. Whitman, *Homer and the Heroic Tradition* (Cambridge, MA: Harvard University Press, 1958), 242.

28. For an analysis of Basil's pagan sources, see, *inter alia*, T. L Shear, *The Influence of Plato on Saint Basil* (Baltimore, MD: J. N. Furst, Co., 1906); G. Büttner, *Basileios des Grossen Mahnworte an die Jugend über den nützlichen Gebrauch der heidnischen Literatur* (Munchen: Druck von H. Kutzner, 1908); L. V. Jacks, *St. Basil and Greek Literature*, The Catholic University of America Patristic Studies, vol. I (Washington: The Catholic University of America Press, Inc., 1920); E. Valgiglio, "Basilio Magno *Ad adulescentes* e Plutarco *De audiendis poetis*," Rivista di Studi Classici. 23 (1975): 67-86. The history of the older interpretations of Basil's address, which has been alternately understood as a defense of and an attack upon the pagan classics, is traced by L. Schucan, *Das Nachleben von Basilius Magnus "ad Adulescentes: ein Beitrag zur Geschichte des christlichen Humanismus,"* Travaux d'humanisme et renaissance vol. 133 (Geneva: Droz, 1973).

29. Cf. T. L. Shear, *The Influence of Plato on Saint Basil*, 42 and 53.

30. For a different assessment, cf. P. de Labriolle, *Histoire de la littérature latine chrétienne*, I (Paris: Les Belle Lettres, 1947), 33: "A vrai dire, on ne voit pas que le sujet y soit développé avec l'ampleur et la précision que l'on souhaiterait. Basil apporte à sa discussion moins de méthode que de bonhommie aimable et d'abondant humanisme."

31. Cf. G. Büttner, *op. cit.*, 28 and 62ff.

32. Very few such parallels are noted by F. Buffière, *Les mythes d Homère et la pensée grecque* (Paris: Les Belles Lettres, 1956), or by J. Pépin, *Mythe et allégorie: les origines grecques et les contestations judéo-chrétiennes* (Paris: Etudes augustiniennes, 1976). H. Herter observes, rightly in my opinion "that Basil's

interpretations are not strictly speaking allegorical"; cf. "Basileios der Grosse und das Problem der profanen Bildung," *Proceedings of the First International Humanistic Symposium at Delphi,* vol. 1 (Athens, 1970), 256.

33. *Ad adul.* IV.17-19.45; IX.7-11.55.

34. *Odyssey* IX.5-10. The same passage is criticized by Plato, *Republic* III.390a-b.

35. A more optimistic appraisal is offered by H. Rahner, *Greek Myths and Christian Mystery,* translated by B. Battershaw (London: Burns and Oats, 1963), esp. Part Three: "Holy Homer," 279-386. The expression, "Holy Homer," is Goethes's (*Das Künstlers Morgenlied,* quoted, 283), and not Rahner's. It is never used to my knowledge by the early Christian writers. For a critical evaluation of Rahner's thesis, see V. Buchheit, "Homer bei Methodios von Olympos," *Rh. Mus.* 99 (1956), 17-36.

36. *Ad adul.* I.24-28.

37. Cf. *Ad adul.* IV.15.

38. *Ad adul.* II.39-46. Cf. Plato, *Republic* IV.429dff.

39. The widely held view (first advanced by Büttner) that Basil was addressing himself to his own nephews rests on questionable internal evidence and has been challenged by A. Moffatt, "The Occasion of St. Basil's *Address to Young Men,*" *Antichthon* 6 (1972), 74-76.

40. *Ad adul.* I.13-18. Cf. Hesiod, *Op. et Dies* 293-97.

41. *Ad adul.* X.33-40.

42. *Ad adul.* II.44; III.9-10; IV.1-2.

43. *Ad adul.* III.11-18. Cf. Daniel 1:4-5; Acts 7:22.

44. J. Daniélou and H.-I. Marrou, *The Christian Centuries: A New History of the Catholic Church,* I: *The First Six Centuries* (New York: McGraw-Hill, 1964), 301. Cf. F. E. Peters, *The Harvest of Hellenism: A History of the Near East from Alexander the Great to the Triumph of Christianity* (New York: Simon and Schuster, 1970), 709.

45. Cf. Daniélou and Marrou, ibid., 302.

46. *Codex Theodosianus* XIII.3.5 (= *Codex Iustinianus* X.53.7), *ap.* J. Bidez, ed., *Oeuvres complètes de l'empereur Julien.* I. 2e partie (Paris: Les Belles Lettres, 1924), 72: *Magistros studiorum doctoresque excellere oportet moribus primum, deinde facundia.* It has been suggested with a good deal of plausibility that Basil's address was written, not late in his career, as has generally been assumed, but as early as the academic year 362-363 and that it represents the author's immediate reaction to Julian's edict; cf. A. Moffatt, *loc. cit.,* 83-86.

47. Julian, *Epistula* (*Letter*) 61.422d-423b. Bidez, 74.

48. *Epist.* 422b-c, 73.

49. *Epist.* 423b, 74.

50. *Epist.* 423a and 424d; cf. *Against the Galileans* 229c-d.

51. *Epist.* 423c-d, 75.

52. On the differences between Iamblichus and Porphyry, whose disciple he had probably been in Rome, cf. A. H. Armstrong. *An Introduction to Ancient Philosophy*

(London: Methuen, 1947), 197-20; Id., ed., *The Cambridge History of Later Greek and Early Medieval Philosophy* (Cambridge: Cambridge University Press, 1970), 293-301; P. Hadot, *Porphyre et Victorinus*, I (Paris: Etudes Augustiniennes, 1968), 91-101. Julian's relationship to Iamblichus's disciples is examined by J. Bidez, *La vie de l'empereur Julien* (Paris: Les Belles Lettres, 1930), 67-72.

53. Cf. Julian, *Against the Galileans* 115d, W. C. Wright transl., *The Works of the Emperor Julian III* (London and New York: Heinemann and Macmillan, 1923), 345: "But now consider our teaching in comparison with this of yours. Our writers say that the creator is the common father and king of all things, but that other functions have been assigned by him to national gods of the peoples and gods that protect the cities, every one of whom administers his own department in accordance with his own nature." The political nature of Julian's ill-fated reform is underscored by A. Kojève, "The Emperor Julian and His Art of Writing," in J. Cropsey, ed., *Ancients and Moderns* (New York: Basic Books, 1964), 95-113. For a summary discussion of the conflicting tendencies within Neoplatonism from this point of view, cf. E. L. Fortin, chapter 11, "The *Viri Novi* of Arnobius and the Conflict Between Faith and Reason in the Early Christian Centuries," 169-97. Plotinus's own, rather more intellectual brand of mysticism is analyzed by A. H. Armstrong, *The Architecture of the Intelligible Universe in the Philosophy of Plotinus: An Analytical and Historical Study* (Cambridge: A. M. Hakkert, 1940; repr. Amsterdam, 1967); 29-47.

54. Cf. Julian, *Fragmenta Breviora* 5, *ap.* W. C. Wright, *loc. cit.,* 299: "They only know how to pray" (said of the soldiers who accompanied him to Gaul in 355). Basil's address, interestingly enough, stresses justice and moderation (e.g., III.13-14), but maintains a strange silence on the subject of courage, a virtue for which Julian shows a lively concern; cf. *Adv. Galil.* 230a, 387: "Yet you are so misguided and foolish that you regard those chronicles of yours as divinely inspired, though by their help no man could ever become wiser or braver or better than he was before; while, on the other hand, writings by whose aid men can acquire courage, wisdom and justice, these you ascribe to Satan and to those who serve Satan!"

55. Cf. Theodoret, *Historia ecclesiastica (A History of the Church from A.D. 322 to the death of Theodore of Mopsuestia, A.D. 427)* III.8.1.

56. Other similarities between Julian's techniques and those of Christianity are mentioned by J. Bidez, *La vie de l'empereur Julien,* 69, and by F. E. Peters, *The Harvest of Hellenism,* 704 and 708-9.

57. E.g., Gregory Nazianzus, *Epistula (Letter)* 58.11-12 (to Basil): "Surely then it is better to use some reserve (*oikonomēthēnai*) in the truth and ourselves to give way a little to circumstances as to a cloud rather than to risk its destruction by the openness of the proclamation. The present company would not receive my economy, as out of date and mocking them, but they shouted me down as practicing it rather from cowardice than for reason. It would be much better, they said, to protect your own people by the truth than by your so-called economy to weaken them while failing to win over the others." John Chrysostom, *De Sacerdotio* I.9: "For great is the power

of deceit, provided it be not introduced with a mischievous intention. In fact, action of this kind ought not to be called deceit but rather a kind of economy, cleverness, and skill, capable of finding out ways where resources fail and making up for the defects of the mind." Cf. ibid., II.1. On the diverse uses of the word *oikonomia* in early Christian literature, cf. G. L. Prestige, *God in Patristic Thought* (London: S.P.C.K., 1952), 57-67 and 97-111; B. Botte, "OIKONOMIA: quelques emplois spécifiquement chrétiens," in *Corona Gratiarum: Miscellanea Patristica, Historica et Liturgica Eligio Dekkers O.S.P. Xll Lustra Complenti Oblata,* Instrumenta Patristica X, I (Bruges: Sint Pietersabdij, 1975), 3-9.

58. E.g., Eph. 1:10; 3:2 and 9; Col. 1:25; I Tim. 1:4.

BASIL THE GREAT AND THE CHOICE OF HERCULES: A NOTE ON THE CHRISTIANIZATION OF A PAGAN MYTH

In his well-known book on the theme of Hercules at the crossroads, Erwin Panofsky observes that, although the writers and artists of the Middle Ages were fond of personifying the various moral virtues, they never went so far as to portray Virtue as such, lest by so doing they should give the impression that she was a goddess.[1] The one exception to this rule, as was later discovered, appears to be the late thirteenth and early fourteenth century Tuscan designer Francesco da Barberino, who announced his intention of making a sketch of moral virtue *in genere,* but not without a good deal of hesitation since he was fully aware of the novelty of his enterprise and of the objections that his contemporaries might have to it. A century and a half later the fashion had not yet caught on. Antonio Averlino, who liked to call himself Filarete, the "Lover of Virtue," could still claim that the only allegorical representations of Virtue and Vice known to him were the ones that occur in the apologue of the choice of Hercules as told by Xenophon toward the beginning of Book II of the *Memorabilia* and by Cicero in his treatise *On Duties.* Filarete's *Trattato d'Architettura* then goes on to describe a projected "House of Virtue and Vice" that was to be crowned by a statue representing Virtue itself.[2]

The thinking behind this reluctance to create images of general virtue is supposedly illustrated by Augustine's attack on the *dea virtus* in Book IV of the *City of God*. Augustine's argument or part of it is that, if the old Romans had really been convinced of the supremacy of virtue, the sole possession of which would have sufficed to make them happy, they could easily have dispensed with the rest of their gods and goddesses. Even so, virtue is not a goddess but a gift of God and is to be obtained from him alone by whom it can be given. For Augustine as for St. Paul, there is only one *virtus dei,* namely, Christ (cf. I Cor. 1:24), the true dispenser of virtue and the bestower of all the good things that accrue to human beings in this life as well as in the next.[3] The same strictures did not apply, on the other hand, to the particular virtues, which, as Augustine remarks, the Romans had never deified and which Christians are required to cultivate here and now inasmuch as they constitute the mandatory precondition of the attainment of eternal life.

One wonders, however, whether the reason alleged for the absence of anthropomorphic figures of general virtue throughout the medieval period is as decisive as Panofsky and others have made it out to be; for it is hard to see why, in a society from which paganism had long been officially banished, anyone would have construed the attempt to depict Virtue through the medium of art as the sign of a desire to elevate it to the rank of a deity. There may be a simpler and more plausible explanation, which is that, prior to Grosseteste's translation of the whole of Aristotle's *Ethics,* ca. 1245, the Middle Ages lacked any determinate or well articulated concept of general virtue. To be sure, general virtue is frequently mentioned from Abelard onward, but only on the basis of the few vague descriptions that one could read of it in what was then known of the literature of antiquity.[4] Both the classical and the Christian traditions occasionally spoke of justice as more or less synonymous with moral rectitude or the whole of virtue in that it extends or can extend to all of one's actions, but they also treated it as one of the four so-called "cardinal" virtues, along with moderation, courage, and prudence.[5] Justice in this restricted sense was the particular virtue whereby one is inclined to render to each his due. The two views appeared to be joined together in a brief passage of Cicero's *De inventione* where justice is defined as that habit of mind which not only gives or restores to individual human beings what properly belongs to them but likewise has as its object the common good or the good of society at large: *Iustitia est habitus animi communi utilitate conservata suam cuique tribuens dignitatem.*[6] Even though this definition, along with the division of justice or right into natural, customary, and statutory that accompanies it, became a *locus classicus* of sorts in medieval literature, the wide variety of discussions to which it gave rise comes across as barely more than a series of academic exercises the sole aim of which was to sort out the various meanings of the term "justice," without much concern for the place that legal justice might occupy within the context of human life as a whole.

It bears noting that even after the rediscovery of the *Nicomachean Ethics*, legal or general justice never quite achieved the status that it enjoys in the Aristotelian scheme. Albert the Great hardly does anything at all with it and is obviously at pains to account for its presence in the economy of the moral life;[7] and, while Thomas Aquinas mentions it from time to time, he can hardly be said to lay any particular stress on it.[8] In the Christian world charity, it seems, tended to replace legal justice or the attachment to the common good of one's society as the virtue that informs all the other virtues and commands their respective acts. True, legal justice will again come into its own at the time of the Renaissance, but only as a result of the challenge that the recovery of Aristotelian philosophy had come to pose in a society that, by and large, was still governed by Christian principles. To my knowledge, the only medieval authors to make a strong case for the centrality of legal justice are Dante and Marsilius of Padua who, on this point at least, speak more for themselves than for the other writers of their generation.[9]

Be that as it may, the qualms about presenting Virtue in the form of an allegory do not appear to have been shared equally by all of the early Christian writers. This much is apparent from the use that is made of the story of Hercules at the crossroads by Basil the Great in his short but illuminating address *To Young Men on the Benefits to Be Derived from the Reading of the Pagan Authors*.[10] Here, to begin with, is the text as it appears in Basil's essay:

And furthermore, somewhere in his writings the sophist from Keos (Prodicus) uttered a doctrine kindred to these others regarding virtue and vice; we must then apply our minds to him as well, for he is not a man to be scorned. His *logos* runs something like this, so far as I recall the man's thought, since I do not know the exact words, but only that he spoke in general to the following effect, without employing meter. When Hercules was quite a young man and was nearly of the age that you yourselves have now reached, while he was deliberating which of the two roads he should take, the one leading through toils to virtue or the easiest, two women approached him, Virtue and Vice. Now at once, although they were silent, the difference between them was evident from their appearance. For the one had been decked out for beauty through the art of toiletry, was drooping with voluptuousness, and led a whole swarm of pleasures in her wake. These things she displayed and, promising others still, she tried to draw Hercules to her. As for the other, she was withered and squalid, had an intense look, and spoke quite differently; for she promised nothing dissolute or pleasant, but countless sweating toils and labors and dangers through every land and sea. The prize to be won by these, however, was to become a god, as the *logos* expressed it. It was this second woman that in the end Hercules followed.

It has not always been sufficiently noted, however, that Basil's rendition of this famous story is far from being as faithful to the original as he himself would have us believe. According to Xenophon, whose work contains the oldest surviving account of the fable,[11] Hercules, having reached the age when young people are ready to become their own masters (*autokratores*) and reveal the path upon which they are likely to embark in life, is confronted by two women of great stature, one symbolizing Virtue and the other Vice. Both of them betray their characters by their demeanor and their attire, the description of which, as Panofsky has shown, was to become a source of endless fascination on the part of Renaissance painters. The first is clothed in white, sober, and dignified in appearance. Her limbs are adorned with purity (*katharotēs*) and her eyes with modesty (*aidōs*). The path to which she points is fraught with greater difficulty at the outset, but in return for his exertions the hero may expect to reap the favor of the gods and the acclaim of his fellow human beings. When death comes at its appointed hour, he will not lie "forgotten and dishonored" but will live on, "sung and remembered for all time" (II.1.33). The second is bolder and far less austere. She is plump and soft with high feeding, open-eyed, filled with vanity, eager to attract attention to herself, and dressed so as to disclose all of her charms. Instead of the pain that accompanies the struggle against one's lower impulses, she promises a lifetime of ease and untold pleasure, allowing her devotees to pluck "the fruits of others' toil" and to seize every advantage that may come their way (II.1.25).

Understandably, Basil has taken upon himself to purge the tale of any and all references to the gods of pagan mythology, but he has also subjected it to a number of tacit emendations the cumulative effect of which is to alter its thrust to a considerable extent. Contrary to what one finds in Xenophon, the first of the two women to be introduced is not Virtue but Vice. The detail would hardly be worth mentioning were it not for the ascetical twist that it straight away imparts to the story. Implied in Basil's procedure is a greater distrust of nature, which he regards as having been wounded by sin, and a stronger desire to counteract its original tendencies. In the Christian version, one is tempted to suggest, the struggle against evil takes precedence over the attraction of the good or the beautiful. The emphasis is less on the possibility of orienting or reorienting the natural inclinations toward more suitable and ultimately more rewarding objects than on the need to overcome them by dint of effort and self-denial. In that regard as well and in many others, the Christian educator found himself in a markedly different position from that of his pagan counterpart. Since he had no choice but to address himself to all indiscriminately, he could not rely exclusively on such motives as are likely to appeal only to generous and well-bred natures who find the virtuous life intrinsically attractive and need no further incentive in order to pursue it.

The same element of asceticism or voluntarism comes into full view with the subsequent description of virtue, which no doubt represents Basil's most notable departure from his pagan model. In addition to being pure and modest, Xenophon's Virtue is "fair to see" (*euprepēs*) and of "noble bearing" (*eleutherios*) (II.1.22). Basil's has lost none of her modesty but she has unexpectedly become "withered" (*katesklēkenai*), "squalid" (*auchmein*), and possessed of a fixed or intense look (*suntonon blepein*). The only immediate prospect that she holds out is that of countless "sweating toils, labors, and dangers through every land and sea." A special effort is thus needed to befriend her and discover her hidden beauty. Accordingly, anyone who would approach her must begin by imposing a harsh discipline upon himself with a view to repressing his desires and overcoming his propensity to evil.

Equally significant is the remark that follows, which is not so much a modification of Xenophon's text as a pure and simple addition to it. In Basil's account, the prize that Hercules stands to win by making the right choice is "to become a god, as the *logos* has it." Xenophon's *logos* mentions no such thing, perhaps because Hercules was already a god or a demigod, or, as seems more likely, because Virtue herself is not a goddess. She merely "consorts" (*suneimi*) with the gods and with good men, as opposed to Vice, who is indeed a goddess albeit a fallen one: "Immortal thou art, yet the outcast of the gods" (II.1.31). Since Virtue is inseparable from toil, she could scarcely be numbered among the easy-living gods, and, from what we know of these gods, was not their constant companion.

The discussion is brought to a fitting close with the observation that Hercules chose Virtue over Vice, which is what Basil's young hearers are likewise urged to do. Such a conclusion might again strike us as trivial except for the fact that it had to be supplied by Basil. In Xenophon, Hercules's felicitous choice is at best implicit. Socrates, who recounts the story, leaves it at saying that his interlocutor, the sophist Aristippus, would do well to ponder what he has just heard and give more careful thought to the kind of life that he proposes to lead (II.1.34). As we shall see in a moment, Socrates and Aristippus have more in common than meets the eye, or so it would seem from the fact that the argument in which they engage is not one that could be carried on between nonphilosophers or between a philosopher and a nonphilosopher. Not that their positions are identical, far from it. Yet there is reason to suspect that for Socrates, if not for Aristippus, the choice between the two lives is perhaps not as clear-cut as one might think.

None of these changes is acknowledged by Basil, who admits that he is reproducing the tale from memory but nonetheless insists on the overall accuracy of his report. Because of the numerous parallels between the two texts, scholars are generally agreed that his source could not have been anyone but Xenophon, even though he is not mentioned by name. The possibility of a lost intermediary cannot be ruled out *a priori*, but if such an intermediary did exist, one finds it strange that it should have left no traces in the abundant literature on this subject in classical and Christian antiquity. What matters in any event is not so much the literary history of the myth as its intellectual content, and on that score there is perhaps something of importance to be learned from a comparison between the two authors. We shall come to a better understanding of the issue at hand if we go back to the *Memorabilia* and look at the context within which it comes up.

As reported by Xenophon, the story forms part of a fairly lengthy discussion between Socrates and Aristippus, the founder of the Cyrenaic school, the first hedonistic school of philosophy in antiquity.[12] The theme in the present instance is continence (*enkrateia*), one of the four virtues ascribed to Socrates in the book, the other three being piety, justice, and prudence. Socrates, who takes the initiative, poses the problem in the form of a question to which Aristippus is invited to reply: if he had two youths to educate, one to become a ruler and the other to lead a private life, which of them would he train in continence as regards food, drink, and the various other bodily pleasures to which human beings are normally attracted? (II.1.1) Aristippus readily agrees that the future ruler is the one who is called upon to develop habits of self-restraint. It soon becomes apparent, however, that Aristippus, who is not himself inclined to continence, has no intention of joining that category, a decision which he justifies on grounds, not of incontinence, but of the troublesome character of the political life (II.1.8-9). Since he is intent only on satisfying his own needs and already finds it hard enough to do so, he is not about to assume responsibility for the needs of others. Rulers are accountable to everybody and are never or only rarely their own masters. They have to sacrifice most of their wishes to those of the community and their subjects invariably end up by treating them the way he, Aristippus, treats his slaves. That being the case, only a fool would want to shoulder the burden of public office.[13] Aristippus, who would rather live pleasantly and comfortably, will have nothing to do with it.

This prompts Socrates to ask whether a nation that is ruled by another nation and thus runs the risk of being oppressed by it lives more pleasantly than one that is not (II.1.10). The question proves slightly embarrassing to his opponent, who has just gone on record as saying that the disadvantages of political rule far outweigh its advantages, but he is not without an answer to it. There is, he thinks, a third possibility, a "middle path" as it were, which consists neither in ruling nor in being ruled but in preserving one's freedom. All one has to do is live "as a foreigner in every land." The best life is not that of the citizen, be he ruler or subject, but that of the resident alien who has no country of his own. It corresponds to what Aristotle would later call the *bios xenikos*.[14] This and nothing else is the "royal road to happiness," for it enables him to enjoy the benefits of political society and at the same time spares him the trouble of making any contribution to it (II.1.11-13).

Socrates again has little difficulty in making it plain that the new solution will not work. If even citizens, who are usually prompt to come to one another's assistance, do not always escape injustice, how much less will a foreigner be able to count on the protection of a city to which he does not belong?[15] Aristippus's middle road would be viable if it did not lead through human beings, the stronger among whom "have a way of making the weaker rue their lot both in public and in private life" (II. 1.12). Life as we know it is inescapably political and seldom favors those who would remain aloof from the affairs of the city. Its harsh teaching is that anyone who refuses to play the hammer will sooner or later be made to play the anvil.[16] Aristippus is not wrong in thinking that citizenship has its unpleasant side, but he has never seriously reflected on the difference between the man who voluntarily undergoes hardships for the sake of a greater good and the one who suffers evils out of necessity (II.1.17). His position is not altogether consistent insofar as it forces him to make use of political institutions while remaining himself entirely unpolitical.

The parable of Hercules at the crossroads, which is introduced at this juncture and which is ostensibly meant to shed further light on the problem, focuses precisely on the choice between what might be called private vice and public virtue. The initial impression conveyed is that the range of human possibilities is somehow exhausted by these two alternatives. Aristippus, at any rate, is convinced that such is Socrates's view and, moreover, that Socrates equates happiness with the art of ruling as opposed to the pleasant life. Whether or not this is true remains doubtful at best. A closer look at the matter reveals a Socrates who is far less simpleminded than Aristippus makes him out to be. Since, as we have just been told, Virtue is excluded from the pantheon of the gods and goddesses, we must conclude that the life wholly devoted to its pursuit is not coextensive with the most divine life and hence perhaps not altogether satisfactory. Furthermore, it is intriguing to observe that, among those who oppose indolence, Socrates mentions not only trainers and poets, such as Hesiod and Epicharmus, but an unnamed third class, about whom nothing is said other than that they are capable of instilling the best kind of knowledge (*epistēmēn axiologon*) into the soul (II.1.20). Finally, and perhaps most strikingly, there is the matter of Socrates's strange silence concerning the decision to which Hercules came after listening to the two women who vie for his allegiance.

We are given to understand by all of this that Socrates, too, may have a third possibility in mind, but one which is less open to criticism than Aristippus's proposed solution and which, instead of sacrificing nobility to pleasure or *vice versa,* seeks to combine them on a higher plane. What this new middle road might be is never specified, presumably for reasons of a prudential nature. A frank disclosure of what Socrates was really like would have done little to rehabilitate him in the eyes of his detractors; and besides, since the life hinted at is not suited to everybody and may even be the preserve of a select few, any more specific reference to it would have been either useless or inappropriate. The reader of Xenophon's Socratic writings and of the Platonic dialogues nonetheless thinks spontaneously of the one life that, in addition to being more truly self-sufficient, has none of the baseness or selfishness of the life that Aristippus dreams of, to wit, the theoretical life, of which Socrates himself is offered as the most perfect embodiment. Such, it would seem, is the teaching to which the conversation between the friendly rivals points indirectly. Beneath the surface of Socrates's edifying speech lurks a subtle intention that is not less important for being less obvious. Appearances to the contrary notwithstanding, the crossroads at which Hercules encounters Virtue and Vice is not a *bivium* but a *trivium.* Where the young hero sees only two roads, Socrates, who contemplates the scene from above, as would for example a person looking at a map, sees three distinct roads, moving toward or away from one another.

That this is the manner in which the story was read by some people in the past is brought to our attention by another Christian writer, Justin Martyr, who characterizes Hercules's crossroads as "a place where three ways met" (*epi triodon tina*).[17] Since this startling remark receives no further elaboration, one can only venture a guess as to what was meant by it. If the comparison between Christ and Socrates that precedes it suggests anything, it is that Christianity, in behalf of which Justin writes, must itself be viewed as a third way, different from and superior to either the political life or the life of philosophic inquiry, both of which have just been alluded to in the text. Interestingly enough, Justin, who is closer to Xenophon in this regard, omits any reference to the choice eventually made by Hercules. The question is whether, for all his apparent lack of subtlety, Basil himself was not thinking of something like a third way, in which Christian virtue emerges as a substitute for the pagan virtue that Hercules is presumed to have sought.

The point to which virtually all of the late ancient writers who deal with this episode call attention has to do with the very possibility of a rational choice of the kind that Hercules is summoned to make. As Cicero rightly observes, that choice must be made in youth, that is to say at a time when the chooser is still relatively inexperienced and hence unable to arrive at a fully enlightened decision concerning what is best for him. In all but the rarest of cases, the young person will decide according to his predispositions, and these in turn are bound to be influenced by his early educators or the opinions of the city in the midst of which he was reared. From that point of view, Hercules's situation was anything but typical. As the "scion of the seed of Jove," he had a distinct advantage over ordinary human beings, the vast majority of whom simply "fall" or "drift" into the "manners and customs" with which they happen to be most familiar.[18] The same point is emphasized even more strongly by Dio Chrysostom, who explains at great length that Zeus had dispatched none other than Hermes to complete Hercules's education and make him fully aware of the implications of his choice between the two women, who in this particular instance stand for kingship versus tyranny rather than for the public life versus the private life.[19] That Xenophon's Hercules had likewise received an excellent training is vouched for by the fact that, whereas he does not appear to be acquainted with Vice and must ask what her name is (II.1.26), he needs no introduction to Virtue, who is not a total stranger to him and who admits to having taken note of his natural dispositions (*physis*) during the time of his education (II.1.27).

It would surely be a mistake to think that Basil was any less intent on securing a proper education for his charges. Since he knew how to quote his authors accurately when he wanted to, he can scarcely have been unaware of the modifications that he introduces into the pagan tale.[20] His purpose, one gathers, was not merely to retell that tale for the benefit of his hearers but to adapt it to their particular needs. The question addressed in his essay, that of the use to which the literature of classical antiquity could be put by Christians, was a delicate one for the obvious reason that on any number of crucial points the way of life reflected in and transmitted through it entered into direct conflict with the ideal of the Gospel. Nowhere perhaps is this more evident than in the Hercules story, in which the practice of moral virtue is linked exclusively to the achievement of worldly glory and other similarly mundane goals.[21]

One way to deal with the challenge was to prohibit the reading of all such works—a dubious enterprise that some of Basil's fellow Christians had been advocating but whose chances of success were practically nil, especially since there were no Christian schools to which young Christians could be sent and since the only formal education open to them at the time was based on the study of the pagan poets. The better and, in the long run, more efficacious solution was to try to defuse the issue by reinterpreting these poets in such a way as to bring their teachings into greater harmony with those of the Christian faith. It is therefore not surprising that practically all of Basil's classical citations have been truncated, distorted, tampered with, or otherwise emptied of their original substance.[22] Nor is it surprising that over the centuries Basil's treatise should have been read by some scholars as a defense of pagan learning and by others as an attack upon it.[23] If the foregoing analysis is accurate, the two assessments may be seen as complementing rather than contradicting each other. Basil was undoubtedly less open to the influence of pagan thought than others among his coreligionists, but even he realized the futility of any attempt to prevent young Christians from coming into contact with it.

This said, one need not exaggerate Basil's originality, any more than one need underestimate it. His own treatment of the Hercules legend conforms to a pattern which by that time already had a long history. He is not the first to present Virtue as "withered" and "squalid"—Philostratus, Maximus of Tyre, and Justin had preceded him,[24] and he is by no means the only one to specify that Hercules chose Virtue—Cicero and Dio Chrysostom had done the same,[25] although Basil probably did not know it. His merit lies rather in the ingenuity with which he managed to place the pagan tale in the service of an ideal that was still being violently attacked by some of his contemporaries, the Emperor Julian among them, and to the triumph of which he himself contributed in no small measure. For generations to come, the passions once aroused by the prize of earthly glory to which Hercules was urged to bend his efforts will have as their object the reward of heavenly bliss promised to the humble followers of Christ.

A full analysis of the spiritual transformation to which his treatment of this subject bears witness would take us much farther afield than the compass of this modest note warrants, and all the more so as it would involve us in a lengthy discussion of the nature of Socratic wisdom and its complex relationship to such notions as the good, the pleasant, and the noble.[26] Suffice it to observe that the position defended by Basil and the one adumbrated by Socrates are not completely at odds with each other, at least to the extent that neither one looks upon the political life as the highest life or prizes the virtues that it calls into play as the greatest of all virtues. Just as, for the philosopher, moral virtue is not an end in itself but the condition and the natural consequence of a way of life that transcends the political realm, so, for the Christian, it is something to be sought, not for its own sake, but as a preparation for and the means to a higher goal, namely, the blessedness of eternal life.

It is equally significant that Socrates, who is said to have been moderate, just, prudent, and in his own way pious, is never called courageous by Xenophon. Courage is the virtue that perfects the spirited part of the soul and that is most directly related to the defense of the political community, whose welfare is contingent on the presence within it of a sufficient number of people who are willing to take up arms in its behalf. It is not first and foremost a virtue of the philosopher, who is not as such a thumotic man. But neither is it a primary concern of pious Christians, as Basil seems to imply by omitting any reference to it in his enumeration of the virtues. On a practical level, this may well be the point at which classical philosophy and Christianity draw nearest to each other since in principle the latter gives little encouragement to spiritedness and refuses to be impressed by the noble objects to which it is mainly directed. For anyone who took the Gospel message seriously, even the most glorious human achievements paled into insignificance. Other human beings could be mesmerized by the splendor of empire and the rewards of earthly glory. The Christian, who knew that kingdoms were clay and that it was paltry to be Caesar, had a better world to look forward to. In Basil's own words,

> neither renown of ancestry, nor strength of body, nor beauty, nor stature, nor honors bestowed by all mankind, nor kingship itself, nor any other human attribute that one might mention, do we judge great; nay, we do not even look with admiration upon those who possess them, but our hopes lead us forward to a more distant time, and everything we do is by way of preparation for the next life.[27]

It might be mentioned, if only in passing, that this depreciation of spiritedness and of the various forms of human greatness to which it can give rise lies at the root of the difficulties that the Christian tradition was often to experience in regard to such matters. Since by definition the philosophic life was not likely to appeal to any but a small number of privileged and essentially nonthumotic souls, there was little chance of it posing an immediate threat to the security of the city. Philosophers do not generally make good soldiers anyway, and their presence in the army might have proved more of a liability than an asset. Not so with Christianity, which attaches less importance to men's natural dispositions and, as a religion of love, has little or nothing to say about the harsher duties they might be required to perform as citizens of a particular society. The result was a tendency on the part of some Christians to look down on military valor and shun all activities involving the use of violence against their fellow human beings. By stressing *erōs* at the expense of *thumos*, however, Christianity left the spirited part of the soul relatively unattended and thus paved the way for its reassertion in the shape of certain excesses against which the classical political philosophers had repeatedly warned.

It is paradoxical at first glance but by no means unfair to say that the dim view of spiritedness reflected in Basil's essay is responsible for both the softness and the fanaticism or the "pious cruelties" for which Christianity has so often been criticized by its modern adversaries.[28]

The more radical contrast between Basil and Socrates nevertheless lies elsewhere, in the theoretical status ascribed to moral virtue on one side or the other. The problem, not a simple one to begin with, is further complicated by the fact that Xenophon, who writes in defense of Socrates, goes out of his way to present his hero as having been morally good and pious in the sense in which these terms were taken by his contemporaries and continue to be taken by decent and pious human beings. His discussion thus deliberately obscures the problematic character that justice assumes the moment the larger issue of its cosmic support or its rootedness in nature as distinguished from mere personal or social utility is brought to the fore. It may well be that in the absence of a legislating God—and there is no unimpeachable evidence that the God of which Socrates speaks is such a God—the question of the natural basis of morality finds no completely satisfying answer. Differently and more cogently stated, one cannot guarantee that justice as the fixed disposition to seek the good of others always redounds to the personal benefit of the one who practices it.[29] As Scripture itself teaches, it all too frequently happens that the race is not to the swiftest, nor bread to the wise, nor favor to those who deserve it.[30]

Basil, needless to say, had no such philosophic doubts about the inner consistency of the moral order, which he saw as firmly grounded in the mind and will of a God who directs all things to their prescribed ends, rewarding or punishing each individual human being according to his just deserts. Moral virtue may have been no more than a means to the higher goal of eternal life, but it was a necessary means, the acquisition of which, though lying beyond the capacity of a fallen human nature, was made possible by the grace of a loving and infinitely generous God. On this particular point, Basil's position differs not only from that of Socrates but that of Dio Chrysostom, for whom virtue is indeed a "veritable goddess" and who, in true Stoic fashion, holds it to be the highest of all human achievements.[31]

This brings us back to the question with which we started and which concerns the basic reason for which the Middle Ages were loath to personify general virtue and consistently refrained from doing so. Whether or not Panofsky was justified in claiming that this striking phenomenon is traceable to the fear that such a personification might have been interpreted as a blasphemous reversion to paganism is a matter that can only be settled on the basis of the historical documents at our disposal. Still, one would be hard pressed to deny that the newly rediscovered notion of universal justice as the social virtue *par excellence* presented a definite threat to a society in which the whole of the political order was thought to be ordered to the common good of the city of God. If justice thus understood encompasses all of man's actions, it could legitimately prescribe even those actions which pertain to divine worship and the duties of religion. Thomas Aquinas, who was not unaware of the problem, tried to solve it by arguing that, while the individual human being is essentially a part of the political community to which he belongs, "he is not ordered to it with regard to the whole of himself and to all that he has."[32] No wonder that he and most of his contemporaries were averse to accepting Aristotle's definition as it stood. To speak of legal justice without any further qualification would have amounted to nothing less than a recognition of the polis and its regime as a total way of life, the primary locus of virtue, the object of the loyal citizen's noblest and most profound attachments, and the sole horizon capable of lending meaning and substance to his highest activities.[33] The pagan gods were dead and so also was the ancient world of politics with which their existence was originally bound up. No one was yet ready to bow once again before the *dea virtus* or restore the temples that Rome, that most political of all nations, had formerly erected in her honor. In this deeper sense, Panofsky was absolutely right. As long as Christendom remained intact, the exaltation of legal justice as the supreme virtue was well-nigh unthinkable. The real break came only with the Renaissance and its endeavors to revitalize the political life, either by advocating a return to Western man's pre-Christian past or by experimenting with the new "modes and orders" to which he was about to be introduced.

NOTES

1. E. Panofsky, *Hercules am Scheidewege und andere antike Bildstoffe in der neueren Kunst* (Leipzig and Berlin: B. G. Teubner, 1930), esp. 150-66.

2. Cf. T. E. Mommsen, *Medieval and Renaissance Studies.* ch. 9: "Petrarch and the Story of the Choice of Hercules" (Ithaca, NY: Cornell University Press, 1959), esp. 175-81.

3. Augustine, *De civitate Dei* (*City of God*) IV.20-21.

4. See on this subject the impressive list of texts compiled by O. Lottin. "Le concept de justice chez les théologiens du moyen âge avant l'introduction d'Aristote." *Revue Thomiste* 44 (1938): 511-21.

5. The use of the word "cardinal" to designate the four main moral virtues appears to have originated with St. Ambrose, *Commentary on Luke's Gospel* V.49 and 62. These were the virtues on which the whole of the moral life in some way turns,

in much the same way that, according to Proverbs 26:14, a door turns on its hinge (*cardo*) and a lazy man on his bed.

6. Cicero, *De inventione* II.53.160.

7. Albert's remarks on this subject are to be found in his *Summa de bono,* in which general justice is said to refer either to the effects of sanctifying grace, or to the totality of the acquired virtues, or else to all human acts insofar as they conform to human nature and the duties incumbent upon it. Cf. Lottin, "Le concept de justice," 519.

8. Thomas devotes a single article to justice as a general virtue in the *Summa Theologiae* II-II, qu. 58, a. 5, but he often alludes to it elsewhere, usually by way of a comparison with charity. Cf. I-II, qu. 60, a. 3, ad 2m; II-II, qu. 33, a. 1, ad lm; qu. 58, a. 6-7; qu. 61, a. 1; qu. 79, a. 1; qu. 81, a. 8, ad lm; qu. 102, a. 1, ad 3m; *De veritate* 28.1; *Commentary on the Ethics of Aristotle* V. lect. 2.

9. Cf. Dante, *Monarchia,* I.11, which draws heavily on Aristotle's thematic discussion of legal justice in *Nicomachean Ethics* V.I; cf. also Marsilius, *Defensor pacis,* I.10-11;II.12, *et passim.*

10. English translation in A. Pegis, ed., *The Wisdom of Catholicism* (New York: Random House, 1949), 8-26.

11. Xenophon, *Memorabilia* II.1.21-34. For a detailed analysis of this passage, see L. Strauss, *Xenophon's Socrates* (Ithaca, NY: Cornell University Press, 1972), 32-39, on which the following interpretation relies extensively.

12. On Aristippus, cf. Diogenes Laertius, *Lives s.v.*

13. For the classic argument against the political life on Epicurean grounds, as well as for the counterargument, cf. Cicero, *De re publica* I.3ff.

14. Cf. Aristotle, *Politics* VII.1324a14-37, where the *bios xenikos* is mentioned but hardly discussed at all as an alternative worthy of consideration.

15. For the manner in which even the most illustrious statesmen—Pericles, Cimon, Miltiades, and Themistocles—are sometimes treated by their own cities, cf. Plato, *Gorgias,* 515c-516e. The reader of the *Memorabilia* cannot help thinking here of the treatment meted out to Socrates by his fellow Athenians.

16. Cf. Strauss, *Xenophon's Socrates* 34.

17. Justin, *Second Apology* II.

18. Cicero, *De officiis* I.32.117-18; cf. III.5.25.

19. Dio Chrysostom, *First Discourse on Kingship* 66ff. The same emphasis on the importance of a good education at an early age reappears in Lactantius, *Divine Institutes* VI.3.6, and St. Jerome, *Letter* 107.6, in both cases with reference to the letter Y, the graphic symbol of the choice between good and evil in the Pythagorean tradition.

20. See on this point the remarks by T. L. Shear, *The Influence of Plato on St. Basil* (Baltimore, MD: J. N. Furst, Co., 1906), 42, 53.

21. The point is well made by Panofsky, *Hercules,* 153, and by Mommsen, "Petrarch," 193-96.

22. For various other examples of the same tactic in Basil's essay, cf. E. L.

Fortin, "Christianity and Hellenism in Basil the Great's Address *Ad Adulescentes*," in ch. 9 of this volume.

23. See, for a survey of these various interpretations, L. Schucan, *Das Nachleben von Basilius Magnus "ad adulescentes": ein Beitrag zur Geschichte des christlichen Humanismus* (Geneva: Droz, 1973). J. Quasten, *Patrology*, vol. III (Utrecht: Spectrum and Westminster, MD: Newman Press, 1966), 214, thinks that Basil's "exhortation is written with extraordinary feeling for the lasting values of Hellenistic learning" and sees its "broadmindedness" as having had "a strong influence on the attitude of the Church toward the classical tradition." A different assessment is offered by H.-I. Marrou, for whom Basil's work is nothing but a "homily" on the dangers of pagan literature and the means of guarding against them; *Histoire de l'éducation dans l'antiquité* (Paris: Editions du Seuil, 1950), 286.

24. Philostratus, *Life of Apollontius of Tyana* VI.10. Maximus of Tyre, *Oratio* XIV.1. Justin, *Second Apology* II. In Xenophon, the verb *auchmeo*, "to be squalid," is used by Virtue to describe the ravages of a life of self-indulgence (II.1.31).

25. Cicero, *De officiis* III.5.25. Dio Chrysostom, *First Discourse on Kingship* 83.

26. See on this whole issue the penetrating remarks by C. Bruell, "Strauss on Xenophon's Socrates," *The Political Science Reviewer* 14 (1984): 263-318.

27. Basil, *To Young Men* 2.

28. Cf. *inter multos alios*, Machiavelli, *The Prince*, ch. 21 (on Ferdinand of Aragon's *pietosa crudeltà*) and *Discourses* II.2 and III.27 (on the lack of spiritedness bred by Christianity). Also Rousseau, *Social Contact* IV.8.

29. Cf. Aristotle, *Nicomachean Ethics* V.1130a3-5.

30. Cf. Ecclesiastes 9:11.

31. Dio Chrysostom, *First Discourse on Kingship* 73 and 83.

32. *Summa Theologiae* I-II, qu. 21, a. 4, ad 3m. On the subordination of the ends of civil society to the common good of the "heavenly Jerusalem," cf. *De virt. in communi*, art. 9, *corp.; On Kingship*, ed. G. B. Phelan (Toronto: Pontifical Institute of Medieval Studies, 1949), II.3-4, 58-67.

33. No one in the modern period has captured the unitary spirit of the classical polis better than Rousseau, even if the terms used to express it betray his own emphatically modern outlook. See, for example, *Social Contract* II.7, in *The Essential Rousseau*, translated by L. Blair (New York: New American Library, 1974), 36: "Anyone who dares to undertake the task of instituting a nation must feel himself capable of changing human nature, so to speak; of transforming each individual, who by himself is a complete and solitary whole, into a part of a greater whole from which he, in a sense, receives his life and his being; of marring man's constitution in order to strengthen it; of substituting a partial and moral existence for the physical and independent existence that we have all received from nature. He must, in short, take away man's resources to give him others that are foreign to him and cannot be used without the help of other men. The more completely these natural resources are annihilated, the greater and more durable are the acquired ones and the stronger and more perfect are the new institutions. If, then, each citizen is nothing, and can do

nothing, without all the others, and if the resources acquired by the whole are equal or superior to the sum of all the individual's natural resources, legislation can be said to have reached its highest possible degree of perfection."

THE *VIRI NOVI* OF ARNOBIUS AND THE CONFLICT BETWEEN FAITH AND REASON IN THE EARLY CHRISTIAN CENTURIES

Book Two of Arnobius's *Adversus nationes* is by far the most theoretical of the seven books that the work as a whole comprises. Its special theme is the objections leveled at Christianity on philosophic grounds, as distinguished from the objections leveled at it on political grounds, which form the subject matter of Book One. The major portion of the book is in fact devoted to a lengthy discussion of the pagan doctrine of the soul. Partly because of the persistent lack of agreement as to its correct interpretation, partly because of the neglect, not to say the contempt, of which the author has been the victim of late, the unique interest of Arnobius's text does not appear to have been fully recognized by modern historians. This enigmatic early fourth-century writer whom Jerome recommended for his learning[1] but who is now generally thought to occupy a kind of no man's land between pagan speculation and the Christian faith, neither of which he supposedly understood very well,[2] could very well be a privileged first witness, if not necessarily a most reliable witness, to the emergence of a new and decisive encounter between revealed religion and philosophy, which was to absorb the energies of the best theologians for the next three centuries and shape the destiny of Christianity down to our time.

The position that Arnobius singles out for particular consideration is ascribed to a group of thinkers to whom he refers cryptically as "new men" or "upstarts" (*viri novi*)[3] and elsewhere, more disparagingly, as "half-baked philosophers" (*scioli*)[4] without ever naming them, in keeping with his habit of preserving the anonymity of the contemporaries against whom his attacks are directed. As we shall see, the identity of the nameless adversary has given rise to considerable speculation on the part of the few scholars who have dealt with the subject in recent years.

In a brilliant and ingenious article originally published in 1922 and later reprinted in his *Aspects mystiques de la Rome païenne*,[5] J. Carcopino attempted to show that the *viri novi,* were Hermetists and that, following an ancient and widely attested tradition, Plato and Pythagoras, whose names also occur in Arnobius's list of pagan authorities, were mentioned only as disciples of Hermes Trismegistus.[6] In spite of his manifest and at times violent opposition to the doctrines of the Hermetists, Arnobius himself, so Carcopino argues, supposedly did not hold views essentially different from theirs. As a recent convert to Christianity, he simply fastened on the Hermetists as the preferred target of his diatribes "because it is always between neighboring schools of thought that the liveliest controversies take place and . . . that the passage from one conviction to another is most easily effected."[7] At one moment in his career, scholars believe Arnobius parted company with his former fellow travelers and transferred his allegiance to the Christian faith, but without substantially altering his position or giving up any of the intellectual weapons with which he had once fought. The paradoxical conclusion at which the article arrives is that the sole doctrinal initiative of this "strange apologist" consisted in reproducing and propagating in the name of Christ—*Christo auctore*—the salutary teachings of Hermes and Asclepius.[8]

Some years later, in a searching analysis of the same text,[9] Père Festugière began by equating the *viri novi* neither with the Hermetists nor the Platonists but with a third group of writers to whom Arnobius refers as "the others" (*caeteri*) and whom Festugière is at first tempted to regard as a specific Gnostic sect united in its acceptance of a common doctrine.[10] This initial assumption is abandoned, somewhat unexpectedly and without warning, in the course of his long essay in favor of a new hypothesis according to which the label *viri novi* is taken to designate, not a distinct sect attached to a particular brand of Gnosticism, but a more or less heterogeneous group professing a mixed doctrine whose elements are traceable to a variety of sources such as Hermetism, Neopythagoreanism (Numenius), Neoplatonism (Porphyry), and the apocryphal literature inspired by Oriental Gnosticism (*Chaldaean Oracles,* pseudo-Zoroastrian works, and the like).[11] In short, Arnobius's attack was aimed at "the principal dogmas propagated in his day by the missionaries of that complex religious movement known as Gnosticism."[12]

Festugière's interpretation was subsequently challenged by Pierre Courcelle,[13] who, in a tightly-reasoned case supported by carefully assembled textual data, was apparently able to demonstrate that the doctrine of the *viri novi* was more coherent than Festugière had in the end been willing to admit and that at least certain sections of Book Two, if not the whole of it, could be adequately explained without postulating the existence of sources as disparate as those to which Festugière had adverted. The philosophers whom Arnobius had in mind are unmistakably Neoplatonists and not Gnostics. Specifically, Arnobius could have found and probably did find in Porphyry's *De regressu animae* many of the theories to which he alludes and particularly the enumeration of the different methods or ways of salvation, namely, asceticism or the way of the philosophers, intercessory prayers (theurgy) or the way of the magi, and animal sacrifices or the way of the Etruscans.[14] Thus, while the doctrine of the *viri novi* does not by itself exhaust the content of Book Two, it can nevertheless be said to be one to the extent to which it corresponds to the doctrine preferred and expounded by Porphyry, as opposed to the other doctrines discussed and presumably rejected by him.[15]

Courcelle's argument, which immediately won Carcopino's verbal support,[16] seemed to have settled the issue once and for all, only to be challenged in turn by M. Mazza, who has since rallied to Festugière's defense and mustered a wealth of new evidence in behalf of what purports to be a slightly modified version of his thesis.[17] According to Mazza, Arnobius's *viri novi* are not Gnostics purely and simply but a definite Gnostic sect invested with special characteristics and possessed of its own physiognomy.[18] The new or refurbished theory emphasizes the distinction between Gnosticism in general, which is at most a loose and essentially syncretistic system erected on the shaky foundation of myth and popular philosophy, and the dissenting or heretical Gnostic sect in question, whose teachings exhibited a substantial unity and posed what may well have been the most formidable threat that Christianity had had to face in the third century. Its members adhered to the scheme of the descent and ascent of the soul, which Mazza regards as the basic and most distinctive tenet of Gnosticism.[19] The word *novus* itself, we are told, belongs in a special way to Gnostic terminology and refers in the present context to the regeneration or conversion which the adherents of the doctrine claimed to have undergone; in which case the *viri novi*—the "converts"—bear a close affinity to the *allogeneis* or "strangers" who likewise play a prominent role in Gnostic speculation.[20] Basing himself on R. Harder's distinction between "source" and "tradition,"[21] Mazza finds convincing proof for the validity of his thesis in the overall agreement between the views which Arnobius attributes to the *viri novi* and the subtle complex of interwoven ideas proper to the Gnostic literature of the period, rather than in Arnobius's demonstrated knowledge and use of any one source from which the bulk of his information might have been derived.[22] Assuming the possible existence of some such single source, Mazza leans toward the once popular but in recent times largely discredited hypothesis according to which Arnobius is indebted either directly or indirectly to Cornelius Labeo, a shadowy figure whose dates remain uncertain and whose thought is known only through a small number of isolated fragments preserved by Augustine and Macrobius.[23]

For all its rich documentation and impressive scholarship, however, Mazza's article raises as many questions as it answers. To mention only a few of the more obvious ones: the framework of descent and ascent, which the author invokes as the touchstone of the Gnostic authenticity of the doctrine under scrutiny, is indeed present in Arnobius or presupposed by him, but since it is common to both Gnosticism and Neoplatonism, it can hardly serve as a criterion to distinguish one from the other. Neither does the fact that Arnobius places the doctrine of the *viri novi* under the patronage of Mercury or Hermes point necessarily to a Gnostic or Hermetic origin. The allusion to Mercury as the original source of Platonic and Pythagorean philosophy could simply conform to an old tradition which has its roots in Plato himself and of which there are traces to be found elsewhere in the Platonic literature of late antiquity.[24] Furthermore, although Mazza tends to make short shrift of them, the precise textual parallels cited by Courcelle would seem to establish beyond any reasonable doubt the existence of specifically Neoplatonic elements in the thought of the *viri novi* and perhaps even the basically Neoplatonic character of that thought. At any rate they provide a more reliable clue to the identity of the *viri novi* than the generic affinities that Mazza detects between the text of Arnobius and the mass of Gnostic materials which he has been able to gather. Courcelle's solution has the added advantage of accounting for the presence of Gnostic ideas in Arnobius, inasmuch as there is reason to believe that these ideas were discussed by Porphyry, whereas some of the doctrines mentioned by Arnobius have no known equivalent in Gnostic speculation and are even directly opposed to it. In particular, one is hard put to find in the position imputed to the *viri novi* any vestige of the radical dualism or acosmism which lies at the heart of the Gnostic conception of the world.[25] This is not to deny the pervasive influence of Platonic thought on Gnosticism or the agreement between the two schools on a wide variety of common issues.[26] But the basic differences remain and Mazza is able to explain them away only by a sleight of hand which consists in transforming an earlier Platonist like Numenius into a Gnostic.[27] Finally, in the absence of a larger context, the three fragments adduced from Labeo present no more than a vague similarity with the corresponding passages in Arnobius and do not warrant anything like a firm conclusion concerning the possibility of a definite link between the two authors.[28]

Regardless of whether or not one agrees *in toto* with the verdict of any of these scholars and despite the many valuable insights which their learned research has yielded, a number of problems remain to which, as far as I can see, no completely satisfactory solution has yet been offered.

First of all, none of the proposed interpretations has succeeded in linking clearly the various themes around which the discussion revolves and which form as it were the warp and woof of Arnobius's argument against the *viri novi*. I refer to such notions as the divine, incorporeal, rational, immortal, and impeccable nature of the soul, its intermediary quality, its preexistence, its innate knowledge, the theory of reminiscence, man's superiority over all the other animals, the descent of the soul, its union with the body and the impediments resulting from that union. All of these notions are obviously related in one way or another to the problem of the human soul. For each one of them, numerous parallels from older or contemporary literature have been produced, and it would be easy to add to the list. The interesting question, however, is whether there is not some strand which would enable us to establish a more precise relationship among them, bring to light the central core around which they cluster, and reveal more clearly the author's method of procedure.

Secondly, it is not fully clear why Arnobius has chosen to call his adversaries *viri novi*. If these adversaries are really the Platonists or, as we would say, the Neoplatonists, it seems unlikely that anyone would think of referring to them as "new" men. Platonism was scarcely considered at the time as a new doctrine. Nor does it suffice to say that the philosophers so designated were precisely Neoplatonists. Although the suggestion has a certain prima facie plausibility, it may be slightly anachronistic, inasmuch as the label is an invention of nineteenth-century scholarship, for which one would be hard pressed to find an exact equivalent in ancient times. If anything, the representatives of the Platonic school of late antiquity always claimed to be the legitimate heirs of Plato and never thought of themselves as anything but Platonists.

Finally, one observes that Arnobius agrees with and often takes over ideas whose Platonic origin cannot be doubted. Like Plato, he insists on the fact that the soul is an intermediate substance.[29] He gives Plato credit for having taught that evildoers would be punished in the afterlife[30] and explicitly contrasts his stand on this point, which he finds more compatible with the teachings of the Christian faith, to that of his own opponents.[31] If these opponents are none other than the Neoplatonists, one would have to suppose either that Arnobius knew Plato well enough to undertake a critique of the interpretation which Plato's own disciples had given of the thought of their master, or else that Arnobius himself finally opted for a position identical or analogous to that of his adversaries. In the latter case, we would be faced with an apparent contradiction similar to the one uncovered with a good deal of penetration by Carcopino, except for the fact that, instead of being a crypto-Hermetist, Arnobius would be a crypto-Platonist fighting on the Christian side with Platonic arms.

Having set out to prove that Arnobius was doing battle either with Gnosticism in general or with a particular Gnostic sect, both Festugière and Mazza were impelled to search for corroborating evidence in earlier or contemporary Gnostic documents. If, reversing the procedure, one operates on the assumption that Arnobius was confronted, as he himself appears to be telling us, with a wholly new adversary or group of adversaries, that is to say, with a school of philosophy which was somehow in the ascendancy, one would normally expect to find more numerous and more accurate parallels in the literature of the following rather than the preceding centuries. The observations that follow will, I hope, confirm that supposition and bring the whole question into sharper focus.

The central and most important section of Book Two is clearly intended as an effort to depreciate the human soul in response to the allegedly exorbitant claims raised on its behalf by the philosophers. Accordingly, after a brief summary of the doctrine of the *viri novi*,[32] Arnobius takes issue with the assertion that the soul is a rational substance,[33] that it is incorporeal,[34] that it is by nature simple and immortal,[35] and above all that it is divine or consubstantial with the divine essence.[36] No one to my knowledge has noticed that these ideas reappear in exactly the same form and the same sequence in a whole series of Neoplatonic treatises or manuals dating from the end of antiquity and constitute what may be regarded as the classic framework within which the Neoplatonic doctrine was customarily set forth.[37]

The first idea to be questioned is that man is a rational being,[38] at least in the sense in which the proposition was understood by Arnobius's opponents. For the sake of convenience, we may begin by setting side by side some of Arnobius's more characteristic statements to that effect and a series of statements by Cassiodorus on the same subject.

Arnobius, *Adversus nationes*, II.17, p. 85, 21 ff. M:	Cassiodorus, *De anima, Patrologia Latina* 70, col. 1284 D:
Sed *rationales nos sumus* et intellegentia *vincimus omne genus*	*Rationem vero homini inesse* quis dubitet? quando divina tractat,

mutorum . . . Vellem tamen scire
quaenam sit haec *ratio, per quam
sumus potiores animalium
generibus cunctis* . . .

Quodsi ministras manus illis etiam
donare parens natura voluisset,
dubitabile non foret, quin et ipsa
construerent moenium alta fastigia
et artificiosas excuderent novitates
. . . . (18) Vestem illa non norunt,
sellas *naves* atque *aratra*
compingere nec denique
superlectilem ceteram quam
familiaris usus exposcit . . . Neque
cum animis *artes* caeli ex
penetralibus ceciderunt . . .

(19) Numquam, inquam, crederent
typho et adrogantia sublevati prima
esse se numina et aequalia principis
summitati, quia grammaticam
musicam oratoriam pepererunt et
geometricas formulas . . .

(40, p. 113,4ff.) imperatas
extollerent *fruges . . . effoderent
altos montes* et viscera ignota
terrarum in materias verterent alieni
nominis atque usus, *penetrarent
abditas* discrimine cum capitis
nationes . . .

humana sapit, *artibus docetur
egregiis, disciplinis eruditur;* et hinc
cetera animalia decenter *excellit*
quod eum *ratio* decora componit
. . . .

Litterarum formas reperit,
diversarum *artium utilitates
disciplinasque* protulit, civitates
defensibili muro cinxit, varii generis
armenta ejecit, meliores *fructus* per
industriam exegit, *terras transcurrit,*
abyssos alato (apto ?) *navigio,
vastos montes* in usum viantium
perforavit, portus ad utilitatem
navigantium lunari dispositione
conclusit, ornavit pulcherrima
fabricarum dispositione tellurem.
Quis jam de ejus ratione dubitet
quando ab auctore suo illuminata
facit arte conspici quod debeat sub
omni celebritate laudari.

(1287 C) Nec de illis sumus qui
dicunt recolere magis animas quam
discere *usuales artes* et reliquas
disciplinas; cum et ad interrogata
sint paratae, ubi potuerint intellectu
perveniente contingere, et nova sic
audiant, quae nihil ex eis ante
didicissent

A careful comparison of these texts reveals certain points of contact
which are all the more striking as they involve precise and minute details.
In both cases the theme of the rationality of the soul is clearly enunciated
at the outset (*sed rationales nos sumus—rationem vero homini inesse*),
although it is approached from two diametrically opposed points of view.

Cassiodorus subscribes to the thesis and proceeds to illustrate it by means of various examples. Arnobius, on the other hand, finds it suspect and brings it up for the sole purpose of criticizing it. Whereas Cassiodorus presents reason as that which distinguishes man from the other animals and accounts for his superiority over them (*et hinc cetera animalia . . . excellit*), Arnobius asks what that reason is worth and what man's alleged superiority over the beasts might be (*vellem . . . scire quaenam est haec ratio per quam sumus potiores animalium generibus cunctis*). Both authors cite as proof of the rational or would-be rational nature of the soul the case of the arts and sciences, which seems to have been topical, judging from its presence in numerous other treatises from the same period.[39] Arnobius elaborates upon the point, enumerating some of the liberal arts (grammar, music, rhetoric, geometry) and alluding later to the musician, the dialectician, the geometer, the orator, the poet, and the grammarian.[40] There follows a list of the different activities and products of human reason. One notices particularly the reference on the part of both authors to the ramparts of cities (*civitates defensibili muro cinxit—construerent moenium alta fastigia*), to the arts of navigation (*navigium—naves*) and of agriculture (*fructus per industrias exegit—imperatas extollerent fruges*), to voyages to distant lands (*terras transcurrit—penetrarent abditas nationes*), and finally to the arts by which man seeks to satisfy his everyday needs (*diversarum artium utilitates—superlectilem ceteram quam familiaris usus exposcit*). While they stand at opposite poles on each of these points, both authors are at one in rejecting the pagan doctrine of recollection,[41] which was inseparable from the notion of the soul's pre-existence and which is often cited in the Neoplatonic treatises as further evidence of its rationality.[42] Even Cassiodorus, who is on the whole sympathetic to the Neoplatonic doctrine, was compelled to modify it on this point in accordance with the demands of the Christian faith.

However significant the foregoing parallels may be, they nevertheless need to be complemented by a series of comparisons with other Neoplatonic texts, especially since Cassiodorus's *De anima* remains for the most part sketchy and incomplete. We shall discover a new set of equally valuable clues if we turn to Nemesius's *De natura hominis,* which deals at greater length with the specific problem of the soul's rationality.

Like Arnobius, Nemesius cites the example of the newborn child[43] and goes on to explain that if reason has not yet manifested itself in him, it will not be long before it does so. Against such a view Arnobius argues that if by any chance the infant were to be secluded from the rest of mankind, reason would never develop in him and nothing would distinguish him from brute animals. Again like Arnobius, Nemesius speaks of the intelligence or foresight of animals, but only to deny that it has its source in reason, since it merely betrays a natural prudence,[44] which God has given to animals in order that they might be able to provide for themselves. That prudence is no more than a shadow or an image of reason,[45] as is evidenced by the fact that their pattern of behavior never changes. Even their tricks are all alike, whereas man's works follow "a thousand different paths."[46] Arnobius, as might have been anticipated, denies that there is an essential difference on this score between men and beasts, inasmuch as the latter display an astonishing skill in building their shelters, in securing their sustenance, and in protecting themselves against dangers of various sorts.[47]

Another revealing detail shows up in the accompanying discussion of the "hands" of animals. Nemesius introduces the idea in the form of an objection: some people contend that if the works of animals are inferior to those of men, it is simply because their bodies lack the proper shape. Take man's fingers away from him and you automatically deprive him of the possibility of practicing any of those arts for which he is justly famous; to which Nemesius replies that God never acts without a purpose and that it would be absurd to think that he would have endowed animals with reason without at the same time giving them the bodily instruments needed for its exercise.[48] The same question is raised by Arnobius, who resolves it in a manner consistent with his own premises. Provided with a pair of hands, animals would be in a position to compete with men in all things. Arnobius readily concedes the existence in animals of an approximation of reason but somehow manages to turn the argument in his favor: that semblance of reason is such that animals are capable of producing works which men cannot emulate, however clever they may be and whatever advantage the possession of hands may confer upon them.[49]

Both authors likewise relate the present doctrine to the problem of the transmigration of souls. Nemesius notes in this connection the dissensions that existed within the Platonic school itself: some Platonists were of the opinion that all souls without exception were rational, including those of brutes, and took Plato's notion of metempsychosis at face value; others maintained that there was a real distinction between rational and irrational souls and interpreted in a metaphorical sense those passages in Plato's works which deal with transmigration: human souls do not literally pass into the bodies of animals but simply become irascible, rapacious, or lascivious, causing men to behave like lions, wolves, or donkeys.[50] Nemesius naturally rejects the idea of metempsychosis and aligns himself with those philosophers, such as Iamblichus, who held that the souls of men and of brutes belonged to different species.[51] Without necessarily approving the doctrine taught by his opponents, Arnobius again looks for a way of using it against them.[52] If they can go so far as to assert that after death the souls of the wicked are reincarnated in the bodies of animals, it must be that the distance which separates men from brutes is not as great as they would have us believe:

> But if this also is true, as is said in the more hidden mysteries, that the souls
> of the wicked go into cattle and other beasts after they have been removed
> from human bodies, it is more clearly demonstrated that we are near them
> and not removed from them by any appreciable difference; for there is a
> factor in both us and them by reason of which animate beings are said to
> exist and to have the power of living motion.[53]

Interestingly enough, Nemesius attributes the doctrine of metempsychosis
and of the rational character of all souls to Cronius, one of the authors
under whose authority Arnobius had from the beginning placed the teachings of the *viri novi*.[54]

Since the treatises of Nemesius and Cassiodorus are mostly doxo-
graphic in character and draw much of their information from Neoplatonic
sources, one cannot fail to be impressed by the convergences noted thus
far. It could still be objected that we are dealing for the most part with
rhetorical or philosophic commonplaces and, hence, that similarities of this
kind, numerous as they may be, are bound to remain inconclusive. Such
is not the case, however, as we shall see.

All of the preceding remarks concerning the rational nature of the
human soul are rooted in the works of the Neoplatonists in the notion of
the soul as an incorporeal or spiritual substance. To insure the efficacy of
his refutation, Arnobius was forced to attack the very foundation of the
rival doctrine, and this he did not neglect to do. Having concluded his
critique of the rationality of the soul, he appropriately turns to the subject
of its incorporeity. The new problem is introduced by a question which
brings the issue clearly to the fore: "And what has happened to that
statement that souls have no bodily substance?"[55]

The idea that the soul is an incorporeal substance was, needless to say,
an integral part of the Platonic doctrine and constitutes one of the habitual
chapter headings of the late Neoplatonic treatises. Its treatment is inevitably bound up with the question of the manner in which a spiritual
substance such as the soul could be joined to a material substance such as
the body. The thrust of Arnobius' argument, which is not immediately
apparent, is perhaps best illustrated by the following comparison with St.
Augustine:

Arnobius, *Adversus nationes* II.7, p. 73, 8 M.:	Augustine, *Epistola* 137.11 Goldb. (*CSEL* 44):
quid sit quod *humores* universi unum corpus efficiant MIXTIONE,	

solum oleum respuat immersionem
in se pati, sed in suam naturam
impenetrabile semper perspicue
colligatur . . .

(II.26, p. 98, 1) quidquid enim
causa ingruente nonnulla ita mutatur
et vertitur UT INTEGRITATEM
SUAM RETINERE NON POSSIT,
id necesse est iudicari natura esse
passivum. Quod autem est
promptum atque expositum
passioni, CORRUPTIBILE esse
ipsa passibilitate interveniente
denuntiat . . . Neque enim nihil
omnino perpessae aut
INTEGRITATEM
CONSERVANTES SUAM possunt
rerum scientiam ponere . . .

in illa ergo persona MIXTURA est
animae et corporis, in hac persona
MIXTURA est dei et hominis, si
tamen recedat auditor a
consuetudine corporum, qua solent
duo *liquores* ita MISCERI UT
NEUTRUM SERVET
INTEGRITATEM SUAM et in
ipsis corporibus aeri lux
INCORRUPTA MISCEATUR.

Augustine, it should be noted, is not interested in the problem of the union of body and soul for its own sake and mentions it only because it furnishes him with a convenient argument with which to defend the dogma of the Incarnation against its pagan detractors. But the underlying doctrine is the same in both cases and it is stated in terms that are remarkably similar. That doctrine is all the more valuable in helping us to pinpoint Arnobius's adversaries as it appears to be totally foreign to Hermetic or Gnostic literature. One observes, to begin with, the recourse to the notion of mixture to illustrate the union of body and soul.[56] In the course of a protracted controversy with Stoicism on this point, and in order to account for the reciprocal action of the soul on the body and the body on the soul, the Neoplatonists had eventually been led to postulate a more intimate connection between the two substances than the one generally described in the Platonic dialogues.[57] The body was no longer thought to be a mere instrument or garment of the soul but to be closely united to it in such a way that the resultant "mixture" did not entail the corruption of either substance or their transformation into a third substance distinct from its original components. In a unique and mysterious fashion, both substances were seen as coming together to form a single being while still retaining their integrity: *integritatem conservantes suam.* Arnobius uses the same expression three times in a row,[58] thereby drawing attention to what he manifestly considers to be the key point of the discussion. In an effort to distinguish that mixture from the mixture which takes place when two bodily substances combine, the Neoplatonists usually cited the example of liquids which, if blended together, lose their identity and give rise to a wholly new substance. Arnobius is undoubtedly alluding to that phenomenon when he speaks of the total mixture of all liquids with the exception of oil. The same example is used by Nemesius and Priscianus in two passages which parallel closely Augustine's text and which can be traced back to the same Neoplatonic source.[59] But whereas Augustine accepts the Neoplatonic doctrine and makes capital of it to explain how the divine and human natures are united in Christ, Arnobius judges it to be of doubtful value: it is not true that the substance of the soul remains unaffected by its union with the body, as the philosophers themselves were compelled to admit, since that contact becomes for it an occasion of suffering and forgetfulness.

The same theory of the hypostatic union of body and soul is developed by means of a second analogy, taken this time from the realm of mathematics:

> Just as a number which is found to exist in bodies remains untouched and secure, even though it be buried in a thousand bodies, so it is necessary that souls, if they are bodiless, as it is claimed, suffer no forgetting of former things, however thoroughly they may be encompassed by material ties.[60]

According to the proposed doctrine, numbers do not have their foundation in bodies. Rather, like the soul to which, in this instance, they are compared, they are incorporeal forms, which exist prior to the body and are not in the least affected by any of the changes that occur in it.[61] One is immediately reminded of the numerical relationships by which bodies are governed in the Pythagorean theory later taken over by the Neoplatonists, or, more simply, of the familiar Platonic theory of lines and geometrical figures, which possess an ideal character and subsist independently of their embodiment in matter. A similar analogy occurs in Priscianus alongside that of the liquids and as part of the same general discussion:

> sed unitur (anima) quidem ut alligata flamma (forma ?), absoluta vero est *ut numerus* numero *appositus,* et neque sic *tacta* additur (*Solutiones*, 52 Bywater).

To be sure, the analogy is not identical in every respect, since, assuming the accuracy of the Latin translation of Priscianus's text, which is the only one to have survived, it has to do with the addition of one number to another rather than with the relation of numbers to bodies. But the mode of union advocated is the same and we are presented with a similar parallel between the soul and numbers as well as with the same fundamental

notion of the spiritual and undefilable character of numbers.
From the incorporeity of the soul Arnobius passes quite naturally and without interruption to the question of its simplicity and its immortality, which formed part and parcel of the Neoplatonic theory as it is developed in most contemporary treatises. The transition from one idea to the other is again explicitly marked: "What of the fact that this same reasoning not only shows they are not bodiless but also deprives them all of immortality and subjects them to the mortal limits of all life?"[62]

The order in which the ideas are taken up and their nexus point, here as elsewhere, to Neoplatonism and perhaps even to Plotinus himself as the chief source of the doctrine which Arnobius combats.[63] In any event, that doctrine is plainly reminiscent of *Enneads* IV.7, on "The Immortality of the Soul," which conforms in the main to the classic scheme of the Neoplatonic treatises to which we have repeatedly alluded.

Arnobius, *Adversus nationes* II.26, p. 98, 13 M.:	Plotinus, *Enneads* IV.7.12.
atquin nos arbitramur quod est *unum*, quod *immortale*, quod *simplex*, quacumque in re fuerit, necessario semper retinere pati . .	Psychē de mia kai haplē energeia ousa en tō zēn physis ou toinyn tautē phtharēsetai

In the first part of *Enneads* IV.7, Plotinus had established that the soul is an incorporeal substance.[64] From that observation, he infers that it is both simple and immortal. "All that is simple intelligence," he adds, "is impassible."[65] Considered in its pure state, the soul is an immortal being inhabiting "an intelligible and pure region."[66] The evils that cling to it "come from without . . . and, once it regains its purity, the greatest goods, prudence, and all the other virtues dwell in it as its property."[67] Its science, like its virtue, is eternal and can never be lost.[68] Its intelligence remains unaffected by the body even though it is itself now in the body and now out of it.[69] The whole discussion culminates in the assertion that such a being "must be divine, since it shares in divine things by reason of its kinship and common essence with the divine."[70]

It so happens that all of these ideas which Arnobius dismisses one after the other—the immortality, the inherent wisdom, and the divinity of the soul, its independence in relation to the body, its impassibility, and its inalienable virtue—are the very ideas which Plotinus had attempted to accredit with unprecedented vigor and conviction. One has only to read in the light of these considerations chapter 15 of Book II, where the doctrine of the *viri novi* is stated in condensed form for the first time:

Wherefore there is no reason that we should be deceived by what promises us vain hopes, something said by certain upstarts (*viri novi*) carried away by an extravagant opinion of themselves, namely, that souls are immortal, very near in degree of rank to the Lord and Ruler of Creation, brought forth by that begetter and Father; divine, wise, learned, and not touchable by any contact with the body. Because this is true and certain and we have been brought forth by the Perfect One in a perfection that is capable of no correction, we are living blameless and therefore incapable of criticism; good, just, and upright, possessing no faults. No passion subdues us, no lust dishonors us. We preserve and renew the practice of every virtue, and because the souls of all of us have flowed out from a single source, therefore we feel alike and are in agreement.[71]

It is barely conceivable that such a concurrence, coupled with the previously cited evidence, could be a simple matter of chance.

Along the same lines, one could show that the doctrine reported and criticized in chapters 29 and 30 of Book Two fits the same Neoplatonic description. The gist of Arnobius's argument is that, by teaching that the soul is naturally virtuous, sinless, and impassible, the *viri novi* have in practice opened the door to all the vices. Once granted that the soul is incapable of punishment, what is there to prevent men from indulging in evil deeds and giving free reign to their selfish impulses?[72] Festugière's conjecture that Arnobius may have been thinking of certain Gnostic sects which preached the *adiaphoria* of human acts misses the crux of the argument altogether.[73] Arnobius does not contend that the *viri novi* deny the intrinsic goodness or badness of human acts and regard all human acts as indifferent; he is merely calling attention to the practical consequences of their teaching. The *viri novi* themselves cannot be accused of immorality.[74] Quite the contrary; they are philosophers who prize virtue and incline to it, not by fear of divine sanctions, but by a natural desire to conform their own lives to the eternal order of things. But philosophers are the exception and not the rule.[75] Experience teaches that most men refrain from evil only when induced to do so by the prospect of divine rewards or punishments. To state publicly that the soul is impervious to suffering is to undermine the cause of virtue. If one accepts Plotinus's views concerning the impassibility of the soul, the conclusion would seem to be entirely justifiable.

Under the circumstances it is not difficult to see why Arnobius stresses the fact that the soul is not immutable, that it is by nature passible and hence punishable,[76] that it is not of itself immortal, and that it cannot in any way be looked upon as a divine being or a portion of the divine substance.[77] The doctrine which in this instance he opposes to that of his adversaries is sometimes known as conditional immortality and consists in stating that the soul is immortal, not indeed by reason of its nature, but "by the gift and favor of the Supreme Ruler."[78] What is peculiar about it is not the doctrine itself, which was fairly common in Christian literature both before and after Arnobius, but the terms in which it is couched. We learn, among other things, that the knowledge of God serves as a kind of "glue" binding together in one, elements that could otherwise be dissociated—*rei dissociabilis glutinum.*[79] Behind this unusual metaphor lies in all probability the thought expressed by Plato in the *Phaedo* to the effect that until such time as philosophy has laid hold of it, the soul is chained and as it were "glued" to the body (*proskekollêmenên*).[80] The Neoplatonic exegesis of that text established a connection between it and the account of the creation of the soul in the *Timaeus* as well as the figurative description of the fall of the soul through the loss of its wings in the *Phaedrus,* two dialogues to which Arnobius himself alludes in the sequel.[81] Arnobius's own adaptation of the metaphor substantially alters its primitive meaning, inasmuch as the glue no longer designates the affection of the soul for the body or its attachment to it but rather the divine action by which the soul, once brought into existence, is preserved from annihilation. To be more precise, it is a direct product of the conflation of two Platonic passages, that of the *Phaedo,* which alone speaks of the "gluing" of the soul, and that of the *Timaeus,* where the demiurge is said to fashion the soul by mixing its various elements in a crater, binding these elements together by an act of his will, and assigning to each soul its proper star.[82] The Neoplatonic pedigree of the doctrine is vouched for not only by the explicit mention of the *Phaedo,* quoted by Arnobius as the dialogue *On the Immortality of the Soul,*[83] but by the allusions to such related themes as the essential divinity of the soul,[84] its fall and subsequent imprisonment in the body,[85] its possible transmigrations,[86] its purification through philosophy,[87] its ascent made possible by the symbolic recovery of its wings, and the eventual return to its starry homeland.[88]

Perhaps the most telling detail in this regard is the sudden appearance in Arnobius's discussion of a second, equally distinctive simile which accompanies that of the glue in the *Phaedo* and is frequently joined to it in the Neoplatonic texts, namely, that of the nail by which pleasure and pain rivet the soul to the body.[89] Since the metaphors of the glue and the nail are both foreign to Plotinus but known to have been employed in combination by Porphyry, one may legitimately infer that Arnobius's source is more directly Porphyrian than Plotinian.[90] The plausibility of the inference is reinforced by Courcelle's demonstration that the section on the three ways of salvation which caps the account of the doctrine of the *viri novi* in the *Adversus nationes* was inspired by Porphyry.[91]

Another piece belonging to the same jigsaw puzzle is supplied by an earlier passage of Book Two in which the philosophers who gibe at the "credulity" of Christians are themselves derided as "jolly wits soaked and saturated with the pure wine (*meracum*) of wisdom."[92] That the same group of adversaries is intended by Arnobius is evident from the fact that the charge of credulity is mentioned and rebutted in virtually the same terms in both passages.[93] The image of drunkenness, which, taken by itself, could easily pass unnoticed, again harks back at least indirectly to the *Phaedo*. The original Platonic text has it that, when the soul hearkens to the body and bodily senses, it is drawn away by them into the realm of the variable, begins to wander about, and becomes confused and dizzy as though it were "drunk with wine."[94] When, on the other hand, it attends to itself, it regains its freedom and reestablishes its lost contact with the absolute and the changeless; which condition, according to Plato, is called wisdom.[95] Arnobius it seems, has simply transposed the metaphor to suit his purpose and rebuked his adversaries for allowing their wisdom to go to their heads. It is significant that the image of drunkenness is utilized in conjunction with that of glue in a passage from Ambrose's *De bono mortis* which bears traces of the same Neoplatonic and most likely Porphyrian influence.[96]

If one concedes the validity of the preceding demonstration, the answers to some of the larger questions raised earlier become somewhat clearer. Apart from the fact that the argument follows a noticeably consistent pattern, one can see without much difficulty why Arnobius reserves for his adversaries the title of *viri novi*. The expression applies remarkably well not to the Platonists in general but to Plotinus, Porphyry, and their immediate disciples, that is to say, to a reasonably well-defined and highly original group of thinkers whose teaching on certain specific points represented a more or less radical departure from what was presumed by others to be the orthodox Platonic position. Mazza is right, against Kroll, in contending that the word *novus* carries more than a purely chronological connotation.[97] But one need not appeal to any special meaning which it may have had in the Gnostic tradition in order to justify its use by Arnobius. There are indications in the *Enneads* themselves that the members of the Plotinian school had come to be regarded as brash innovators and were at pains to refute the charge of deviationism directed against them by the more conservative Platonists.[98] The implicit irony or sarcasm of Arnobius's argument is that, while the *viri novi* were quick to fault Christianity for its novelty,[99] they themselves were not immune to the same reproach. Modern research has long since established that, despite the existence of common characteristics, the Platonic school of late antiquity showed signs of an internal diversity which became more pronounced as time went on and attained its high point in Plotinus, the greatest philosophic genius since Aristotle and the representative par excellence of what is today called Neoplatonism.[100] Albinus already notes the lack of agreement among Platonists on the question of the rationality of the soul, some holding, as we have seen, that all souls were rational and others that the human soul alone was to be considered such.[101] The divergences become blatant the moment we turn to Iamblichus, Proclus, Simplicius, and Priscianus, all of whom are outspokenly critical of Plotinian psychology, accuse Plotinus of newfangling Plato's thought, and reproach him specifically with having overestimated the perfection of the human soul. Contrary to what Plotinus had taught, they deny that the soul is impeccable and prefer to dwell on its passible and changing nature.[102]

One can readily understand, then, why Arnobius was prompted to use Platonic arguments against the Neoplatonists and insist in his own right on the medium and hence inferior quality of the soul.[103] By so doing, he was merely taking his cue from those Platonists who rejected the Plotinian interpretation in the name of traditional Platonism. Carcopino has very shrewdly brought to light the seeming inconsistency of Arnobius's procedure, but he mistakenly takes the theory of the mid-rank position of the soul to be specifically Hermetic.[104] It is initially a Platonic doctrine, even if it eventually found its way into the *Corpus Hermeticum* and, for that matter, countless other philosophical or pseudo-philosophical texts of late antiquity.

If, as the evidence at hand suggests, the *viri novi*, against whom the *Adversus nationes* inveighs, are first and foremost the Neoplatonists, Arnobius's position in the history of early Christian thought may be quite different from that assigned to him by most modern scholars. The rare and hitherto largely ignored significance of Book II lies in the fact that it presents us with the first reasonably coherent and formally complete account of the confrontation between Christianity and the most important philosophic school of late antiquity. Far from being engaged in a rear guard action against the scattered remnants of a once-powerful Gnostic army, the author, long mistaken for a latecomer to the old and by then somewhat exhausted controversies of the second and third centuries,[105] has all the earmarks of a pioneer whose appearance on the scene coincides with the dramatic moment of the impact of Neoplatonism and who may be credited with having discerned, however imperfectly, the essential features of a challenge which, by virtue of the towering stature of the opponent, turned out to be incomparably greater than any with which Christianity had previously had to cope. His achievement is the more noteworthy as with the advent of Neoplatonism the conflict between faith and reason—a conflict precipitated by the uncompromising intellectualism of Neoplatonic thought and the overt hostility of its foremost representatives toward religious belief in general and the Christian faith in particular[106]—reaches what appears to have been a decisive climax.

One could, of course, point to the numerous encounters which had already taken place between Christianity and classical philosophy, especially within the Alexandrine school. But both traditional Platonism and Stoicism were less outwardly antireligious than Plotinian Neoplatonism. This is not to suggest that on a deeper level Plato's own thought might not prove to be as irreconcilable with orthodox religious belief as was Plotinus's rigid dogmatism, but only that in Plotinian philosophy, more than in any previous philosophy, the self-idolizing and essentially pharisaical tendency of the philosophic enterprise becomes fully apparent.[107] If such is the case, there is a very specific sense in which the head-on clash between Christianity and Greek philosophy, uncushioned by any accommodation to popular opinion, occurs only within the context of the situation created by the emergence of Neoplatonism as the dominant philosophic force of late antiquity.

The difference between Plato and the radical wing of Platonism in this crucial respect must be interpreted with a certain amount of caution. One cannot leave it at asserting that Neoplatonism is simply less religious than Platonism, if only because Plotinus's own philosophy is itself more often than not cast in a pious mold and shot through with religious imagery. The real issue lies elsewhere, in the attitude which the Plotinian school assumed toward the political life. At the risk of considerable oversimplification, one could say that Neoplatonism first comes to sight as an attempt to solve the problem raised by the famous discussion of the Good in the *Republic*.[108] The remarkable feature of Plato's method of procedure is that, while it describes the ascent to the Good or superessential principle which, like the sun in the visible world, is the cause of the being of all things and their knowability, it does not furnish any indication as to how one descends from that highest principle to the lower levels of everyday existence. The hiatus was pointed out by Aristotle, who objected to the Platonic approach on the ground that it was incapable of providing practical guidance in human affairs.[109] Neoplatonism countered the objection in a novel way, not by attempting to fill the lacuna, but by replacing the imperfect constructions in which human initiative and freedom play a preponderant role with an eternal and unchangeable model articulating the structure of the intelligible world. In the process, however, the properly political dimension of Plato's thought was to all intents and purposes discarded.[110] The net result was a natural, metaphysical, and mystical Platonism, inspired in largest measure by the *Timaeus*, the *Parmenides*, or the *Phaedo*, and all but totally divorced from the political context in which Platonic philosophy in its native form was imbedded.

This conspicuous lack of concern for the political life and the political conditions of the philosophic life accounts for the absence, in the works of the Neoplatonists, of the zetetic or propaedeutic quality which characterizes Plato's own works. It is indicated among other ways by the substitution of the Neoplatonic treatise for the Platonic dialogue as the preferred medium of written communication. It is reflected above all in the new stance and posture which the Neoplatonists saw fit to adopt toward religion. What is sometimes called Plotinian rationalism is, in reality, just another name for the apolitical character of the *Enneads,* which address themselves exclusively to a small group of philosophers or potential philosophers whose ears are more attuned to the music of the cosmic spheres than to the din of actual cities.[111] In his sublime self-sufficiency and indifference to the fate of empires, the Neoplatonic philosopher was under no compulsion to speak with deference of the gods of the city or, more generally, to adapt himself outwardly to the religion of his time.[112] The spiritual cosmopolis which he inhabited, unlike Plato's ideal city, no longer stood in need of the services of Thrasymachus.[113] Philosophy, it was thought, could henceforth dispense with the rhetorical art by which it once sought to relate itself to the nonphilosophic life.

The fact remains that, by severing its ties with civil society, philosophy could easily have jeopardized its own existence. The danger was sensed by the later Neoplatonists, whose works display a greater sensitivity to the political implications of philosophy and anticipate the return to a more integral Platonism such as the one that we observe among the Arabic philosophers of the Middle Ages, who deliberately combined, as Plato had done, the method of Socrates with that of Thrasymachus, tempering the intransigence of the one with the flexibility of the other.[114]

On the basis of the admittedly sparse but nevertheless useful information supplied by Arnobius, one could go a step further and submit at least tentatively that, by the reaction which it provoked, the rise of revealed religion and its gradual conquest of the Greco-Roman world was itself partly responsible for the turn of Platonic philosophy in the direction of a militant rationalism. Christianity, whose destiny it was to develop within a society distinguished from all other societies by the presence of philosophy or science in its midst, did not find a ready-made adversary along the way; it produced it. The devil of Western thought, one might venture to state, is a child of the biblical God. By giving birth to what was at once potentially its most powerful ally and its greatest rival, Christianity forced both itself and Greek philosophy to render explicit the absolute claim that each makes on the allegiance of its followers.

The external victory of Christianity in the troubled and politically disastrous years that followed does not allow us to prejudge the ultimate outcome of a contest that has lasted down to our time. What may be said with some degree of assurance is that that contest has engendered a creative tension in which the conflicting tendencies of Western civilization find their deeper and more mysterious unity.

NOTES

1. Jerome, *Epistula* (*Letter*) 62 (*Ad Tranquillinum*). Jerome also describes the seven books of the *Adversus nationes* as "splendid books" (*luculentissimi libri, Chronicon*, A. D. 326-7) but finds Arnobius "uneven and prolix and without clear divisions in his work" (*Epistula* [*Letter*] 58.10). According to *De viribus inlustribus* (*On Illustrious Men*) 79, Arnobius's work was commonly available in Jerome's day.

2. See, for example, B. Altaner, *Patrology* (New York: Herder and Herder, 1958), 205-7. Cf. Arnobius of Sicca, *The Case Against the Pagans*, newly translated and annotated by George E. McCracken, *Ancient Christian Writers* 7-8 (New York, NY and Mahwah, NJ: Paulist Press, 1949), vol. I, 3. For a more positive appraisal cf. E. Rapisarda, *Arnobio* (Catania: G. Crisafulli, 1946).

3. *Adversus nationes* II.15, pp. 82.24. All page and line references are to the critical edition by C. Marchesi, *Arnobii adversus nationes* (Turin: Corpus Scriptorum Latinorum Paravianum, 1953).

4. *Adv. nat.* II.62, p.138,6.

5. J. Carcopino, "Le tombeau de Lambiridi et l'hermétisme africain," *Rev. arch.* 15 (1922): 283-90. J. Carcopino, *Aspects mystiques de la Rome Païenne* (Paris: Artisan du Livre, 1941), 293-301.

6. *Aspects mystiques*, 294.

7. Ibid., 295.

8. Ibid., 300.

9. A. J. Festugière, "La doctrine des *Viri novi* sur l'origine et le sort des âmes," *Mémorial Lagrange* (Paris: J. Gabalda, 1940), 97-132; reprinted in *Hermétisme et mystique païenne* (Paris: Aubier-Montaigne, 1967). See also by the same author, "Arnobiana," *Vigiliae Christianae* 6 (1952): 208-54, and *La Révélation d'Hermès Trismégiste*, vol. III: *Les doctrines de l'âme* (Paris: J. Gabalda, 1953), 50-2. The main points of Festugière's analysis are summarized by McCracken in *The Case Against the Pagans*, 309-10. A similar position is adopted by G. Quispel, *Gnosis als Weltreligion* (Zurich: Origo, 1951), 28.

10. *Mémorial Lagrange*, 99 and note 1. Cf. *Adv. nat.* II.13, p. 80,11: "vos, vos appello qui Mercurium, qui Platonem Pythagoramque sectamini, vosque ceteros, qui estis unius mentis et per easdem vias placitorum inceditis unitate."

11. Ibid., 127.

12. Ibid., 132. Cf. 127: "Cette doctrine a une parenté si nombreuse qu'il semble difficile de l'attribuer à une seule secte et de la faire dériver d'un seul ouvrage."

13. P. Courcelle, "Les sages de Porphyre et les *Viri novi* d'Arnobe," *Revue des études latines* 31 (1953): 257-71. Also by the same author, "Anti-Christian Arguments and Christian Platonism: from Arnobius to St. Ambrose," in A. Momigliano, ed., *The Conflict Between Paganism and Christianity in the Fourth Century* (Oxford: Clarendon Press, 1963), 151-92.

14. *Adv. nat.* II.62.

15. Courcelle, ibid., 271. The view that Arnobius was attacking Plotinus is suggested by A. Roehricht, *Die Seelenlehrer des Arnobius nach ihren Quellen und ihrer Entstehung untersucht* (Hamburg: Agentur ies Rauhenhauses, 1893), 30ff. Roehricht's thesis is rejected by F. Niggetiet, *De Cornelio Labeone* (Muenster [Lipsiae]: R. Noske Bornensis, 1908). W. Kroll, "Die Zeit des Cornelius Labeo," *Rhein. Museum*, n. F. 71 (1916), 351ff., thinks that Arnobius's adversary may have been Porphyry.

16. Reported in *Bulletin de la Société Ernest Renan*, nouvelle série 3 (1954): 122-23.

17. M. Mazza, "Studi Arnobiani I: La dottrina dei *Viri novi* nel secondo libro dell'*Adversus Nationes* di Arnobio," *Helikon* 3 (1963): 111-69.

18. Ibid., 120; cf. 124.

19. Ibid., 132, quoting A. S. Ferguson, in W. Scott, *Hermetica*, vol. IV (Oxford: Clarendon Press, 1936), 476: "Now the core of this doctrine is the descent and ascent of the soul, its fatal star-given burden."

20. Mazza, ibid., 121-24; cf. 148-49.

21. R. Harder, "Quelle oder Tradition?" in E. R. Dodds et al., *Les sources de Plotin, Dix Exposés et Discussions*, Tome V (Geneva: Foundation Hardt, 1960), 325-39.

22. Cf. Mazza, ibid., 148, 160.

23. Ibid., 156-69.

24. Mercury (Hermes) is mentioned only once (II.13), along with Plato and Pythagoras, as the leader of the school. Festugière and Mazza to the contrary, it is by no means evident that two different groups of philosophers are intended by Arnobius, the followers of Hermes on the one hand and those of Plato and Pythagoras on the other. The rest of chapter 13 makes it clear that Plato is *the* authority; cf. p. 80.17: *Plato vester.* The Greek Hermes was identified with the Egyptian Theuth, the god of inventions (Plato, *Philebus*, 18bff.; *Phaedrus*, 274cff.; Cicero, *De natura deorum*, III.22) and came to be regarded as the embodiment of reason and the inventor of all knowledge (cf. Clement of Alex., *Stromata* VI.4). The designation of Hermes as the source of Plato's philosophy apparently originated as an attempt to parry the objection that, because of its relative newness, Greek philosophy did not share the prestige which attached to the ancient lore of Egypt by reason of its hoary age; cf. Plato, *Timaeus* 22bff. Mercury, Plato, and Pythagoras are listed in the same order by Iamblichus, *De mysteriis* I.2: "If also you should propose any philosophic inquiry, we shall discuss it for you according to the ancient pillars of Hermes, which Plato and Pythagoras knew before, and from thence constituted their philosophy." Cf. *De mysteriis* I.1: "Hence our ancestors dedicated the inventions of their wisdom to this deity, inscribing all their own writings with the name of Hermes." Hermes's inventions were reported to have been engraved on pillars, from which the knowledge of them was passed on to later generations.

25. Cf. Plotinus, *Enneads* II.9.17 et passim. On radical dualism as the cardinal

feature of Gnostic thought, see, *inter alia*, H. Jonas, *The Gnostic Religion* (Boston: Beacon Press, 1963), 42ff., and 241-65.

26. Plotinus, *Enneads* II.9.9 and 17, on the Platonic derivation of much of Gnostic speculation.

27. Mazza, "Studi Arnobrari," 134-35. On the place and use of Numenius in the Platonic school, cf. Porphyry, *Vita Plotini* 14, 20, and 21, where, as in Arnobius's case (II.11), the name of Numenius occurs side by side with that of Cronius.

28. For a brief summary of the literature on Labeo, cf. in addition to Mazza, McCracken, *The Case Against the Pagans*, 38-40, who considers the Labeo myth to have been thoroughly exploded and concludes his discussion with the remark: "Let us hope that the ghost of Labeo has now been laid." Also ibid., 336-37. The ghost of Labeo has since been resurrected by P. Hadot, *Porphyre et Victorinus* (Paris: Etudes Augustiniennes, 1968), 82-3, who raises the interesting possibility that Labeo's lost book may have been adapted from a work by Porphyry. For a more recent account of this whole issue, cf. P. F. Betrice, "Un oracle antichrétien chez Arnobe," in *Memorial Dom Jean Gribomont* (1920-1986), (Roma: Institutum Patristicum Augustinuum, 1986), esp. 120-23.

29. *Adv. nat.* II.14, p. 82,10; II.31, p. 103,11; II.36, p. 108,10; II.53, p. 126,24, et passim.

30. *Adv. nat.* II.14, p. 81,14ff.

31. *Adv. nat.* II.36, p. 107,23ff.

32. *Adv. nat.* II.15, p. 82,24ff. This is the only passage in which the expression *viri novi* occurs. Somewhat analogous expressions are used in II.25, p. 95,9 (*o viri*); II.29, p. 100,16 (*veros . . . auctores*); II.35, p. 106,24 (*o isti*); II.43, p. 116,9 (*o suboles ac primi progenies numinis*). Cf. Courcelle, loc. cit., 259, n. 2.

33. *Adv. nat.* II.17-26, p. 85,21-97,6.

34. *Adv. nat.* II.26, p. 97,7-16; cf. II.28, p. 99,20; II.30, p. 102,20.

35. *Adv. nat.* II.7, p. 73,12; II.14, p. 82,1; II.15, p. 83,2; II.24, p. 94,11; II.26, p. 97,18; II.28, p. 99,21, et passim.

36. *Adv. nat.* II.7, p. 73,14; II.15, p. 83,4; II.19, p. 87,22; II.22, p. 91,15 and 23 (*principalis esse substantiae portionem*); II.25, p. 95,11; II.26, p. 96,17ff., et passim.

37. Further proof of this assertion could be found by studying the structure of the Neoplatonic treatises on the soul.

38. *Adv. nat.* II.17-26, p. 85,21-97,6 and II.40, p. 112,22, where the same ideas are often developed. Compare, for example, p. 86,7: *Nonne alia (animantia) cernimus . . . construere mansiones*, with p. 112,22: *ut cum animantia cetera . . . domorum aut vestium tutamina . . . conquirerent*; also p. 86,22: *superlectilem ceteram quam familiaris usus exposcit*, with p. 113,1: *superlectilem variam diurnorum contraherent egestati.*

39. Cf. Ps.-Gregory Thaumaturgus, *De anima* (Migne, *Patrologia, Series Graeca* or *PG* 10: col. 1144c); Nemesius, *De natura hominis* (*PG* 40, col. 584a-b).

40. *Adv. nat.* II.19, p. 88,15; cf. II.37, p. 110,14.

41. Cf. II.19, p. 88,17; II.22, p. 91,16; II.24, p. 94,1ff., etc.

42. *De natura hominis* (*PG* 40, col. 581a-589a). Cf. Aenaeas of Gaza, *Theophrastus* (*PG* 85, col. 901).

43. *De natura hominis* col. 584b; *Adv. nat.* II.21, p. 90,9: *accipiamus deinceps modo aliquem natum* . . . The word *modo*, "newly," is conjectured by McCracken to fill an obvious lacuna in the lone manuscript of the *Adv. nat.* at this point; McCracken, ed., *The Case Against the Pagans*, 318, n. 138 and "Critical Notes to Arnobius's *Adversus nationes*," *Vigiliae Christ.* 3 (1949): 41. The conjecture would seem to be borne out by the parallel with Nemesius's text, which reads: *komidê neoi.*

44. *De nat. hom.* col. 585c: *phusikê ou logikê sunesis.* On the "intelligence" (*sunesis*) of animals, cf. Plato, *Menex.* 237d.

45. *De nat. hom.* col. 585c: *technês eikona kai skian logikên.*

46. *De nat. hom.* col. 588a.

47. *Adv. nat.* II.17, p. 86,7.

48. *Adv. nat.* 585a-b.

49. *Adv. nat.* II.17, p. 86,15: "Yet even in those things which they make with their beaks and claws, we see that there are many images of reason and wisdom (*rationio et sapientiae simulacra*) which we human beings are unable to copy with any amount of thought, although we have hands that work for us and are masters of every sort of perfection."

50. *De nat. hom.* col. 581b. Cf. Aenaeas of Gaza, *Theophrastus* (*PG* 85, col. 893); Augustine, *De civ. Dei* X.30. Additional references in Courcelle, "Anti-Christian Arguments," 161-65.

51. *De nat. hom.* col. 584a.

52. On "retorsion" as one of Arnobius's favorite dialectical devices, cf. McCracken, ed., *The Case Against the Pagans*, 45.

53. *Adv. nat.* II.16, p. 85,14.

54. *De nat. hom.* col. 581b; *Adv. nat.* II.11, p. 76,17. On Cronius, cf. McCracken, ed., *The Case Against the Pagans*, 310, n. 66.

55. *Adv. nat.* II.16, p. 97,17, reading with Réifferscheid, *Arnobii adversus nationes*, Corpus Scriptorum Ecclesiasticorum Latinorum (CSEL) 4, p. 69,19: *CORPORALEM animas susbstantiam non habere,* rather than *INCORPORALIS animas substantiam non habere,* to which Marchesi unjustifiably reverts on the basis of the corrupt manuscript text. The same thought is expressed by Arnobius in II.28, p .99,20 (*et sciunt animas se esse et CORPORALEM substantiam non habere*), as well as in II.30, p. 102,20 (*et qui poterit pollui CORPORALEM quod substantiam non habet*). The defenders of the spirituality of the soul asserted, against the Stoic view, that the soul was indeed a substance, albeit an incorporeal substance. Cf. Chalcidius, *In Timaeum c.* 227.265.2 Wrob.: *Sed quia duplex essentia est, altera corporea, altera carens corpore, consequenter docebimus quod sit anima essentia carens corpore.* Plotinus, *Enneads* IV.9.4: the soul is both "an incorporeal being" (*asômaton*) and "a substance" (*ousia*). Hence one should not translate, as does Festugière (*Mem. Lagr.,* 109), followed by McCracken, ed., *The Case Against the Pagans* 139: "And what has happened to that statement that bodiless souls have no substance?"

56. Note also the charasteristic use of *admixtio* by Augustine, ibid., p. 110, 13 and Arnobius, p. 99.3.

57. For a fuller discussion of this issue, cf. E. L. Fortin, *Christianisme et culture philosophique au cinquième siècle* (Paris: Etudes Augustiniennes, 1959), 111-28; Id., in chapter 14 of this volume, "The *Definitio Fidei* of Chalcedon and Its Philosophic Sources," 199-207. J. Pépin, "Une nouvelle source de saint Augustin: le *Zêtêma* de Porphyre sur l'union de l'ame et du corps," *Revue des études anciennes* 66 (1964): 53-107. Wm. O'Neill, "Augustine's Influence upon Descartes and the Mind/Body Problem," *Revue des études augustiniennes* 12 (1966): 255-60. John T. Newton, Jr., *Neoplatonism and Augustine's Doctrine of the Person and Work of Christ* (dissertation, Emory University, 1969), 71ff.

58. *Adv. nat.* II.26, p. 98,2: *ut integritatem suam retinere non possit*; II.27, p. 98,10: *aut integritatem conservantes suam*; p. 98,15: *semper suam retinere naturam*. Also II.26, p. 97,1: *retinentem res suas.*

59. Cf. Fortin, *Christianisme et culture philosophique*, 119-21.

60. *Adv. nat.* II.26, p. 97,11, reading with Festugière (*Mém. Lagr.* 109): *ut numerus IN corporibus constitutus*, against Reifferscheid, Marchesi, and McCracken, who amend the text to read: *SINE corporibus constitutus*. Cf. II.28, p. 99,18: *animas . . . IN corporibus ipsis quemadmodum constitutas*: p. 99,2: *IN ipsis corporibus positae*. Augustine, *C. Fortunatum*, 20, *PL* 42, col. 122: *si sola versatur anima IN corpore constituta*. Reifferscheid's and Marchesi's emendation is in no way required by the general meaning of the passage and is even contrary to it since it destroys the analogy established by Arnobius between the soul, which is occasionally bound to a body, and numbers, which are occasionally bound to material forms.

61. Nemesius, *De natura hominis* PG 40, col. 549b. "The line, being incorporeal, touches the body and yet has its existence apart from it." Cf. Aristotle, *Metaphysics* I.6.987b23ff.

62. *Adv. nat.* II.26, p. 97,16.

63. It is unlikely, however, that Arnobius had direct access to the *Enneads,* which were published by Porphyry in 301. The *Adversus Nationes* appears to have been written not much before or after 300; cf. McCracken, ed., *The Case Against the Pagans*, 7-12.

64. *Enneads* IV.7.2ff.

65. *Enneads* IV.7.13.

66. *Enneads* IV.7.10.

67. *Enneads* IV.7.10.

68. *Enneads* IV.7.12.

69. *Enneads* IV.7.13.

70. *Enneads* IV.7.10.

71. *Adv. nat.* II.15, p. 82,23ff.

72. *Adv. nat.* II.29, p. 101,3: "What man is there, although he be of a character that ever flees from the realm of infamy and shame, who, when he hears expressly stated by the wisest of men that souls are immortal and not subject to the laws of the

fates, would not rush headlong into every kind of shameful deed—would not, free from fear and without qualms, engage in and trespass into unlawful things—would not, finally, gratify his desires in everything commanded by incontinent passion, emboldened even still more by freedom from punishment?" Cf. II.54, p. 128,7ff.

73. *Mémorial Lagrange*, 130.

74. *Adv. nat.* II.49, p. 121,22ff.; II.50, p. 123,5ff.

75. *Adv. nat.* II.49, p. 122,9: "But the proper thing is to appraise and weigh humanity not by the standard of a very few good men, but by all the rest."

76. *Adv. nat.* II.26, p. 98,2ff.; II.35, p. 107,6, et passim.

77. *Adv. nat.* II.22, p. 91,23: *principalis esse substantiae portionem*; II.19, p. 87,21: *numquam . . . crederent typho et adrogantia sublevati prima esse numina et aequalia principis summitati;* II.15, p. 83,2: *domino rerum ac principi gradu proximas dignitatis; et passim.* Similar reservations about the pagan doctrine of the immortality and the divinity of the soul are expressed by Cassiodorus, *De anima* (Migne, *Patrologia, Series Latina* or *PL*) 70, col. 1287a: *Quapropter haec anima . . . non intelligenda est pars Dei, ut quidam dementium irreligiosa voluntate putaverunt;* col. 1286b: *verum hanc immortalitatem animae non talem debemus advertere, quae nullam recipiat passionem: est enim mutabilitati obnoxia et maeroribus pervia; sed tamen inter quaevis taedia vel anxietates continuationis beneficio perseverat. Singulariter autem immortalis Deus est.* See also Courcelle, "Les sages de Porphyre," 261, n. 11; Fortin, *Christianisme et culture philosophique,* 93ff.

78. *Adv. nat.* II.32, p. 104,4; II.36, p. 107,17. On conditional immortality, cf. Mazza, *Studi Arnobiani*, p. 113 and 129, with the references cited in the footnotes.

79. *Adv. nat.* II.32, p. 104,6.

80. Plato, *Phaedo* 83e.

81. *Adv. nat.* II.34, p. 105,24ff.; II.36, p. 107,23ff. The Neoplatonic doctrine of the soul was to a large degree a systematization of various Platonic texts taken from such dialogues as the *Phaedo,* the *Phaedrus,* the *Timaeus,* the *Theaetetus,* and the *Republic;* cf. Plotinus, *Enneads* IV.8.1. Since the same set of texts is quoted over and over again by different authors, there is no need to suppose that Arnobius was always reading Plato in the original. On the metaphor of the glue and its use in Neoplatonic literature, cf. P. Courcelle, "La colle et le clou de l'ame dans la tradition néo-platonicienne et chrétienne," *Revue belge de philologie et d'histoire* 36 (1956): 72-95. A similar alliance of the two Platonic images of the glue and the wings of the soul is again found in Caesarius of Arles, *Sermo* 34.6, *Corpus Christianorum* 103, p. 150 (= Ps. Aug., *Sermo* [Sermon] 276.6. [*PL* 39, col. 2266]): Certum est . . . quod nisi quisque de peccatorum *glutine* et nimiis impedimentis ac laqueis mundi huius *animae suae pennas* contenderit expedire, ad veram requiem numquam poterit pervenire. Cf. Pseudo Aug., *Sermo* 368.4. (*PL* 39, col. 1654) ad usum assumenda sunt ista, non eis vinculo amoris *quasi glutino* haerendum est.

82. *Timaeus* 41a-d, also quoted by Augustine against Porphyry in *Sermo* 241.7; *De civitate Dei* (*City of God*) X.29 and XXII.26; *Retractiones* (*Retractions*) I.4.3; and by Aenaeas of Gaza, *Theophrastus* (*PG* 85, col. 952). Cf. J. O'Meara, *Porphyry's*

Philosophy from Oracles in Augustine (Paris: Etudes Augustiniennes, 1959), 146-48; P. Hadot, "Citations de Porphyre chez saint Augustin," *Revue des études augustiniennes* 6 (1960): 216, n. 17; E. TeSelle, *Augustine the Theologian* (New York: Herder and Herder, 1970), 252-53.

83. *Adv. nat.* II.14, p. 81,3.

84. Cf. Plato, *Phaedo* 80b and 82c; *Phaedrus* 246e.

85. *Adv. nat.* II.13, p. 81,5; II.28, p. 99,1, et passim. Cf. Plato, *Phaedo* 81e; *Phaedrus* 250c.

86. Cf. *Phaedo* 81eff.; *Phaedrus* 248cff.; *Timaeus* 91e; *Republic* X.620a-b.

87. *Adv. nat.* II.30, p. 103,1; cf. *Phaedo* 82d.

88. *Adv. nat.* II.33, p. 105,4: "You, the moment you are freed from the bonds of your bodies and depart, think wings will be ready for you to enable you to hasten to heaven and soar to the stars." Cf. *Phaedrus* 246aff.

89. *Phaedo* 83d. *Adv. nat.* II.13, p. 81,3: "As for the fact that you refrain from every fault and passion, is not this the fear which possesses you, that you may cling to your bodies as if nailed to them with spikes (*velut trabalibus clavis adfixi*)?" Cf. Porphyry, *De abstinentia* I.38, p. 114,19ff. Nauck. To the image of the glue and the nail should be added that of the chains and the knot which bind the soul to the body. Cf. *Timaeus* 41b and 43a; *Adv. nat.* II.30, p. 103,10: *corporalibus vinculis;* II.33, p. 105,5: *soluti membrorum. . . e nodis;* II.36, p. 108,4: *vinctum et nodis perfectissimis conligatum.* Cf. Courcelle, "La colle et le clou," 93, n. 1

90. Cf. Courcelle, ibid., 73ff. Also, id., "Variations sur le clou de l'ame," *Mélanges offerts à Mlle Christine Mohrmann* (Utrecht: Spectrum, 1963), 38-40.

91. Courcelle, "Les sages de Porphyre" 265ff.

92. *Adv. nat.* II.8, p. 74,1.

93. Ibid., II.8, p. 73,19ff.; II.34, p. 105,14ff.

94. *Phaedo* 79c. On wine as the means by which the philosopher limits his horizon and accepts the perspective of the city, cf. *Laws* 636eff., where the achievement of harmony between the excellence of man and the excellence of the citizen is presented as the most noble exercise of the virtue of moderation.

95. *Phaedo* 79d.

96. Ambrose, *De bono mortis* IX.40: Unde et nos si volumus post mortem corporis huius in bonis esse, caveamus ne *adglutinetur* anima nostra huic corpori, ne commisceatur, ne inhaereat, ne trahatur a corpore et *tamquam ebria* perturbationibus eius vacillet et fluiet nec se ei credat et eius delectationibus, ut committat se eius sensibus. Cf. Courcelle, "La colle et le clou," 76.

97. Mazza, *loc. cit.*, 121.

98. Cf. Plotinus, *Enneads* V.1.8: "These teachings are therefore no novelties, no inventions of today, but long since stated, if not stressed; our doctrine here is the explanation of an earlier and can show the antiquity of these opinions on the testimony of Plato himself."

99. *Adv. nat.* II.66, p. 143,15ff.; cf. II.36, p. 108,13. For the philosophic implications of the objection as formulated by Porphyry, cf. Augustine, *Epistula (Letter)*

102.8-15.

100. See, among other useful studies, K. Praechter, "Richtungen und Schulen in Neuplatonismus," *Genethliakon C. Robert* (Berlin, 1910), 100-56, with the reservations expressed by J. Bidez, "Le philosophe Jamblique et son école," *Revue des études grecques* 32 (1919): 29-40. E. Bréhier, "Platonisme et néoplatonisme," *Revue des études grecques* 51 (1938): 489-98. E. R. Dodds, "Theurgy in Its Relation to Neoplatonism," *Journal of Roman Studies* 37 (1947): 55-69. H. Dörrie et al., *Porphyre, huit exposés suivis de discussions* 12 (Genève: Vandoeuvres, 1965). W. Theiler, *Forschungen zum Neuplatonismus* (Berlin: de Gruyter, 1966). A. H. Armstrong, ed., *The Cambridge History of Later Greek and Early Medieval Philosophy* (London: Cambridge University Press, 1967), 53 ff. and 272 ff. J. Daniélou, "Grégoire de Nysse et le néo-platonisme de l'école d'Athènes," *Revue des ét. grecques* 80 (1967): 395-401.

101. Albinus, *Epitome* 25.5.

102. Cf. Proclus, *Commentary on the First Alcibiades*, translated by Wm. O'Neill, (The Hague: M. Nijhoff, 1965), 149: "Nor will we admit the view of those who assert that the soul is a part of the divine being, and that the part is like to the whole and always perfect, and that the disturbance of the passions is concerned with the living organism, since those who hold these views make the soul ever perfect, ever wise and never in need of recollection, ever free from passion and never corrupted." Id., *In Timaeum* III, p. 333,28 Diels: "What is it then that sins in us when, yielding to an irrational impulse, we lunge toward a licentious image? Is it the decision of the will ? . . . But if the decision is guilty of sin, how could the soul be sinless? . . . On the basis of these considerations, we shall take a stand against Plotinus and the great Theodore (of Asine), who hold that there is in us, beyond all reach, something impassible and ever engaged in the act of thinking." Simplicius, *In Arist. de anima* 5.38 Hayd.: "Hence we shall concede neither, as Plotinus would have it, that there is a part of the soul which remains ever pure and identical to itself, nor that, as the soul proceeds toward generation, its fall is ever complete." Ibid., 89.22 Hayd.: "Let us acknowledge that the soul can in some way be moved as to its essence, so that, in this manner, too, it lies midway between the divisible and the indivisible." Priscianus Lydus, *Metaphrasis in Theophrastum* 32,13 Byw.: "Surely, according to Iamblichus, the individual soul comprises these two things, the immutable and the mutable, so that in this fashion also it retains its intermediate quality . . . It is not only according to its modes of being that it changes but in a certain way according to its essence as well."

103. E.g., *Adv. nat.* II.31, p. 103,16: "Hence it is that among scholars and men endowed with superior ability there is a controversy about the nature of souls and some say that they are mortal and cannot partake of divine substance, but others that they are everlasting and cannot degenerate into mortal nature. This is the result of the law according to which they have an intermediate character: some have arguments ready at hand by which it is found that they are subject to suffering and perishable, and others on the contrary have arguments by which it is shown that they are divine

and immortal." On the notion of the mid-rank position of the soul in Neoplatonism, cf. R. J. O'Connell, *St. Augustine's Early Theory of Man, A. D. 386-391* (Cambridge, MA: Harvard University Press, 1968), 155ff.

104. Carcopino, *Aspects mystiques* 298.

105. Manichaeism, which flourished in the West and became a major concern of the Christian writers in the fourth century, was not seen at the time as a variant of the Gnostic movement.

106. Cf. Macrobius, *In Somnium Scipionis* I.11.11, where the Neoplatonists are described as a sect particularly "devoted to reason." *Adv. nat.* II.34, p. 105,22: *Si tenetis alioqui sequiminique rationem, et nobis aliquam portionem ex ista ratione concedite.* The intellectualism of the *viri novi* is noted by Festugière, *Mém. Lagr.*, 120. Olympiodorus, *In Phaedonem* (*On the Phaedo*) 123,3 Novins, observes that Plotinus, Porphyry and their followers honored philosophy above all else, while others (Iamblichus, Syrianus, Proclus, etc.) deferred to theurgy (*ieratikê*). The seriousness of Iamblichus's hierophantic divagations and "spiritualistic drivellings" has long been a matter of controversy among scholars. Dodds concludes a famous article on "The *Parmenides* of Plato and the Origin of the Neoplatonic 'One'," *The Classical Quarterly* 22 (1928): 142, with the remark that Plotinus was "the one man who still knew how to think clearly in an age which was beginning to forget what thinking meant." Cf. on this point, P. Hadot, *Porphyre et Victorinus* I (Paris: Etudes Augustiniennes, 1968), 91-101.

107. On the deep-seated "arrogance" (*typhus*) of the *viri novi*, cf. *Adv. nat.* II.3, p. 68,8; II.12, p. 79,20; II.16, p. 84,1; II.19, p. 87,21, and II.63, p. 140,11. For the meaning of *typhus*, which occurs only in Book Two, cf. McCracken, ed., *The Case Against the Pagans*, 303, n. 13.

108. Plato, *Republic* VI.505aff.

109. Esp. Aristotle *Nicomachean Ethics* I.6.

110. The same shift from the political to the apolitical is observable in Plotinus's reinterpretation of the "cave" (*Republic* VII.514aff.) as synonymous with "this world" (*tode to pan*) rather than with the "city"; cf. *Enneads* IV.8.1 and 3. On the apoliticism of the Neoplatonic school in general, cf. R. Hathaway, "The Neoplatonist Interpretation of Plato: Remarks on Its Distinctive Characteristics." *Journal of the History of Philosophy* 7 (1969): 19-26. See also, on Julian's relation to Neoplatonism and the political nature of his attempt to restore "hellenism," the penetrating remarks by A. Kojève, "The Emperor Julian and His Art of writing," in J. Cropsey, ed., *Ancients and Moderns* (New York: Basic Books, 1964), 95-113.

111. Plotinus, *Enneads* II.9.13.

112. Cf. *Alfarabi's Philosophy of Plato and Aristotle*, trans. M. Mahdi (New York: Cornell University Press, 1962), I.4.60 p. 48.

113. Cf. Plato, *Republic* V.450a and esp. VI.498c, where Socrates and his enemy are finally reconciled. Thrasymachus, once tamed, becomes an indispensable part of the new city in speech which has just been founded.

114. *Alfarabi's Philosophy of Plato and Aristotle*, II.10.36 in Mahdi, p. 66. The

"method of Socrates," as Alfarabi understands it, is characterized by its emphasis on "the scientific investigation of justice and the virtues" and is appropriate only in the philosopher's dealings with the elite. Its radicalism led in Socrates's case to nonconformity and death. The "method of Thrasymachus" or the art of rhetoric, on the other hand, is appropriate in dealing with the youth and the multitude. cf. Plato, *Phaedrus* 266b-c. By cleverly combining both methods, Plato was able to escape the fate of his master without prejudice to philosophy.

12

THE *DEFINITIO FIDEI* OF CHALCEDON AND ITS PHILOSOPHICAL SOURCES

The gains registered by Patristic studies in recent years have led scholars to emphasize more than in the past the influence exerted on early Christian literature by such philosophical schools as Stoicism, Neopythagorianism, and Aristotelianism. The result has been, along with a better knowledge of the intellectual background of the first centuries, a tendency to undervalue in some cases the role of Neoplatonism, to which earlier generations of scholars attributed an overwhelming importance in the shaping of Christian ideas and dogma. A general readjustment is thus slowly taking place which is destined to add at once breadth and perspective to our view of the evolution of Patristic thought as a whole. This change in attitude is particularly noticeable in the current literature on the Council of Chalcedon and, more specifically, on the celebrated formula by which it attempted to put an end to the raging controversies concerning the union of the divine and human natures in Christ. It is immediately evident that this formula is not a mere restatement of the teaching of sacred Scripture but a theological exposition of this teaching which makes liberal use of terms and concepts borrowed from contemporary philosophy. One would search in vain, however, for any reference to Neoplatonism in this connection in Dr. R. V. Sellers's recent book on the subject.[1] Such references are also conspicuously absent from the chapters on the Incarnation in Professor H. A. Wolfson's monumental study of the *Philosophy of the Church Fathers.*[2] In like manner, it is clearly not in terms of Neoplatonic doctrine that the contributors to the collective work on the same Council edited by Fathers Grillmeier and Bacht have sought to interpret the phraseology of the *Definitio.*[3] Yet, despite the presence of elements that unmistakably hark back to Stoic or Aristotelian sources, it is doubtful whether in the final analysis either one of these two schools provided the tool used by the Fathers to express the mystery of the union of the two natures. The best evidence that we have been able to gather points to the fact that we must once again turn to Neoplatonism if we wish to gain a full understanding of the problem at hand.

A brief survey of relevant Patristic texts reveals that the analogy to which Fathers and heretics alike resorted most frequently in order to manifest Christ's dual nature is by and large that of the union of soul and body in man. The analogy occurs repeatedly in the works of Gregory of Nazianzus, John Chrysostom, Cyril of Alexandria, Theodoret, Nestorius, Augustine, Pope Leo I, Leontius of Byzantium, John of Damascus, as well as in many lesser theologians such as Abuccara, Peter Mogilas, Critopoulos, Theorianus, and Anastasius the Sinaitic, to mention only the writers of antiquity.[4] It received new prestige and a kind of semi-official recognition when in time it found its way into the so-called Athanasian Creed, which states unequivocally that Christ is "one, not as a result of the conversion of the divinity into flesh, but as a result of the assumption of the humanity unto God, one altogether not by reason of the confusion of the substances, but by reason of the unity of person; or just as rational soul and flesh are one man, so God and man are one Christ."

As one reflects on that doctrine, however, it soon becomes apparent that neither the Aristotelian nor the Stoic conception of the union of soul and body could lend itself perfectly to the application made of this analogy or shed much useful light on the present discussions. Apart from the fact that it remains very scanty, the information furnished by Aristotle's *De anima* on this subject[5] refers us directly to his doctrine of matter and form, which, if properly understood, hardly squares with the teaching of the Council on the union of the two natures in Christ. According to the Aristotelian view, matter and form, although occasionally spoken of as substances, are not complete substances in themselves but rather substantial principles that combine to form a single complete nature. Thus neither the form of man, that is to say his soul, nor his matter is man, but together they constitute one human nature or essence distinct from either of these two components taken individually. The Council of Chalcedon, on the other hand, distinguishes clearly between nature and person (*prosōpon*) or hypostasis and goes on to explain that the divine and human natures of Christ are joined without being fused and without giving rise to a *tertium quid* compounded of one and the other. The mode of union advertised suggests a much closer relationship than the one implied in the traditional Platonic concept of the union of soul and body, and at the same time it differs from the essential union alluded to a moment ago in that it involves two complete natures, both of which are maintained in their integrity and retain their own properties. Thus, it is extremely difficult to see how, as Professor Wolfson has written, "the solution arrived at by the Fathers reduces itself to the analogy of (the) Aristotelian conception of the unity of matter and form."[6] If anything, one would rather expect any endeavor to pattern the doctrine of the union of the two natures in Christ on that of Aristotle to miscarry or to deviate sooner or later into Monophysitism, as it seems to have done in the case of the Aristotelian John Philoponos. It is also significant that the expression *asygchytos henōsis*, by which the Council characterizes this union, is not to be found anywhere in the works of Aristotle.

If we turn to Stoicism, we shall discover that its own doctrine of the union of soul and body was hardly more suitable, albeit for different reasons. The type of union advocated in this instance is that of a "total mixture,"[7] according to which the soul or *pneuma* is diffused throughout the body and comes into contact with each one of its parts without increasing its weight or size and without undergoing any transformation in the process. Unlike that of Aristotle, the present doctrine teaches that two complete substances are intimately associated and bound together in what the Stoics themselves had already labeled an unconfused union; but it also had its shortcomings, the main one being that both of these substances are corporeal, whereas in the case of the Incarnation, at least one of the natures was in every respect incorporeal. Just how a corporeal substance could be united in this manner to an incorporeal substance was far from clear,[8] and Stoicism, with its doctrine of the materiality of all existing things, was in no position to supply the answer. It is not surprising therefore that the enlightenment sought by the Fathers should ultimately have come from an altogether different source.

Happily, there existed at the time another highly important and more appropriate conception; I refer to the Neoplatonic view of the union of soul and body. This doctrine, which seems to have been disregarded or misconstrued by the bulk of modern scholarship, represents an effort to supplement the ideas set forth by Plato on this vexed question and constitutes one of Neoplatonism's most distinctive and fruitful contributions to contemporary philosophical speculation. Historically, it evolved out of a series of endeavors to answer what appears to have been the two most cogent objections raised against the Platonic dogma of the spirituality of the soul. If, on the one hand, the soul is a spiritual substance and is not in any way extended in space, how can it be imprisoned in a tridimensional body and animate its various parts? The question, we may remember, is discussed at some length in Augustine's *De quantitate animae* and adverted to in the very title of that work. On the other hand, how can a spiritual substance possibly affect a body and in turn be affected by it?[9] That there exists a reciprocal action of the body on the soul and of the soul on the body is a matter of everyday observation. Fear, for example, although originating in the soul, may produce visible transformations in the body and, likewise, the pain resulting from a wound inflicted on the body is experienced by the soul. Both the animal and the corporeal passions, therefore, bespeak a more intimate connection between body and soul than the one allowed for by the classic concept of a purely accidental union. Everything leads us to believe that the being thus affected is not a mere aggregate of two independent substances existing side by side, but a composite entity exhibiting a physical unity and behaving in every respect as an organic whole. These objections presented no serious difficulty for the Stoics inasmuch as there was nothing to prevent the soul, conceived by them as a material substance, from being diffused in space or from coming into contact with and acting upon another material substance; but they could not be taken lightly by those philosophers who contended that the soul is spiritual or incorporeal and, as such supposedly immune to any contact of this kind.

The Platonic school eventually countered with a theory of its own which may be described in round terms as that of the hypostatic union of soul and body, and wherein two complete substances, one of which is purely spiritual, are knit together so as to form a single being while remaining unmixed and preserving their identity. The term *asygchytos henōsis* used to designate this union, although originally popularized by the Stoics and presumably borrowed from them, thus takes on a new meaning and neutralizes, as it were, the Stoic doctrine against which it was competing. The main lines of this specifically Neoplatonic theory may be gleaned from the passages of the *Enneads* which deal with the problem of the union of soul and body.[10] We find it expressed with even greater clarity perhaps in some of the later Neoplatonic or Neoplatonically-minded writers such as Porphyry, Proclus, Chalcidius, Nemesius, Augustine, and Priscianus.[11] It may at times be couched in terms reminiscent of Plato or Aristotle; nevertheless, the insistence of these writers on the newness of their doctrine should warn us against identifying it purely and simply with the older Platonic view, or with the Aristotelian conception, which occasionally comes in for some sharp criticism on the part of the Neoplatonists, or with both at the same time.[12] The Neoplatonists themselves are the first to concede that this position is an extremely subtle and difficult one; yet there seemed to be no other way by which the principles to which the Platonic tradition had always adhered in regard to the spirituality of the soul could be reconciled with the acts of experience. They will endeavour to clarify it and render it more palatable by means of the analogies of sunlight and air, iron and fire, or wine and water,[13] all of which are admittedly very imperfect since they involve only material substances, but which help us nonetheless to form a mental picture of this particular *unio inconfusa* insofar as these substances unite without apparently suffering any alteration.

The reader who is sufficiently acquainted with the theological controversies of the fifth century will have sensed by this time the relevance of the Neoplatonic doctrine to the discussions concerning the incarnate union. In their efforts to gain an insight into the "ineffable and indescribable mystery"[14] of Christ and to forestall further heresies by formulating that mystery with the utmost precision, the orthodox Fathers had suddenly stumbled upon a remarkably perfect instrument. Here at last was an egregious example, indeed the only one available, of a mode of union that could account for the dual nature of Christ without prejudice to the unity of personal subject or to the integrity of the two natures concerned. If ever a philosophical doctrine appeared to dovetail into the faith, it was this one. With very little pruning or sifting, the Neoplatonic concept and its phrasing could be inserted into an entirely new framework and made to express a theological truth in a manner fully consonant with the teaching of Revelation, as the very words of the Chalcedonian formulary suggest:

We unanimously teach therefore, in conformity with the holy Fathers, that one and the same is confessed to be Son and Our Lord Jesus Christ; the same perfect in divinity, and the same perfect in humanity. He is true God and true man, the same with a body and a rational soul. He who is consubstantial with the Father in divinity is the same who is consubstantial with us in humanity, "in all things like unto us, save sin." He who, in truth, was begotten of the Father in divinity before all time is the same one who in these times for us and for our salvation was begotten of the Virgin Mary, Mother of God, according to humanity. In one and the same Christ, Son, Lord, only-begotten, must be acknowledged two natures without confusion, without change, without division, inseparable. The differences in the natures are not suppressed for a moment by reason of the union; rather, the properties of each are guarded intact. Yet they are joined together in one Person and subsistence, not divided or veiled apart in two persons. He is one and the selfsame Son, only-begotten, God, Word, Lord, Jesus Christ, as the Prophets taught in times past, as Jesus Christ taught us about himself and as the Creed of the Fathers teaches us.

The Neoplatonic doctrine was all the more attractive since it stood roughly in the same relation to the Aristotelian theory on the one hand and to the former Platonic conception of an accidental union on the other as the Chalcedonian faith to Monophysitism and to Nestorianism. It is not surprising therefore that, once applied to Christ, it was used as an antidote to both of these heresies. This is not to imply that the mystery of the Incarnation was thereby evacuated or its awesome profundity in any way lessened. It is one thing to teach the possibility of the hypostatic union of two created and finite substances such as the soul and the body and another thing altogether to accept the union according to a similar mode of a divine and of a human nature. The Fathers, more than anyone else, were alive to the deficiencies inherent in any comparison of this sort. Whatever their limitations, however, these comparisons, as Cyril of Alexandria had previously noted, "afford a feeble image of reality and by means of what is known lead us to what has been revealed and lies beyond the pale of the human intellect."[15] Simply by giving us an inkling as to the manner in which the Word of God had been able to assume an individual human nature and become one with it without any danger of its being "filched or squandered away," the doctrine of the philosophers had already rendered an invaluable service to Christian theology and helped it to reach another watershed.

These brief remarks enable us to understand more easily perhaps the esteem voiced, with what may seem undue enthusiasm, by the Fathers for a philosophical school whose *floruit* coincided roughly with the heyday of Patristic literature and which soon became notorious for the violent opposition of some of its writers to the Christian faith. It is worthy of note that Neoplatonism has met with considerably less success at the hands of modern scholarship. When Coleridge entitled his lecture on Plotinus and his followers, "Corrupt Philosophy,"[16] he was merely echoing an opinion that has since won the support of many eminent critics and historians. Despite an increasingly large chorus of dissenting voices, it is still fashionable in some quarters to look upon Neoplatonism as a "failure of nerve"[17] or as a kind of philosophical and mystical Noah's ark into which elements flowing from the most diverse sources, Greek and otherwise, would have sought refuge at a time when ancient culture had already begun to show signs of weakness and decay. In the end, it would be nothing more than an essentially syncretistic system compounded of heterogeneous doctrines never fully brought into the unity of breathing life. These views, expressed with all the brilliance and incisiveness desirable, underlie the article by Harnack which the *Encyclopedia Britannica* continues to reprint year after year and in which Neoplatonism appears as the "collapse of ancient philosophy," as an intellectually bankrupt system that has "failed as signally in its religious enterprise as it did in its philosophical," and which finally "extinguished" the ancient philosophy that it was seeking to perfect. Even more sympathetic critics like Bréhier will detect in some of its important phases an "offensive return of very ancient ideas, a return to 'prelogical thinking' which confounds all distinct representations."[18] Surprisingly enough, this critical and hostile attitude towards Neoplatonism is often shared by men who profess the greatest admiration for those whose work betrays a strong Neoplatonic influence. When Augustine proclaimed the Neoplatonists "able and acute men," "the most esteemed of the pagan philosophers," and the ones who were "not undeservedly exalted above the rest in fame and glory,"[19] he may very well have been suggesting that Christianity was indebted to them for more things than he could prudently admit, as the veiled presence of the Neoplatonic doctrine in the Christological formula was to bear out a few years later.

Even if these observations should prove accurate, however, there is another question which may be asked legitimately and which will bring the problem into proper focus. To what extent are the position of the Council of Chalcedon and that of Neoplatonism interdependent and does the value of the one necessarily affect the truth of the other? The question is not an idle one, for, whereas the Chalcedonian doctrine is still regarded as a definitive expression of the orthodox faith and may be used as a yardstick to evaluate any new position in regard to the Incarnation, philosophers in the main no longer accept the Neoplatonic view according to which soul and body are united hypostatically. It may be felt perhaps that the subsequent rejection of the Neoplatonic doctrine, assuming that it has played an important part in the formulation of the Christian dogma, will cast some discredit on the solution proposed by the Council. Yet further reflection will convince us that this need not be so, since the philosophical doctrine in this case is in no sense a principle invoked to discriminate between orthodoxy and heresy but merely an instrument or tool employed by the Fathers to convey in terms accessible to the human mind a divinely revealed truth. For that reason it could be used without any fear of diluting the wine of the Gospel with the water of secular philosophy. The value of this instrument lay solely in its capacity to serve a given purpose and was not at all contingent upon its truth or falsity. There is no contradiction in the statement that a proposition may be false philosophically and still remain true on a theological plane. The use made of any philosophical doctrine by theology does not of necessity contain even an implicit judgment regarding the intrinsic value of that doctrine. Indeed, if one had to choose between a doctrine that is known to the hearer to be false and one that is unknown to him, although true, one might be compelled to prefer the former. It is entirely permissible, for example, to appeal to the Manichaean theory of good and evil to bring home to another person the mentality reflected in a typical Western without assuming any responsibility for that theory or urging its acceptance by others. There is no reason to suppose that the problem changes when the vehicle in question is called upon to manifest a truth pertaining to a higher order.

That the teaching of Neoplatonism on this point should then be judged erroneous by human standards matters little in the last analysis. On the contrary, it is even more remarkable that, although jettisoned by later philosophy, this teaching should have found a permanent home in the Christian dogma which it was admirably suited to express. The fires which, at the time of Eunapius, still burned on the altars of Plotinus have not been extinguished entirely but simply removed to other altars where they continue to blend with the light that shines forth in the Chalcedonian confession.

NOTES

1. R. V. Sellers, *The Council of Chalcedon: A Historical and Doctrinal Survey* (London: S. P. C. K. , 1953).

2. H. A. Wolfson, *The Philosophy of the Church Fathers*, vol. I: *Faith, Trinity, Incarnation* (Cambridge MA: Harvard University Press, 1956), 364-493.

3. A. Grillmeier and H. Bacht, "Das Konzil von Chalkedon," *Geschichte und Gegenwart*, 3 vols. (Würzburg: Echter-Verlag, 1951-1954).

4. References to these and many other authors may be found in E. Schlitz, "La comparison du Symbole Quicumque vult," in *Ephemerides Theologicae Lovanienses* 24 (1948): 440-454.

5. Aristotle, *De anima* II.1.412b 6sq.

6. H. A. Wolfson, *The Philosophy of the Church Fathers*, 373.

7. See the discussion of this doctrine by Plotinus in *Enneads* II.7, trans. E. Bréhier (Paris: Les Belles Lettres, 1924-1938), 91.

8. Cf. Augustine, *De anima et eius origine* (*On the Soul and Its Origin*) IV.5.6; *De civitate Dei* (*The City of God*) XXI.10.1, etc.

9. Cf. Tertullian, *De anima* 5.5; Plotinus, *Enneads* I.1.3.12; Nemesius, *De natura hominis*, Migne, *Patrologia, Series Graeca* (or *PG*) 40.548a and 593b, etc.

10. See especially *Enneads* I.1; IV.3 and 7.

11. Proclus, *In Timaeum* 131b, 199a, 218c; Chalcidius, *In Timaeum* chap. 221, 257, 4sq. Wrobel; Nemesius, *De natura hominis PG* 40, 649b; Augustine, *Epistula* (*Letter*) 137.11; Priscianus, *Solutiones*, 51, 4sq. Bywater. For supplementary details the reader may consult E. L. Fortin, *Christianisme et culture philosophique au cinquième siècle: la querelle de l'âme humaine en Occident* (Paris: Etudes Augustiniennes, 1959), 111-128.

12. Cf F. M. Sciacca, *Saint Augustin et le néoplatonisme: la possibilité d'une philosophie chrétienne* (Louvain and Paris: Publications Universitaires de Louvain, 1956), according to whom Plotinus shared Plato's view of a purely accidental union:

"Elle (l'âme) ne s'unit pas, mais au contraire elle tombe dans un corps (elle vit en lui dans un rapport accidentel et extrinsèque) pour expier une faute" (p. 44). Yet he states that Augustine favored the Aristotelian conception which he received through Plotinus: "Avec Aristote (à travers Plotin), Augustin soutient l'union substantielle de l'ame et du corps" (p. 46). For Plotinus's criticism of Aristotle's hylomorphic theory of the union of soul and body, cf. *Enneads* IV.3.20.36, 88; *Enneads* IV.7.8⁵.40, trans. E. Bréhier, 204.

13. Plotinus, *Enneads* IV.3.22.1.89; Augustine, *Epistula* 137.11; Nemesius, *De natura hominis* (*PG* 40, 592Bsq.); Chalcidius, *In Timaeum*, chap. 227, 265, 4 Wrobel, etc.

14. Cyril of Alexandria, *Ad Succensum* 2.143b.

15. Cyril of Alexandria, *Quod unus sit Christus PG* 65.1357c.

16. Samuel Taylor Coleridge, *The Philosophical Lectures, 1818-1819*, edited by Kathleen Coburn (New York: Philosophical Library, 1949), 227.

17. See Gilbert Murray, *Five Stages of Greek Religion*, (New York: Columbia University Press, 1925), chapter 4.

18. E. Bréhir, *The Philosophy of Plotinus*, trans. Joseph Thomas (Chicago: University of Chicago Press, 1958), 102.

19. Augustine, *Epist.* 118.33; *De civ. Dei* VIII.6; *Contra academicos (Against the Academics)* III.18.41.

III

THE MEDIEVAL ROOTS OF
CHRISTIAN EDUCATION

13

THE PARADOXES OF ARISTOTLE'S THEORY OF EDUCATION IN THE LIGHT OF RECENT CONTROVERSIES

The reader who examines closely the passages in which Aristotle discusses the teaching of philosophy to young men may well wonder whether the practice of the ancients was not at variance with their principles in this matter. According to a well-established custom to which the Platonic dialogues already bear witness and of which various traces are discernible at that time, the young student who wished to take up the study of philosophy under the tutorship of a competent master did so immediately upon completing the cycle of preliminary studies at the school of the grammarian and the rhetorician. Yet on two occasions at least, Aristotle, who seems to have conformed to that tradition, questions the advisability and, indeed, the very possibility of teaching philosophy to a boy of that age. Prof. Étienne Gilson, who, with his customary brilliance and flair for the paradoxical, has recently brought this difficulty to the attention of his colleagues,[1] assumes that it has not been adequately answered by Aristotle himself and expresses wonder at the fact that it has never been noticed or, if noticed, not felt as serious by students of classical and Scholastic philosophy. Whether Prof. Gilson's eloquent plea will prompt any professor of philosophy to drop his courses and start searching for another job is more than doubtful. It does invite us to look into the problem, however, and that, after all, is perhaps the only point the author was really trying to make.² A more careful scrutiny of the texts invoked will not only reveal that the alleged inconsistency is merely an apparent one but will also bring to light an important and often neglected aspect of classical education. For the sake of clarity, let us begin by relating briefly and without commentary the contents of the two passages in question.

In Book I, chapter 3, of the *Nicomachean Ethics,* Aristotle deals succinctly, by way of introduction to the whole treatise, with the manner in which moral science should be studied and then asks to whom this science should be taught. We are told in this connection that the young man is not an apt student of moral and political philosophy for two reasons. On the one hand, he lacks the experience of life and of men; this experience can come only with time and it is indispensable in this case, since it is precisely human actions that constitute the subject of ethics and provide its proper principles.³ On the other hand, the young man does not dominate his passions sufficiently; from a purely speculative point of view moral philosophy presents little interest. The only real profit that may be gained from its study is that it helps us become better human beings by facilitating the development of the moral virtues. In order to obtain this result, however, one must be prepared to regulate his conduct according to the dictates of reason. It so happens that the young man, and the description here fits the person who is young in character as well, is easily led astray by the unruliness of his lower appetites. Rather than follow the injunctions of reason, he is more likely to pursue each object as passion directs.⁴

Book VI, chapter 8, reverts to the same topic from a slightly different point of view. Dealing this time with the intellectual virtues, Aristotle again stresses the fact that young men, being inexperienced, are not yet in a position to acquire practical wisdom.⁵ To this consideration he now adds that, for that matter, they are not good metaphysicians or good natural philosophers either. The science of metaphysics is not readily accessible and presupposes a training that they can hardly be expected to possess at that early age. At best, they will be able to repeat the words they have heard, without any true understanding of their meaning. As for natural science, it embraces the entire realm of nature, which, by reason of its vastness, requires years of investigation. Aristotle himself, as we know, spent much of his life exploring it, cataloguing its various species and subspecies, and tracing their "history." What the young student lacks this time is an adequate experience, not of life, but of nature, on which this science rests.⁶ There is, in reality, within the province of philosophy, only one field in which he has any chance of being distinctly proficient at that age, namely, mathematics. Less abstruse than metaphysics, and less dependent upon the knowledge of singulars than natural philosophy, this discipline can be mastered without too much difficulty and become the object of a truly scientific inquiry even on the part of an adolescent.[7]

If one accepts this reasoning, the efforts of the philosopher who attempts to communicate his knowledge to young minds are doomed in advance to failure. Instead of wasting his time and that of his students, he would be better off, as Hamlet says, to buy a cart and conduct mules. One could only smile indulgently at the naiveté of a teacher who, with owlish seriousness, would begin by explaining to his pupils the futility of his trying to impart to them any real knowledge of philosophy, and then calmly set about the task of exposing his science in great detail to these same and by now utterly bewildered students. Not only ancient education but a large portion of medieval education and of our own as well, in the degree to which it takes its lead from Aristotle, would be the victim of a gross illusion. The question, we gather, is more complex than the foregoing remarks suggest. What we should like to show is that it had not escaped Aristotle and that it is possible to find within the framework of his doctrine the elements of a solution.

The key to our problem, it seems, lies in a notion which modern scholarship has generally overlooked or to which it has not given due prominence. I refer to the Aristotelian concept of *paideia*. The word *paideia* has, of course, become very familiar to us, and Prof. Jaeger's classic work, *Paideia, The Ideals of Greek Culture*,[8] has done much in recent years to popularize it. Prof. Jaeger's book, however, does not encompass Aristotle, and, in any case, merely takes the term *paideia* in its broadest acceptation, without making an effort to ascertain its various meanings. We may concede immediately that the expression has been put to a wide variety of uses in the course of its long history, from its humble appearance in Aeschylus[9] as a synonym for *trophē*, the older and more traditional word for child rearing, down through the Hellenistic period, at which time its meaning is extended in such a way as to include, finally, the totality of man's intellectual and moral development.[10] In Aristotle himself, it is applied to the training of animals[11] as well as to all the degrees of the physical, intellectual, and moral formation of the human being from the earliest childhood to the age of twenty-one or thereabouts.[12] Elsewhere is his works, however, the same term has clearly received new impositions, the exact significance of which is not at once apparent. Although Aristotle has never treated the question exhaustively and for its own sake, at least in the works that have come down to us, it is still possible, by gathering the various texts in which *paideia* is employed in this narrower and more specialized sense, to determine the main articulations of his thought.

We shall discover a first element of that thought if we turn to the famous discussion concerning the first principle of knowledge in Book IV, chapter 4 (1006 a 4 sq.), of the *Metaphysics.* This principle, on which all subsequent knowledge depends in a certain manner, is not demonstrable, says Aristotle, not because it is false, but for the simple reason that it is immediately evident. To try to establish its truth by way of deduction from previously known premises would be absurd. It is impossible that there should be demonstration of absolutely everything. Sooner or later, lest one be faced with an infinite regression which would preclude all demonstration and all science, one must arrive at a proposition that is a principle and in no way a conclusion, that is to say, a proposition whose truth does not depend upon that of another proposition that would be prior to it. Among these self-evident principles none is more obvious than the one which enunciates the opposition between being and non-being, or, as it is commonly called, the principle of noncontradiction. And yet there are some persons who insist that even this principle be the object of a demonstration in the strict sense. Such an attitude betrays an incapacity to discern what is evident and can only be explained, adds Aristotle, by a lack of education, *apaideusia.*

From these remarks it is permissible to infer that the student who wishes to acquire *paideia* must first learn to recognize a principle as opposed to a conclusion or, to put it very simply, be able to distinguish between what is known and what is unknown. He will be disciplinable, i.e., capable of receiving a discipline, to the extent that he possesses this aptitude.[13] An example taken from natural philosophy may serve to illustrate the point. Before attempting to demonstrate anything in that science, it is necessary to accept the existence of nature as Aristotle defines it in the *Physics.*[14] That there is such a thing as nature in this precise sense is immediately evident.[15] Anyone pretending to prove the existence of nature would be striving to establish what is manifest by what is not and would do away with the entire science of nature by destroying its very principle. A man blind from birth might just as well try to reason about colors.[16]

It is not difficult to see that this initial capacity already presupposes a certain training on the part of the student. There are, of course, principles that are rooted in very common notions and that, upon being enunciated, are readily understood by all men. Anyone who knows what a part and a whole are, or is familiar with the meaning of the word equal, will agree that the whole is greater than the part and that two things equal to a third are equal to each other. To deny these truths would be to stop thinking altogether. The matter is somewhat more complicated when we come to the proper principles of each science. It is not enough here that we learn what the terms signify. Albeit indemonstrable, these principles require an explanation. The teacher who manifests their truth by means of examples or in any other way is already making a valuable contribution to the intellectual advancement of his students. Thus, strictly speaking, one does not demonstrate that all mobile beings are composed of matter and form or that nature acts for an end; yet the painstaking examination to which these principles are subjected in the *Physics*[17] is in itself a sufficient indication of the fact that they are not within the reach of any chance comer. An accurate grasp of these truths is all the more important since even a slight error with respect to them may have far-reaching consequences later on. Any attempt to impart a philosophical discipline should, therefore, begin with an elucidation of the proper principles of that discipline, and it is only once this preliminary work has been accomplished that the student will be ready to go on to something else.

This determination, however, important though it may be, still represents only the first component of the philosophical *paideia* set forth by Aristotle. We shall encounter another component of that doctrine if we revert to the passage of the *Nicomachean Ethics* which originally gave rise to our discussion. The issue this time is no longer that of the principles of the various sciences but of their proper modes. Working from the premise that the mode according to which the truth is manifested in a given science is contingent upon the subject of that science, Aristotle reminds his reader that he must not expect the same measure of precision in all the philosophical disciplines. It again pertains to the *pepaideumenos* to be acquainted with these different modes and, by the same token, with the degree of accuracy that may be anticipated in each one of these sciences.[18] Moral philosophy in particular, by reason of the extreme contingency of its matter, namely, human actions, offers little certitude. Whoever undertakes to write a treatise on this subject will hardly be able to do more than to indicate the truth "broadly and in outline."[19] Whereas natural phenomena present a remarkable uniformity at all times, and are for the most part the same everywhere—the properties of fire, for instance, are identical in Greece and in Persia—the just, the noble, and the lawful may vary from one country to another.[20] It is on the grounds of this variability of ethical standards, observes Aristotle, that some people have been led to deny the existence of natural right and the validity of even the most common principles of morality. While carefully shunning this extreme, the moral philosopher must bear in mind that particular circumstances may cause the proper principles of this science to change when they are applied to concrete cases. Generally speaking, it is true that a deposit should be returned to its owner; this is practically the definition of justice. Yet there are times when it would be dangerous and even unjust to return an object to its lawful proprietor. Such examples could be multiplied at will. The general principles of moral science can never dispense the man who acts from taking into account the indefinitely changeable circumstances attendant upon each one of his actions.[21] A doctor cannot prescribe the same treatment to all his patients even if they are afflicted with the same illness;

it may be that, for reasons peculiar to himself, one of these patients is incapable of withstanding this treatment.[22] Likewise, a trainer cannot form in an absolutely identical manner all the athletes entrusted to his care, if only because they do not all have the same physical dispositions.[23] His art consists precisely in his ability to use to the best advantage the virtualities inherent in each subject. Thus, it would be unwise, to say the least, to teach moral philosophy to a student who would have no idea of the mode of that science and, consequently, of the nature and value of the conclusions reached therein.

Each science, then, possesses its proper mode, with which one must become familiar before any effort is made to come to grips with the problems it strives to resolve. Were we to pursue this inquiry and extend it to the other philosophical disciplines, we should discover, for example, that mathematics, thanks to the rigor and precision of its mode, is the science that presents for us the highest degree of certitude and stands as the prototype of all the other sciences; that, contrary to mathematics, which prescinds from sensible matter and motion, natural philosophy demonstrates from all four principal causes, but must be satisfied in most cases with *a posteriori* demonstrations;[24] that First Philosophy, whose object is entirely free from matter and therefore immutable, studies all things in the light of the most universal causes and remains the highest, most divine, and most inaccessible of the sciences.[25] There are manifestly some very significant divergences among these various disciplines. The fact that we refer to them indiscriminately as sciences should not delude us into thinking that they are all sciences in exactly the same fashion. The *pepaideumenos,* as Aristotle describes him, is precisely the man who has become aware of these differences and who knows to what kind of proof he may look forward in each case, who will not demand of an orator, for example, the rigorous procedure typical of the mathematician, any more than he will be content with probable arguments in geometry.[26]

These considerations help us to understand, among other things, the use of the word *paideia* in an important and often misconstrued passage of the treatise *On the Parts of Animals,* which reads as follows:

> In every speculative inquiry, the humblest as well as the most noble, there are, it seems, two distinct habits of mind (*hexis*): one that may be called science (*epistēmē*) of the object, and the other a certain *paideia.* For it pertains to the *pepaideumenos* to be able to form, with accuracy, a judgment concerning the mode (*tropos*), whether good or bad, employed by the speaker in his treatment of a question. To be well-trained (*pepaideusthai*) is precisely to have this capacity; such is, indeed, the man of whom we say that he possesses a general formation (*ton holōs pepaideumenon*).[27]

The *paideia* that the present context distinguishes clearly from science (*epistēmē*) is here again a habitus or determination[28] having as its proper object the method or mode of procedure proper to a particular discipline. Since the young student presumably has not had the opportunity to investigate the subject thoroughly himself, he cannot boast of a perfect knowledge of it and is not prepared, in consequence, to formulate a judgment bearing specifically on the truth or falseness of the conclusions proposed by the speaker.[29] In this respect, his position remains inferior to that of the master. But he is not in a state of complete ignorance either. His knowledge of the principles and of the proper mode of that science already enables him to assess or judge (*krinein*),[30] from this more restricted standpoint, the views put forward by another person. This capacity may be limited to a single discipline or it may extend to a number of other branches. The true *pepaideumenos*, as Aristotle remarks, is obviously the one who is thus competent in all or nearly all fields of knowledge.[31]

One is hardly justified, therefore, in equating purely and simply *paideia* with dialectic, defined as the "method or art or reasoning about any given problem,"[32] or in looking upon it as being roughly synonymous with our own conveniently vague "general culture," as other more recent scholars have done.[33] Aristotle had something far more definite in mind. His older translators showed greater penetration when they either resorted to a paraphrase to suggest its meaning[34] or, as in the case of William of Moerbeke, simply transliterated the word,[35] thereby intimating that they were dealing with a properly philosophical term for which no exact equivalent could be found in their own idiom.

Thanks to this preparation, the young man will be able to penetrate more deeply into the study of the different sciences and gradually become more proficient in them as time goes on. It is scarcely possible from this moment forward to determine down to the last iota the contents of a program that may comprise many degrees. The sum of knowledge that a student who is hardly more than a beginner in philosophy can assimilate will depend on numerous factors, such as his native ability, his previous education, the quality of his teachers, and his own personal efforts.[36] What matters here is that we realize that between *apaideusia* or the total lack of education, and wisdom, which remains the preserve of a small number of exceptionally gifted natures and which is attained only after many years of study, there exists a preliminary stage designed to supply the budding philosopher with the tools indispensable to the attainment of his goal.

Since this initiation is normally acquired during the adolescent years, the term *paideia* adopted by Aristotle is fully justified and offers an example, among many others, of the philosophical promotion from which current language has frequently benefitted. On this score, the ancients manifested greater restraint than many of our more sophisticated contemporaries. Instead of having recourse to strange or unknown expressions to convey new thoughts, they simply borrowed the "words of the tribe," on which they made further impositions. This procedure has the undeniable advantage of allowing the beginner to use notions firmly grounded in everyday reality as stepping-stones toward more abstract, and therefore less familiar, ideas. The term *hylē*, raised in the *Physics* to the level of "prime matter," originally meant "timber." Similarly, the verb *logizesthai*, which reappears in a slightly modified form in the formidable "syllogism" proper to the third operation of the mind, had first of all designated the very simple act by which young Greeks counted their pebbles. A philosopher could just as easily appropriate a word like *paideia* and make use of it to express a new phase of the multiple education to which the young man was subjected throughout the entire first part of his life.[37]

Taken as a whole, the program just outlined is far more diversified than these willfully brief remarks suggest. We have limited ourselves to the strictly philosophical part of the *paideia* envisaged by Aristotle. A more exhaustive investigation would have to take into account other elements that pertain to it directly, and more particularly the liberal arts, the traditional gateways to philosophy, as the words *trivium* and *quadrivium* by which they were commonly referred to in the Middle Ages indicate. Such an inquiry might give us a better insight into the true nature of the *engkyklios paideia* devised by the ancients: not just a grab bag or an accumulation of superficial and poorly assimilated bits of information, but a clearly defined and well-organized whole, endowed with its proper finality and possessing its own relative perfection. There can be no doubt that the student who has received this type of education, although he is still only in the early stages of his intellectual development, is better equipped for life and for the more advanced studies that lie ahead than the one who has amassed huge stores of material knowledge in a haphazard and chaotic manner.[38] Having been duly instructed with regard to the general principles that govern the various sciences as well as to the respective modes of these sciences, and having been trained to a greater or less degree in the use of these modes, he will derive greater benefit from the experience that time will bring and will find the progressive acquisition of these disciplines considerably easier in the long run.

It is precisely to the fact that it favors the development of the intellectual virtues and strives to generate in the mind of the young man a genuine *hexis* that this form of education owes its superiority to that of the Sophists, the great initiators of the pedagogical revolution that marked the fifth century B.C. The avowed aim of these Sophists, as we know from Protagoras, was to educate men, *paideuein anthrōpous*.[39] Instead of inculcating principles and relating their ideas to these principles, however, they adopted for the most part a form of teaching based solely on practice and experience.[40] This method may be valid as far as it goes, and it no doubt represents an advance over what existed before; but it also has its disadvantages. Aristotle compares it to that of the shoemaker who presents to his client a variety of shoes from which he may choose the one that fits him best.[41] By so doing, he is certainly being helpful, but if the buyer should happen to suffer from sore feet later on, he will again be compelled to seek the services of the shoemaker. There is another course, the one which consists in imparting the art of shoemaking, thereby enabling the person to whom this instruction is given to meet his own needs as they arise. It is to this second alternative that the *paideia* advocated by Aristotle corresponds in the intellectual sphere.[42] The young student who has received his education in this more universal form already has the power to move forward in his quest for new knowledge and to solve his own difficulties without having to be constantly assisted by the master.

If, with these ideas in mind, we now return to the problem raised at the outset, we shall find that it is perhaps not as insoluble as it may have appeared at first glance. That a young man should still be a far cry from what we should label a philosopher in the full sense of the word will surprise no one. His knowledge necessarily remains very scanty by comparison with the vastly superior acquirements of the wise man. It does not follow, however, nor does Aristotle imply that he should not be exposed to philosophy at a relatively early age. Nothing is to prevent him from acquiring the rudiments of that science or, to use Aristotle's own term, its *paideia*, even if he cannot hope to gain a complete mastery of it until much later. What is more, there is every reason to suspect that the student who has not received the proper formation at this privileged moment will be hard pressed to attain wisdom at a more advanced age. The great educators of the past had sensed, long before our modern psychologists, the importance of these decisive and irreplaceable years. The love of Socrates for the elite of the Athenian youth, whatever suspicions it may have awakened in the minds of the multitude, cannot be explained otherwise. That he should have persistently sought the company of young men in the gymnasium and in the market place is no mere coincidence. Any hope that he may have had of recruiting prospective philosophers rested almost exclusively with them. It is less than likely that a man whose mind has already been warped by erroneous opinions and unscientific thinking habits, which the years have only intensified, will ever undergo the branch-and-root change that an authentically philosophical life would require.

Of this truth there is no finer illustration perhaps than Plato's *Parmenides,* in which, for the first and last time in the *Dialogues,* the resourceful Socrates, presented here as a young man, does not have the upper hand. Pitted against the now aging and white-maned Parmenides, "awe-inspiring and venerable, like Homer's hero,"[43] he grows increasingly silent and merely stands by as what had begun as a friendly conversation evolves into a monologue that will come to an abrupt end, leaving both parties further than ever away from each other. The upshot of the whole abortive discussion, one finally gathers, is that the old Eleatic philosopher, who is already reluctant to defend his own position, will never be induced to cross the "vast ocean of discourses"[44] by which he might eventually be able to give to his thought an entirely new orientation.[45]

Wisdom, insofar as it is accessible to man, may be the prerogative of old age, but even so, it remains the "ultimate flowering of seeds planted in youth."[46] This could very well be the reason why true philosophers, like the devil in *Faust*, have always felt for the young men of the city a profound and mysterious attraction.

NOTES

1. E. Gilson, "Note sur un texte de saint Thomas," in *Revue thomiste*, vol. LIV (1954): 148-52, in which no attempt is made to provide a solution. In a lecture on this topic, published almost simultaneously under the title, *Thomas Aquinas and Our Colleagues* (Princeton: Princeton University Press, 1953), the same author takes a more positive stand: having apparently succeeded in casting out St. Thomas with Aquinas, he proceeds to reintroduce him into the classroom by suggesting that, in the case of the Christian, faith may come to the rescue of reason and assist it in grasping the more abstract notions of metaphysics; cf. 17. He is the first to grant, however, that this answer, which he regards as tentative, would have no value for a pagan like Aristotle. Cf. the discussion of Prof. Gilson's views by D. H. Salman, "L'enseignement de la philosophie aux jeunes d'après Aristote, Saint Thomas et M. É. Gilson," in *Laval théologique et philosophique*, vol. XI (1955): 9-24. The present article reproduces in slightly expanded form some remarks found in E. L. Fortin, *Christianisme et culture philosophique au cinquieme siècle: la querelle de l'âme humaine en Occident* (Paris: Etudes Augustiniennes, 1959), 177-89.

2. E. Gilson, *Thomas Aquinas and Our Colleagues*, 25, n. 10: "It is always untimely to question the wisdom of current practice. One of the most frequent answers to such questions is: then what do you suggest we should do? My only answer to this is: we should put our heads together and consider the problem . . ." Cf. ibid., 18: "It may well be that . . . (my) conclusion does not prove satisfactory. Then one should not waste any time on refuting it. The only useful thing to do would be to find another answer to the problem raised by the texts of Thomas Aquinas."

3. Aristotle, *Nicomachean Ethics* I.3.1095a2.

4. *Nic. Ethics* 1095 sq. Cf. Shakespeare, *Troilus and Cressida*, act 2, sc. 2, lines 163-171.

> Paris and Troilus, you have both said well;
> And on the cause and question now in hand

have gloz'd, but superficially; not much
Unlike young men, whom Aristotle thought
Unfit to hear moral philosophy.
The reasons you allege do more conduce
To the hot passion of distempered blood
Than to make up a free determination
'Twixt right and wrong . . .

5. *Nic. Ethics* VI.8.1142a14 sq.

6. *Nic. Ethics* VI.8.1142a18 sq.

7. Cf. *Nic. Ethics* 1142a12 and 17, where, as regards mathematics, the young man is called *sophos*.

8. English translation by Gilbert Highet, 3 vols. (Oxford: Oxford University Press, 1939-1945).

9. *Seven against Thebes* 18.

10. It is this idea that Cicero has rendered in Latin by the word *humanitas*. On *paideia* in this sense, see H.-I. Marrou, *Saint Augustin et la fin de la culture antique* (Paris: E. de Boccard, 1938), 552-55.

11. See, for instance, in the *History of Animals* IX.46.630b19, the story of the elephant who had been taught (*paideuein*) to kneel in the presence of the king.

12. Thus in the treatise *Peri paideias* which takes up the whole last part of the *Politics* VII.13 to the end.

13. Cf. St. Thomas, *In Metaphysica Aristoteles* Book IV, lesson 6, n. 607. I am indebted to Prof. Maurice Dionne, of Laval University, for much of the information contained in the pages that follow immediately, but wish to assume full responsibility for any error of interpretation that I may have committed.

14. *Physics* II.1.192b22.

15. *Physics* II.1.192b22.

16. *Physics* II.1.193a7.

17. *Physics* I.7.189b30 sq.; ibid., II.8.198b10 sq.

18. *Nic. Ethics* I.3.1094b24.

19. *Nic. Ethics* 1094b20.

20. *Nic. Ethics* V.7.1134b25; I.3.1094b4. Cf. Plato, *Laws* X.889e: "In the first place, my dear friend, these people would say that the Gods exist not by nature but by art, and by the laws of states, which are different in different places, according to the agreement of those who make them; and that the honourable is one thing by nature and another thing by law, and that the principles of justice have no existence at all in nature, but that mankind are always disputing about them and altering them; and that the alterations which are made by art and by law have no basis in nature, but are of authority for the moment and at the time at which they are made. These, my friends, are the sayings of wise men, poets and prose writers, which find a way into the minds of youth . . . " (Jowett translation.) On the mutability of these moral principles, see St. Thomas I-II qu. 94, a.4.

21. For this reason, observes Aristotle (ibid., VI.11.1143b11), one should always

take into consideration the advice of older and more experienced persons, even if they are unable to support this advice with rational arguments. Their experience, if nothing else, often allows them to judge soundly with regard to practical matters. The "intellectuals," about whom so much evil has been spoken in our time, are precisely the armchair philosophers who pretend to solve in a purely abstract and theoretical manner, and without reference to the particular conditions of human existence, the most concrete problems of moral and political life.

22. *Nic. Ethics* X.9.1180b7.

23. Ibid., 1180b10. Whence, concludes Aristotle, the superiority of private *paideia*, which adapts itself more easily to the particular needs of each subject.

24. For the distinction between the natural philosopher and the mathematician, see *Physics* II.2.193b22 sq.; *Metaphysics* II.3.995a15, etc.

25. Cf. *Metaphysics* I.2.982a5 sq.; 1.1026a7 sq.

26. *Nic. Ethics* I.3.1094b24. See the corresponding passage in the *Metaphysics*, II.3.995a6 sq., where, as befits the context, the question is posed in the most general terms: "Some people do not listen to a speaker unless he speaks mathematically, others unless he gives instances, while others expect him to cite a poet as witness. And some want to have everything done accurately, while others are annoyed by accuracy, either because they cannot follow the connexion of thought or because they regard it as pettifoggery. For accuracy has something of this character, so that as in trade so in argument some people think it mean. Hence one must be already trained (*pepaideusthai*) to know how to take each sort of argument, since it is absurd to seek at the same time knowledge and the way of attaining knowledge; and it is not easy to get even one of the two. The minute accuracy of mathematics is not to be demanded in all cases, but only in the things which have no matter. Hence its method is not that of natural science; for presumably the whole of nature has matter. Hence we must inquire first what nature is: for thus we shall also see what natural science treats of . . . "

27. Aristotle, *On the Parts of Animals* I.1.639a1 sq.

28. The word *hexis* is taken here in the second of the two senses indicated in the *Metaphysics* (V.20.1022b10), and designates the quality by which a subject is well or ill disposed in itself or with regard to something else. Cf. *Categories* 8b27-9 a12.

29. *On the Parts of Animals* I.1.639a13. It is one thing to criticize a conclusion, and another to criticize the method by which an author pretends to arrive at that conclusion.

30. The *pepaideumenos* is always presented as having this power to "judge." See, in addition, *Nic. Ethics* I.3.1094b29; *Politics* III.6.1282a7.

31. *On the Parts of Animals,* I.1.639a9; *Nic. Ethics,* I.3.1095a1.

32. Aristotle, *Topics* I.1.100a18; cf. J.-M. Le Blond, *Aristote, philosophe de la vie: le livre premier du Traité sur les parties des animaux* (Paris: Aubier, 1945), 129, with whom we are presently taking issue. According to our interpretation, Aristotle's *paideia* obviously includes dialectic or, better still, logic, which it presupposes and which has as its object the mode *common* to all the sciences; but it also embraces, as

we have seen, the mode *proper* to each science.

33. E.g., P. Louis, *Aristote, Les parties des animaux, texte et traduction* (Paris: Les Belles Lettre, 1956), XXI. There is no reason whatever to suppose that Aristotle is writing here for the benefit of the general public, as opposed to students and specialists (cf. in the same vein, Le Blond, op cit., 128, n. 3). An interpretation such as this one mistakes completely the meaning of *pepaideumenos*. Aristotle simply begins, as he usually does, by exposing the *paideia* of the science with which he proposes to deal, before delving into the science itself. Louis's suggestion, according to which one should henceforth distinguish three types of Aristotelian writings instead of two, namely, the esoteric or acroamatic treatises, the exoteric books, and the works intended for the general public, harks back to the same basic misconception and scarcely deserves a better fate.

34. Cf. W. Ogle, *Aristotle On the Parts of Animals*, translated, with an Introduction and Notes (London, 1882) [reprinted in R. McKeon, *The Basic Works of Aristotle*, NY: Random House, 1941, 643 sq.], who renders *paideia* by "educational acquaintance." Despite minor shortcomings, Ogle's text appears to be far more satisfactory than any of the other modern translations of this treatise. The author is fully aware of the problem posed by the use of *paideia* in the passage under scrutiny, even if he does not dwell upon it; cf. ibid., 141, n. 1.

35. William of Moerbeke, *De partibus animalium, ad locum.*

36. On the three principles of education: nature (physis), habit (*ethos*), and reason (*logos*), cf. Aristotle, *Politics* VII.12.1332a40; Plutarch, *On the Education of Children*, 2a.

37. Needless to say, the manner in which this investigation is being conducted and its presuppositions, as exemplified in the above remarks, stand in sharp contrast with the views shared by many Aristotelian scholars today and expressed, for instance, with enviable assurance, by Ingemar Dühring, *Aristotle's De partibus animalium, Critical and Literary Commentaries* (Göteborg: Garland Pub., 1943), 7: " . . . Every account of Aristotle's opinion or doctrine on this or that question, based on citations indiscriminately chosen from the whole *Corpus Aristotelicum*, starts—this may be openly confessed or not—from the erroneous presumption that there is an unchangeable Aristotelian system. To those who are firmly convinced that Aristotle's views not only on biological but also on metaphysical and ethical problems and questions concerning the theory of cognition, nay, even his conceptions of the methods of science have undergone a gradual change, every such account must seem hopelessly obsolete. Nowadays nobody dreams of dealing with Plato's writings as a manifestation of one unchanged and fixed philosophical system. And similarly must he who wants to take up a position towards one of the preserved writings of Aristotle meditate the problem of designing its approximate place in Aristotle's philosophical development."

38. One is reminded, by contrast, of the character of Sartre's *La nausée* who longed for the education that he had not received as a boy, and who decided to make up for lost time by reading all the books in the municipal library in alphabetical order.

39. Plato, *Protagoras* 317b; cf. Aristotle, *Soph. Refut.* chap. 34.183b36 sq.

40. Aristotle, ibid. On the methods used by the Sophists and their contribution to higher learning, cf. H.-I. Marrou, *Histoire de l'éducation dans l'antiquité*, Paris: Editions du Seuil, 1950), 81 sq.

41. Ibid., chap. 34.184a2 sq.

42. The three levels of knowledge: experience, *paideia,* and science, are again listed with all the desirable clarity in the *Politics* III.6.1282a1 sq.

43. Plato, *Theaetetus* 183e6. The praise contained in these words is more apparent than real, as may be seen by turning to the passage in Homer's *Iliad* (III. 172) from which they are taken. Helen is speaking, and the "awe-inspiring and venerable" hero is none other than Priam, who is already an old man at the time of the Trojan War, who plays only an insignificant part in it, and who will soon be humiliated and forced to pay an exorbitant price for the body of his son, Hector. Priam's reign has reached its end, and, by implication, so has Parmenides's. Such is the meaning of the encounter, invented by Plato, between Socrates and his illustrious predecessor. The quotations of Plato are never chosen at random!

44. *Parmenides* 137a7.

45. On the necessity of unlearning before being able to learn properly, cf. St. Augustine, *Contra Academicos* III.17.38: "Now, when Zeno, the founder of the Stoic School, had heard and accepted some of the teachings, he came to the school which had been founded by Plato and which Polemon was then conducting. It is my opinion that he was held suspect there. I believe he did not seem to be the kind of man to whom those Platonic and sacrosanct teachings ought to be disclosed and entrusted—at least, before he had unlearned what he had received from other schools and had brought with him to this school."

46. The same thought occurs in St. Jerome, *Epistula* 52.2-3, p. 414,16 sq. Hilberg (*Corpus Scriptorum Ecclesiasticorum Latinorum,* 54), who finds an illustration of it in the episode of the Sunamite narrated in I Kings I:1 sq. This mysterious woman, at once virgin and spouse, turns out to be wisdom, which the young man must cultivate early in life, but which is fully possessed only in the serene and passion-free atmosphere of later years.

14

GLADLY TO LEARN AND GLADLY TO TEACH: WHY CHRISTIANS INVENTED THE UNIVERSITY

The title and part of the content of this essay are inspired by the charmingly ironic description of the Oxford Cleric in the Prologue of Chaucer's *Canterbury Tales*:

> An Oxford Cleric, still a student though,
> One who had taken logic long ago,
> Was there. His horse was thinner than a rake,
> And he was not too fat, I undertake,
> But had a hollow look, a sober stare;
> The thread upon his overcoat was bare.
> He had found no preferment in the church
> And he was too unworldly to make search
> For secular employment. By his bed
> He preferred having twenty books in red
> And black, of Aristotle's philosophy,
> To having fine clothes, fiddle or psaltery.
> Though a philosopher, as I have told,
> He had not found the stone for making gold.

Whatever money from his friends he took
He spent on learning or another book
And prayed for them most earnestly, returning
Thanks to them thus for paying for his learning.
His only care was study, and indeed
He never spoke a word more than was need,
Formal at that, respectful in the extreme,
Short, to the point, and lofty in his theme.
The thought of moral virtue filled his speech
And he would gladly learn and gladly teach.

My subject should not be that complicated since, for better or for worse, the university is a Christian invention. Although not without remote antecedents in classical and Christian antiquity, universities as we know them are indeed a product of Western Christendom, but, I am not convinced that my task is all that easy. It suffices to read one book on the subject to realize how complex it soon becomes, and two books to realize how far apart scholars can be in their analyses of it.

Be that as it may, there is not much doubt that the Middle Ages represent the highwater mark of Christian higher learning. No other period in the history of the Church matches this one in the magnitude of its educational accomplishments. Early Christianity never developed a school system of its own on any level, let alone the highest. At most, we find in St. Augustine's treatise *On Christian Doctrine*, a blueprint of what a *bona fide* Christian university might look like and to a large extent became nine hundred years later, even though, given the constraints of Augustine's time, any attempt to institutionalize such a program was out of the question. This is the program according to which all the arts and sciences, including philosophy, are enlisted in the service of Christian revelation, Bonaventure's classic *reductio artium ad theologiam*. As for the modern period, no one thinks of it as being particularly glorious in this regard since it is the period that witnessed the decline of the once dominant Christian universities and their subsequent involvement in a series of rear guard actions against the assaults of philosophic and scientific modernity. Toward the end of the Middle Ages, there were eighty-odd universities in Europe, many of them famous. I will not venture to guess how many of them survive in recognizable form.

One cannot scan the vast literature on the medieval university from Denifle and Rashdall to Ferruolo—for starters I would still recommend Charles H. Haskins's delightful little book, *The Rise of Universities* (1923)[1]—without being impressed by its structural resemblances to the modern university. Differences there are, to be sure, the main one being that the original university had no assets or physical facilities of its own, such as a clearly marked campus, a building or set of buildings, a library, laboratories, or even a modest endowment. Professors taught wherever they could: in their homes, in rented accommodations, or in colleges where students, who often came from distant places, could reside but which did not offer any courses or have their own teaching staffs. Paris had forty of these colleges at one time, the best known being the Sorbonne and the College de Navarre. The term "university" itself did not designate an institution of higher learning. It referred to a legally established guild or corporation organized for the protection of its members. One did not speak of the "university" as such; it was always the university or totality of the professors, or the students, or both of this or that city. Only much later, toward the end of the Middle Ages, did the term begin to be used without further qualification.

Aside from these peculiarities, the main features were roughly the ones with which we have been familiar ever since. These include such matters as duly promulgated statutes defining the university's mode of governance, its officers, its division into smaller academic units or faculties (of which there were four: arts, theology, law, and medicine), admissions procedures, tuition fees, a well-ordered program of studies, regularly scheduled classes, public examinations, doctoral defenses, commencement exercises and the granting of degrees, namely, the baccalaureate, the licentiate, or the doctorate. Never before had anything of the kind been seen. There had been schools devoted to the cultivation of the arts and sciences—the School of Athens and the School of Alexandria stand out among others—but the scholars who frequented them, being under no obligation to instruct students, were apparently more eager to learn than to teach. The combination of these two complementary activities is what gave the medieval university its unique character.

A sure sign that, on this purely external level, the medieval university is the prototype and legitimate progenitor of its modern successor is that the complaints of which it was the object are barely distinguishable from the ones most commonly heard today; academics, one gathers, have a tendency to grumble. Baudelaire may have said the last word on the subject when he wrote: "This breed complains, therefore it exists." What kind of complaints? Everything from the decline of learning or the tension between liberal education and professionalism to inadequate faculty salaries (Chaucer's Oxford cleric, living in more or less genteel poverty, was thin as a rail), substandard living conditions, a perennial housing shortage, rising tuition costs, chronic student absenteeism, indebtedness, delinquency, rowdiness, and run-ins with the local population—in short, many, if not most, of the problems that universities have been plagued with ever since. One way to solve a few of these problems was to do what Milan and Venice did: keep the students at a safe distance by locating the university in some outlying place, such as Pavia or Padua.

None of this takes us to the heart of the medieval university, which is more likely to be remembered for its differences from the modern university than for its similarities to it. These more profound differences have a lot to do with what the university stood for and understood itself to be. Medieval universities are generally thought to be a natural out-growth of the cathedral and monastic schools that had sprung up in the West during the so-called "Dark Ages," once the barbarian invasions had wiped out the old Roman school system in all but a few remote and well protected localities, such as southern Italy and southern Spain. The type of education provided by these schools was at best elementary. Its aim was to equip the student with what he minimally needed to live as a priest or a member of a monastic order. Christianity, it has been said, is a learned religion. It presupposes on the part of its ministers the ability to read, if not necessarily to understand, the Bible and other such liturgical texts as may be required to say mass or administer the sacraments. What is not completely clear is how these modest schools were transformed into institutions dedicated to the pursuit of the highest forms of learning.

One explanation is that the growth and progressive urbanization of medieval society from the twelfth century onward created a demand for the services of professionals with a solid training in law, government, and public administration. Accordingly, the new educational centers would have had as their primary purpose to produce the corps of civil servants indispensable to the proper functioning of the various political units of Christendom.

The problem with this explanation is that similar social conditions had existed elsewhere in the past without giving rise to universities or their equivalent; for the needs in question can be met in other ways, through the establishment of palace schools, civil service examinations, and the like. The latter are known to have existed long before the Middle Ages in places as far away as China and Persia, where public offices began to be filled on the basis of competence rather than patronage. This suggests the presence within Christian society of other factors that called for a different kind of education.

Two such factors played a decisive role in the affair. The first is the unique political structure of Christendom, a society ruled by two distinct powers, one spiritual and the other temporal, whose relationship to each other had never been defined with any degree of precision and perhaps did not admit of any clear definition. As long as the Church was the only effective political authority in the West, as it was destined to become once the Roman Empire was overrun by barbarians, the task of clarification was not urgent. With the consolidation and rise to prominence of new national entities in the course of the twelfth century, the situation changed rapidly.

Roman Law was officially adopted by the countries of continental Europe and the Church itself acquired its own constitution, so to speak, in the form of Gratian's *Decree*, where for the first time an attempt was made to sort out the ecclesiastical laws from the civil laws, with which, since the promulgation of Justinian's *Code*, they had been intermingled. All of this called for a more accurate delimitation of the respective jurisdictional spheres, a task that fell to the canon and the civil lawyers of the period. It is not surprising that one of the oldest universities, if not the oldest, Bologna, the home of the great Irnerius, was renowned throughout Europe for its faculty of law.

Still, when one talks about the medieval university today, one does not think primarily of its achievements in this field, important as they may have been at the time and for the development of legal theory. Without the slightest doubt, the heart of that university lay elsewhere, in the faculties of arts and sciences and of theology, the twin disciplines in which the University of Paris was to distinguish itself. If it is not surprising that one of the two oldest medieval universities was noted for its faculty of law, it is even less surprising that the other was most famous for its faculty of theology.

Why philosophy and theology should have been central to the medieval educational enterprise becomes evident when one recalls that Christianity first comes to sight as a nonpolitical religion or a "sound doctrine," as St. Paul repeatedly calls it (I Tim. 1:10; 3:3; Tit. 1:9; 2:1) rather than as a God-given law. In the absence of any divinely promulgated legal and social system, unity was secured by a commonality of belief. Henceforth, one would be justified, not by the performance of lawful deeds, but by faith. As Montesquieu observes, no other religious tradition has ever placed a greater premium on purity of doctrine or been so much on its guard against heresy. It is no accident that the internal history of Christianity, in contrast to that of either Judaism or Islam, is dominated by doctrinal rather than juridical disputes. Orthodoxy was thought to be more important than orthopraxy and what one held as a believer took precedence over any of the political or legal arrangements by which human beings are wont to order their temporal lives. The word "heresy" itself in its now customary meaning is a specifically Christian term. The only non-Christian Latin author to use it, as far as I can tell, is Cicero, in whose works it means nothing more than a philosophical sect (*Ad familiares* XV.16.3). E. M. Forster exaggerated only slightly when he suggested that calling one religion false and another true is an essentially Christian idea.[2] Granted, dogmatic speculation was not part of the primitive New Testament message—the Apostles would not have understood a word of the Athanasian Creed—but the inner dynamics of that message invited it and made it impossible to dispense with it in the long run.

Why so? For one thing, the Bible, although written in principle for everyone, is anything but self-explanatory. Its statements often contradict one another at first glance or lend themselves to more than one interpretation. In one place, it tells its followers that they are to obey their rulers (Rom. 13:1), and in another that they are to obey God rather than men (Acts 5:29). Christ has nothing but praise for the few soldiers who come to see him; at the same time, he warns us that "all who take the sword will perish by the sword" (Mt. 26:52). The New Testament teaches that with the coming of Christ, the law has been abrogated; it also teaches that Christ "did not come to abolish the law" and that "till heaven and earth pass away, not an iota, not a dot will pass from the Law until all is accomplished" (Mt. 5:17-18). I do not wish to imply that these conundrums and others like them are unanswerable, but since the Bible itself does not supply the answers, one has no choice but to look elsewhere, to one's reason, for them. The task of theology, that Christian "guide of the perplexed," to crib a phrase from Maimonides, is precisely to provide the necessary guidance in this matter. As one early Scholastic, Hugh of St. Cher, put it with refreshing candor, its role is to dispel the "confusion" (*confusio*) that pervades the sacred text. (Commentary on the *Historia scholastica* of Petrus Comestor, Cod. Reims 59, f.1vo.) In different and slightly less reverent terms, the trouble with God is that he has a hard time expressing himself clearly.

To this intrabiblical perplexity was added another, having to do with certain obvious conflicts between the doctrines of the faith and the "external wisdom," *exô sophia*, of the pagan philosophers, with which, as a Mediterranean religion, Christianity was bound to come into contact. The earliest medieval case in point is the quarrel between Lanfranc and Berengar of Tours over the doctrine of the transubstantiation, which seems to violate the most basic canons of logic. A second case is the controversy between Roscelin and Abelard concerning the status of universals. Such controversies made it plain that a proper understanding of Christian dogma was contingent on the rigorous use of prescribed methods of argumentation. Just as there are no heresies outside the Christian world, so, strictly speaking, there is no theology outside of it. Philosophy never became an integral part of the Islamic and Jewish religious traditions, neither of which gave birth to a full-blown system of university education; it did become a canonically mandated part of Christian higher education.

The Copernican moment in the history of this vast movement came with the appearance of Aristotle on the scene during the course of the thirteenth century. With Aristotle, Latin Christianity discovered not just a new philosophy but philosophy *tout court*. What had been available prior to that time were scattered fragments of Platonic, Aristotelian, or

Stoic philosophy that the Church Fathers had bequeathed in predigested and Christianized form to their medieval heirs. Aristotle was different. Augustine had said of Plato—"our Plato," *Plato noster*, as he calls him affectionately—that he would have been a Christian had he lived in Christian times. No one ever said the same of Aristotle, a paradigmatic naturalist who had little use for the trappings of religion and, because of his teaching on the substantial union of body and soul, once had the reputation of being a materialist.

These obstacles notwithstanding, Aristotle did manage to make his way into the fold and enjoy his day in the Christian sun. The old suspicions were momentarily laid to rest and the Parisian Arts Faculty was gradually transformed into a faculty of Aristotelian philosophy. By 1255, virtually all of Aristotle's major works, many of which had previously been declared off limits, had become a mandatory component of its official syllabus. The one exception was the *Politics*, which had yet to be translated, but it would not be long before it too was added to the list. The Arts Faculty suddenly came to life; students who had once been eager to leave it for the nobler realms of theology stayed in it for as long as twelve years—from the age of fourteen to the age of twenty-six. Some never left it at all. The Oxford Cleric, who preferred Aristotle to a psaltery and, by implication, the Book of Psalms itself, was apparently one of them.

Technically, the study of philosophy came in under the heading of logic or dialectic, the backbone of the Arts curriculum insofar as it constituted the tool of the other sciences and epitomized the type of education that was in the ascendancy. Chaucer's Oxford Cleric had specialized in logic "long ago." Nor could he could have done otherwise. The university, now reconciled with Aristotle, looked askance at the Muses and banished them from its precincts. The literary taste of the age was such that it preferred the minor Latin poet Statius to Virgil, one of the great poets of all times. Not that the Middle Ages failed to produce its own literary masterpieces: we all know about the *Song of Roland* and the other *Chansons de Geste*, written just as the science of theology was coming into being, as well as about *Tristan and Isolde, Parsifal*, and numerous other courtly romances dating from a slightly later period. But these works, intended for the entertainment of aristocratic audiences, never made it into the schools. The charms of literary expression mattered little to people who had fallen in love with the syllogism in all of its variegated forms and used it as the sole means of intellectual communication. Not even Dante, who did more than anyone else to reaccredit the Muses in the Christian world, was able to secure a place for them in the academy. A hundred years after him, the Italian humanist Leonardo Bruni could still complain bitterly about the contempt in which the humanities, the *studia humanitatis*, were held. In all typical cases, the noblest education consisted in an ascent, not from the theology of the city and its poets to philosophy, but from philosophy itself to Christian theology.

The whole idea was to make use of philosophy to impart ever greater logical rigor to the study of the divinely revealed mysteries. Theology was called a "science" for the first time, albeit a special kind of science, one that received its principles from on high and was thus subalternated to the science of God himself and all those who shared in it. Without its consent, philosophy became, as the saying went, theology's handmaiden. In return for surrendering its title as queen of the sciences, it was guaranteed a permanent place in the new order of things. Henceforth, its highest achievement would be, not indeed to prove the possibility of divine revelation, let alone its truth, or even to prove the falsity of the arguments leveled against it by philosophers—this could not have been done without prejudice to the supernatural character of the divine word—but to show that these arguments are not compelling or demonstrably true.

Novel as it may have been, the medieval university was not entirely without roots in the past. Schools in which advanced training in the ecclesiastical disciplines could be acquired had existed in antiquity and played a significant role in the preservation and transmission of Greek learning. The most famous of these was Alexandria, which under the empire had supplanted Athens as the hub of the intellectual world and was celebrated everywhere for its magnificent library—over a half million volumes, duplicates included. Although Alexandria frequently exchanged teachers with Athens, the two schools appear to have been markedly unlike in their orientations. Athens remained pagan to the core, even though it attracted numerous Christian students and some illustrious ones at that. Alexandria was more responsive to the winds of change, even though not all of its teachers were Christians. Its readiness to accommodate itself to the new climate of religious opinion (from its foundation under Alexander, it had been a center of religious speculation) is probably what insured its survival. As for Athens, it was long thought by modern historians to have died a natural death and been shut down for that reason by Justinian in 529. Yet recently uncovered archaeological evidence suggests that at the time of its closure the school was anything but moribund. Its teachers and students were forced to flee in haste, burying their art treasures as they left in the hope of retrieving them when and if the city recovered from the "malignant fever" that had swept over it.

If I mention the School of Alexandria, it is not because it deserves to be regarded as a forerunner of the medieval university but because, as the cradle of intellectual Christianity, it is the place from which Greek philosophic learning was eventually transmitted to the Middle Ages. To a limited extent this happened directly through Boethius, the son of a Roman diplomat, who accompanied his father to Alexandria where he studied Aristotelian philosophy; he is the only late-ancient Latin writer to have benefitted from any formal instruction in philosophy, and later wrote a number of treatises on logic through which the Latin West received its first instruction in that discipline.

The same thing happened on a broader scale, albeit circuitously, via the Arabic philosophers, thanks to whom the Western world eventually became acquainted with the whole of the Aristotelian corpus or just about. It is not uninteresting to note that the Arabs had themselves received their Aristotle from the Christians with whom they came into contact on the fringes of the Empire. Some medieval sources speak in this connection of a large collection of Greek manuscripts donated by the Byzantine emperor to the Caliph Al-Mamoun of Baghdad during the first half of the ninth century. From this material would have come the Arab world's initiation to Greek philosophy. The texts were translated first into Arabic by Syrian Christians and, some three centuries later, into Latin for the benefit of the Schoolmen. Although uncorroborated by independent sources, the story is not incompatible with Farabi's, Maimonides's, and Boccaccio's accounts of the migration of philosophy from Alexandria to Antioch and thence to Baghdad, where Farabi was able to study it under the guidance of his Christian teachers. Farabi adds that the Christian students were not allowed to read beyond Book I, chap. 7, of the *Prior Analytics*, presumably because what follows in that work, namely, the treatise on science, could pose a threat to the integrity of their faith. No such restriction applied to their Muslim counterparts. Their faith was obviously at risk too, but from a Christian standpoint there was nothing wrong with that.

As the medieval sequel to this intriguing story shows, the misgivings about philosophy were not wholly unfounded. There is no denying that the newly rediscovered Aristotle helped propel scholastic theology to hitherto unattained heights. From this period date the great syntheses of Thomas Aquinas, Bonaventure, Scotus, Ockham, and their innumerable disciples. A comparable flowering of top-notch theological speculation had not been seen since the golden age of patristic literature, and has not been duplicated since then. At the same time, however, the stage was set for the confrontation that had been brewing since the early part of the century and that came to a head in 1277, when 219 propositions excerpted or condensed from the works of a group of Aristotelians associated with the Arts Faculty were condemned by the bishop of Paris, Etienne Tempier. The cat was finally out of the bag. It had become visible to the naked eye that, if philosophy could be enlisted as an ally in the pursuit of theological wisdom, it could just as easily transform itself into a dangerous rival. The Socrates of the *Republic* had once asked how a city that lays its hands on philosophy could avoid destruction. The question now was whether theology could avoid a similar fate.

The unvarnished truth of the matter is that on some of Aristotle's most basic teachings no reasonable compromise could be negotiated. Foremost among these are the eternity of the world, God's knowledge of particulars, and the personal immortality of the soul. Either God is the omnipotent creator of the universe, who continues to govern it and orders all of his creatures to their appointed ends, rewarding the good and punishing the wicked, or he is the "thought that thinks itself," supremely indifferent to everything that goes on here below and incapable of entering into any kind of personal relationship with us. The implications for the way in which one lives one's life as a human being were enormous. Aristotle, whom an earlier generation of Christian teachers had passed on as a gift to their Arabic students, had surreptitiously come back to haunt the donors. Some of his devotees were using him as a ladder with which to escape from what they now saw as a theological cave that held them prisoners. Precarious as it may have been, the situation was not simply to be deplored. The unresolvable tension to which it gave rise between biblical faith and philosophic reason, those two great guides to life that human consciousness at its best has uncovered, could still be fruitful as long as one had the courage to face up to it and learned to live with it.

There was a subtle downside to all of this, for in the process, higher education had undergone a radical change. It lost its Socratic or zetetic character and became progressively more doctrinaire. In particular, it ceased to be an erotic enterprise involving small, self-selecting conventicles whose members shared a common life, held together as they were by the bonds of friendship and a passionate love of the true and the beautiful. Unlike their ancient predecessors, the students who populated the new university were motivated by a different set of concerns. They were in the business of earning degrees and, again like Chaucer's cleric, were worried about finding jobs. The academic questions with which they were made to deal were likewise different. They were not necessarily the natural questions with which reason left to itself seeks to come to grips, but were dictated to a large extent by the religious agenda to which the society was committed. As a result, medieval education was marked by an abstract character that became more pronounced as time went on.

In the end, both components of medieval thought, the religious and the philosophic, were weakened and rendered more vulnerable by the conflict in which they were locked. The saddest part of the story is that, by expelling the Muses from its midst, the Christian university forfeited the weapons with which it might have been able to blunt the attacks that were being mounted against it with increasing intensity by its enemies. So secure was it in its triumph that it never felt pressed to make a case for itself before the bar of public opinion. The policy may have been adequate in a situation of Christendom, that is, a situation in which societal institutions are Christian through and through. It was less well suited to a crisis situation such as the one in which the university was now entangled. As it turned out, the initiative gradually passed in a subterranean way to the other side. For all I know, Dante, Marsilius, Boccaccio, Petrarch, Chaucer, and others like them did more to shape the mentality of the next generations than did the singularly unerotic Nominalists of the late Middle Ages.

This treatment has dealt in the main with the rise and triumph of the university. The foregoing would be incomplete if it did not allude at least in passing to its decline. When did the medieval university die? Surely not all at once. In a sense, it is still with us in diminished form and there have been numerous, if not very successful, attempts to reinvigorate it. It is not farfetched to say that there lurks in the souls of many of our contemporaries a deep-seated longing for the glories of the Middle Ages. Haskins's book is only one example of it. Whatever its deficiencies, the medieval university had a principle of unity and order, taken from either the biblical or the philosophic tradition. The same cannot be said of the typical modern university, which, like our modern liberal democratic societies, has a lot of *pluribus* but not much *unum*. Given the onesidedness of the contest in which they are engaged, finding the proper balance between these two poles of university life today promises to be a long and arduous task.

NOTES

1.   Charles Haskins, *The Rise of Universities* (Ithaca, NY: Cornell University Press, 1957 and 1969). Reprint of the ed. published by H. Holt and Company, New York, 1923.

2.   E. M. Forster, *Alexandria: A History and a Guide* (London: Michael Hoag, 1982), 20.

15

THOMAS AQUINAS AND THE REFORM OF CHRISTIAN EDUCATION

My story begins where it ends, with a few remarks about Umberto Eco's international best seller, *The Name of the Rose*,[1] a novel dealing with a series of strange murders that disrupt the life of a once peaceful medieval monastery whose library, presided over by a blind and aged monk, was reputed to be the finest in all of Christendom. The dark mystery surrounding these murders is pierced by a philosophical sleuth named William of Baskerville, who represents a cross between William of Ockham and Sherlock Holmes, two men of outstanding intellectual virtue. We eventually discover that the hideous crimes were perpetrated by none other than the librarian himself, not for any selfish motive, but in the name of religion and for the sake of its preservation. By a fortuitous turn of events, the monastery had come into possession of the missing portion of Aristotle's *Poetics*, the one devoted to comedy, which the old man was determined to keep out of everybody's reach because its recovery boded nothing but evil for the Christian faith.

Comedy, he reasoned, extols the base at the expense of the noble, the low at the expense of the high. By heaping ridicule on things that ought to be held sacred, it foments doubt and functions as a tool with which to dismantle "every holy and venerable image" (p. 476). The laughter that comedy provokes is a vile sport, fit for "villeins" and fools, who indulge in it for the sole purpose of allaying their secret fears. The true name of fear is fear of God. Whereas tragedy instills that fear into our hearts, comedy cancels it. Comedy teaches that to free oneself from fear is the beginning of wisdom. And yet Christ did not laugh and neither should we. That the rabble should do so is of no consequence since nobody takes them seriously anyway. But the case of Aristotle was different. His treatise made comedy respectable, an object of esteem on the part of the wise and the learned. Aristotle elevated it to the rank of an art and conferred upon it a dignity to which it is not entitled and that it would never have enjoyed otherwise. Therein lay the danger. Allowing such a book to become known was "the Luciferine spark that would set fire to the whole world" (p. 475).

The pious monk was not entirely mistaken. If he was afraid of Aristotle, it was not because he had misunderstood him but because he had understood him only too well; for it was certainly the case that the recovery of Aristotelian philosophy had led, by an implacable logic, to numerous encroachments on the domain of faith. His shortsighted strategy nevertheless backfired. The futile attempt to halt the diffusion of the new ideas resulted only in the destruction of the monastery and, therewith, of the whole world of faith and learning for which it stood. As William explains earlier in the novel, the hiding of books may be of some use in a space of years or days, but "over the centuries it is no use at all" (p. 286).

Eco's novel illustrates in vivid fashion the problem that lies at the heart of the educational endeavors of the Middle Ages: that of reconciling the truths that come to us from divine revelation with the philosophical wisdom of Greece and Rome. The medieval university, which has no exact equivalent in antiquity and out of which grew our own modern university with its formal program of studies, its division into faculties, and its practice of awarding degrees, was originally created for the express purpose of dealing with this problem. By and large, the new institution sought to promote the twin goals of classical education, namely, the formation of the human being and the citizen, but with the understanding that these goals would henceforth be subordinated to the higher goal of forming Christians. Three terms sum up the ideals to which it was dedicated: "humanity," "civility," and "Christianity"—*humanitas, civilitas, christianitas*. Although the three overlapped to some extent, they were by no means identical. Human nature is the same always and everywhere, whereas citizenship inevitably varies from place to place and from one moment in history to another. As for Christianity, it was but one of the religions among which the medieval world in its totality was divided. The object was to determine how all three goals could be made to support one another and collaborate in reasonably harmonious fashion.

How this state of affairs had come about is a long story only the main lines of which need to be recounted for present purposes. The first point to note is that the Christian tradition is the only one of the great religious traditions of the West to have incorporated the study of philosophy into its curriculum. The reason it was able to do so is that, unlike Judaism and Islam, Christianity presents itself first and foremost, not as a sacred law or a divinely mandated social system encompassing every aspect of human life and thought, but as a "faith" or a sacred doctrine the basic tenets of which lend themselves more readily to, and in a sense invite, the kind of rational investigation that is associated with the notion of theology. Significantly, the use of the word "theology" to designate the scientific study of the divinely revealed truth dates only from the twelfth century and is a direct product of the novel efforts that were then made to clarify, organize, and if need be defend the datum of Revelation. Prior to that time, "theology" had meant, as it does for Plato and Aristotle, the teachings of the poets regarding the gods, or else that part of Christian dogmatics which concerns itself with the nature of God in contradistinction to the "economy" or the divine governance of the universe.

It should be added that much of groundwork for these efforts had been laid by the early Church Fathers, to whom belongs the honor of being the first to introduce philosophy into the fold and transform it into an instrument capable of leading to a more penetrating grasp of the content of their religious beliefs—the so-called "intelligence of the faith," *intellectus fidei*, as distinguished from the simple "rule of faith," *regula fidei*. Not everyone was convinced of the legitimacy of such an endeavor. Some Christian writers were vehemently opposed to the study of the pagan classics on grounds similar to those of Eco's librarian and would gladly have boycotted them altogether. To anyone who already possessed the whole truth, the philosophical "quest" (*zêtêsis*) for wisdom was impious or, at the very least, superfluous. St. Paul himself had repeatedly warned against it, and with good reason (e.g., Col. 2:8; I Tim. 1:4 and 6:4; II Tim. 2:22; Tit. 3:9). Nowhere in his Letters was it possible to find an element of praise for it. Pagan literature and learning were the pods that one gave to swine and on which the Prodigal Son had fed after squandering his share of the paternal heritage (cf. Luke 15:16). In Tertullian's famous phrase, Athens had nothing whatever to do with Jerusalem:

Poor Aristotle, who invented dialectics, the art of building up and tearing down; an art so evasive in its propositions, so farfetched in its conjectures, so harsh in its arguments, so productive of contentions—embarrassing even to itself, retracting everything and really treating of nothing! Whence spring those "fables and endless genealogies," "sterile questions," and "words that spread like a cancer?" From all these, when the apostle would restrain us, he expressly names "philosophy" as that against which he would have us be on our guard. Writing to the Colossians, he says, "See that no one beguile you through philosophy and vain deceit, after the tradition of men and contrary to the wisdom of the Holy Spirit." He had been at Athens and had become acquainted with that human wisdom which pretends to know the truth, while it only corrupts it and is itself divided into its own manifold heresies by a variety of mutually repugnant sects. What indeed has Athens to do with Jerusalem? What concord is there between the Academy and the Church, between heretics and Christians? Our instruction comes from "the porch of Solomon," who had himself been taught that "the Lord should be sought in simplicity of heart." Away with all attempts to produce a mottled Christianity of Stoic, Platonic, and dialectic composition! We want no curious disputation after possessing Jesus Christ, no inquiry after enjoying the Gospel![2]

To the question of whether Christians ought to be educated or not there was a ready answer: they had only to read the Bible, which was admirably suited to the fulfillment of every intellectual need. Anyone interested in first principles could turn to the Book of Genesis, which contained a sublime account of the origins of all things. For moral philosophy, there was the wisdom literature of the Old Testament; for history, all of its historical books; and for poetry, the Psalms, the sheer beauty of whose language was unmatched by anything that might be encountered elsewhere.

Others found the argument less than persuasive and decided that more would have to be done if Christians were to equal their pagan counterparts in intellectual achievement. The Bible was, after all, a bit short on rational discourse. Important as it may have been in every other respect, it did not back up its assertions with any sort of argument and made no pretense of supplying the disciplines through which the human mind is perfected. As has been observed, the only biblical character to give a reason for anything is the serpent in Genesis, and he is not generally held in odor of sanctity. Unlike Aristotle's unmoved mover, the God of sacred Scripture does not come across in the first instance as a thinking being. This did not mean, however, that his children were forbidden to think. The cult that he demanded was a "reasonable cult," *logike latreia* (Rom. 12:1), one that entailed the use of reason. Paul's strictures relative to the quest for new knowledge were to be taken seriously, but they were not the New Testament's last word on the subject, for Christ himself had said: "Seek (*zêteite*) and you shall find."[3] Hence pagan wisdom could not simply be equated with the pods eaten by the Prodigal Son. It was more like the captive woman of Deuteronomy, whom the faithful Israelite was legally permitted to take as a wife once the battle had been won and all the male enemies duly slaughtered (Deut. 21:1-14). Granted, there were certain conditions to be met: the poor woman had to shave her head, pare her nails, get rid of her pagan ornaments, and be given a full month to bewail her kin; but if, at the end of that relatively mild ordeal, the romance was still on, the marriage could take place. The same wisdom was also needed to fight the opponents of Christianity with their own weapons, in which case it could be compared to the sword that the young David managed to wrest from his more powerful adversary and with which he then proceeded to cut off his head. (Cf. *inter alia*, St. Jerome, *Letter* 70 [to Magnus].)

The problem might have been less acute were it not for the fact that Christians had no schools of their own and were therefore totally dependent on the pagan schools for their formal education. Like it or not, all young students had to read Homer or Virgil at the risk of being exposed to a way of life that stood at a considerable remove from the moral ideal of the Gospel and was often in open conflict with it. The only remedy was to interpret these authors in such a way as to give the impression that what they taught was not really that different from what Christians believed.

One of the finest examples that we have of this "Christian" reading of the pagan classics, as we saw in chapter 9, is Basil the Great's address *To Young Men on the Benefits to Be Derived from the Reading of the Pagan Authors*,[4] which is all the more remarkable as it contains a large number of references to classical texts, rendered literally or more often in the form of a paraphrase, from a wide range of poets and prose writers. What is peculiar about it, as we have seen, is that these citations have been subtly distorted and given a Christian, or pre-Christian, or quasi-Christian meaning. Even Odysseus is held up as a model of outstanding moral virtue and praised for, of all things, his truthfulness. It does not take much ingenuity to realize that, far from bearing out Basil's contention, the original text proves the exact opposite.

Basil's pedagogy had much to recommend it.[5] By reflecting on it, one catches a faint glimpse of the enormous spiritual transformation that the passage from a pagan to a Christian civilization demanded and in turn effected. Before three centuries had elapsed, the lowly Christians whom Celsus, the earliest philosophic critic of the new faith, had mocked as "theologizing fishermen" had become the intellectual elite of the Roman Empire.

The only ancient writer to draw up a blueprint of what a Christian school might look like if it were to be established is Augustine, who, in Book II of his treatise *On Christian Doctrine*, lists all of the human disciplines as they were then known with a view to showing how they can contribute to a better knowledge of the truths of the Christian faith. It is, therefore, not surprising that Augustine's work, on which the medieval university was largely based, has been read by modern scholars as a treatise of "Christian culture." Its aim is less to resolve the difficulties inherent in any attempt to bridge the gulf between pagan and Christian thought than to sketch the type of education that is called for in a society that takes the Bible as its ultimate norm. Accordingly, the whole of the *enkuklios paideia* or liberal arts program of the ancients, which included the mathematical arts on one side—mathematics proper, geometry, astronomy, and music—and the arts of language on the other—grammar, rhetoric, and dialectic—is inserted into a larger framework and provided with a new rationale. Already at work in this scheme, in theory if not in actual practice, is the famous "reduction of the arts to theology," *reductio artium ad theologiam*,[6] that characterizes medieval education at its peak. It is typical of Augustine's rather more Platonic than Aristotelian approach to this matter that it views all things in the light of their very highest principles. In the end, there is one and only one wisdom, *una sapientia*, which is informed and governed by divine revelation. Any other knowledge to which the human mind may have access, including the whole of pagan philosophy, is at best partial and uncertain. Christianity and it alone is the highroad to human wholeness or perfection.

The trouble that later writers would have with this view is that it takes for granted that the Christian faith is the only true faith and hence that anyone who rejects it after having known it is necessarily at fault. As long as Christianity was all but universally acknowledged in the West, there was no reason to quarrel with it, and indeed it remained the dominant view among theologians to the end of the Middle Ages. The first great challenge to it came with the rediscovery and the Latin translation of Aristotle's works during the first half of the thirteenth century. It has been rightly pointed out that, in the person of Aristotle, the West was confronted, not just with a new philosophy, but with philosophy simply. Here for the first time was a complete, fully developed, and coherent account of human life that owed nothing to divine revelation and could conceivably be construed as an alternative to it. The Arts Faculty, where philosophy was taught and whose role had previously been limited to that of a propaedeutic to the study of theology, suddenly assumed greater prominence and became the focus of the liveliest debates among scholars. Its Masters, who had been in the habit of moving up to theology as soon as circumstances permitted, were no longer quite so eager to leave philosophy and began to make a lifelong career of teaching it.

The crisis that ensued shook the foundations of Christendom and has been described by a distinguished historian with a penchant for sweeping generalizations as one of the four major crises of recorded history, the other three being the Aryan invasions of the second millennium B.C., the fall of the Roman Empire, and the still unresolved crisis of present-day Western civilization.[7] The whole issue came to a climax in 1277 with the condemnation by the bishop of Paris, Etienne Tempier, of 219 Propositions culled or condensed from the works of the Arts Masters and judged to be totally at odds with the basic truths of the Christian faith.[8] Tempier, whose action has been severely criticized by modern scholars, was in fact more broad-minded than most of them are willing to grant. What he objected to was not that these controversial matters were being debated in the schools, but that the Masters engaged in the debate had chosen to make a public issue of them, thereby endangering the faith of simple Christians. The irony is that by promulgating his syllabus Tempier unwittingly did as much as anyone to bring the infamous doctrines to the attention of a larger audience. From that moment on, no educated person would be ignorant of them.

Be that as it may, the challenge had already been met to some extent by Thomas Aquinas, who undertook to reform the whole of theology in accordance with the situation created by the rising tide of Aristotelianism. Whereas Augustine had thought only in terms of a "single wisdom"—*una sapientia*—which included all of the truths uncovered by the pagan philosophers and brought them to completion, Thomas spoke of two wisdoms or two perfect wholes, one governed by principles that are available to the unaided human reason, and the other by principles that exceed the mind's natural capacity and are thus knowable only through divine revelation. With or without any further intervention on God's part, the universe had its proper perfection inasmuch as it contained within itself that by means of which it is capable of attaining its end or of returning to its principle. Grace does not destroy its nature; it merely elevates it by assigning to it an end that is higher than any to which it might aspire or even be aware of when left to itself. With unprecedented boldness, the very first article of the *Summa theologiae* (I, qu. 1, a. 1) asks "whether, besides the philosophical sciences, some other science is needed," namely, sacred science—*Utrum sit necessarium, praeter philosophicas disciplinas, aliam doctrinam haberi*[9]—almost as if to imply that divine revelation was somehow expendable. The question was not without far-reaching practical implications. Speaking figuratively, Augustine has warned that one cannot safely appropriate the spoils of the Egyptians, that is to say, pagan learning and philosophy, without first observing the Passover (*On Christian Doctrine* II.40-41). Thomas, on the other hand, evinces a greater willingness to postpone the celebration of the Passover until the Egyptians have been despoiled and even until such time as the whole land of Canaan has been duly annexed. It goes without saying that, since the order of nature and the order of grace both stem from God, they are necessarily in harmony with each other. If, by any chance, human reason should perceive a contradiction between them, it can only be because it has gone astray and rashly assented to propositions that are neither self-evident nor demonstrably true.

The great merit of the new approach was that, by recognizing the legitimacy and the integrity of the natural order, it provided a common ground of discussion between Christians and other believers as well as between believers and nonbelievers. It also supplied the natural foundations of political rule and thus made for a clearer distinction between the spiritual and temporal powers. Although Thomas seldom dwells on this problem, his use of Aristotle's *Politics* gave a new impetus to political philosophy and encouraged others to delve more deeply into it. As a result, the notion of citizenship regained some of the importance that it had lost over the centuries and became a major concern of such prominent writers as Dante and Marsilius of Padua. Dante himself would soon resurrect the term *politizare* in order to describe the type of political activity that had again become possible (see esp. Dante, *Monarchy* I.12).

These general observations call for a series of additional remarks, which, I hope, will bring the problem into sharper focus. The first is that Thomas's attempt to harmonize biblical faith and Aristotelian philosophy needs to be interpreted judiciously and in the light of the theological context to which it belongs. Thomas himself appears to have been fully cognizant of the limits of any such enterprise. It is by no means evident, for instance, that Aristotle's notion of virtue as expounded in the *Nicomachean Ethics* is compatible with the true spirit of the Sermon on the Mount. There is, after all, a world of difference between the magnanimous man who takes pride in his noble deeds, seeks above all to please himself, and finds his greatest reward in the honor bestowed upon him by his fellow human beings, and the humble follower of Christ who despises honors, is taught to think of others rather than of himself, and joyfully accepts to be held in contempt and even die for his divine master— *contemni et mori pro te*; just as there is a world of difference between the courageous warrior who sacrifices himself and everything that is dearest to him for his country and the saintly Christian who gives up his earthly life in exchange for a greater reward in heaven. The actions may be materially the same in both cases, but, as Pascal would later say, they belong to two formally different and incommensurable orders.

The second remark has to do with the Aristotelian notion of nature, which Thomas was the first to exploit to the full and which met with fierce opposition on the part of the other theologians inasmuch as it posed a direct threat to the biblical notion of divine omnipotence. If God is the supreme master of all and if the whole of creation depends on him not only for its coming into being but for its internal structure, it is hard to think of nature as endowed with an intelligible necessity over which no one, not even God, has any control. Between divine freedom and philosophical necessitarianism there seemed to be no middle ground and hence no possible compromise. Scotus tried valiantly to find a way out of the dilemma by positing the existence of an indefinite number of ideas in the divine mind, among which God was free to choose if he decided to create, as in fact he did. This means, however, that the universe as we know it is only one of a variety of possible and equally contingent universes. The same tendency was carried to its logical conclusion by William of Ockham, who denied the existence of intelligible natures or universal ideas altogether. On this telling, God is at liberty to do or command whatever he likes. He could even order us to hate him if he so desired. There are no limits, intrinsic or extrinsic, to the exercise of his absolutely free will.

Thomas's own solution to this thorny problem avoids the extremes of intellectualism and voluntarism insofar as it seeks to preserve both the intrinsic intelligibility of the universe and its total dependence on God as creator. One of the consequences of this more moderate stance is that it understands virtuous behavior as essentially a matter of reason rather than of blind obedience to the commands of a capricious God. Education has a crucial role to play in it and can be pursued without any offense to the divine majesty. It is nonetheless true that, even as he strives to preserve the thrust of Aristotle's analysis of the moral life, Thomas subverts it by capping the natural virtues with a constellation of infused or supernatural virtues; for the person who believes in the superiority of these supernatural virtues is bound to differ in character from the one who thinks that the only virtues worth cultivating are the ones to which nature points as the highest of all possible human achievements.

This brings me to my next point, which is that Thomas's philosophy and, for that matter, the whole of medieval philosophy assumes a tone that is rather more doctrinaire than that of classical philosophy. This should not cause any great surprise, given the extreme importance that attaches to the unity of doctrine, as opposed to the unity of social structures, in the Christian world. Three great issues came to dominate the intellectual scene: the notion of creation, divine providence and foreknowledge, and the personal immortality of the human soul. Those were the issues on which the theological tradition and the nonreligious philosophic tradition parted company and understandably so, since they touched upon the rational premises on which belief in divine revelation was predicated. If it could be shown conclusively that God has nothing to do with this world, has no knowledge of or control over human affairs, and does not mete out justice in the next world, theology was in ruins. Because it took these possibilities seriously, philosophy was singled out by some theologians as the enemy par excellence, the very "tree of the knowledge of good and evil," as Bonaventure went so far as to call it:

Philosophy must bow before the dictate of eternal truth and not before that of mere rational thought in the worthless manner of the ancient (pagan) thinkers. Do you seek to enjoy God's threefold mercy? Be a humble servant by despising yourself, assisting your neighbor, and respecting God. What is Christian philosophy? It is humility . . . Those who love Holy Scripture also love philosophy insofar as it strengthens their faith; but philosophy is the tree of the knowledge of good and evil, for its truth is mixed with error. If you are an imitator of the philosophers, you say, 'How could Aristotle be mistaken?' and you do not love Holy Scripture; you necessarily fall away from faith. If you say the world is eternal, you know nothing of Christ. If you say there is but one intelligence in all things, no happiness after this life and no resurrection of the dead—if you eat of this tree of the knowledge of good and evil, you are falling away from faith. Those who study the philosophers must be on their guard; everything contrary to Christ's teaching must be avoided as being deadly for the soul.[10]

The problem was more subtle than it appears to be at first glance, for it lay not so much in the fact that the philosophers rejected these pivotal doctrines, although they sometimes did, as in the fact that they questioned their demonstrability. What distinguishes the philosophical mind at its highest is its determination to withhold judgment on any issue in regard to which human reason alone is unable to arrive at a definite conclusion. In the final analysis the contest was not between two mutually exclusive and equally dogmatic positions but between theological dogmatism on the one hand and a peculiar brand of philosophical skepticism on the other.

The same skepticism inevitably spilled over into other domains and particularly into the domain of morality, where its potentially dangerous implications were even more obvious. Centuries earlier, John Chrysostom had observed that if the farmer and the blacksmith, the carpenter and the pilot, and all those who live from the work of their hands had to wait for Plato to tell them what justice is, they would have to abandon their trades and would die of starvation before ever having had a chance to perform a just deed.[11] The practical advantage of the theological position was that it removed any lingering doubt concerning the ultimate goodness of justice and thus offered the clarity and firmness of direction that for the most part constitute the prerequisites of decent human behavior. Its vision was that of a morally consistent universe in which the good are always rewarded and the wicked always punished. The disadvantage was that its teachings rested on theoretical premises whose certitude left something to be desired. The "dogmatism" on which it had to fall back recalls in some manner the dogmatism of the early modern period, for which it may have remotely paved the way, although it is important to observe that this dogmatism has its roots in divine revelation and thus differs sharply from the dogmatism based on radical skepticism that typifies so much of modern thought.

What we finally come to is a conflict or, if not that, at least a permanent tension at the heart of the Western tradition, with neither side being in a position to establish its own claims or refute those of the other. Only a completed or "systematic" philosophy, that is to say, a philosophy that has succeeded in giving an adequate account of the universe in terms of its intrinsic causes, as distinguished from a philosophy that understands itself as an unfinished and unfinishable quest for the truth, can claim to have ruled out the possibility of divine revelation; and, conversely, only a theology that has succeeded in dispelling the mystery in which it is ultimately grounded, even if by so doing it should destroy itself, can command universal assent. This tension between the two most noble guides to life that human consciousness at its highest level has brought to light is not necessarily something to be lamented. It can be fruitful as long as one knows how to live it, or as long as philosophy remains open to theology and theology to philosophy. It may even account for the enormous intellectual vitality that Western thought has demonstrated across the centuries.

My fourth and last comment concerns the predominantly dialectical tone of medieval university education. To anyone trained in the classical tradition, one of the most striking features of Scholasticism, as it came to be called, is its unerotic or "unmusical" character. By that time, the Bible had replaced the Muses and a true story had been substituted for the beautiful lies of the poet as the mandatory starting point of one's ascent to the higher realms of learning. Homer and Virgil were no longer authorities to be reckoned with and the view of the world reflected in their works had ceased to be a live option. The West, of course, had never known Homer save through the mediation of the Latin poets, and the infinitely more gentle and pious Virgil had long been co-opted as an unconscious precursor of the new age. Whereas the Church Fathers wrote books that still had a distinctly rhetorical cast, their Scholastic followers produced philosophical commentaries and theological disputations. Dogma was subjected to the regime of dialectics and the cold syllogism in all its forms became the preferred medium of intellectual communication. It is symptomatic of the spirit of the age that, in the Thomistic scheme, poetry is treated as a part of logic and not as a part of politics, as it had been by Plato and Aristotle. Its chief interest resides in its being a mode of discourse among others, a first feeble attempt at knowledge, the lowest in fact of the disciplines—*infima disciplina*—inferior even to rhetoric insofar as the poet uses images or metaphors rather than plausible arguments to convey his thoughts (Thomas Aquinas, *Commentary on the Posterior Analytics of Aristotle,* Prooemium). In a world that was already overwhelmingly Christian, both rhetoric and poetry had lost their real *raison d'être* and survived only in the form of sermons and liturgical hymns calculated to reinforce a faith that practically everyone accepted. The days were past when one had to make a case for that faith and win people over to it by appealing to their passions. Medieval Christendom is one of the few great civilizations known to us which had God and not some outstanding poet as its educator. There was a price to be paid for this extraordinary privilege. As time went on, theology itself became ever more abstract, indulging in refinements that sapped its vitality and had little significance beyond the quarrels that pitted rival schools of thought against one another. The spirit of genuine inquiry was gradually lost, as was the insight into the problems that had given rise to it two centuries earlier.

The crucial turning point came toward the end of the thirteenth century and the beginning of the fourteenth. Heralded by the crisis of 1277 to which I have already alluded (p. 241), it found its literary expression in Dante's *Divine Comedy,* the poetic masterpiece of the Middle Ages and the encyclopedic work in which the various strands of medieval thought come together in a new and dazzling synthesis. In no other medieval work are the goals of humanity, civility or citizenship, and Christianity more deftly interwoven and brought into finer harmony with one another. Original in its literary form, the *Comedy* is no less novel in its attempt both to introduce the Muses into the Christian world and to revalidate the notion of citizenship. It is a matter of chance that northern Italy, with its plethora of small communes, had begun to experience a rebirth of the political life, but it is not a matter of chance that the *Comedy,* which is thoroughly political in its inspiration, should have done so much to foster that rebirth. That political horizon is nevertheless only the first of its three great horizons. Beyond it lay the larger horizon of the philosopher, whose Olympian gaze ranges from beginning to end of the universe and who, from the lofty vantage point of the heaven of the fixed stars, can look back toward that "little threshing floor" called Earth on which the endless drama of human passion is played out, sometimes with astonishing fierceness:

> With my sight I returned through all and each of the seven spheres, and saw this globe such that I smiled at its paltry appearance; and that counsel I approve as best which holds it for least; and he whose mind is turned elsewhere can truly be called righteous.[12]

Finally, this philosophical horizon, vast as it may have been, is itself encompassed by the presumably larger horizon opened up in the last ten cantos of the *Comedy,* that of divine revelation.

The old ambiguities remain, however, and they haunt Dante's poem as much as they had haunted the works of his classical mentors. We know from Aristotle and his medieval disciples that it is only in the best regime that the good man and the good citizen coincide, and we know from not a few of Dante's contemporaries that an analogous question was being raised in regard to the relationship between the good man and the good Christian. Since no one has ever seen the best regime except in books, human beings rarely have any choice but to make the best of the flawed political arrangements under which they are called upon to live. Given the right education, by which I mean the kind of education that is geared to the development of our common nature and not just education in the spirit of the regime, the more fortunate or gifted ones could aspire to a degree of intellectual and moral perfection far superior to that of society at large. Admittedly, the scheme was not foolproof, for it was unable to guarantee that noble and decent human beings would never have to suffer at the hands of some tyrant or tyrannical mob. Part of the ambition of the Christian Middle Ages was precisely to guard against such an eventuality by subjecting government to the rule of natural law. With that, the necessary conditions of a just life would always be present and the possibility of a clash between the requirements of humanity, civility, and Christianity would be greatly reduced, if not eliminated once and for all.

The cloud in the distance was that human perfection is subject to different understandings according as it is examined in the light of reason alone or in the light of reason illumined by faith. We again come face to face with the problem that had shadowed the efforts of the medieval theologian from the start: the apparently unresolvable conflict between divine revelation and philosophic reason conceived not merely as two bodies of doctrine but as the grounds of two distinct and irreducibly different ways of life. Where Dante stood on this key issue is a problem that preoccupied his early readers more than it does the vast majority of his twentieth-century commentators. No one doubts that he wrote as a Christian, and to this day his poem stands as the greatest Christian poem in our tradition. To what extent he also thought as a Christian is another matter. The sudden reappearance of the Muses in the midst of a society from which they had supposedly been banished forever comes as a timely reminder of the distance the medieval mind had traveled from its religious beginnings to the increasingly secular orientation of its later years. The gigantic effort to bring the entire realm of politics under the aegis of religion had, it seems, turned against itself and given way to a concerted attempt on the part of influential thinkers to reinsert the whole of religion into a political context. Dante himself could find no better way of negotiating the issue of the relationship between divine faith and natural reason than by leaving it to thoughtful readers to make up their own minds as to how that relationship might best be articulated.

In this roundabout fashion we come back to the problem with which we began and which is so aptly formulated by the librarian in Eco's novel. The librarian's mistake was to equate laughter with derision. To be sure, comedy is not without its dangers and can easily become a deadly weapon in the hands of an unscrupulous or irresponsible writer, but this is not its only function and it is certainly not its highest one. As William explains and as the example of Dante demonstrates, there is nothing to prevent it from being placed in the service of truth, nobility, or piety and quite possibly all three at once. In this regard, its status is no different from that of the other intellectual disciplines, which can likewise be put to a variety of uses, some good and some bad. Augustine had said as much about rhetoric, the art of the sophist as well as that of the statesman, which others had accused him of employing and which he was obliged to defend against his detractors:

> Since by means of the art of rhetoric both truth and falsehood are urged, who would dare to say that truth should stand in the person of its defenders unarmed against lying, so that those who wish to urge falsehoods may know how to make their listeners benevolent, or attentive, or docile in their presentation, while the defenders of truth are ignorant of that art? Should they speak briefly, clearly, and plausibly while the defenders of truth speak in such a way as to tire their listeners, make themselves difficult to understand, and render what they have to say dubious? Should they oppose the truth with fallacious arguments and assert falsehoods, while the defenders of truth have no ability either to defend the truth or to oppose the false? Should they, urging the minds of their listeners into error, ardently exhort them, moving them by speech so that they terrify, sadden, and exhilarate them, while the defenders of truth are sluggish, cold, and somnolent? Who is so foolish as to think this to be wisdom? While the faculty of eloquence, which is of great value in urging either evil or justice, is in itself indifferent, why should it not be obtained for the uses of the good in the service of truth if the evil usurp it for the winning of perverse and vain causes in defense of iniquity and error?[13]

Eco's librarian was a fanatic whose animosity toward Aristotle was rooted in fear, which he could detect in others but not in himself. That is why he was willing to go to any extreme, not excluding murder, to achieve his otherwise commendable goal. What he failed to see is that in this instance the proposed remedy was worse than the disease. His physical blindness is only a symbol of the blindness that afflicted the eye of his mind. Dante was more clever and more successful. His solution had the advantage of preserving both Aristotle and the Christian faith instead of sacrificing one to the other.

What in the end is the legacy of the Middle Ages and what light does it shed on the issues that face us at the present moment? My all too sketchy remarks may or may not provide the basis for an adequate answer to this broad question. Still, it should be obvious that our own age, which seems to have lost confidence in itself and in which conviction, to the extent that it exists, is grounded in neither reason nor Revelation, has much to learn from a civilization that prized them above all else. I know of no university today where the Bible and the philosopher whom Dante called "the master of those who know" are taken with anything like the seriousness that our medieval predecessors brought to their study. The paradox in all of this is that the age that is customarily referred to as the "age of faith" is also the age in which Aristotle was held in highest honor. I take it as a sure sign of our predicament that the only two religious thinkers of the modern period to enjoy almost universal respect are Pascal and Kierkegaard, both of them notorious critics of reason. Religion and philosophy are still with us, but in their present form they hardly give us an inkling of what it might mean to live in a world that is permeated with divine and human meaning. The former is either divorced from reason or condescendingly subsumed under the category of myth; the latter, even when not reduced to a desiccating empiricism or the mere therapeutization of our language games, has retreated into a metaphysical and ethical neutrality that deprives it of any possibility of guiding our choices as human beings and citizens. "Values" are the order of the day, and each individual is free to choose his own or to refuse the choice if that happens to be his personal value. Little wonder that the modern university should have decided to call itself a "multiversity." It has no principle of order, and without such a principle, there is no wisdom. Hopeless as it appears to be, the situation nevertheless has a relative advantage over other, more stable situations. Insofar as it is characterized by the shaking of all traditions and cultural horizons, it allows for a reconsideration of the fundamental human alternatives in ways that would have been unthinkable at other moments in our history. The sense of disintegration that so many of our thoughtful contemporaries have experienced is itself an invitation to undertake a fresh or nontraditional assessment of the tradition to which the ruling consciousness of our day is the mostly unconscious heir.

NOTES

1. Umberto Eco, *The Name of the Rose*, trans. W. Weaver (New York: Harcourt Brace Jovanovich, 1983).

2. Tertullian, *On the Exclusion of Heretics*

3. Matt. 7:7. See, on this subject, J. Danielou, "Recherche et tradition chez les

Pères du IIe et du IIIe siècles," *Nouvelle Revue Théologique* 94 (1972): 449-61.

4. English translation in A. Pegis, *The Wisdom of Catholicism* (New York: Random House, 1949), 9-26.

5. For further details concerning Basil's method of procedure, cf. chapter 9 of this volume, "Christianity and Hellenism in Basil the Great's Address *Ad adulescentes*," 137-151.

6. Cf. St. Bonaventure, *St. Bonaventure's De reductione artium ad theologiam*, trans. Sister Emma T. Healy (St. Bonaventure, NY: The Franciscan Institute, St. Bonaventure University, 1955). St. Bonaventure uses the phrase *reductio artium ad theologiam* to indicate that the arts or all secular studies "must be grouped under theology; that theology is the unifying and clarifying science of all the other sciences; that no philosophical knowledge is complete and adequate unless it is studied in the light of theological truth" (Sister Emma T. Healy, p. 18).

7. S. Mazzarino, *Aspetti sociali del quarto secolo: Ricerche di storia tardo-romana* (Rome: L'"Erma" di Brechtachneider, 1951), Introd.

8. See, for an English translation of Tempier condemnation, *Medieval Political Philosophy: A Sourcebook*, edited by R. Lerner and M. Mahdi (New York: The Free Press of Glençoe, 1963), 335-54.

9. Thomas Aquinas, *Summa theologiae* I, qu.1, a. 1.

10. St. Bonaventure, "Third Sunday of Advent," Sermon 2, in *Opera Omnia*, IX.62-63.

11. St. John Chrysostom, *Homilia in Matthaeum* I.11.

12. Dante, *Paradiso* XXII.133-38.

13. St. Augustine, *De doctrina christiana* (*On Christian Doctrine*) IV.ii.3.

IV

DANTE AND THE POLITICS OF CHRISTENDOM

16

DANTE AND THE REDISCOVERY OF POLITICAL PHILOSOPHY

Political philosophy is a relative newcomer to the intellectual tradition of the Christian West. As late as the early decades of the fourteenth century, Dante could still bemoan its neglect on the part of his contemporaries and plead for its restoration to the place of honor that it once occupied among the human disciplines. Only through it would a proper solution be found to the nagging dilemmas of a society governed by two distinct and often competing authorities, one spiritual and the other temporal. It and it alone could teach his fellow countrymen to live, not as the "Babylonians" whom they had chosen to follow, but as the noble "Romans" whose descendants they claimed to be.[1] Yet Dante himself was not without knowing that sooner or later the newly rediscovered science was bound to come into conflict with biblical revelation, that other great guide to life and the one to which most of the Western world had been committed for centuries. With the Latin translation of Aristotle's *Politics* in the 1260s, the Middle Ages was introduced for the first time to a fully developed view of human existence that not only owed nothing to divine revelation but could plausibly be construed as a viable alternative to it. Just how the two rivals were to be reconciled is the theme of virtually all of Dante's major works, including his poetic masterpiece, the *Divine Comedy*. Unfortunately, the

numerous exegetical problems created by the *Comedy's* use of the allegorical mode make it extremely difficult to determine his exact position in
regard to this matter. If a careful reading of the poem suggests anything,
it is that that position may be less conventional than the one that is most
often ascribed to him by modern scholars.

It is generally taken for granted by admirers and critics alike that
Dante's views on this, as well as on all other important issues, however
personally expressed, were in substantial agreement with the common
beliefs of his time. The majority of the studies devoted to him in recent
years fall into two broad categories answering roughly to the two most
prevalent forms of contemporary historical scholarship, which for want of
better terms, I shall label theoretical historicism and active or radical historicism. The first of these, represented preeminently in this country by
Charles S. Singleton, argues that the only valid approach to Dante's works
is the one that leads through the great theological literature of the Middle
Ages, with which Dante himself could not fail to have been acquainted
and by which he presumably took his bearings. This implies among other
things that the content of the body of literature in question can be
apprehended with strict objectivity and that, by adopting the methods of
modern research, one is able to arrive at an understanding of it which is
not essentially different from that of its authors. Singleton's aim is thus
to retrace the pattern of Dante's thought "as established in the theology of
Dante's day." It is assumed from the start that "the poet did not invent the
doctrine," for "what (he) sees as poet and realizes as poet" is nothing
other than "what (was) already conceptually elaborated and established in
Christian doctrine."[2]

The second widely held position is the one articulated by D. S. Carne-
Ross on the occasion of a critical assessment of Singleton's work which
appeared in the May 1, 1975, issue of *The New York Review of Books.*
Following Gadamer's hermeneutics, Carne-Ross questions the feasibility
of a detached and self-forgetful appropriation of Dante's thought of the
kind advocated by Singleton. Any endeavor to speak "as though from
inside Dante's world" is illusory and self-annulling, inasmuch as the interpreter is himself one of the structural elements in a game that could not
be enacted without him. What Singleton and his fellow travelers have
naively mistaken for a genuine recovery of the past is at most the product
of an unavoidable "fusion of horizons," entailing both a creative reinterpretation of Dante's cultural horizon and a corresponding expansion of our
own. There is in fact no such thing as *the* correct interpretation of the
Comedy since, once severed from the contingencies of its origin, the text
"has been freed for new relations of meaning exceeding those which may
have been intended by the author" (Theodore Kisiel's phrase).

For all his misgivings about our ability to recapture Dante's thought world in its primitive form, Carne-Ross, like Singleton, is convinced that Dante's works mirror faithfully the Christian orthodoxy of the Middle Ages. The only point at issue between the two interpreters is whether we as moderns can reinstate in our minds the global outlook that the poet shared with his age and, if not, on what ground his thought could still be an object of legitimate concern to us. The answer is again given in terms of hermeneutical theory: Our own world, we are reminded, is neither identical with nor totally different from the premodern world out of which it evolved by a series of gradual rather than cataclysmic changes. Insofar as the process allows for the survival of numerous elements handed down to us from the old and now abandoned universe of discourse, some glimmer of recognition remains possible and the medieval text is free to address us without forfeiting its historical identity or exacting from us a "conversion" that, in our present socio-cultural context, could never be anything more than a mockery or a pretense.

No one seriously doubts that Dante dealt with the problems of his time in a spirit which was likewise that of his time, and that both the problems and the terms in which they are posed are as far removed from us as the assumptions of modernity are from those of Dante and his contemporaries. But this still leaves open the questions as to whether the general principles in the light of which he discussed those problems apply only to his time and as to whether it ultimately makes any more sense to speak of an elusive insight into the inescapable "historicality of all understanding" than it does to speak of principles whose universality transcends the particular horizon of experience from which all inquiry necessarily begins.

Be that as it may, both Singleton and Carne-Ross are a good deal more confident about the unimpeachable orthodoxy of Dante's views than is an older and longer tradition of Dante scholarship whose origins can be traced back to the time of the poet himself. The fact of the matter is that, although Dante enjoys the reputation of being perhaps the greatest of all Christian poets, his status in the Christian world was from the beginning and has always remained somewhat ambiguous. To this day, he is more often praised than read and more likely to be admired from a distance than studied at first hand, except perhaps by a small band of dedicated Dantophiles who have long since claimed him as their special preserve. Relatively few people have had the urge or the patience to accompany him all the way on his lengthy journey through hell, purgatory, and heaven, and fewer still have allowed themselves to be profoundly influenced by his teachings. Like Pascal, albeit for different reasons, Dante was never fully absorbed into the mainstream of Christian thought or fully integrated into its curriculum of studies. Pascal was blamed for denigrating human reason and for having contributed to the demise of the cosmology in which Christianity had traditionally sought its rational underpinnings. If Dante was suspected of anything, it was not of underestimating the power of reason but of placing too much trust in it. The differences run deeper however. Whereas Pascal's Christian faith was never in question, doubts have frequently been voiced concerning the sincerity of Dante's religious convictions. Not long after his death he was accused of Averroism by some of his contemporaries. The charge was never substantiated, but that it should have been made is itself symptomatic of the kind of mistrust he was capable of arousing. His *Monarchia* was, after all, condemned by the Church in 1329 and we know that copies of it were burned in a number of Italian cities at the time. The record also shows that, had it not been for the patriotic zeal of the Italian clergy, the *Comedy* itself would have been placed on the *Index of Prohibited Books* by the Council of Trent.[3]

The chief reason for the mistrust is not so much that people disagreed with him as that they did not know whether they should agree with him or not. For, the *Comedy,* as anyone who delves into it soon discovers, is not an easy book to decipher. In his short but illuminating *Life of Dante,* Boccaccio tells us that it was not written solely for the purpose of "charming" its readers but of "instructing" them as well and, furthermore, that the teaching which it imparts was addressed to two distinct classes of persons: (a) the "prelates, priests, and preachers" whose duty it is to look after the "frail souls" entrusted to their care, and (b) "the people of excellent learning who, either by reflecting on what the men of the past have written or by supplementing their writings on points that may have been neglected or that beg for further clarification, seek to inform the minds and souls of their hearers and readers."[4] Accordingly, Dante's work is open to two different and at times widely divergent interpretations, one "theological" the other "moral." In one and the same act it is able to "discipline the wise" and "strengthen the foolish." Its poetry is comparable to a river "wherein the little lamb may wade and the great elephant freely swim."[5] This means, however, that its deepest meaning is not necessarily or not always its most obvious meaning. Dante, in short, is an esoteric writer. Part of his teaching remains submerged and hence inaccessible to the casual or uninformed reader. To be more precise, his work contains not just one but two or more teachings all of which were intended by the author, but for specifically different and, one might add, unequal audiences.

The views set forth by Boccaccio did not originate with him. They merely echo and clarify Dante's own well-known statements about the "polysemous" character of his writings in the *Letter to Can grande,* the *Convivio,* and the *Comedy* itself. These statements are often taken to mean that Dante has deliberately set out to give concrete and even mystical expression to the dogmas of Christian theology by clothing them in a veil of allegory. On that telling, the nucleus of hidden truth in the *Comedy* would be coextensive with the sum of the truths expounded discursively and nonmetaphorically in the theological treatises, sermons, and liturgical texts of the period. It cannot be denied of course that all or most of the great religious doctrines of the Middle Ages reappear in some form or other in the *Comedy* and Dante himself occasionally suggests as much. The basic question is whether one can come to an adequate understanding of the poem by reading it simply as a document of the age or an allegory of the Christian faith.

The issue is further complicated by Dante's frequent remarks to the effect that the matters with which he deals had not yet been touched upon or, as he puts it, that the waters on which he moves had never been sailed by anyone before (cf. *Par.* II.1-6). If he means what he says, and there is no reason to doubt that he does, one may be even more inclined to think that the doctrinal substance of the *Comedy* does not coincide in all particulars with the generally accepted views of his day. In order to be sure of it, however, one would have to have a better idea of what these supposedly novel truths are. But then where does one begin to look for them?

The answer to that question can only be, "within the *Comedy* itself," for there would be no point in calling attention to the presence of some mysterious teaching in the text if that teaching were destined to remain forever beyond our reach. Assuming that Dante wrote with the hope of being understood by at least some of his readers, he could not leave them without any inkling as to what his real meaning might be; and assuming that he wrote for future generations as well as for his own, as we know he did, he could hardly rely on such information as would be available only to the people of his time. It was therefore incumbent on him to provide us with all of the clues necessary to a proper interpretation of his work or see to it that no important piece of evidence was left out which could not be supplied by the judicious exercise of one's reason or imagination.

Furthermore, the thematic discussion of poetry in the *Convivio* makes it clear that inner meaning and outer form are so bound up with each other as to constitute an organic whole from which no element, however trifling in appearance, can be dissociated without some loss of intelligibility,[6] Within the purviews of Dante's vast realm, nothing indeed is "left to chance" (*Par.* XXXII.52-3).[7] As one critic has recently stated, "Each new form of address, figure of speech, method of proof, or event is in itself purposive and subsumes, contributes to, or augments the effects of smaller, larger, and collateral divisions."[8] The reader may sometimes fail to perceive the relevance of this or that detail, but unless he prefers to think that the author was negligent or confused, he has no choice but to proceed on the assumption that each one is consonant with the rest of the text and designed to reveal, enhance, or otherwise qualify its meaning.

This is as much as to say that one cannot approach the *Comedy* as one might approach any other book and certainly not as one tends to approach most modern books. If, for reasons of his own, Dante has chosen to conceal his intention, we are constantly left to wonder whether or not what he says is to be taken at face value. The likelihood is that upon inspection some of his statements will turn out to be ironic and hence expressive of ideas that are contradicted by their literal sense. True, it would never occur to us to speak of these statements as ironic if we had not begun to detect the irony or seen beyond what is actually said; but this only proves that the person who reaches this stage has already overcome his initial indifference or the merely "historical" curiosity that had attracted him to the *Comedy* in the first place and has assumed the role of a silent participant who is compelled to take sides on the issue at hand.[9] The experience in store for him is unique. It involves nothing less than his transformation into an accomplice who raises himself to the level of the author's thought by reproducing within himself the genesis of that thought. Thanks to the collusion thus forged between the two minds, what may have started out as just another pleasant foray into Dante's fanciful "other world" rapidly develops into a strange spiritual adventure in which one is willy-nilly caught up, with no clear foreknowledge of where it could lead and no guarantee that he will still be the same by the time he reaches his destination.

With these ideas in mind let us turn, not to the whole of the *Comedy*, to which one could not possibly do justice in a few pages, but to one particular episode that has thus far eluded every attempt at an interpretation, namely, the meeting between Virgil, Dante, and the Latin poet Statius in Cantos XXI and XXII of *Purgatorio*.[10] The enigma posed by these two cantos is all the more tantalizing as the role assigned to Statius in the action of the *Comedy* is second in importance only to those of Virgil and Beatrice. Once introduced, Statius figures in no fewer than thirteen cantos and is, along with the other two, the only character to move from one level to another. The reader has been prepared for what is about to happen by the allusion in the preceding canto to an earthquake that has just caused the mountain to tremble. Nowhere else in the *Purgatorio* is there any mention of such an event. We soon learn that the quake heralded Statius's release from purgatory, to which he had been confined for upwards of nine hundred years in order to atone for his sins. It is worth noting that Canto XXI, where Statius makes his first appearance, marks the mathematical midpoint of purgatory proper, through which the travelers have been moving since Canto IX, and hence the ideological center of the whole of Dante's figurative odyssey. What exactly is the significance of Statius's presence in the overall economy of the poem and to what does he owe the high honor conferred upon him by Dante? We may begin by recalling the salient details of the initial encounter between the three poets.

In the course of their journey toward the top of the mountain of purgatory, Virgil and Dante come upon Statius on the ledge of the avaricious. Statius, still ignorant of the identity of the pilgrims, proceeds to give a brief account of his literary career and especially of his admiration for Virgil, to whom he graciously acknowledges his debt as a poet. There follows a touching recognition scene in which, forgetting for a moment that they are shades, Statius rushes to embrace his revered master.

Virgil's first reaction is one of surprise at the thought that a man of Statius's "wisdom" should foolishly have allowed himself to be carried away by avarice; whereupon Statius explains that the sin for which he was just now being punished was not really greed but its no doubt less contemptible opposite, prodigality; and that he was associated with the avaricious because vices opposed to the same virtue, in this case liberality or moderation in the use of wealth, are purged together on the same ledge (XXII.25-54).

We are subsequently informed by Statius himself that, enlightened by the famous prophecy of the *Fourth Eclogue,* he had converted to Christianity but that, out of fear of being persecuted, he had refrained from any public profession of faith, remaining to the end of his life a secret Christian, *chiuso cristian* (XXII.90), and eschewing any reference whatever to Christianity in his two epic poems, the *Achilleid,* which had not yet been written, and the *Thebaid,* which was only half completed at the time of his conversion.

Since there are no traces anywhere in the literary tradition of Statius's prodigality or avarice, whichever it may be, or for that matter of his pretended Christianity; we must assume that both details have been invented by Dante for some definite, though as yet unknown, purpose which would have to be taken into account in any final or reasonably complete interpretation of the relevant passages. It is likewise obvious that, in the total absence of independent witnesses, any such interpretation will have to be derived from the *Comedy* itself. Fortunately, there is in Dante's text sufficient evidence to show that Statius had indeed been the victim of the vices to which he confesses, but not in the way in which one would normally have anticipated.

First of all, it is almost certain that the initial letters of the four tercets in which Statius's avarice is described, V-L-O-E, should be read as an acrostic spelling the word *velo* or "veil," a standard device employed by Dante to signal the existence of a covert meaning in the text.[11] We also observe that the first of these four tercets specifically adverts to the knowledge by which the doubtful or the amazing is rendered intelligible and thereby ceases to be an object of doubt or amazement: "Truly, things often take on appearances that excite false wonder because their true causes are hidden" (XXII.28-30). The antithesis between the truth and its deceptive semblances is further accentuated by the manner in which the terms designating the true and the false—*veramente, falsa, vere*—are intertwined in the phrasing of the sentence. In typical Dantean fashion a correspondence has been established between the intention of the passage and its literary form.

There comes next a brief but equally mysterious statement in which Statius grossly misinterprets the following verse from the *Aeneid*: "To what (extreme of wickedness) dost thou not drive mortal hearts, accursed hunger for gold!"—*Quid non mortalia pectora cogis / Auri sacra fames!* (III.56). The exclamation is called forth by Aeneas's accidental discovery of the crime perpetrated by the Thracian king, Polymestor, a one-time ally of the Trojans who had later shifted his allegiance to the Greeks, treacherously murdered Priam's son, Polydorus, and confiscated the treasure entrusted to him by his father. Statius gives to Aeneas's words a meaning that is plausible if one takes the sentence by itself but which is clearly ruled out by the context and is in fact the very opposite of the one intended by Virgil. Instead of excoriating the loathsome desire for gold that lurks in the hearts of people, he laments the fact that it should have so little power over them. "Why," he says, "O blessed hunger for gold, dost thou not govern mortal appetite!" The misreading is all the more striking as Statius is at pains to explain that he has finally "understood" what Virgil wanted to say. The verb that he uses is *intendere*, which in the *Comedy* often signifies "to penetrate the hidden meaning of a text."[12] Since Dante had intimated on a previous occasion that he was cognizant of all the sordid details of the story,[13] one is loath to accuse him of inadvertence. The error in all probability is deliberate. Like the acrostic detected in the preceding verses, it points to the possibility that his own text could lend itself to more than one interpretation.

Assuming, as Virgil unmistakably does, that miserliness is not the characteristic vice of a "wise" poet, one is prompted to look for some other type of avarice or prodigality to which Statius could have succumbed. The nature of this new vice is not all that difficult to imagine. If a poet qua poet is called lavish or stingy, it is most likely to be in regard to what he has to say. The poet's coin is not gold or silver but words, and words, too, like money, can be dispensed or withheld inappropriately, along with the thought they convey. The little that is said about Statius in the *Comedy* suggests that, while there is no reason to suspect him of having been a spendthrift in the ordinary sense, he had fallen prey to a less common but no less important form of prodigality. As the author of two epic poems notable for their unabashed paganism—*lungamente mostrando paganesmo* (XXII.91)—he may be said to have been prodigal in words, a defect from which in time he sought to cure himself, only to fall by reaction into the antipodal vice of taciturnity. Having once spoken too much, he ended up by saying too little and incurred the blame of thrift.

The suggestion, farfetched as it may sound at first hearing, becomes more credible when we consider the likely connection between the avarice gratuitously imputed to Statius by Dante and his presumed hidden Christianity. It could well be that the two fictions belong together and are intended to illumine each other. By shunning any open avowal of his newly found Christian faith, Statius practiced what was known in the Middle Ages as the "economy of truth," *oeconomia veritatis*. His avarice is of a piece with, if not actually identical to, the "lukewarmness" (*tepidezza*) with which he reproaches himself in the same passage (XXII.92). An ardent Christian would doubtless have been less fearful and more forthright, even at the risk of his life. Not so with Statius. The subterfuge to which he resorted guaranteed his survival, but by the same token it robbed him of the one opportunity that he might have had of leading others to the truth. No one reading his poems would have learned anything about the Christian faith. His position is the exact opposite of that assigned to Virgil, who, "like one carrying his light behind him at night," showed the way to those who came after him but was unable to help himself (XXII.67-9).

Our suspicion regarding Statius's verbal avarice and prodigality is confirmed in retrospect by the peculiar interplay of silence and speech with which the preceding canto had ended. Statius has just declared his unbounded esteem for Virgil but is as yet unaware that one of his interlocutors is that same Virgil, for the pleasure of whose personal acquaintance he would gladly have spent an extra year in purgatory (XXI.100-2). Dante is about to reveal Virgil's identity but is restrained by a sign from his master and suddenly sees himself pulled in opposite directions by the two poets, one of them begging him to speak, the other urging him to remain quiet. Observing Statius's eagerness to know, Virgil finally relents and the disclosure takes place. What this playful and apparently idle tug-of-war signifies is not altogether clear. If we recall, however, that the composition of the *Comedy* exhibits a sequence of interlocking scenes that parallels the scheme of interlocking rhymed verses within each canto, we are given a hint as to its possible meaning. The otherwise unexplainable interlude is a subtle but direct anticipation of the next and crucial episode in the drama. Its function is to ready us for the curious blend of speech and silence or boldness and reserve which, as we have seen, constitutes the focus of the ensuing canto.

Even if, for the sake of argument, one were to grant the validity of the foregoing interpretation, one might feel that little has yet been done to dispel the obscurity in which the whole incident is shrouded. What does it matter after all that Statius should have been a coward who demonstrated his lack of courage by purposely withholding the truth about his conversion to Christianity? His role in the *Comedy* could still strike us as purely adventitious and add nothing to our understanding of either the internal structure or the doctrinal content of the poem. There is more to the story, however. A moment's reflection will edge us closer to the reason that accounts for the lofty position to which Statius, a relatively minor poet compared to Virgil, is elevated at this critical juncture of Dante's voyage.

Statius's most obvious function is to serve, along with Virgil, as Dante's guide in the upper regions of purgatory. His role in this respect is analogous to the one that Virgil alone had fulfilled throughout the earlier part of the journey. But if such is the case, the composition of the poem is bound to impress us as strangely asymmetrical. Given Dante's fondness for symmetry, one would normally expect a third epic poet to assume the role previously discharged by the other two poets once the threshold of heaven is reached. No doubt Beatrice will be on hand to accompany Dante on the rest of his journey; but as a shadowy figure who cannot by any stretch of the imagination be thought to belong in the same category as Virgil and Statius, she hardly qualifies as the missing guide.

The key to the riddle is furnished in part by the positions which the three poets who travel together occupy in relation to one another and which Dante is always careful to note with the utmost precision. In the scenes that immediately follow the first encounter with Statius, both Virgil and Statius are shown leading the way and Dante, who is still in need of a guide, walks reverently behind them (XXII.127; XXIV.143). As they prepare to cross the wall of fire, the positions shift: Dante moves ahead of Statius and is portrayed comically as a goat between two shepherds, with Virgil in front and Statius bringing up the rear (XXVII.46-8 and 85-6). By the time they reach the end of purgatory a second change occurs and we notice that without much fanfare Dante has all of a sudden taken the lead (XXVIII.82 and 145). The third canticle, it turns out, will not be without its epic poet, to wit, the author himself, who has now become so to speak his own guide. It is significant that at this moment Dante is referred to by name for the first and only time in the poem, and with particular emphasis at that, inasmuch as we are told that this was done out of necessity—*di necessità* (XXX.63).[14]

In light of these observations and bearing in mind what was said earlier about Statius, we can at last address ourselves to the unresolved problem of the symbolic value attached to each of the three major poets. The simplest case is undoubtedly that of Virgil, the non-Christian who writes a non-Christian epic. The case of Statius, the poet par excellence of purgatory, is slightly more complex but no longer as bewildering as it once seemed to be, since on the basis of Dante's literary fiction he now stands for the Christian who produces what must likewise be described as a non-Christian epic. Dante's own case would appear to exhibit a simplicity analogous to that of Virgil, for one immediately thinks of him as a Christian who sets out to write a Christian epic. By this elementary procedure the symmetry that was originally thought to be lacking is restored and the three parts of the poem are adjusted to one another without any discernible hiatus. Or are they?

The only trouble with that explanation is that it again confronts us with an incomplete enumeration. One fascinating possibility has been tacitly passed over and thereby brought in a forceful if somewhat roundabout way to our attention, namely, the hypothetical case of the non-Christian who writes a Christian epic. At this point the reader is thrust in the situation of having to reexamine the various alternatives since neither Virgil's nor Statius's position appears subject to revision. Dante's own status is cast in a rather more dubious light. Could it be that he, too, felt the need to resort to a strategy similar to the one that he fancifully ascribes to Statius? It would be interesting to say the least if Dante, the author of the most famous Christian poem in our tradition, had slyly refused to pronounce himself on so crucial a matter.

Needless to say, the contention that the deeper layers of the *Comedy* leave room for doubt concerning the religious convictions of its author runs counter to the bulk of contemporary opinion and is apt to be greeted with a fair amount of skepticism by most readers. Even if it could be proved to everybody's satisfaction that Dante had reservations about the truth of the Christian faith, one wonders why he should have gone to such great lengths to veil his thought. We forget all too easily the severe restrictions imposed by the societies of the past on the public expression of ideas and opinions judged to be at odds with their most cherished beliefs. Statius's crypto-Christianity, which finds its rationale in the open hostility of the pagan rulers to the new faith, has its parallel in the reticence displayed by his medieval counterpart, who lived at a time when heretics and apostates had become liable to the harsh penalties once reserved for avowed Christians.

We know by now that there is at least one expedient to which a confirmed rebel can resort in order to avert a head-on collision with the established authority without abdicating his freedom or jeopardizing his power to act, and that is to conform in deed and speech to the conventions of the society in which he happens to live. By deftly covering his tracks, he automatically creates a presumption of innocence in his favor and shifts the burden of proof to the offended party. From then on it is no longer up to him to exculpate himself but up to others to demonstrate his guilt. Even if he remains suspect, there is little likelihood of his being convicted; for it is virtually impossible to impeach someone for holding or propagating subversive views which he has never actually voiced and which, moreover, can be shown to be at variance with numerous other statements that he did make.

That Dante was keenly aware of the dangers that he faced is readily established from a variety of texts and allusions scattered throughout the *Comedy.* One of the literary devices that he utilizes in the *Purgatorio* consists in relating the seven deadly sins to the beatitudes of the Sermon on the Mount. Each time a "P" (for *Peccatum*, "sin") is removed from the pilgrim's forehead, the corresponding beatitude is chanted in the background. No sooner has Dante undergone a series of tests calculated to rid him of, say, pride or anger than he is reminded of the blessedness promised to the "poor in spirit" or the "peacemakers" (cf. *Purg.* XII.110; XV.38; XVII.68-69; XXVII.8). In general the parallelism between sin and beatitude poses no major problem. The situation becomes a bit more complicated when we reach the fourth beatitude, "Blessed are those who hunger and thirst for righteousness," which the poet has split into two parts, one dealing with the "hungry" and the other with the "thirsty" (*Purg.* XXII.6 and XXIV.151-4). According to Grandgent, echoed by Singleton, the separation was necessitated by the desire to obtain the requisite number of beatitudes. Why that should be so is not all that evident, especially since by availing himself of all eight beatitudes Dante would already have ended up with one too many. It is more to the point to observe that in the process two other beatitudes have been silently dropped, the "meek" and the "persecuted," the praise of whose virtues would have been out of place in a discussion bearing precisely on the means by which one can escape oppression and persecution.

Nor is this all. The lacuna created by the omission of these two beatitudes is remedied by the addition of a new one, taken not from the Sermon on the Mount but from Psalm 31:1 (Vg.): *Beati quorum tecta sunt peccata,* "Blessed are they whose sins are covered" (*Purg.* XXIX.3). The trick this time lies in the poet's having quietly suppressed the first part of the verse, which speaks not of the "covering" of one's sins but of their "remission": *Beati quorum remissa est iniquitas.* One is tempted to infer that Dante was more intent on not being caught than on being forgiven. It should be added at once that the veil which "covers" his own sins is not such as to preclude the possibility of their being uncovered by the wise, just, and sympathetic reader (cf. *Par.* XVII. 104-5).

The same concern is evinced with even greater clarity in the famous Canto XVII of *Paradiso,* in which the course of the poet's life is foretold. The prophecy, oddly enough, is uttered, not by Beatrice, as we had first been led to expect (cf. *Inf.* X.130-2), but by Dante's ancestor, Cacciaguida, to whom he simply refers as his "father." Dante has just listened to Cacciaguida's account of the internal strife that has long racked his native city and immediately proceeds to inquire about his own future, for which he rightly fears. The reason alleged is that if he is apprized beforehand of the misfortunes that lie ahead, he may find them easier to bear than if they were to fall upon him abruptly; for, as he says, "an arrow foreseen comes more slowly" (v. 27).

From Cacciaguida he learns first of all that he will be banished from Florence and experience the unremitting harshness of a life lived in exile (v. 48). He will discover for himself "how salty bread tastes in other people's houses and how hard the path leading up and down other people's stairs can be" (v. 58-60). He is also told that in his misery he will be able to count on the benefits of an unnamed savior whose noble deeds will bring about a reversal in people's fortunes and, finally, that notwithstanding the grave perils to which it is exposed "his life has a future far beyond the punishment of his enemies" (v. 97-8).

If this were the whole of Cacciaguida's prophecy we should have every reason to be disappointed, since practically all of the events referred to either had already come to pass or never materialized. The real burden of the prophetic speech, one surmises, lies elsewhere. It has to do neither with the known past nor the uncertain future but with that part of the future whose outlines may be discerned by a man of wise counsel. Hearing that his fame is assured, Dante is perplexed. Upon reflection, however, he gradually comes to understand that, once Florence is taken away from him, he must not "by reason of his songs" risk the loss of other cities that might still be open to him. The things that he has learned in the course of his journey, if he were to relate them, would most certainly arouse the antagonism of many of his hearers. The alternative is to remain silent; yet to do so would be to forgo any chance of being remembered by posterity. A "timid friend of the truth" would have no trouble preserving his own life now, but only at the price of losing it among those "who will call this time ancient" (v. 118-20).

The effect of Dante's remarks is to elicit a smile of approval on the part of his illustrious ancestor. The opening lines of the canto had alluded ominously to the plight of Phäeton, whose failure to heed the advice of his father, the sun, was the occasion of his downfall. Only once Cacciaguida is convinced that his own advice will not be misused does he encourage Dante to lay all falsehood aside and reveal what he has seen. Some people will inevitably be offended by what he has to say; but if that should happen, they and not he will be the ones to suffer: "Let there be scratching where the itching is" (v. 129). His words, however bitterly resented, will provide a vital nourishment for those who can digest them and, without prejudice to his present situation, win him the acclaim of future generations.

Cacciaguida's obscure prophecy, inserted at the very center of the *Paradiso,* is a commentary on what Dante had previously described as "the art of coming back" (*Inf.* X.49-51, 77, 81).[15] Its significance may be summed up by saying that if Dante wishes to avoid being persecuted for his impiety, he must accommodate his speech to the religious beliefs of his contemporaries, and if he has any hope of living beyond his time, he must in some subtle way let it be known that his own horizon is not defined by those beliefs. Therein lies the superiority of his "wisdom" to that of Statius. By steering a middle course between verbal avarice and verbal prodigality, the *Comedy* demonstrates the kind of "measure" that was still wanting in the works of his allegedly Christian predecessor. Unlike Statius, Dante cannot be blamed for saying too much or too little. He neither completely reveals nor completely conceals the inner depths of his thought. The stratagem was doubly successful in that it enabled him not only to save himself and his reputation but at the same time to instruct others regardless of what their level of understanding, degree of preparedness, or personal dispositions may have been then or were likely to be in the centuries that followed.

Whether or not one accepts this general interpretation will depend in large measure on how well it squares with the rest of the poem and how much it contributes to the elucidation of its numerous and seemingly insoluble enigmas.[16] In the meantime, we have at least some evidence that Dante, who so often speaks of himself by indirection in the *Comedy,* had learned to wear the mask of orthodoxy, lifting it occasionally, to be sure, but only as much as was necessary to carry out his purpose. The history of the recovery of this ironic mode of communication is not without its own brand of irony. Having at last triumphed over the enemies by whom it had long been threatened from without, the Christian society of the Middle Ages will henceforth harbor in its midst an increasingly large number of thinkers bent on pursuing a course of action that would lead them further and further away from the path that clerical officialdom had marked out for itself. The adversary this time will be the more dangerous as he will be hidden within the ranks of the faithful and, so to speak, invisible to the naked eye.

What this strange adversary may have been like is hinted at in a variety of ways by Dante himself. Readers of the *Comedy* have long been puzzled by the presence among the blessed in *Paradiso,* Canto XX, of an obscure Trojan hero named Riphaeus, who, as it happens, is the only unconverted pagan to be canonized by the author. Riphaeus is of course praised for his exceeding righteousness in the *Aeneid,*[17] but there were other equally virtuous and more renowned pagans who could just as easily have been selected to illustrate the unfathomable mystery of divine predestination that the *Comedy* makes bold to explore at this point. What we notice is that, in addition to being just, Riphaeus was part of a small band of Trojans who, in the thick of the battle, disguised themselves as Greeks in order to fight against the Greeks.[18] Riphaeus's justice was not his only title to the eternal glory of Dante's heaven. It went hand in hand with a certain craftiness or duplicity similar to the one that would be used to good advantage by the new spiritual warriors of the late Middle Ages.

To speak of adversaries or warriors in this connection may not be wholly appropriate; for, unlike their early modern successors, the political writers of the Middle Ages never mounted a direct attack on Christianity and never tried to discredit it publicly. Most of them recognized both its grandeur and its usefulness, and had no qualms about lending their support to it. In accordance with the tradition of classical antiquity whose spirit they sought to revive, they would have considered themselves amply rewarded if, by renouncing its worldly ambitions, the religion under which the West had lived for so long and with which it could not conveniently dispense were to become at once more spiritual and more humane.

Admittedly, the thesis defended in these pages oversimplifies matters and leaves untouched a number of equally important strata of the *Comedy*. If it should prove to be substantially correct, however, a Christian might well be tempted to write Dante off as an archvillain the study of whose works bodes nothing but ill for his faith. Yet to draw this conclusion would be to fall into an even greater oversimplification. It is certainly not a matter of chance that each of the three canticles of the *Comedy* ends with the word "stars" and that the work as a whole is brought to a fitting close with a reference to "the love that moves the sun and the other stars." The mood generated by this constant reminder of what is divine in the universe again invites a comparison with Pascal, "that strange Christian who did not find his father in the heavens,"[19] whose modern eyes could no longer perceive anything splendid, lovely, or enchanting in a world that had lost its center along with its circumference,[20] and for whom the spectacle of the starry sky above was a source of frightened anguish rather than of serene wonder.[21] If the religious core of Dante's poem is to be discovered anywhere, it is in its concentration on the single most profound longing of the human soul, a longing once described by the author himself as "the inborn and perpetual thirst for the godlike kingdom" (*Par.* II.19-20). To that longing the *Comedy* bears what is beyond the shadow of a doubt one of the most exquisite testimonies ever given. As such, it poses in all its force the problem to which, for a Christian, Christianity alone offers the ultimate answer.

The modern theologian is ordinarily inclined to view things in a rather different perspective. Chastened by a long history of religious feuds and pious cruelties, he is more likely to challenge Christianity's claim to exclusivism and demand the same measure of sympathetic consideration for all religions or, at the very least, all great religions. Whether this goal of universal sympathy is achievable and how much one stands to gain by pursuing it are, nevertheless, questions that bear careful scrutiny. The problem with which it confronts us from a confessional as well as from a nonconfessional viewpoint is that it not only tends to dilute the substance of the faith but precludes any genuine encounter between people of different religious persuasions. The seeming humility from which it draws its appeal necessitates a bracketing of one's attachment to one's beliefs in favor of a provisional espousal of another's attachment as one's own. To that extent it may be said to operate on the principle of an histrionic rather than a serious identification with the other. Like Descartes's methodical doubt, to which it bears an epistemological affinity, it must begin by negating what it seeks to preserve without being able to guarantee its subsequent retrieval. As a consequence, it inevitably misses what is most vital in the other, for only the totally committed person is in a position to appreciate the depth of someone else's commitment. Its end result would thus appear to be a subtle demotion of, and hence an implicit disrespect for, all religious positions. Upon close examination, it reveals itself as more superficial than profound, more arrogant than humble, and more provincial than truly universal.

Where Dante stood on this issue of belief versus unbelief will probably never be known with any degree of finality and is at best a matter of idle curiosity. What can be asserted with some assurance is that he himself took Christianity and its claim to truth more seriously than many and perhaps most of its latter-day advocates or critics and that he was painfully aware of all that was to be won or lost by embracing it or giving it up. For that reason if for no other, the probing of the *Comedy's* disquieting underside has more to teach us about what it means, or once meant, to be a Christian than any naive but comforting acceptance of its Christian surface. The faith to which such a probing can lead will be all the stronger as it is tempered in the blast furnace of the most searching critique to which it has ever been subjected.

Our own generation does not take well to the idea of an irreducible though possibly creative tension between revealed religion and philosophy of the kind that is adumbrated in *Comedy*. It generally prefers either Etienne Gilson's attractive thesis, which collapses these two originally independent components of Western thought into the notion of a "Christian Philosophy" (for the more broad-minded a "religious philosophy"), or else an older "enlightened" theology, most familiar today in the guise of Tillich's concept of "ultimate concern," which obliterates the distinction between them altogether. The basic perplexities remain, however. Against the first alternative one might urge, as Heidegger does, that the idea of a Christian philosophy is just another stillborn attempt to square the circle,[22] and against the second that, under pretense of transforming us into "rational Christians," the enlightened theology of the modern period has only succeeded in making us "extremely irrational philosophers," as Lessing predicted it would.[23]

The objection that was thought to compel the abandonment of the position taken by Dante is that it seemed to foreclose the possibility of a final reconciliation between biblical faith and philosophic reason. Even so, one is entitled to ask whether in the last analysis the unbelief occasionally engendered by that position is more offensive to the religious mind than such present-day forms of unbelief as respectful indifference or a kind of nostalgia for lost faith that goes hand in hand with the inability to distinguish between a theological truth and a pious myth.

NOTES

1. Dante, *Epistolae* VI.2. 5-8, *Opere Minori*, ed. A. del Monte (Milano: Rizzoli, 1960), 764-65.

2. Charles S. Singleton, *Dante Studies 2: Journey to Beatrice* (Cambridge, MA: Harvard University Press, 1967), 7.

3. Cf. G. H. Putnam, *The Censorship of the Church of Rome* (New York: G. P. Putnam's Sons, 1909), II 308.

4. G. Boccaccio, *Life of Dante* in F. Basetti-Sani ed., *The Earliest Lives of Dante* (New York: Frederick Ungar, 1963), 74-75.

5. Ibid., 50.

6. Dante, *Convivio* II.1.9-15.

7. The point is acknowledged by Carne-Ross, who adds wistfully, *New York Review of Books*, (May 1, 1975), 6: "The trouble is that nothing in the *Comedy* is finally problematic . . . More than any other great work of the imagination, the *Comedy* confronts us with a world that is ordered and meaningful from top to bottom. A recurring phrase of Singleton's is 'It is no accident that . . .' One sometimes wishes it were. What Dante says in paradise, *'casual punto non puote aver sito'* (32, 53) is true of his poem as a whole: there is no place there for a particle of chance, for the randomness of things. No place, then, for the unexplained gift to the moment when, in Stevens's words, 'Life's nonsense pierces us with strange relation.' The relations are all there, plotted in advance, waiting only for reason to discover them or grace to reveal them."

8. R. S. Haller, *Literary Criticism of Dante Alighieri* (Lincoln, Nebraska: University of Nebraska Press, 1973), xxxix.

9. See, on the subject of irony, the remarks by J. Klein, *A Commentary on Plato's Meno* (Chapel Hill: The University of North Carolina Press, 1965), 5-6.

10. An earlier and shorter version of the interpretation that follows was

published under the title "Dante and Averroism," in *Actas del V Congreso Inter-nacional de Filosofia Medieval* (Madrid: Editora nacional, 1979), II 739-46.

11. *Purgatorio* XXII.28-39. The cryptogram follows the customary rules of the genre, which require that the proper order be restored by taking the first letter first (V), then the last (E), the second (L), and the next to the last (O). Cf. W. Arensberg, *The Cryptography of Dante* (New York: A. A. Knopf, 1921), 50.

12. Dante Alighieri, *La Divina Commedia*, edited and annotated by C. H. Grandgent, revised by Charles S. Singleton (Cambridge, MA: Harvard University Press, 1972), 506, *ad* v. 38.

13. Cf. *Purg.* XX.114-5.

14. Dante appears to be apologizing for speaking about himself in such a personal way in his own book, thus violating the rules of decorum; cf. *Convivio* I.2. Even as he does so, however, he manages to poke fun at the reader. The expression *di necessità* contains the poet's name in the form of a cryptogram, which is to be deciphered in accordance with the rule explained above: *D*[i] *NEcessiTA*. In the present case the Italian spelling of the letter "d" (*di*) has been used. We are told how to read the cryptogram by the accompanying verses, in which Dante, startled by the sound of his name, looks to the left and to the right, like the captain of a ship who rushes "aft and fore" (*di poppa in prora*) to see what the men of his crew are doing (XXX.58-60). The poet puts himself forward again in the unusual rhyme scheme displayed in this passage. Of the fifteen verses that it comprises, twelve end in "a"; the remaining three, which stand out that much more prominently, end in *io*, the Italian "I."

15. The art in question is the theme of one of Boccaccio's stories, *Decameron*, III.7, which has sometimes been interpreted as a secret life of Dante.

16. For further details on this point see my *Dissidence et philosophie au moyen âge: Dante et ses antécédents* (Montreal: Bellarmin, and Paris: Vrin, 1981), 147f.

17. Virgil, *Aeneid* II.426-7. Riphaeus and his companions come upon this tactic accidentally when they are mistaken for Greeks by their opponents at nightfall.

18. *Aeneid* II.386-97.

19. P. Valéry, "Variation sur une pensée," in *Oeuvres* (Paris: Gallimard, Bibliothèque de la Pléiade, 1957), I, 461.

20. Pascal, *Pensées*, frg. 199.

21. *Pensées*, frg. 201.

22. M. Heidegger, *An Introduction to Metaphysics*, trans. R. Manheim (Garden City: Doubleday, 1961), 6.

23. G. E. Lessing, Letter to his brother Karl, 2 Feb., 1774, in *Gesammelte Werke*, ed. P. Rilla (Berlin: Aufbau Verlag, 1956), IX, 596-97.

DANTE AND THE STRUCTURE OF PHILOSOPHICAL ALLEGORY

Contemporary Dante scholarship continues to be dominated in large measure by the age-old controversy over the nature and function of allegory in the *Divine Comedy*. To the different stands taken by commentators on this issue may be traced all or most modern accounts of Dante's poem, which has been variously interpreted as the work of an orthodox Christian, a Thomist, a mystic, a defiant heretic, or a Neoplatonist tinged with Averroism, to list only some of the more plausible theories put forward in our century. The persistence of such widely divergent views raises doubts as to whether the problem has always been posed in suitable terms by those who have attempted to deal with it.

In the *Convivio,* Dante himself calls attention to two distinct types of allegory, one of which is ascribed to the poets and the other to the theologians. In the case of the former, a spiritual meaning is conveyed by means of a story that lacks historical truth and is not to be regarded as anything more than a "comely *lie*"—*bella menzogna* (II.i.3). When Ovid tells us, for instance, that Orpheus was gifted with such outstanding musical talents as to tame wild beasts and cause even trees and stones to run after him, there is no question of taking what he says at face value. His sole purpose is to teach that by using his powers of persuasion to good advantage a wise man is sometimes able to subdue the cruel hearts of his fellow human beings and win the allegiance of people who, by reason of their coarseness, deserve to be likened to stones.

As distinguished from poetic allegory, theological allegory, or what is commonly referred to today as typology, is founded on a literal sense that is no less true than the spiritual meaning that it is made to bear. The events narrated in Scripture were not invented by the sacred writers; they are themselves historical, even though they occasionally serve as types of a higher reality in which they find their ultimate fulfillment. Foremost among them is the crossing of the Red Sea, which in the biblical and Christian tradition eventually came to signify the moral liberation of the Israelites or the redemption of the human soul through baptism.[1] By and large, the debate has thus far tended to focus on the question of which of these two basic forms of allegory Dante would have adopted in his own works.

Against an older generation of scholars, Charles S. Singleton has argued that the allegory exemplified in the *Comedy* is clearly theological and not poetic. True, in the *Convivio*, Dante professes to side with the poets rather than with the theologians: *prendo lo senso allegorico secondo che per li poeti è usitato* (II.i.4); but one cannot infer from this statement alone that the method at work in the *Comedy* is identical to that of his earlier poems. Under the probable influence of Thomas Aquinas, Dante's thought could have undergone an evolution from the *Convivio* to the *Comedy*, or it may simply be that the subject to be treated in the latter work called for a different mode of procedure. What matters in either case is that the *Comedy* confronts us with an allegory that follows in all essentials the rules laid down in Christian theology. The allegorical scheme referred to in the *Letter to Can Grande*, which was written as an introduction to the *Paradiso*, is beyond any doubt that of the theologians, and the only example to which Dante appeals to make his point—again the departure of the Israelites from Egypt—is itself drawn from the Bible.[2]

Although Singleton's thesis has gained widespread support in recent years, it cannot be said to have settled the issue once and for all. The main objection to which it is exposed is that it claims for the *Comedy* something hitherto regarded as the proper preserve of sacred Scripture. According to traditional hermeneutics, God alone is capable of using events as types of other events and hence of writing in a manner that is allegorical *in re* and not merely *in verbis*. The objection cannot be countered by saying, as Singleton does, that the poet can "imitate" God's way of writing,[3] since human beings have no final control over the events of history and are not free to invest them with an inner meaning that is fully disclosed by what will happen only at a later date. If the *Comedy* were nothing more than a restatement or an amplification of the biblical report, one could perhaps maintain that it, too, shares in the prerogative of divine foreknowledge. But this is obviously not the case. Even a superficial reading of the poem should be enough to convince us that many of its characters—Achilles, Ulysses, Diomedes, Riphaeus—to say nothing of such monsters as Phlegyas, Charon, the Minotaur, Geryon, Cacus, the Centaurs, the Furies, and a host of other picturesque figures scattered throughout the infernal dungeons, have no reality outside of the poet's imagination. It is useless to point out that these characters enjoy a kind of preexistence in pagan literature, since they were never real to begin with and have not become any more so as a result of their being taken over at second hand by a medieval writer. Nor does this observation apply solely to the mythological figures encountered in the *Comedy*. It is equally valid for the whole of Dante's fanciful journey through hell, purgatory, and heaven, which never actually took place, however vividly and concretely it may have been portrayed by the author.

Having reached what appears to be an impasse, one is forced to look for some untried solution that would more readily account for all of the facts at hand. A careful reconsideration of the matter suggests that Dante himself may have viewed the problem in a somewhat different light. The *Convivio* had already alerted us to the fact that of the three spiritual senses, the allegorical proper, the moral, and the anagogical, the moral sense is the one that must be sought out with the greatest diligence;[4] and the *Letter to Can Grande* adds that the discipline to which this investigation rightly belongs is ethics or moral philosophy and not moral theology, as might have been expected if the substance of the poem were entirely or primarily theological: *Genus vero philosophiae sub quo hic in toto et parte proceditur est morale negotium sive ethica* (XVI.40). On this premise, it is at least conceivable that the division of allegory into poetic and theological was not meant to be exhaustive and is designed to leave room for a third, as yet unspecified kind of allegory, which one might appropriately call philosophical allegory.

Such at any rate appears to be the position taken by some of Dante's early commentators. Both Boccaccio and Benvenuto da Imola inform us that Dante may be read, and was in fact read by his contemporaries, either as a poet, a theologian, or a philosopher.[5] His *Comedy* was thus written in such a way as to lend itself to three broad types of interpretation, all of them willed by the author, albeit for readers of divergent interests and uneven capacities.[6] In short, Dante is not a poet *tout court* but a philosophical poet, beneath the surface of whose works lurks a wealth of hidden meanings that only the most painstaking analysis has any chance of bringing to light.[7]

If this is indeed so, one immediately begins to wonder why Dante would have deemed it necessary to withhold his thought on matters of crucial significance to him. The question was to have been taken up *ex professo* in the next to the last book of the *Convivio*,[8] which has not been preserved and may never have been written. His extant works nevertheless provide us with a number of useful hints, the gist of which, according to Boccaccio, is that wise men often have recourse to poetry for the sake of intimating certain truths which they could not have voiced publicly without incurring the wrath or displeasure of the constituted authorities.[9]

Assuming, then, that Dante deliberately avoided any forthright disclosure of his most private thoughts, the reader is prompted to inquire what those private and potentially dangerous thoughts might be. The first answer that offers itself is that, as a confirmed imperialist and a staunch opponent of papal theocracy, Dante was bent on attacking the ecclesiastical politics of his time but prudently refrained from doing so in an open or straightforward manner. A striking illustration of this procedure occurs at the beginning of Canto XVII of *Inferno*, where Geryon makes his heralded and spectacular appearance. The Geryon of classical mythology was a three-headed and three-bodied monster well known to us through the descriptions of Virgil, Horace, Ovid, and other Latin poets.[10] Dante has simplified his anatomy to a considerable extent, leaving him with a single body surmounted by a single head, and a human head at that. His paws are furry all the way up to the armpits and his breast is adorned with knotted bands and medallions.[11] His face, oddly enough, is that of a kindly man, while the lower part of his body, which has not yet been hoisted onto the bank, has the form of a reptile:

> *La faccia sua era faccia d 'uom giusto, tanto benigna avea di fuor la pelle,*
> *e d'un serpente tutto l'altro fusto (Inf.,* XVII.10-12).

The beast, we were told at the outset, is endowed with the most remarkable attributes: it crosses the highest mountains, destroys fortresses, defeats armies, and afflicts the whole world.[12] What does it represent? Fraud perhaps, since the text speaks of it as a *sozza imagine di froda* (XVII.7) and since the sins punished in the infamous Malebolge into which our travelers are about to descend are sins of fraud.

But Dante may have had something more specific in mind. If there exists in the Middle Ages an institution whose power is felt beyond the mountains and to which even the thickest walls are not impervious, it can hardly be anything but the papacy. Could Geryon have been seized upon as a cover to speak of the Church? The hypothesis, tempting as it sounds, remains unproved, at least until such time as one's attention is drawn to another feature of the text, which nobody to my knowledge has noticed and which bears a direct relationship to the problem at hand. The key to its meaning, it seems, lies in two words which, though forming a grammatical unit, have been artfully separated by means of a subordinate clause, *faccia* and *benigna,* or, to be more explicit, *benigna faccia*— "Boniface," that "serpent" whose official kindness masked a heart supposedly bursting with malice, intrigue, and duplicity.[13] In light of this finding, the description of the monster's body loses much of its strangeness, inasmuch as the furry paws and ornate breast recall the papal vestments of the time, whose arms were covered with ermine and whose front and sides were decorated with cords and medallions.

Even this explanation is bound to appear unsatisfactory, however, for it fails to take into account the fact that Dante had few qualms about criticizing the papacy whenever the occasion arose and was never sparing of bitter invectives against it.[14] There can be no mistaking what he thought about Boniface and the other popes of his day, all but one of whom have been consigned to the lower regions of hell in punishment for their real or alleged misdeeds.[15] Why, one may ask, would he have gone to such lengths to conceal in one place what he proclaims with astonishing boldness in so many others?

Such a procedure makes sense only if the superficial criticism displayed in *Inferno* XVII and related texts was really intended as a decoy for a deeper and less innocent form of concealment. We all know that a disguise is effective only to the extent to which it is itself disguised, and also that one can disguise one's thought in a variety of ways, not the least common of which is to create a diversion causing the reader to lose sight of what otherwise could not easily pass unnoticed. There was nothing to prevent Dante from using boldness to conceal his boldness, thereby turning the attention of the hasty or heedless critic away from the far more daring teaching imbedded in the interstices of his book.

What this teaching might be is suggested to us, among other ways, by the peculiar use that is made of numbers in Canto XXVI of *Paradiso.* The pilgrim, who has just undergone a rather dubious examination in faith, hope, and charity, encounters a new light, that of Adam, to whom he is eager to put a series of disparate and seemingly innocuous questions. He wants to know what the age of the world is, how much time Adam spent in the Garden of Eden, what the nature of his sin was, and what language he spoke.[16] Adam, who is already aware of these questions without their having to be formulated, is happy to reply to them, but he does so only indirectly and without the slightest concern for the order in which they were originally listed. The sin for which he merited "so great an exile"— *tanto essilio*—consisted, not in any intrinsic wrongdoing, but only in his exceeding the limits that had been prescribed for him. In limbo, he spent 4,302 years before being liberated by Christ. He had previously lived to be 930 years old. The language that he created and used has disappeared altogether and is no longer spoken anywhere today. Finally, he remained barely more than six hours in the Garden of Eden prior to his abrupt and unfortunate banishment.[17]

Scholars have long been puzzled by Adam's chronology, which, except for the 930 years of his life on earth (Gen. 5:5), has no firm foundation either in Scripture or in the theological tradition.[18] On what could it possibly rest? The mystery in which it is shrouded vanishes the moment we observe that the figures given refer, not to the actual age of the world or the length of Adam's sojourn in Eden, but to the *Comedy* itself and, more precisely, to the amount of time that Dante spends, first in the *Inferno*, and then in the earthly paradise, which the topography of the poem situates at the top of the mountain of purgatory. If we count the number of verses from the beginning of Canto IV of *Inferno*, where Dante and Virgil penetrate into hell proper, to the end of the Canticle, we discover that they come up to exactly 4,302, provided we leave out the last four verses, in which the two pilgrims emerge on the shores of purgatory after having made their escape from the nether world. The same goes for the duration of the stay in Eden, which the wayfarer reaches at six o'clock in the morning and from which he departs just as the sun was changing quadrants, that is to say, promptly at the hour of noon.[19] For all practical purposes, Dante has chosen to identify himself with Adam. He has become a "new Adam," speaking a different and more cautious language, and intent above all on avoiding the plight of his predecessor, who had suffered the pain of "exile" for his failure to observe the bounds of propriety in speech. Little wonder that Adam should have known beforehand the questions that Dante was about to put to him. The two characters are one and the same, notwithstanding the different guises in which they are made to appear.

This still leaves us with the problem of ascertaining why Dante's questions were not answered directly but in a roundabout and supposedly desultory manner. In order to obtain the desired response to the initial question regarding the age of the world, one has to go to the trouble of adding all of the figures cited separately in the text. Since, on the basis of the information vouchsafed to us, Adam died in his nine hundred and thirty-first year, since he spent 4,302 years in limbo from which he was rescued in the thirty-fourth year of the Christian era, and since the action of the poem is situated in the one thousand three hundred and first year of the same era, we arrive at a grand total of 6,500. It can likewise be shown from the chronological data supplied elsewhere in the *Comedy* that, according to Dante's calculations, based largely on artistic or symbolic considerations, the world in its present state was to last another 6,500 years.[20] The memorable voyage undertaken by the pilgrim would thus occupy the center of human history. It literally occurs "in the middle of the journey of *our* life," as is cryptically asserted in the famous first verse of the poem. Dante, one is led to conclude, is not only *a* "new Adam," he is *the* "new Adam," whose saving work is placed at the figurative mid-point of time and who replaces in a subtle and more than slightly blasphemous way the new Adam of Christian theology.

Needless to say, this highly heterodox teaching was unlikely to meet with the approval of the religious authorities or for that matter of most of Dante's contemporaries. Under the circumstances, it is hardly surprising that he should have taken such pains to keep it from all but the most industrious and inquisitive of readers. The allegory that he invented for this purpose is considerably more complex than most scholars have imagined. It exhibits a dual structure, one of whose elements corresponds to the immediate intention of the poem, which was to humanize the papal politics of his day, and the other to its larger intention, which was to restore philosophic thought to its erstwhile status as an independent and essentially transpolitical activity. The use that is made of this new allegory in the *Comedy* reveals in unsuspected ways what Dante considered to be the true nobility of his character. That nobility, as the *Convivio* explains, was based on ancestry as well as on wealth, both admittedly of an unconventional sort. The ancestry is traced back to Plato and Aristotle, the foremost representatives of the philosophy which Dante sought to reinstate over against the Christian interpretation that prevailed in his day, and the wealth that accompanies it is to be reckoned less in terms of the money or property of which his politically more powerful enemies had once managed to deprive him than in terms of the philosophical wisdom that he claimed as a permanent possession.[21]

NOTES

1. Cf. Dante, *Convivio* II.i.6-7; *Letter to Can Grande*, 7,21.

2. Charles S. Singleton, *Dante Studies 1: Commedia, Elements of Structure* (Cambridge, MA: Harvard University Press, 1954), 1-17 and 84-98.

3. Ibid., 15.

4. *Convivio* II.i.5: "Lo terzo senso si chiama morale, e questo è quello che li lettori deono intentamente andare appostando per le scritture, ad utilitade di loro e di loro discenti."

5. Boccaccio, *Trattatello in Laude di Dante*, ch. 2, ed. Ricci (Milano: R. Ricciardi, 1965), 576; Benvenuto da Imola Rambaldi, *Commentum super Dantis Comoediam*, ed. J. P. Lacaita (Florentine: G. Barbera, 1887) vol. 1, 12: "Ab aliquibus vocabatur poeta, ab aliis philosophus, ab aliis theologus."

6. Boccaccio, *Trattatello*, ch. 17, 645-646.

7. Ibid., ch. 2, 74; ch. 9, 617. Dante refers to himself as *vir philosophiae domesticus* in *Epistula* XII.3.6.

8. Cf. *Convivio* II.i.4.

9. Boccaccio, *Trattatello*, ch. 9, 616; id., *Esposizioni sopra la Comedia di Dante*, ed. Padoan (Verona: A. Mondadora, 1965), 33-36.

10. Cf. Virgil, *Aeneid* VI.289; VIII.202,; Horace, *Carmina* II.14.7-8; Ovid, *Heroides* X.91-92.

11. *Inferno* XVII.13-15; *Due branche avea pilose insin l'ascelle; lo dosso e 'Ipetto e ambedue le coste dipinti avea di nodi e di rotelle.*

12. Cf. *Inferno* XVII.1-3.

13. See, among the more obvious references to Boniface's character, *Inferno* XIX.52-57; XXVII.85-111; *Paradiso* XII.88-90; XII.22-27; XXX.146-148.

14. See, for example, *Inf.* XIX.104; *Purg.* VIII.130-132; XVI.82-129; XX.8-15.

15. The only medieval pope to have been judged worthy of the honors of Dante's heaven is John XXI (Peter of Spain), who is present in *Par.* XII.134.

16. Cf *Par.* XXVI.109-114.

17. *Par.* XXVI.115-142.

18. Dante's timetable comes closest to that of Eusebius, according to whom the birth of Christ would have occurred in the year 5, 119; cf. *Chronicon*, ed. Helm, 169 and 173-174. On the various theories concerning the age of the world, see V. Grumel, *La chronologie* in: *Traité d'études byzantines,* publié par P. Lemerle, t. I (Paris: Presses Universitaires de France, 1958), 3-25.

19. Cf. *Purg.* XXVIII.3.12 and 16; 33.103-105.

20. Cf. R. Benini, *Scienza, religione ed arte nell'astronomia di Dante* (Roma: Reale academia d'Italia, 1939), 16-35.

21. Cf. *Convivio* IV.x-xvi; xvii.11; xx-xxi.

18

DANTE'S *COMEDY* AS UTOPIA

It is not at all common to think of the *Divine Comedy* or any part thereof as a utopia, and, in fact, Dante's name rarely shows up in any of the studies that have been made of this important literary genre. J. O. Hertzler was speaking not only for himself but for the bulk of twentieth-century scholarship when he wrote over a half a century ago: "Following the appearance of Augustine's *City of God* there was a period of nearly a thousand years during which there was no instance of even the most meager and insignificant utopian literature."[1]

The reason for the omission is not far to seek. Overwhelmed by the magic of Dante's poetry, we tend to equate the *Paradiso* with the heaven of Christian theology. But the heaven of Christian theology cannot properly be defined as a utopia, that is to say, a perfect society that exists only in the imagination of some poet or political thinker. It is coeval with creation and hence always actual. Any suggestion to the contrary would border on impiety.

THE DANTEAN INVERSION

The trouble with this view of the *Paradiso* is that it misunderstands the use that is made of the allegorical method in the poem, a use characterized by what I shall call the "Dantean inversion." Whereas in medieval theology the material world is seen as an image or reflection of God's manifold *perfection—invisibilia Dei per ea quae facta sunt conspiciuntur* (Romans 1:20)—in the *Comedy* the opposite is the case: the world to come functions as an image of our world. To quote Dante's *Letter to Can Grande della Scala* (written as an introduction to the *Paradiso* and therewith the *Comedy* as a whole), the poet's overall aim is to "remove those living in *this* life from a state of misery and lead them to a state of happiness."[2] Accordingly, his poem has two meanings, one literal and the other figurative or spiritual. Taken literally, its subject is "the state of souls after death." Taken figuratively—and we may assume that the figurative sense is the higher of the two—its subject is the human being "earning or becoming liable to the rewards or punishments of justice through the exercise of his free will."[3]

It matters little for present purposes that the Dantean authenticity of this letter has been contested and continues to be contested by modern scholars,[4] for one easily comes to the same conclusion by reading the *Comedy,* the whole of which is permeated by a thoroughly intramundane or thisworldly spirit. This is true even of the *Paradiso,* which, as I shall argue, is not a description of heaven but a picture of what, in Dante's opinion, the perfect Christian society on earth might look like if it were to come into being. Paradoxically, the poem that has done more than any other work to fix in our imaginations the contours of the next world is concerned exclusively with the modalities and vicissitudes of life here below. The assumption on which it rests is that the perfect society in question has never existed in reality and probably never will. The poet's sole intention is to offer a model by which human beings may be guided in their efforts at political reform while at the same time making them aware of the limits of human justice and hence of the need for moderation in its pursuit.

Needless to say, Dante himself does not employ the term "utopia," which would not be coined for another two centuries (by Thomas More in 1516), but the notion that it conveys was as familiar to him as it was to the great political thinkers who had preceded him. This much becomes evident when we reflect on the etymology of the word, which is formed on the basis of the Greek expressions *ou topos,* meaning "no place," and *eu topos,* meaning a "good place," the implication being that the good or perfect society is not to be found anywhere in the world as we know it. Plato spoke in this connection of a "city in speech,"[5] in contrast to actual cities, all of which were judged to be more or less defective or corrupt. Dante's language is different. The poet adverts instead to the four senses according to which his poem is to be interpreted: the literal or historical, the allegorical, the moral, and the anagogical.

The literal sense, which is presupposed to the others and with which any interpretation of the poem must begin, is, as its name indicates, the one imparted by the letter of the text; to this literal sense may then be added one or more of the three. The point is illustrated by means of a single example borrowed from Exodus 14, the crossing of the Red Sea. Taken in its literal sense, Exodus 14 is an account of the rescue of the Israelites from Egypt at the time of Moses, but Christians believe that this historical event was also intended by the Holy Spirit as a prefiguration or "type" of baptism, through whose waters the soul is rescued spiritually and ushered into the life of grace. Such is its allegorical meaning. In its moral sense, it may be seen as a figure of humanity's deliverance from its enslavement to sin. Finally, the same event can be viewed as an anticipatory image of the events reserved for the end-time, at which moment the saved among us will pass from the sorrows of this life to the joys of eternal life. This is what in the Christian tradition was known as the *sensus anagogicus* or "anagogical sense" of the text.

Thus understood, Dante's doctrine has nothing original about it. It has its roots in Pauline typology and had been the most commonly used method of biblical interpretation since the age of the Fathers.[6] What *is* new is that for the first time someone has chosen to apply it to a text other than the Bible, but not without a number of subtle modifications of which the reader is not immediately aware. The best way to approach the problem is to ask ourselves how, concretely, the method is supposed to work in the poem.

For the most part, students of the *Comedy*, beginning with Dante's early commentators, have been remarkably adept at uncovering all sorts of allegorical and moral meanings in it. If anything, the harvest, in this regard, is apt to be too plentiful. There is virtually no end to the ingenious interpretations that have been proposed of the characters, objects or incidents that fill the pages of the poem; so much so that it is occasionally necessary to warn the allegorizers that the slope is more slippery than they think. Take, for instance, the case of Beatrice, Dante's guide in *Paradiso*, who has been made to stand for any number of strange and often incompatible realities: baptism, the minor orders, the monastic tonsure, the priestly vocation, the ideal woman, the bishop of Florence, the agent intellect, reason illumined by faith, the light of glory, the essence of Christian theology, and the list goes on and on. Believe me, it would be a mistake to think that the allegorical and moral senses of the *Comedy* are wholly unproblematic.

My own concern is not with these two senses but with the anagogical sense, which has always proved more elusive, and on which there is little agreement among critics. Where exactly are we to look for it in the poem? One's instinct is to equate it with the so-called "beatific vision" that awaits Dante at the end of his journey through life; but this explanation is not altogether convincing, first of all because it refers to an event that, at this point, has no reality outside of the poet's imagination, and secondly, because it runs counter to Dante's repeated assertion that the poem deals with *this* life and not the afterlife.

There is a more plausible explanation, which is that Dante's subdivision of the spiritual sense into allegorical, moral, and anagogical has as its purpose to call attention to the specific character of each of the three main divisions of the poem: hell, purgatory, and heaven. It can be shown, I think, that the subject matter of the *Inferno* is treated for the most part according to the allegorical mode; that in the *Purgatorio*, where Dante's ethics is laid out, the moral sense predominates; and that the *Paradiso* reveals its true meaning only when read in terms of what Dante understands by the anagogical sense. These are not necessarily hard and fast lines, and a certain amount of crisscrossing takes place throughout the poem, but not to the extent of depriving the three labels of any determinate meaning. No one can reasonably look for, say, an anagogical sense in the *Inferno* as a whole or for an allegorical sense in the *Paradiso* as a whole.

My thesis in a nutshell is that what Dante means by the anagogical sense is what we mean today when we speak of a utopia. The poet, after all, did not know any more than we do about the heaven promised to us at the end of our days, but as a political thinker he had a good idea of what constitutes a well-ordered society. His *Paradiso* is, in effect, a blueprint of what, under the circumstances of his time, a society of this kind would look like if it were to be realized. Such an assertion is bolder than may seem at first hearing; it comes down to saying that politics rather than religion is the core of Dante's enterprise and that the *Comedy* makes complete sense only when read in that light. This is not to imply that the poem is devoid of any religious significance, but only that the religious significance, whatever it may finally be, is firmly imbedded in a political context from which it cannot be divorced. Dante may or may not have wanted to prepare us for the joys of heaven, but one thing is certain: he was passionately interested in restoring a measure of unity and strength to a Christian world that suddenly found itself threatened by powerful enemies without and increasingly sharp divisions within.

THE STRUCTURAL WEAKNESS OF THE HOLY ROMAN EMPIRE

The task at hand, a difficult one at all times, was rendered doubly difficult by the unique character of medieval society, the most distinctive features of which owed their origin to a series of complicated historical accidents resulting in the establishment of a new empire in the West under Charlemagne in the year 800—a momentous event precipitated by the conflict between the papacy and the Byzantine emperor, Leo III, the Isaurian, over the religious use of images. The matter bears some investigation inasmuch as its main lines tend to disappear beneath the plethora of minute details unearthed by modern historians.[7]

The heart and soul of the Byzantine Empire had been for centuries and remained its so-called *romanitas* or "Romanness." Its capital, Constantinople, the world's first Christian city (it had no pagan temples), looked upon itself as the "new Rome," and its political head, who bore the title of "Ruler of the Romans"—*Basileus tôn Romaiôn*—had never relinquished his legal title to the Western part of the Empire. To counteract his universal authority a more powerful figure was needed, for whom the Latin name of *imperator* or "emperor" was made to order, and the more so as it had no exact equivalent in the Greek language.[8]

The sad fact of the matter, however, is that from its inception the artificially created superstructure had few chances of ever becoming more than a pale replica of the ancient Roman Empire. As an intellectual offspring of the papacy, the new emperor was literally a ruler without a throne and had no real status beyond that of an ancillary organ. Throughout most of his existence, he remained a tragic figure, floating in a kind of vacuum and impeded in the exercise of his duties by the simultaneous presence of a higher authority. Unlike his rival, the Byzantine *autocrator*, he was not the image of God on earth but was expected to display the virtues of devotion and humility that befit a ruler who has delivered himself into the hands of churchmen, a member, like everyone else, of the people of God and subject to the jurisdiction of its official representatives.

Prior to his anointment, which was administered at the discretion of the Pope, he was only the Emperor-elect. No throne was present at his coronation. Instead, he was given a sword, symbolizing his role as the Pope's universal, if at times recalcitrant, policeman. Whereas the priestly "character" was indelible, his could be removed at any moment, and sometimes was. What would have been unthinkable in the East had suddenly become the rule in the West. By a strange confluence of unforeseeable circumstances, the ecclesiastical power had deftly managed to sandwich itself between the divinity and the temporal power. Papal theocracy had emerged as an alternative to Caesaropapism, with the successor of Peter arrogating to himself temporal functions for which he had no divine mandate (the extravagant claims were mostly based on forgeries, such as the *Donation of Constantine* and the ninth-century collection of papal or synodal decrees known as the *Pseudo-Isidore*) and which he was not necessarily competent to discharge. In short, a new foundation was needed if effective political rule was to be reestablished in the Western lands.

The consequences of this less than desirable state of affairs are vividly depicted throughout the *Comedy*, beginning with the first scene of the poem, which shows Dante lost in a dark wood and trying to climb to the summit of a mountain whose shoulders are bathed in sunlight. His efforts are thwarted by the sudden appearance of a leopard, a lion, and a she-wolf, the last being by far the most fearsome of the three beasts, for it is the one that "kills." The leopard with the spotted hide recalls Dante's native Florence and its warring factions, the Whites and the Blacks, constantly vying not with but against each other for control of the city. The lion, the traditional symbol of royalty, represents the king of France, and the she-wolf, Rome or the papacy, the two foreign powers then most directly involved in Florentine politics. It is significant that the text links them together as partners, so to speak, in a succession of intrigues that led to the triumph of the Blacks over the Whites as well as to the poet's indictment and subsequent condemnation. At the sight of the she-wolf, Dante, who had once found cause for good hope in the beast with the gaily painted hide, loses heart and is ready to admit defeat. He is then rescued by Virgil, who announces that, in order to escape from that evil place, he will have to take another road. The new and longer road is of course the one that leads through hell, purgatory, and the heavenly spheres all the way up to the empyrean.

What follows in the *Inferno* and the whole first half of the *Purgatorio* is for the most part a thinly-disguised account of the major events of Dante's life and a graphic description of the relentless strife that had been tearing Florence, the rest of Italy, and the whole of Christendom apart for over a century. If, as I have suggested and hope to demonstrate, the *Paradiso* is Dante's utopia, the *Inferno* has all the attributes of a "dystopia." The picture that it presents is the very antithesis of what a rational society is expected to be. The majority of its inhabitants, having lost the "good of the intellect" (*Inf.* III.18), are actuated by the basest and most selfish of passions. Violence and fraud dominate the scene, and, abetted by the thirst for gain, grow stronger by the hour. The consequences both for individuals and for society at large are disastrous.

Among the victims is Dante himself, whose personal odyssey is told between the lines of the successive cantos. It has not been sufficiently observed that the order of these cantos, which often seems arbitrary, is dictated less by the nature of the sins portrayed in the various circles of hell than by the chronology of the poet's life. To cite only three examples chosen more or less at random: in Canto XIII, Pier delle Vigne, the poet who had served as Frederick II's secretary and was falsely accused of embezzlement, is Dante, who had likewise served as secretary of the Florentine republic and was charged with a similar crime. The hapless but by no means helpless Ulysses of Canto XXVI, who cannot or will not return to Ithaca, is again Dante, the exile who was prevented from returning to Florence by the sentence of death that was twice pronounced against him. In Canto XXVII, Guido da Montefeltro, the retired captain of the Ghibbeline League, whom Boniface VIII had absolved in advance for his collusion in a treacherous deed plotted by the Pope himself, is none other than Dante, whom the Florentine leaders, now desperate for help, tried to entice back with an offer of amnesty or pardon *in absentia*.[9]

The whole matter comes to a head in Canto XVI of *Purgatorio*, the fiftieth canto of the *Comedy* and the one in which the entire first half of the poem culminates. The gist of that famous canto is that human beings have themselves and not their stars to blame for the evils from which they suffer. The seeds of virtue have been implanted in them from birth, but they will not bear fruit unless they are properly nurtured (v. 66-82). If so few virtuous people remain, it is less because of the corruption of human nature than because of the absence of good government. Just as the source of the present wickedness is not original sin but bad leadership, so the cure is not divine grace but a return to sound political rule. The laws exist and they are good. Alas, no one is around to enforce them and repress evildoers (v. 85-105; cf. VI.76-78). The last of the emperors was Frederick II, who died, deposed and excommunicated, in 1250. His successors, never having been anointed or granted full recognition, were emperors in name only. For a period known as the *interregnum*, which lasted close to twenty-five years (1250-1273), there was no Emperor at all, not even an Emperor-Elect.

The problem has deeper ramifications, however, for the failure of princes to carry out their responsibilities is traceable to the constant impingements of the ecclesiastical authority. It used to be that the world was ruled by two suns, the Pope and the emperor. By combining within itself both sovereignties, the former has usurped the place of the latter and soiled itself with the burden. Of the vices that plague human existence, there is none more prevalent than greed and none to which the Church, by reason of its lack of material self-sufficiency, is more prone. Rome's habit of forging political alliances for the sake of its own aggrandizement not only sets a bad example for its followers but effectively neutralizes the efforts of the one agency by which its worldly ambitions might be contained (v. 116-29). Little wonder that courtesy and valor have ceased from the land and that the world, deserted by every virtue, should go astray (v. 58-60; 82).

In fairness, it should be added that the papacy is not the only culprit in the matter. Dante makes it clear that the emperors, who were often more interested in securing and expanding their own domains than in carrying out their public duties, bore their share of the blame for the present woes. Canto VII of *Purgatorio* shows them gathered in a peaceful valley where they spend their lives in idleness, unable but perhaps also unwilling to exercise their proper authority, or so it would seem from the reproaches that Dante heaps upon them.

THE MONARCHIC IDEAL

Such, in barest outline, is Dante's diagnosis of the fundamental illness of his time. What is the remedy? To be sure, one can always preach a return to the old-fashioned virtues of courage and self-restraint, and the *Comedy* is not short on exhortations of this kind. But efforts at persuasion are rarely successful without the support of some authority capable of enforcing standards of public morality. When it comes to that, Dante's *Monarchia* has more to offer at first glance. Its specific proposal, which is also the point on which it is thought by many to deviate conspicuously from the *Comedy*, is the establishment of a world government that would maintain peace among the various elements of Christendom and foster a way of life in which justice and freedom can thrive. Why Dante would have abandoned this proposal, if he did abandon it, is not at all evident since the situation envisaged in the *Comedy* does not appear to be any different from the one with which he tries to cope in the *Monarchia*. One gathers as much from the rather irreverent manner in which the *Comedy* still speaks of the papacy, as it does, for example, in the Geryon episode (*Inf.* XVII), on which we commented earlier (pp. 272-3).

It is worth noting that this comical interlude is again autobiographical in nature. The scene that it evokes took place in 1301, when Dante and two other Florentine dignitaries were sent to Rome on a mission the purpose of which was to work out a solution to the conflict that had arisen between the two rival factions, the Whites, who sided with the Emperor, and the Blacks, who were partial to the Pope. The ambassadors were duly received by Boniface but the meeting achieved no tangible results. Two of the emissaries were allowed to go back to Florence, but not Dante, from whom, as a contemporary chronicler notes, the Pope had more to fear. In the interval, he was accused of embezzlement by his fellow Florentines and summoned before the tribunal. When he refused to appear, he was sentenced to death and went into perpetual exile.

The Geryon episode may be the most humorous episode of its kind in the *Comedy*, but it is not the only one. The poem, as anyone who has read it knows, teems with all kinds of gibes at the Papacy, each one funnier or more virulent than the others. All of the medieval Popes named in it have been consigned to hell in the company of simonists or heretics, with one exception: John XXI, the Scholastic philosopher Peter of Spain, who reigned for a total of nine months.[10]

If, as we are given to understand, the papacy is as powerful and given to political intrigue as ever, by what means is it to be restrained? A closer look at the *Paradiso* reveals that the solution to which the *Comedy* points, although couched in more pious terms, is remarkably similar to the one advanced in the *Monarchia*. One of the key passages in this regard is Canto XVIII, where, having reached the heaven of Jupiter, the emblem of justice, Dante and Beatrice witness a dazzling astronomical spectacle that is nothing less than the apotheosis of world-monarchic rule. More than a thousand brilliant lights come together to spell the first verse of the Book of Wisdom, "Love righteousness, you rulers of the earth": *Diligite iustitiam, qui iudicatis terram.* Soon other lights assemble on top of the "m" of *terram* in such a way as to assume the form, first of the Florentine lily, and then of the imperial eagle. This brilliant display is followed by what purports to be a discussion of the theological problem of predestination, which was debated at considerable length in Cantos XIX and XX. Which predestination? Not the one that a Christian theologian spontaneously thinks of, but the one whereby the various nations of the world are now destined to become incorporated into an all-encompassing political organization ruled by a single head.

In retrospect, one discovers that the whole first part of the *Paradiso* is nothing but the unfolding of a vast scheme by means of which all the segments of a Christendom that was being rent asunder by powerful centrifugal forces might be pulled together and made to cooperate in the pursuit of a common goal. Cantos III and IV speak to us about a group of nuns who supposedly left their convents to be married and now have to compensate for their broken vows. This ingenious fabrication is Dante's roundabout way of suggesting how the rebellious kingdoms of southern Italy (represented by the Empress Constance, the mother of Frederick II) and the Blacks of Florence (represented by Piccarda Donati) might make amends for their rebellion and return to the imperial fold. Cantos VI to X invite us to think in terms of a possible reconciliation between Guelphs and Ghibellines (mentioned by name for the only time in VI.103-108), between Eastern and Western Christendom, as well as between the Emperor and the newly emancipated kingdoms of northern and central Europe.

The same strategy is adopted in regard to the deepening rifts that had begun to manifest themselves in intellectual circles. Canto X, in which the theological luminaries of the Middle Ages are gathered, is particularly striking insofar as it places side by side people who were bitter enemies in life but now speak as if they had always been the closest of friends. Thomas Aquinas, Scholasticism's most distinguished theologian, pays tribute to the "eternal light" of his erstwhile rival, Siger of Brabant, the leader of a dissident school of thought known since the nineteenth century as Latin Averroism (v. 133-38). In another delicately ironic passage, St. Bonaventure, who had once mercilessly attacked Joachim of Flora as a false prophet, points to him as one "endowed with the spirit of prophecy" (XII.141).

From the theologians the *Comedy* turns next to the monastic orders, the Dominicans and the Franciscans in particular, and to the endless controversies that had marked their relationship, as well as the divisions that had opened up within their own ranks. The trick this time consists in having Thomas Aquinas, a Dominican, extol the virtues of St. Francis, the founder of the Franciscan Order, and Bonaventure, the Master General of the Franciscans, sing the praises of St. Dominic, the founder of the Dominican Order. Anybody who knows anything about the history of monastic orders does not have to be told that this vision of unity is again highly utopian—something to be prayed for but never fully achieved in practice.

Later on, in Canto XXX, Beatrice and her disciple reach the empyrean or the heaven of pure light. Their eyes gaze for the first time on all the seats that the "great city" comprises, seats already so full that only a few more people are wanted (v. 130-32). In the midst of them is a throne surmounted by a crown, which unexpectedly turns out to be the throne reserved for "the imperial soul of the lofty Henry," the ruler on whom Dante had once pinned his hopes for the renewal of the empire (v. 133-38).

Scholars have often been taken aback by what some of them judge to be the inappropriateness of this startling symbol of mundane sovereignty in the highest heaven. Singleton's observation that since, for Dante, the imperial power is divinely ordained, it could fittingly be represented even here,[11] does little to alleviate the shock, inasmuch as one would then have to look for a corresponding symbol of papal authority, which is likewise ordained by God. What we find instead is the exact opposite; for at that moment, Beatrice delivers her parting speech, the burden of which is not only to extol the emperor but to excoriate the treachery of his adversary, Clement V, the pope who stealthily betrayed him.[12] The presence of Henry's throne in the empyrean may be deemed incongruous in the extreme degree, but only if one inclines to the view that the *Comedy* was intended as a revision of Dante's imperial ideal. It is anything but incongruous when read within the context of the author's vision of a refurbished and enlarged Roman Empire presided over by its legitimate and divinely appointed ruler, precisely in accordance with the teaching of the *Monarchia*.

If my interpretation of these passages and others like them is correct, one must conclude that the teaching of the *Comedy* is not fundamentally different from that of the *Monarchia*. This should not come as any great surprise to us, especially if we remember that the two works were written within the last decade of Dante's life and may even have been completed at approximately the same time, that is, within three years of his death. Contrary to popular opinion, I see no reason to think that Dante changed his mind on this subject and every reason to think that the *Monarchia* should be read as a commentary on the *Comedy*, however much it may differ from it in form or tone. What the former says explicitly the latter states only slightly less forthrightly and less didactically.

THE NATURE OF DANTEAN IMPERIALISM

This brings us to the massive difficulty with which any student of Dante's political thought must sooner or later come to grips: how can Dante, who hails Aristotle as the "master of those who know"[13] and claims to be his faithful disciple, part company with him on a matter of such extreme importance? It suffices to read the *Politics* once to realize that for Aristotle the society that is most conducive to human perfection is neither a world empire nor a large nation, but the city and a relatively small city at that. Human beings are by nature "political," that is to say, born to live as members, not of an empire, but of a polis, the only association within which their potential can be fully actualized. It, and only it, corresponds to our capacity to know and love, and thus makes possible their total participation in the life of the community. Nothing could be further from Aristotle's thought than the notion of a government that would hold sway not only over the whole of Christendom, but over all the nations of the earth. Experience teaches that large-scale imperialism is usually synonymous with brutal repression and tyranny. People accustomed to their own laws, customs, traditions, and particular ways of life do not willingly give them up for the sake of something alien and often profoundly abhorrent to them. All things considered, it is almost inconceivable that so ardent a lover of freedom as Dante should have endorsed and looked forward to the growth of the one political organism that is most inimical to its exercise. What induced him to do so?

Two major factors lay behind this otherwise inexplicable decision. The first was the necessity to provide for the defense of the Christian West in the face of the persistent threat posed by Islamic expansionism, one of the fundamental facts of medieval politics. We forget too easily the seriousness of this threat, which did not abate until two and a half centuries later. In Dante's own day, the Muslims still occupied not only all of North Africa and the Middle East, including the Holy Places, but roughly half of the Iberian peninsula, from which they were expelled only in 1492. Interestingly enough, Dante was not the only medieval Aristotelian to flirt with the idea of a universal empire. His proposal has its parallel in Averroes, who likewise found himself in the situation of having to adjust his speech, if not necessarily his thinking, to the demands of a religion that shared in some way Christianity's universal outlook.[14]

The second reason is internal to Christianity, whose victory over pagan polytheism had introduced into the political life a complication of which Aristotle had no direct experience and which he does not discuss in the *Politics.* Unlike the so-called "city-states" of Aristotle's day, the nations of the West now shared a common religion whose spiritual leader could claim an authority that transcended all national boundaries and thus completely overshadowed that of any local ruler. One way to remedy the situation, and it may have been the only feasible one at the time, was to broaden the scope of imperial rule so as to make it coextensive with that of the Pope, but only as long as this could be done with a minimum of prejudice to the freedom of each nation.

In point of fact, Dante's world monarchy is anything but the mono-lithic structure or the harsh despotism that we associate with the notion of a world empire. It is a political arrangement that respects the national character of its individual components and allows for a notable degree of diversity among them. Its visible head is an Emperor who would at long last be installed in his own capital, Rome, over whose territory he himself would rule and from which he would exercise indirect rule over the rest of Christendom, granting to local kings and princes as much latitude as is necessary to legislate for their own constituencies.[15] As the first canto of the *Comedy* puts it, in terms that are amazingly precise,

> In all parts he commands (*impera*) and there he rules (*regge*)
> there is his lofty city (*città*) and his lofty throne (*seggio*).
> O, happy is he whom he elects thereto! (v. 127-29)

Nowhere in the *Comedy* is there any suggestion that the separate entities that then made up the *respublica Christiana* would be robbed of their identity and summoned to transform themselves into a universal and homogeneous society. Surely the last thing Dante wanted was the abolition of the Florentine republic, whose freedom he was more eager than anyone else to preserve.

It is probably in this perspective that one should read *Paradiso* XXVIII and XXIX, two cantos devoted to the subject of angels. At this point, Dante and Beatrice penetrate into the *primum mobile*, which separates the heaven of the fixed stars below from the empyrean above and to which, in the economy of the poem, the angelic hierarchies have been assigned. Few parts of the *Comedy* are likely to strike us as more quaintly medieval than the disquisition that follows on the nature and function of these separated substances, their various orders, and the recondite speculations in which on these points Scholastic theology was wont to engage. In his introduction to Canto XXIX, Grandgent notes that "to the modern reader such speculations seem otiose" and that "we are perhaps justified in believing that they did not seem very important to Dante."[16] It is doubtful, however, whether Dante, who prides himself on having left no detail to chance in his poem (cf. *Par.*, XXII.53), would have spent as much time as he does on this topic if it had so little to contribute to the development of his theme.

There may again be a simple solution to the problem, which is that the superior beings about whom the poet suddenly has so much to teach stand for the local rulers who in the new order of things have pledged their unbounded allegiance to the emperor, entertain the closest of relationships with him, extend the benefits of his rule to all parts of the world, and have no existence apart from their own subjects. This seemingly odd portrayal of rulers as angels or angel-like creatures is by no means uncommon in the literature of the Middle Ages. It conforms to an old and well established practice that has its twin roots in the biblical and the hellenistic traditions. The Second Book of Samuel had already spoken of King David as being "like the angel of God" and as having been granted "wisdom like the wisdom of the angel of God to know all things that are on earth": *sicut enim angelus Dei, sic et dominus meus rex* (14:17). The same image recurs in a large number of ancient and medieval texts in which kings and princes are endowed with quasi divine attributes and which speak in like manner of what Ernst Kantorowicz calls their "angelic character." If, in his physical being, the ruler is subject like everyone else to the limitations of mortality, in his corporate being he transcends the purely human order and appears, in Gilbert of Tournai's words, as a likeness of the "holy spirits and angels."[17]

DANTE'S UTOPIANISM

This much being said, one has to admit that, both in the *Monarchia* and in the *Comedy*, the concept of a civil society that takes the old Roman empire or, as others prefer to think, the papacy, rather than the Aristotelian polis, as its model is not nearly so transparent as it is sometimes made out to be. It does not take long to realize that Dante's world monarch far exceeds anything that has ever been seen or is likely to be seen in real life. He is nothing less than the embodiment of reason, combining in his person the perfection of wisdom and moral virtue and graced with all the attributes of Plato's philosopher-king, to whom he has often been compared. The point was already made by Guido Vernani, Dante's early adversary, who argues quite rightly that so excellent a human being is not to be found anywhere.[18] What Vernani fails to note is that Dante himself did not think otherwise. His imaginary ruler remains at best a shadowy figure who is not to be identified with any particular incumbent of the office but rather functions as a general standard by which all actual rulers are to be judged. Only by means of such a fiction was it possible to accredit the notion of an overarching political authority that could counterbalance the universal authority of the Pope and thus effect what no local ruler would ever be strong enough to accomplish by himself.

Further evidence for the utopian character of Dante's scheme is to be uncovered in the unforgettable story of Count Ugolino in *Inferno* XXXIII, which serves as a prelude to the long-awaited encounter with Lucifer at the bottom of the pit. Ugolino was a Guelf leader who had served as *podestà* of Pisa for a period of ten years. Falsely accused of treason, he was imprisoned in the tower at Pisa, where he was left to die of starvation with his five sons. The vague hint that some of the prisoners resorted to cannibalism only adds to the horror of the tale, which is all the more noteworthy as the details pertaining to the conversation that went on inside the tower had to be invented by the poet. Why this gruesome story has been inserted at this particular juncture of the poem is a question that is not even asked by most interpreters. Like all the other riddles of the *Comedy*, it too has its answer. What we have before us is a figurative account of the demise of Henry VII, once the embodiment of Dante's political hopes. Not coincidentally, the scene is laid in Pisa, Henry's headquarters in Italy and the place where he is still buried. Henry's death occurred in 1313, eight years before the completion of the *Comedy* and Dante's own death. When, in the text from *Paradiso* XXX to which reference was made a moment ago, Dante spoke of the Roman throne prepared for the "lofty soul of the imperial Henry," he was well aware that Henry would never mount that throne. The statement is another piece of fiction, rendered plausible only by the fact that the year 1300 has been chosen as the dramatic date of the poem. After 1313, Dante could not possibly have had any illusions about the outcome of Henry's Italian expedition. To repeat what was said earlier, his goal was to present, not a future reality, but a standard or a model by which in making political choices his contemporaries could take their bearings.

But we do not need any of these subtle hypotheses in order to convince ourselves that Dante did not anticipate the coming into being of the intrinsically most desirable society. He knew, both from Aristotle and from common human experience, that men's attachment to what belongs to them as individuals will always stand in the way of their becoming perfect lovers of justice. To use the language of *Paradiso*, "I" and "mine" will never mean the same thing among us as "we" and "our" (cf. *Par.*, XIX.10-12.). Perfect justice would be attainable if the goods that human beings require for their physical well-being could be shared equally by all, but this is not so. Anyone who appropriates these goods for his own use necessarily deprives others of them and sets up a situation wherein they may be coveted against reason. There are absolute limits, imposed by our bodily nature, to the sharing of material goods, that is to say, of such goods as must be divided before they can be appropriated. In Dante's *Comedy*, as in Plato's *Republic*, perfect justice is achieved only by pretending that the body does not exist.

There was a more specific obstacle to the triumph of justice in the Christian West, namely, the dualism of the spiritual and temporal powers and the nagging tensions to which it continued to give rise. At first glance, Dante's program appears to be equidistant from the caesaropapism of the Eastern Empire, which subordinates papal rule to imperial rule, and the papal theocracy of the Western Empire, recently reasserted by Boniface VIII in the Bull *Unam Sanctam*, which subordinates imperial rule to papal rule. That program, as outlined in the *Monarchia,* calls for the harmonious collaboration of the two highest authorities, each one of which is considered supreme in its own domain. The Pope's mission is to lead the human race to the blessedness of eternal life by means of spiritual teachings; the Emperor's mission is to lead it to the blessedness of this life by means of philosophic teachings.[19] In the words of *Purgatorio* XVI, God wanted the world to be illumined by "two suns," the Pope and the Emperor, and considered both of them indispensable to its well-being. In practice, this meant that the Church was to renounce its worldly ambitions, divest itself of its wealth and territorial possessions, leave politics to the temporal rulers, and, with the support of the Emperor, attend exclusively to spiritual matters.

The only thing wrong with this proposal is that it takes for granted the continuity between imperial rule and papal rule, and, ultimately, between the teachings of natural reason and those of Sacred Scripture, in which these two rules are grounded. Conflicts between the two powers had repeatedly arisen in the past and it was a foregone conclusion that they would not cease unless some provision was made for their adjudication. On Dante's own telling, things are well-ordered when they are reduced to a single principle.[20] Yet his scheme reduced them to two independent principles, adding only that, while neither is subject to the other, Caesar owes to Peter the reverence that a first-born son owes to his father.[21] This last assertion is obviously more of a pious wish than a principle on which emperors can be counted upon to act. Any experienced observer sees right away that Dante's proposal places the Church entirely at the mercy of the temporal ruler, in whose hands all effective power has been concentrated.

POETRY AND PHILOSOPHY

This is not the only side of the story, however, for the argument as we have developed it overlooks the fact that a disarmed and spiritual church can be as politically disruptive as a worldly one. This much we know from the example of Savonarola and countless religious reformers across the ages. Something else was needed if the proposed solution was to have any chance of success. With such considerations we come to what, I submit, is the *Comedy's* most original contribution to the theologico-political problem of the Middle Ages.

Historians and students of medieval political theory often complain about Dante's "conservatism," as they like to call it, and dismiss his views as reactionary and nostalgically committed to a conception of society that would soon be relegated to the dustbin of history.[22] One can certainly agree that, by comparison with his illustrious fellow countryman, Machiavelli, Dante would have to be labeled a conservative, although in this instance the term hardly seems appropriate. A conservative in the modern sense is one who resists change because he thinks that all change is bad, and this Dante never accepted. However much he may have felt that Italian life had deteriorated, he was emphatically not in favor of a simple return to the *status quo ante*. The proof is that the society projected in the *Comedy* contains an element that had hitherto been missing from medieval society and that can be designated by means of a single term: philosophy.

It may be objected that philosophy was not totally foreign to earlier generations of theologians, who since the days of the Church Fathers had managed to integrate it into the fabric of Christian intellectual life. Pertinent as it may be, however, the objection obscures the fact that up to the middle of the thirteenth century or thereabouts, what passed for philosophy in the Western world was not philosophy in its pure state but a philosophy that had been defanged, as it were, and tailored to the needs of the Christian faith. With the rediscovery of Aristotle, that picture was radically altered. The Christian Middle Ages encountered not just a new philosophy but philosophy *tout court*. [23]

This applies to Aristotelian natural philosophy to begin with, but it applies even more to the *Politics*, the last of Aristotle's great treatises to be translated into Latin during the 1260s, the decade in which Dante was born. There is a strong case to be made for the view that Dante himself was the first genuinely political philosopher of the Latin Middle Ages insofar as it fell to him to call philosophy down from the empyrean and introduce it, not indeed into Athens, as Socrates had done, but into the cities and nations of Christendom. No doubt, the groundwork for this endeavor had been laid by Thomas Aquinas, but Thomas is not generally regarded as first and foremost a political thinker. It is not without significance that his commentary on the *Politics* is the only one of his commentaries on Aristotle's major treatises that was never completed. From Thomas one learns next to nothing about the dominant structures and inner tensions of medieval society. What was for Dante the central political issue of the Western world is not even a minor theme of Thomas's works. Although the beginning of his academic career coincides with the death of the brilliant Frederick II (in 1250), one scours his voluminous corpus in vain for any allusion to the fate of the Empire or, for that matter, any mention of the Emperor. As Etienne Gilson puts it, "This theologian views everything as if the Emperor did not exist."[24] In Thomas's opinion, the legitimate heir of the Roman Empire was not the Holy Roman Empire but the spiritual kingdom into which the Rome of old had since been transformed: *transmutatum est de temporali in spirituale* (*In epistulam II ad Thessalonicenses 2.1.1*). Never or only very rarely are the standards of political judgment that were part of his Aristotelian legacy brought to bear on a situation from which, as a thinker who sees all things in the light of eternity, he appears to have been only too eager to prescind. Any use of politics as a practical science is at best latent in him.

Not so with Dante, who found in Aristotle's account of the natural foundations of civil society and the principles of right rule the key to the most pressing problem of his age. In an important but obscure passage of the *Monarchia* (III.11), Dante indicates that, since the Pope and the Emperor exercise different kinds of authority, they necessarily belong to different species. From this observation, he infers that their harmony can be secured only by means of a common relationship to a higher being, who is either God himself or a substance lower than God but superior to all other creatures. The term used elsewhere to identify this mysterious substance is the "Point"—*il Punto*—on which, we are told, the heavens and all of nature depend (*Par.*, XXVIII.41-42) and from which the powers of Peter and Caesar are independently derived (cf. *Epist.* 5.5).

What is meant by this point, it seems, is either reason itself, the highest principle in the universe—its "empress," as it is called in the *Convivio*—or the embodiment of reason, who could be either God, or, short of that, the human being in whom reason finds its fullest expression, the philosopher. Simply stated, the Pope and the Emperor would best be able to discharge their functions and would cooperate most effectively with each other if they both accepted to be guided by perfected reason or philosophy. The notion that we finally arrive at is something like the secret royalty of the philosopher, the only person who, because he straddles both worlds, is capable of harmonizing them, reconciling whenever necessary the demands of the Bible with those of the political life.

But this could very well be the most utopian of all the proposals made or hinted at in the *Comedy*; for nothing assures us that the true philosopher will be on hand when needed, or, if he should be, that he will be listened to by either the Pope or the Emperor. We know not only from Plato's *Republic* but from the events of Dante's time that, far from being welcomed with open arms, philosophers are liable to be held in suspicion, if not actually persecuted, by the religious and political establishments under which they happen to live. The example of Siger of Brabant, so aptly laid before us in *Paradiso* X—Siger, who, because he was so badly treated, found death "slow in coming" at the early age of forty-four—is there to remind us of this unpleasant fact. St. Bonventure, who had more than his share of misgivings about philosophy, went so far as to identify it with the knowledge of good and evil, the very knowledge that Adam and Eve had been forbidden to seek.[25] Recent condemnations, such as those of 1270 and 1277 by the bishop of Paris, Etienne Tempier, had served notice that in such matters only a certain amount of freedom could be tolerated. No, philosophy was not about to make a triumphal entry into the new Jerusalem. In many ways, the tide in high ecclesiastical circles was running against it. Red flags were going up all over the place.

Enter the poet, who in this respect has a decided edge over the philosopher in that he alone can move entire nations, educate the tastes of his fellow countrymen, redirect their affections, and, without their being aware of it, charm them into acquiescing in the vision of beauty and harmony that he wishes to accredit. The task was a gigantic one; it called for a special kind of poetry that would destroy prejudice by building on it and forge a viable consensus out of the *membra disjecta* of a disintegrating Christian society. That logical contradiction of the modern period, philosophical poetry, became the privileged instrument by means of which, as the legislator of legislators, the poet sought to effect an intellectual revolution designed to instill new vitality into the hollow shell of imperial rule.

The new founding achieved its most splendid expression in the *Comedy*, the charter of a regenerated Christendom, in which the timeless wisdom of Greece is rescued from the limbo of Christian theology and seized upon as the integrating principle of a synthesis whose depth and beauty the breakdown of the medieval world and the triumph of modernity have sometimes obscured but never completely erased from our consciousness.

One may still be tempted to ask why, if the specific political program outlined in the *Comedy* had so little chance of success, the poet went to the trouble of elaborating it. The objection, a familiar one, has been leveled not only at Dante but at the entire premodern tradition, which was rejected by the early modern thinkers on the ground that its proponents spent most of their time talking about things that are seldom if ever seen in practice.[26] Better to take Machiavelli's advice and go to the "effectual truth" of the matter than to its imagination.

To this criticism there was a ready answer, which is that human beings usually accomplish more when they are encouraged to raise rather than lower their sights. It is also possible to take the issue a step further and argue that Dante's success was not contingent on the result of his efforts to reform medieval society. In the last analysis, his goal was more philosophic than strictly political. He himself intimates as much when, from the lofty summit of heaven of the fixed stars, he looks back on what lies behind him and says:

> I turned my eyes down through all the seven spheres
> and I saw this globe of ours such
> that I smiled at its mean appearance.
> And I approve that opinion as best which esteems it
> of least account; so that those who think
> of something else can be called righteous.
>
> (*Par.* XXII.133-8)

With these words the poet returns to the highest theme of classical political philosophy. He acknowledges that the political life is inherently incapable of satisfying the deepest longings of the human heart and gives us to understand that the joys which it affords are paltry by comparison with those of the theoretical life. The remarkable thing is that even as regards the theoretical life itself the studied ambiguity of the poem is maintained to the very end. The choice with which we are finally confronted is between a philosophy that owes its greatest dignity to its status as the handmaiden of theology and one that refuses to bow to any higher authority. By and large, I have limited myself to an examination of the political dimension of the poem and especially of the relationship between Peter and Caesar as Dante conceives it. A more complete analysis of his masterpiece would necessitate a parallel study of the relationship between Jerusalem and Athens or between divine revelation and philosophic wisdom, the absolutely highest theme of the *Comedy* and, indeed, of the Western tradition as a whole.

NOTES

1. J. Hertzler, *The History of Utopian Thought* (New York: Macmillan, 1926), 121.

2. Dante, *Epistolae* 10 (to *Can Grande*), No. 15.

3. *Epistolae* No. 8.

4. See, most recently, P. Dronke, *Dante and Medieval Latin Traditions* (Cambridge, MA: Cambridge University Press, 1988), 103-11.

5. Plato, *Republic* IX.592b.

6. See, for a summary of the classic teaching on this subject, Thomas Aquinas, *Summa Theologiae* I qu. 1, art. 10.

7. For a concise statement of the problem, cf. esp. W. Ullmann, "*Medieval Monarchy*," *Sewanee Mediaeval Colloquium Occasional Papers*, 1 (Spring, 1982): 19-59.

8. The Greek term *Basileus* was used to designate both the king (Latin: *rex*) and the emperor (Latin: *imperator*).

9. Dante rejected the offer because accepting it would have been tantamount to an admission of guilt.

10. The pope died accidentally when the ceiling that supported his library collapsed on him at the papal palace of Viterbo.

11. Charles S. Singleton, *The Divine Comedy, Paradiso 2: Commentary* (Princeton University Press, 1975), 505, ad v. 133-38.

12. Clement, badly in need of Henry's help, had summoned him to Rome to be anointed. Shortly thereafter, having entered into a new coalition with Robert of Naples, he withdrew his support of the emperor, who was left to die with his decimated and ailing army in the plains of Tuscany.

13. *Inferno* IV.131. Cf. Maimonides, *Guide of the Perplexed*, I.54; II.28; III.12; III.54.

14. Cf. *Averroes on Plato's Republic*, 45, 20-46, 22, trans. R. Lerner (Ithaca and London: Cornell University Press, 1974), 44-46.

15. E.g., *Monarchia* I.14, where Dante explains that "minute regulations for each city cannot come from the supreme ruler alone, for common laws are sometimes defective and need to be amended, as the Philosopher makes clear in his praise of equity in the *Nicomachean Ethics*. Thus, nations, kingdoms, and cities have their own customs, which must be regulated by different laws."

16. Dante Alighieri, *La Divina Commedia*, edited and annotated by C. H. Grandgent, revised by Charles S. Singleton (Cambridge, MA: Harvard University Press, 1972), 884.

17. E. Kantorowicz, *The King's Two Bodies: A Study in Mediaeval Political Theology* (Princeton: Princeton University Press, 1957), 8, 271-72, 495, et passim. Gilbert of Tournai, *Eruditio regum et principum*, III.2.A. de Poorter, ed., (Louvain: Institut supérieur de Philosophie, 1914), 84.

18. *De reprobatione Monarchiae*, N. Matteini, ed. (Padova: Il Pensiero medioevale, 1958), la serie, vol. 6, 98, 7.

19. *Monarchia* III.15.

20. Ibid., I.5.

21. Ibid., I.15.18.

22. E.g., J. Goudet, *Dante et la politique* (Paris: Aubier-Montaigne, 1969), 190-91. J. LeGoff, *La civilisation de l'Occident médiéval* (Paris: Arthaud, 1967), 587.

23. Cf. E. Gilson, *Etudes de philosophie médiévale* (Strasbourg: Commission des publications de la Faculté des lettres de l'Université de Strasbourg, 1921), 53.

24. E. Gilson, *Dante and Philosophy*, trans. D. Moore (Gloucester, MA: Peter Smith, 1968), 172.

25. Third Sunday of Advent, *Sermo* 2, in *Opera*, vol. IX, 62-63.

26. See, *inter multa alia*, Spinoza, *A Political Treatise*, chap. 1: Introduction: "They (the philosophers) conceive of men not as they are but as they themselves would like them to be. Whence it has come to pass that they have generally written satire and have never conceived a theory of politics that could be turned to use but only such as might be taken for a chimera, or might have been formed in Utopia, or in that golden age of the poets when, to be sure, there was least need of it."

19

DANTE AND THE POLITICS
OF NEUTRALITY

Partly as a result of the emergence of the so-called Third World and its ambiguous relationship to the superpowers since the end of World War II, the problem of political neutrality has acquired a prominence that far surpasses any that might have attached to it at other moments in our history. Yet we know from Thucydides's account of the dealings between some of the lesser Greek cities and the superpowers of his day, Athens and Sparta, that it was already familiar to the great writers of classical antiquity; and there is reason to believe that it was equally familiar to the political thinkers of the Middle Ages, although in this instance it took on a new form owing to the peculiar character of medieval society, which, unlike most other societies, was ruled by two distinct and often competing authorities, one spiritual and the other temporal.

How this unique state of affairs had come about is a long story that led to the establishment in 800 of the Holy Roman Empire, a novel political arrangement of which we have already spoken,[1] and which set the stage for the frequent confrontations between the two powers in the centuries that followed.

Far from unifying the various segments of western Christendom, the constant intrusion of the papacy into its temporal affairs had the unfortunate effect of intensifying the divisions within it. It awakened passions that no one was able to control and, particularly in the small communes of northern Italy, whose political life underwent a brilliant renascence from the thirteenth century onward, it more or less forced local rulers and their constituencies to align themselves with either the Pope or the Emperor. But it also invited some of these rulers, who had as much to fear from the former as from the latter, to adopt a course of action that would spare them the necessity of choosing between them.[2] There is much evidence to suggest that this tempting if somewhat precarious neutrality is precisely the one that is examined in Canto III of Dante's *Inferno*.

This famous canto deals for the most part with the uncommitted souls whom Dante and Virgil encounter just as they are about to penetrate into hell proper, a mournful crowd made up entirely of individuals who are destined to remain eternally nameless. Assembled under an anonymous banner that circles overhead without ever pointing in any specific direction, they have fallen prey to a frantic but aimless agitation. The only criticism leveled at them is that they failed to distinguish themselves in either goodness or badness, for which reason they are now made to languish before the gate of hell, deprived forever of the praise or blame that eluded them on earth. Their fate is a mild one compared to that of the damned in hell, but it is no less pitiable than any other. Having never really lived, they are incapable of dying and are henceforth condemned to a life of complete oblivion, envious of all others but without the faintest hope of being themselves remembered, let alone envied. To their company, Dante has joined the angels who refused to take sides at the time of the revolt against God and who are now disdained by the pity of heaven no less than by the justice of hell. Since these angels were neither "faithful" nor "rebellious," no one will have anything to do with them. Virgil has nothing but contempt for them and advises Dante to move on without addressing them or taking any further notice of them.

We hardly need to remind ourselves that the situation envisaged in this canto represents a significant departure from the theology of the Middle Ages, according to which there are in all only four places to which the human soul, once separated from the body, may be consigned: heaven, purgatory, hell, or limbo. Nowhere outside of the *Comedy* is there any mention of Dante's strange new category. All indications point to the fact that what we have here is a pure and simple invention of the poet, harmless in appearance and full of picturesque detail, but bereft of any theological foundation or significance. The question is why Dante, whose knowledge of Christian theology is rarely at fault and who could very well have dispensed with this piece of fiction, chose to insert it at this point in his poem.

To that question no one to my knowledge has yet been able to offer a satisfactory answer. Most commentators refer us to chapter 3 of the

Book of Revelation, which inveighs against the angel of the church at Laodicea, who is neither warm nor cold and of whom it is said that he will be spewed from the mouth of God if he persists in his lukewarmness; but the link between the two texts is at best tenuous. First of all, luke-warmness is not the same thing as neutrality, and in any event the Book of Revelation speaks of a single angel only, who is presumed to be the local bishop. Nor does it imply that, once rejected by God, this individual will also be turned down by hell. The severe rebuke addressed to him is meant only to incite him to a higher degree of fervor and contains no suggestion to the effect that his status might be different from that of any other Christian who fails to live up to his responsibilities. Scholars have likewise adverted to other possible sources, such as the *Stromata* of Clement of Alexandria, the *Life of St. Brendan,* and the legend of Parsifal, from which Dante's information could conceivably have been drawn; but the parallels are vague and, given their contextual disparity, hardly conclusive.

A more ingenious interpretation has been proposed by Professor John Freccero, who claims to have found in the theological literature of the time a theory that lends support to Dante's conceit.[3] Freccero notes first of all that one of the key terms used to describe the situation of the neutral angels is ambiguous and hence subject to misinterpretation. Dante says of this "choir of wicked angels" that they were neither faithful nor rebellious but *per se (Inf.,* III.39). Most modern translators take the preposition *per* in this phrase to mean "for" and interpret the passage as signifying that said angels were neither for nor against God but "for themselves." Such, however, is not Dante's intention. On the basis of data supplied elsewhere in the *Comedy,* it can be shown that the expression *per se* is more properly and more intelligibly rendered by "apart." Unwilling either to profess their loyalty to God or join the ranks of those who revolted against him, the neutrals resolved to form a group by themselves, and it is this isolation or separation from everyone else that defines their present position. Dante's *per se* would thus correspond to the *da se* of modern Italian. The same formula reappears in *Paradiso* XVII.69, where Cacciaguida predicts that during his exile Dante will sever his ties with all existing political parties and form as it were a party "by himself": *a te fia bello averti fatta parte PER TE stesso.*

What could the poet possibly have had in mind? Always according to Freccero, medieval theology distinguished two successive moments in the angelic revolt. In the first of these, the rebellious angels rejected God as their final end. As a result, the bond of charity that would have united them permanently to their Maker was never formed and they were forever excluded from the joys of the beatific vision. This deprivation of a good that would otherwise have been theirs must be regarded as an evil, albeit only a physical evil, one that does not imply any guilt on their part. For their condition to become morally evil or sinful, a second act was required in virtue of which they opted for an inferior good, namely, themselves or some other created object, as their final end or supreme good. Only this second act was morally culpable, and the more so as the chosen object stood at a greater distance from God.

With the help of these subtle distinctions, one would finally be able to account for the apparent anomaly contained in the notion of angelic neutrality. In the case of the neutral angel, no positive act followed the rejection of the promised beatitude. Summoned to choose God above all else, the angel would have refused to do so and thereby renounced the beatific vision, but without allowing himself to be attracted to any other good, as if he had been free to forge for himself a destiny different from the one prescribed by God. His whole being would thus be characterized by a "double negation," and it is this double negation that caused him to lose the place originally set aside for him in the order of creation.

As to the question of whether he is morally better or worse than the other angels, it does not arise since he cannot even be called a sinner. By refraining from any further action, he deprived himself of the one element that could have guaranteed his insertion into the cosmos as God had willed it. As a result, he now finds himself in a state of total alienation from God as well as from all other beings. Nothing distinguishes him from the nothingness out of which he was created. Dante had every reason to relegate him to that strange vestibule which does not strictly speaking form part of the spiritual universe of the *Comedy*. The total detachment of these neutrals would serve no other purpose than to complete the gamut of possibilities that Dante lays out before us by disposing all the beings of creation along a ladder that extends from the glacial pit of hell to the intense ardor of the celestial spheres.[4]

Freccero's thesis has the advantage of linking the problem at hand to the discussions in which medieval theologians were wont to engage regarding the sin of the angels, but it is not without its drawbacks both from the point of view of Christian doctrine and from that of the *Comedy* itself. For one is at a loss to explain how an act of the will can remain unspecified by any object and be wholly constituted by an "irreducible negation." The Scholastics were careful to distinguish between the negative aspect of the sinful act, by virtue of which the creature turns away from its supreme good, and the positive aspect, by virtue of which it turns toward an inferior good. Accordingly, they spoke not of two consecutive acts but of two distinct formalities of one and the same act. The will has the good as its sole object and can never be moved by anything else. Even when it chooses evil, it is only because it mistakes a particular good for its total good. There is no such thing as an act that is defined by pure nothingness. The angel was not metaphysically free to abstain from the choice that he was called upon to make. If he rejected God's offer, it is because he had first chosen himself. This was enough to remove him from the society of the blessed in heaven and merit for him the pains of eternal damnation. Dante would have been justified in adding angelic or human neutrality to the spectrum of options open to creatures if that alternative had been a real one, but since it is inherently contradictory, Freccero's argument loses much of its force.

It is nevertheless permissible to think of another kind of neutrality in regard to which everything that has just been said about the double refusal or the double negation of the neutral angels is verified in a manner that is at once simpler and more consonant with the historical coordinates of the poem. The burning question to which Dante addresses himself in the opening cantos of the *Comedy* is without any doubt the bloody conflict that pitted the Whites against the Blacks in his native Florence. At the moment to which the *Comedy* takes us back, the situation had become so inflamed that it was virtually impossible to avoid siding with one or the other of the two factions. Yet, as in all such circumstances, some people found themselves ill at ease. The choice was not an easy one to make, especially since the Whites seemed weak and badly fitted for the battle. We know that Dante himself supported the White cause only because he dreaded the consequences of a Black victory even more. For various motives, not all of them noble, others preferred to remain aloof from the fray.

Needless to say, the problem went well beyond the narrow confines of a local feud ignited by recent events. Since at least the time of Frederick I, the whole of northern Italy had become the scene of an ongoing struggle that the strained relations between the Empire and the Papacy did much to aggravate. Interestingly enough, the resentment harbored toward a German emperor who seemed only too eager to exploit his Italian subjects was often matched by an equally strong distrust of the Holy See and its temporal ambitions. It is therefore not surprising that, caught between these two great powers and desirous of preserving a measure of independence for themselves, some of the Italian communes should have attempted to shake off the imperial yoke, but without transferring their political allegiance to the Church. These, one surmises, are the people that the *Comedy* alludes to under the image of the neutrals whom Dante takes to task for pursuing a policy of strict nonalignment in the midst of a situation that called for a firm if at times painful decision on their part. The God with whom they refused to ally themselves is not the biblical God, with respect to whom any such neutrality is out of the question, but the figure who in Dante's fictional universe embodies His supreme authority in the political sphere, namely, the emperor. In like fashion, the angels who are lumped together with the souls of deceased human beings in Canto III are not literally angels but, in accordance with contemporary usage, the leaders of these same communities, who can neither be called glorious nor infamous inasmuch as, out of weakness, lack of resolve, cowardice, or self-interest, they withdrew from the contest and thereby passed up the opportunity to play a significant role in the great events of their day. This and nothing else is what caused them to forfeit their right to a place in Dante's hell, purgatory, or heaven, where, as we are later told, only the souls who deserve to be remembered for their noble or base deeds are shown to us (cf. *Par.,* XVII.138).

The use of the word "angel" in this context should come as no surprise to us. It merely conforms to a practice that has its twin roots in the biblical and the hellenistic traditions, from which it was borrowed at the time of the establishment of the Holy Roman Empire. From that moment on, it became customary in the West, as it had been in the East, to endow kings and princes with quasi-divine attributes.[5] Faced with the embarrassing fact that Charlemagne was something of a usurper, the apologists of the Carolingian empire had already made abundant use of this theo-phanic conception of kingly rule. The logic that supports it has nothing particularly mysterious about it. Human beings are not easily persuaded to surrender their freedom and the control of their lives to people whom they do not regard as their superiors. To have the right and the capacity to rule others, a prince ought to have a superior nature. He must be a god or, short of that, God's own personal representative. Because he must be, he is. The problem is well stated by Rousseau in the form of an argument attributed to Caligula:

> As a shepherd is of a nature superior to that of his flock, the shepherds of men, i.e., their rulers, are of a nature superior to that of the peoples under them. Thus, Philo tells us, the Emperor Claudius reasoned, concluding equally well either that kings were gods or that men were beasts.[6]

The word "angel" reappears only once in the *Inferno,* this time in connection with the "black angels" of the fifth ditch of Malebolge (*Inf.* XXIII.131), who appear to stand for the leaders of the Black party at whose hands the poet had already suffered much and who remained adamant in their refusal to allow him back into his own city. In an analogous sense, Canto VIII uses the paraphrase, "the thousand fallen from heaven," again to describe the rulers or guardians whose vigilance Dante and Virgil will have to circumvent before making their entry into the City of Dis. What is significant is that these creatures are called angels by reason of their political function rather than by reason of their specifically angelic nature.

The foregoing analysis of *Inferno* III could conceivably shed some light on the open riddle with which that canto presents us and advance our understanding of the much-neglected political dimension of the poem. It leaves untouched its deeper riddle, which has to do with the unfinished character of Dante's partly imaginary typology. Three classes of persons are mentioned explicitly: the faithful, the rebellious, and the neutrals. To complete the series, assuming that it needs to be completed, a fourth class must be added, that of the person who is at once faithful and rebellious. One's initial impulse is to dismiss such an eventuality out of hand inasmuch as it postulates the simultaneous presence in the same individual of two mutually exclusive attributes. The contradiction may be only superficial, however. It vanishes the moment one takes seriously the possibility of an internal rebellion that is covered over by an outward show of loyalty. Reference was made earlier to the fact that the only parallel to the *per se* of the neutral angels in the *Comedy* is the *per te* of *Paradiso* XVII. The difference between the two passages is that, whereas Dante regards the position of the neutrals as contemptible and self-defeating, his own "neutral" position is presented by Cacciaguida as both noble and, to the extent to which the spiritual success of his endeavors was not contingent on their material success, eminently viable. What that position might be is a question that mercifully lies beyond the limited aim of the present analysis.

NOTES

1. Cf. supra, 276-78.

2. See on this subject the pertinent remarks by Q. Skinner, *The Foundations of Modern Political Thought*, vol. 1: *The Renaissance* (New York: Cambridge University Press, 1978), 4f.

3. J. Freccero, "Dante and the Neutral Angels," *The Romanic Review* 51 (1960): 3-14. Id., "Dante's 'per se' Angel: The Middle Ground in Nature and in Grace," *Studi Danteschi* 39 (1962): 36-387.

4. See for further references and a fuller analysis of Freccero's position, E. L. Fortin, *Dissidence et philosophie au moyen âge: Dante et ses antécédents* (Paris: Vrin, and Montreal: Bellarmin, 1981), 115-21.

5. Cf. supra, 256.

6. Jean Jacques Rousseau, *Social Contract*, I.2.

V

SELECTED REVIEWS

Peter Brown. *Augustine of Hippo: A Biography*. Berkeley and Los Angeles: University of California Press, 1967. 463 pp.

Peter Brown's book is far and away the best comprehensive biography of Augustine to have appeared thus far in any language. The enterprise is one that had already discouraged many a seasoned Augustinian scholar. To appreciate its magnitude, one needs only to be reminded of the 5,502 items included in van Bavel's bibliography for the 1950-60 period alone, or of the 430-odd titles listed each year in the Bulletin published by the *Revue des études augustiniennes*.

Brown's approach is at once chronological and topical. The book is divided into thirty-six short or relatively short chapters, each one of which focuses on some important theme, issue, or event relating to the life and thought of Augustine. Although obviously well-acquainted with the more important recent disputes among historians and scholars, Brown has generally refrained from entering the lists on one side or the other and has preferred to deal with controversial points in an expository and non-polemical manner. The same serene objectivity marks the unusually thorough and well-balanced treatment of such complex issues as the Donatist and Pelagian controversies. Not the least of the book's many attractive features is the manner in which Augustine's thought is constantly related to the historical situations that constitute the matrix within which it took shape or out of which it evolved. The result is not only an up-to-date account of Augustine's life but a new assessment of his entire literary activity and of his many-sided personality, based on a judicious use of ancient sources and the best findings of modern scholarship. As such, the book could serve as an excellent point of departure for the study of virtually every major aspect of Augustine's life or thought. Its usefulness is further enhanced by a series of tables which relate the major events

of Augustine's life to contemporary events and list his works in chronological order, along with all existing English translations of these works.

As the Preface indicates, the plane on which Brown has chosen to
move lies somewhere between the routine of Augustine's daily life and the
heights of his philosophic and theological speculations. The question that
immediately arises concerns the extent to which one can exclude Augustine's highest principles from one's purview and still do full justice to the
subject matter at hand. A case in point is the somewhat misleading, if not
erroneous, statement that for Augustine "the 'highest pitch' of wisdom
was available to any moderately educated and serious mind" (p. 120).
Augustine appears to have been anything but an egalitarian in that sense,
as he himself has often intimated (cf. *De ordine* I.1.1; II.5.16; IV.16.44;
De beata vita I.1, etc.). The fact that the characters of the early *Dialogues*
do not at first glance constitute a particularly promising group is no proof
to the contrary, since one of the purposes of the dialogue form in the
ancient philosophic tradition is precisely to draw attention to the natural
differences among men and to the crucial significance of these differences
in any philosophic or theological discussion. Equally perplexing to this
reader are Brown's remarks about prayer as a recognized vehicle for
philosophic enquiry or of philosophy as a concentrated act of prayer (pp.
165-66). A closer examination of the famous statement to that effect in
Enneads V.1.6 would probably reveal that for Plotinus, as for Plato, true
piety is philosophy or the very antithesis of prayer as Augustine
understands it.

Brown's analysis of Augustine's allegorical method of interpretation
is likewise open to criticism on certain points. It would perhaps be more
accurate and helpful to say that the position taken by Augustine is analogous to that of Plato rather than to that of Freud (cf. p. 261).
Augustine's conception of the Bible as an organic and perfectly intelligible whole, whose obscurities and apparent contradictions are an
invitation to ferret out hidden meanings in the text, draws heavily upon
sources that may be traced back to Plato's thematic discussion of books
and book writing in the *Phaedrus* and has little in common with Freud's
anal science of interpretation. What is really at stake in this matter is
Augustine's whole theory of hermeneutics, of which unfortunately there
exists no first-rate treatment at the present moment. Brown observes
rightly, as others have done before him, that Augustine hardly ever attacks
contemporary forms of pagan worship and that his lengthy critique of
pagan cults in the *City of God*, based for the most part on Varro, is
largely anachronistic. According to Brown, Augustine's method of procedure is explained by his conviction that the pagans of his time could
best be reached through their libraries (p. 305). There are reasons to
believe, however, that Augustine and his audience were less bookish than

some recent scholars are inclined to think. In keeping with Augustine's own principles, one might venture to suggest that this great "secularizer" of the pagan past (p. 266) showed classical restraint in dealing with civil religion and was considerably less "secular" in his approach to this problem than most of his latter-day disciples.

Finally, Brown detects an inconsistency in the fact that Augustine occasionally ridicules certain popular attitudes (e.g., the belief in the value of dreams), while appealing elsewhere to these same beliefs to bend the shocking hardness of reasonable pagans (p. 415). It cannot be denied that Augustine contradicts himself; but these "contradictions" do not necessarily imply a compromise with the opinions of the multitude or an evolution in his thought. They are often explained by the different audiences to whom his remarks are addressed. This simple rhetorical device was by no means an uncommon one. It reminds us, among other things, of the method used by Plato, who sides with the vulgar against the Sophists or with the Sophists against the vulgar, as the circumstances of the case demand.

The foregoing observations are offered less as a criticism than as an example of the limitations inherent in Brown's approach. They leave intact the many other merits of this outstanding and timely book. Augustine lived in an age of rapid and dramatic change. As a learned, indefatigable, and unusually penetrating man, he was able to renew Christianity by adapting it to the circumstances of his time and thus shape its destiny for centuries to come. In Augustine, more than in anyone else, traditional or so-called Hellenized Christianity may be said to have received its classic expression. In this important respect, Brown's book adds a much-needed historical dimension to the current debate concerning the de-Hellenization of Christian thought.

Robert J. O'Connell, S.J. *St. Augustine's Early Theory of Man, A.D.* 386-391. Cambridge, MA: Belknap Press of Harvard University Press, 1968. 320 pp.

O'Connell's monograph is the latest in a long and impressive series of works dealing with what might be called the riddle of the early Augustine. The terms in which the problem is posed are basically those of O'Connell's predecessors (Bouillet, Alfaric, Theiler, Henry, Courcelle, et al.) but the reader soon discovers that in reopening the debate, O'Connell has enlarged it to a considerable degree. Without minimizing the role of Porphyry, the essay reverts to the older thesis according to which Plotinus rather than his disciple represents the decisive philosophic influence on

Augustine's intellectual development. For O'Connell, the proper way to understand Augustine, then, is to read him against the background of the *Enneads*. The method employed to establish that thesis consists not only in tracking down textual or doctrinal parallels between the two authors but in analyzing closely the subtle structure of overlapping images in which Augustine's thought is more often than not imbricated. Particular importance is attached to Plotinus's treatise on omnipresence (*Enneads* VI.4-5), which, O'Connell thinks, removed the last great intellectual impediment to Augustine's acceptance of the Christian faith.

O'Connell is not only an able philosopher; he is a master sleuth who excels at uncovering larcenies where none was suspected and who is capable of solving complex literary mysteries on the basis of the most tenuous but nevertheless unmistakable evidence. Parts of his book read like a genuine Maigret. O'Connell knows better than anyone else that he is dealing with a clever crook. Augustine is anything but a bungling schoolboy who simply pirates or slavishly apes his pagan models. O'Connell sees him as an incipient and groping genius with an uncanny ability to assimilate, transmute, and hence conceal his sources. One would never have guessed, e.g., that Augustine's biblical metaphor *fovisti caput nescientis* ("You soothed my head, unknown to me") was overlaid in his mind with the pagan image of Athena forcefully turning or twisting the head of the budding philosopher toward the light of truth. Nor would anyone have thought that St. John's "triple concupiscence" had been transformed by Augustine into the familiar triad of pride, curiosity, and bodily desire only with an assist from Plotinus and his view of the restlessness or curiosity of the fallen soul.

There is no denying that O'Connell's inquiry greatly expands the sphere of recognized Plotinian influence on Augustine. O'Connell is no Alfaric, however. He is not about to raise doubts concerning Augustine's conversion to Christianity. What is at stake is not the sincerity of that conversion but the content of Augustine's beliefs at that early date. Augustine could very well have adhered unflinchingly to the faith of the *Catholica* without being fully aware of all its implications or without seeing the incompatibility of its basic tenets with some of the Plotinian doctrines that he had recently and so avidly embraced. After all, did he not confess to having once held that Christ was a mere teacher who carried no more than an exemplary value?

Still, it is difficult to ward off the impression that O'Connell is a more severe judge of the young Augustine than was the later Augustine himself. For all its enormous persuasiveness, his study confronts us with an inescapable paradox: if the Christianity of the dialogues is as undeveloped as O'Connell apparently thinks it is, why did Augustine bother to reedit or "revise" these works for posterity instead of simply denouncing or withdrawing them? By so doing, was he not enshrining for future generations the falsehoods that he himself had come to recognize and repudiate during his own lifetime? At this point it becomes advisable not only to enlarge but to transcend the limited perspective within which the polemic has thus far tended to move. A possible clue as to how this might be accomplished is furnished indirectly by O'Connell himself in the epilogue, which raises the interesting issue of Augustine's relevance to our time. Like Dietrich Ritschl (*Memory and Hope,* 1967), with whom he seems to concur implicitly, O'Connell all but blames Western Christianity's addiction to Augustinianism for the woes that have lately beset the house of theology. Specifically, he reproaches Augustine with showing little concern for the political or secular aspects of human life. The statement is astonishing in view of the fact that Augustine is ostensibly the only Latin Father to present us with anything like a sophisticated political theology. It is true, of course, that the political dimension, so conspicuous in Plato, is largely absent from the metaphysical and mystical Platonism of Plotinus, that *Plato dimidiatus,* as he has been called. But Augustine had access to Plato's political teaching through other sources and notably through Cicero, who in a different way was as much his master as Plotinus. One fears that in this respect O'Connell's Augustine is himself an *Augustinus dimidiatus.*

There is more to that story. Augustine's thought is political in an even deeper sense, being wholly imbedded as it were in a decidedly political context; for Augustine had learned from both Plotinus and Cicero that the quest for the highest truth can never be divorced from a prudent reserve in the expression of that truth. The Protean disguises (to use his own image) in which he often appears in the dialogues do not easily lend themselves to the kind of analysis favored and made possible by the tools of modern historical research. Until the zetetic quality of these dialogues is fully appreciated and explored, it is doubtful whether the mystery that they pose can be resolved in a completely satisfactory manner.

Having said this much, the reviewer readily "confesses" that O'Connell's book is a first-rate study which fully deserves a place alongside those of Alfaric and Courcelle as a milestone in Augustinian scholarship.

Oliver O'Donovan. *The Problem of Self-Love in St. Augustine.* New Haven and London: Yale University Press, 1980. 230 pp.

O'Donovan's gracefully written book is a late but welcome addition to an already large body of literature spawned directly or indirectly by A. Nygren's epoch-making *Agape and Eros,* the first installment of which

appeared in 1930. Most of the ground that it covers is aptly described as
a battlefield "on which the smoke still hangs heavy" (p. 10). Interestingly
enough, Augustine is the first Latin writer to make extensive use of the
expression *amor sui* or "self-love," which occurs some one-hundred and
fifty times throughout his voluminous corpus. Although once accepted virtually without question, his views on this crucial subject have not met
with universal approval in our century. Nygren was convinced that
Augustine had dealt a lethal blow to the self-denying *agape* of the Gospel
by synthesizing it with the essentially self-regarding *eros* of Platonic
philosophy. Others have since rallied to Augustine's defense, but without
always doing full justice to the complexity of his thought. Hence the need
for a global assessment of the problem based on a careful scrutiny of the
evidence at hand. Chapter 1 lays the groundwork for such an assessment
by sorting out the various meanings of *amor* and its analogues, *dilectio*
and *caritas,* in Augustine's works. Four kinds or, better, "aspects" of love
emerge as distinct but related: the cosmic, the positive or subjective, the
rational, and the benevolent. The rest of the essay is devoted to an
exploration of the manner in which, on the basis of this division,
Augustine managed to reconcile self-love with the twofold commandment
of the love of God and neighbor. Chapter 2 makes the point that, even
though the love of God and the desire for happiness are not coextensive,
they are not always or not necessarily antithetical. One of the keys to a
proper understanding of their relationship lies in the distinction between
right and wrong or perverse self-love, which is further explicated in
chapters 3 and 4, entitled respectively, "Self-Knowledge and Self-Love"
and "The Primal Destruction." Chapter 5 refutes Holl's contention that
Augustine's teaching regarding the "love-of-neighbor-as-self" leads to a
questionable "double-standard" theory and then goes on to make the case
for a maximalist rather than a minimalist interpretation of that teaching,
which is shown to be founded on the love of the three Divine Persons for
one another and on a "collectivist metaphysics" that stresses the primacy
of the universal common good (cf. p. 133). The concluding chapter, with
which the reader who is eager to strike pay dirt may wish to begin,
attempts to draw out the broad philosophic and theological significance of
Augustine's doctrine via a head-to-head confrontation with such notable
contributors to the ongoing debate as Rousselot, Holl, Nygren, Gilson, and
Holte.

Patristic scholars and Christian ethicists alike will be grateful for this
able defense of Augustinian eudaemonism, which reflects a growing trend
away from Kantian moralism among recent scholars. As O'Donovan
points out, quoting an anonymous writer, if Christian love were strictly a
matter of duty as opposed to inclination, one would be left with the
paradox of a heaven that is "full of people who are not particularly

interested in being there" (cf. pp. 8, 155). By loving themselves rightly, human beings do not yield to a selfish or egotistical impulse, but merely conform to an ontological order that has its ultimate source in God himself. Nygren's denial of the legitimacy of self-love in any of its forms amounts to a rejection, if not of the doctrine of creation, as is sometimes said, at least of the teleology that goes hand in hand with it (cf. p. 158). Yet Nygren was right in insisting on the uniqueness of the New Testament concept of love. O'Donovan's own analysis makes it clear that the movement from self-love to the love of God is neither simply continuous, as the classical tradition would have it, nor simply discontinuous, as Nygren prefers to think. Augustine had no qualms about incorporating natural love into his scheme, but the role that he assigns to it is never such as to preclude the need for divine authority or divine grace.

One may be inclined to agree with this general thesis without necessarily accepting all of the particular judgments that accompany or support it. The provocative characterization of Book I of the *De doctrina christiana* as a "false step" (p. 29) on Augustine's part is liable to raise a few eyebrows among the *periti*, who will undoubtedly demand further proof before giving up this *locus classicus* of the Augustinian teaching on love. It is hard to believe that Augustine was as fickle a writer as O'Donovan occasionally makes him out to be. The substitution of one analogy or of one logical instrument for another (e.g., with respect to the Trinity) does not automatically betoken a lack of consistency within the same work or from one work to the next. Different contexts call for different formulations; and, besides, there is nothing to prevent a subtle writer from using a series of provisional formulas as steppingstones to a more perfect articulation of his thought. Experience has taught us more than once that Augustine himself is a generally more reliable guide to his own mistakes than the common run of interpreters.

Elsewhere, the analysis of self-knowledge could have benefited from a more thorough investigation of Augustine's notion of memory as the repository of the basic truths on which the acquisition of all further knowledge depends, and hence as an essential component of the rational soul. As for the discussion of Augustine's *iustitia minor* and the so-called "double-standard" theory to which it later gave rise (cf. pp. 126, 141, 151), it might have gained in sharpness if greater attention had been paid to the way in which the principle of dilution functions in the Platonic and Augustinian approach to ethical matters. Augustine was not a fanatic, but neither was he prone to underestimate the power of evil among human beings. Whether or not the robustness of his thought is fully brought out in O'Donovan's account is doubtful, especially since so little is said about the role of *disciplina* or punishment in relation to brotherly love. One does well to bear in mind that even the celebrated maxim, "Love and do as you will," belongs to the context of the Donatist controversy and was probably meant to justify the use of force against recalcitrant schismatics. Finally, it was inevitable, I suppose, that the great themes of love, friendship, and beauty, which still occupy a prominent place in Augustine—they have all but disappeared from modern thought—should lose some of their luster as a result of their being treated in so professorial and academically competent a manner.

Ronald H. Nash. *The Light of the Mind: St. Augustine's Theory of Knowledge.* Lexington, KY: The University Press of Kentucky, 1969. 147 pp.

Ronald Nash's short monograph has the obvious merit of being the first study in English dealing exclusively and comprehensively with Augustine's theory of knowledge. An accurate assessment of Augustine's views on this subject is all the more important in Nash's opinion as Augustine has not only allegedly stamped with his influence such giants as Descartes and Malebranche but has actually anticipated some of the most original insights of Berkeley and Kant. The topic is on the whole notoriously controversial, as the persistent divergences of interpretation among scholars, both past and present, abundantly testify. Nash has nevertheless faced the difficulties of his enterprise courageously. Pitting himself against Portalié, Boyer, Gilson, Copleston, and other established authorities, whom he accuses of having scholasticized Augustine, he presents an account of Augustine's thought which claims the double advantage of being more consonant with Augustine's own statements and more intelligible to the modern reader.

The opening chapters of the book deal in the main with a number of preliminary issues all intimately connected with Augustine's "epistemology," such as his repudiation of skepticism, his views on the role of faith in human life and its relation to reason, and his theory of sense perception and cognition. Of particular interest is chapter 2, which focuses on the *Contra academicos* and traces the line of reasoning which led to the rejection of the materialistic or mechanistic cosmology on which skepticism was based in favor of Platonic teleology or the notion of an intelligible universe governed by a divine mind. This reviewer's sole regret is that Nash has not taken greater pains to indicate how Augustine not only used the Platonic theory to refute skepticism but reshaped the Platonic theory itself to suit the requirements of the Faith.

The remainder of the essay is devoted to an analysis of the doctrines of divine illumination and of intellection, which, as the author rightly points out, form the core of Augustine's theory of knowledge. The competing interpretations advanced by contemporary scholars are reduced to four broad types, which Nash labels respectively the Thomistic, the Franciscan, the Formal, and the Ontological. The first and least acceptable of these, defended by Boyer, identifies the divine light of which Augustine speaks with the agent intellect and falsely ascribes to Augustine a theory of abstraction analogous to that of Aristotle. The second, to which the name of Portalié is attached, argues that the ideas are impressed on the human mind by God himself but leaves the mind with only a passive role to play in the act of knowing. The third, which finds its chief proponents in Gilson, DeWulf, Copleston, and Kaelin, sees the role of illumination as that of imparting a quality of certitude or necessity to the ideas but is unable to account for their content. There remains the ontological interpretation, hitherto shunned by most historians, which alone would do full justice to the complexity of Augustine's thought and which combines among other things the benefits of conceptualism and realism. In essence, it postulates an immediate awareness of the eternal truths on the part of the human mind. This statement is not to be taken to mean that man sees all things in God, as Malebranche later contended, but that man's reason has been so structured by God as to be capable of knowing the ideas in the divine mind as well as the creation that is patterned on them. Only by having recourse to such an isomorphism, Nash suggests, is it possible to resolve what he calls the three great paradoxes with which any account of Augustine's views must come to grips, namely, how the human intellect is both active and passive, how the archetypal forms are at once distinct and not distinct from the mind itself, and how the mind is and is not at the same time the light that makes knowledge possible. A brief synthesis of the most pertinent Augustinian texts accordingly reveals 1) that the ideas in the mind are *a priori,* that is to say, not derived from experience, 2) that they are *virtual* or not always actually thought, and 3) that they constitute the necessary *precondition of science.*

Nash shrewdly observes that the preference exhibited by scholars for one or the other of these interpretations is by and large a function of the prior assumptions to which they are committed or with which they approach Augustine's works. Yet one does not see clearly how he is able to exempt himself from his own verdict. Although there is much to be said for his position, the terms in which it is expressed are often more redolent of modern thought than of Augustine and his models. It is misleading, if nothing else, to speak of the importance of epistemology for Augustine and to stress the kinship in this regard between his views and those of either Descartes or Kant, inasmuch as epistemology is predicated on the very denial of the teleology on which, by Nash's own admission, Augustine's final position rests. If the universe is teleological or, what amounts to the same thing, if there is a natural harmony between it and the human mind, one can dispense, as Augustine did, with the artificial intellectual tools to which philosophers were compelled to resort at the dawn of the modern period once that harmony had been rejected and once the intrinsic intelligibility of the universe had been questioned.

There are more subtle ways in which Nash's own bias occasionally comes to the surface. He is undoubtedly justified in taking issue with those contemporary theologians, such as Alan Richardson, who argue that faith as Augustine understands it is devoid of any propositional content (p. 31), but he in turn oversimplifies matters when he remarks that for Augustine practical reason directs and guides the theoretical reason (p. 34), thus unwittingly making of him an advocate of moralism, which he most emphatically was not. Assuming the advisability of stating the problem in these non-Augustinian terms, the most that can be said from Augustine's point of view is that religious knowledge, as distinguished from purely philosophic knowledge, is in one and the same act both speculative and practical. This is not to deny that the will exercises a great influence on the intellect or that some kind of faith is presupposed on the part of the student especially during the early stages of the learning process.

The irony of the book, in this reviewer's judgment, is that Nash could have found much better support for his interpretation in a sound and penetrating analysis of Plato's theory of knowledge than in the parallels that he is so eager to draw between Augustine and the modern epistemological tradition. Unfortunately, he still clings to a textbook understanding of the separation between the physical and intellectual worlds in Plato and fails to see—in the celebrated analogy of the cave, for instance—an effort on Plato's part to show how the same world can be viewed in two radically different ways or a dramatic illustration of the fundamental distinction between mere opinion and true knowledge. He likewise takes at face value Plato's statements on reminiscence or recollection instead of discerning in them a figurative expression of the microcosmic nature of the human soul or of the pre-established accord between the mind which knows and the universe which it knows (cf. p. 69, 81ff.). The same mistake was, of course, made by Augustine, who nevertheless managed to capture with admirable profundity the true spirit of the Platonic argument and at least had the excuse of not having read most of Plato's dialogues, including the *Meno,* which he knew only at second hand.

Finally, the overall quality of the essay is marred at times by a number of minor but still annoying defects. The author sheds little light on the issues at hand when he defines "word" (*verbum*) as a symbol, as opposed to a sign, in what may be one of the least satisfactory parts of the book (p. 85ff.), and his constant recourse to Latin words or phrases, presumably for the sake of clarity, is to say the least far from unimpeachable; witness, for example, the frequent use of the plural for the singular or of the genitive when the context obviously calls for the nominative form (pp. 63, 72, 75, 87, 89, *et passim*).

The preceding strictures are formulated for the sole purpose of furthering the dialogue which Nash has auspiciously reopened and which has yet to yield its choicest fruits. Whatever the merit of these strictures, there is no denying that the book assembles a wealth of profitable information which philosophers and theologians whose interests reach back to the wellsprings of Western thought will mine with delight.

Robert J. O'Connell, S.J. *Art and the Christian Intelligence in St. Augustine.* Cambridge, MA: Harvard University Press, 1978. 275 pp.

R. J. O'Connell's latest book has all the sterling literary qualities of its predecessors, *St. Augustine's Early Theory of Man* (1968) and *St. Augustine's Confessions: The Odyssey of the Soul* (1969). The task in the present case was fraught with new and graver perils; for, although considerations on art abound in Augustine, the subject never receives the full-blown treatment to which modern aesthetic theory has accustomed us. The one possible exception to this rule is the *De musica,* but even it deals with music as a science rather than as an art and does little to alter the perspective established in the other dialogues. The bulk of the essay traces the evolution of Augustine's theory of art through the early dialogues, the *Confessions,* and, in less detailed fashion, the works of his mature period.

As is so often the case, O'Connell sheds a flood of welcome light on riddles that have long baffled seasoned scholars. His investigations extend considerably our knowledge of Augustine's indebtedness to Plotinus and the Neoplatonic tradition. To that tradition is attributed the notion of the liberal arts as rooted in the "fall of the soul" and as serving no real purpose other than that of preparing its reascent to God. This, more than anything else, accounts for Augustine's excessive "rationalism," his desensualized and somewhat "otherworldly" approach to the aesthetic experience, and a persistent tendency to reduce the work of art to the outward expression of an inner reality. Fortunately, the rigor of his theoretical pronouncements is tempered, indeed "contradicted," by his obvious sensitivity to beauty, both natural and artistic, and the consummate artistry of his writings.

Even though O'Connell rightly cautions against the danger of judging an author by the standards of another age, it is not clear how he himself has managed to avoid the pitfall. His attempt to "retrieve" (Heidegger's *Wiederholung,* p. 7) Augustine's overall view is followed by a reformulation of that view in keeping with the demands of present-day aesthetics and O'Connell's own, rather more "incarnational" understanding of Christianity. Accordingly, the last chapter, entitled characteristically, "Toward a Contemporary Augustinian Aesthetic," sets forth what a more "consistent" Augustine should have said and probably would have said had he had access to the superior wisdom of, let us say, Kant or some later aestheticist (cf. pp. 166-67). The proposed solution pleads, among other things, for a greater "ingredience" of the spiritual into the temporal than Augustine was apparently willing to allow. The matter would be of little consequence if the modern outlook could be shown to be a mere refinement of the classical outlook; but the gulf between them may not be all that easy to bridge. Modern aesthetics has its twin roots in the emergence of feeling as a wholly independent theme of psychology (Rousseau) and the Hegelian assertion that art rather than nature is the true seat of beauty. As such, it implies a much more radical break with the classical (or Augustinian) tradition than O'Connell would have us believe. The question is whether the product of the mating of these two powerful traditions is finally superior to either of its individual components. One doubts that the heights to which Augustine's "odyssey of the soul" rises could ever be attained on the basis of an aesthetic theory that binds us more closely to the ephemeral beauties from which his torn soul struggled so valiantly to wrench itself.

The further question is whether one can divorce Augustine's theory from its original context and still do full justice to it. In that regard, it is significant that O'Connell barely alludes to the famous discussion of poetic theology in book VI of the *City of God*. Closer attention to this discussion might have suggested other reasons for which Augustine did not see fit to dwell at length on the nature of the affective state induced by the contemplation of a work of art. The battle for the subordination of poetry and art in general to either theoretical or practical wisdom had long been fought and won. Poets, it was agreed, are not mere entertainers. Their power is such that they are able to mold the character of an entire nation. Reading the *Aeneid* was thus more than a matter of shedding a few idle tears over the plight of the abandoned Dido; through it one learned what it meant to be a citizen of the Roman empire. The challenge that it posed to Christian faith was not one to be readily ignored. At stake was the ultimate worth of the ideal of humanity embodied in the way of life of the pagan hero, conceived as a total way of life. Little wonder that, in spite of his deep admiration for the sheer loveliness of the *Aeneid*, Augustine should have continued to view it with suspicion. The point was not to attack art or to defend it but to determine how it could be placed in the service of an ideal that was even loftier than that to which in its unadulterated form the subtle charm of Virgil's poetry was likely to lead; a new

Aeneas and a new Dido were called for. Both were provided by the *Confessions,* where, as O'Connell notes perceptively (p. 128), Monica herself is portrayed in the guise of Aeneas's memorable lover. Augustine could not possibly foresee how future generations would react to his work, but that it should have become the most moving spiritual classic of the Western world is hardly a matter of chance. The opposition between Augustine the theorist and Augustine the practitioner, one suspects, is a figment of O'Connell's imagination or that of the revered master (H.-I. Marrou) to whose memory his engaging and otherwise highly meritorious book is thoughtfully dedicated.

Dom C. Baur. *John Chrysostom and His Time,* vol. I, *Antioch,* Sister M. Gonzaga, trans. Westminnster, Md.: The Newman Press, 1959. 399 pp.; vol. II, *Constantinople,* 1960. 488 pp.

Fourth-century Antioch was a proud and fair city, second in size only to Alexandria and equal to it in splendor and magnificence. Cicero had once extolled it as the "Queen of the East." There for the first time the faithful had been called "Christians" shortly after 40 A.D., and there St. Paul had begun his journeys. In the centuries that followed, the inroads made by Christianity were such that when the Emperor Julian arrived there, he found the famous temple of Apollo attended by a single impoverished priest with only one goose to sacrifice. Of all the scholars, exegetes, and preachers whom the city harbored in its theological heyday, none embodied its noblest aspirations more perfectly than one John, soon to be known to the world as Chrysostom because of the golden stream of his eloquence.

    Although Chrysostom seldom speaks of himself in his works, more is known about him than about any other Greek Father and no Christian doctor has found a more impressive number of biographers and panegyrists. For reasons difficult to ascertain, however, his life story has not tempted English speaking scholars in our century. In undertaking a translation of Dom Chrysostomus Baur's monumental work, *John Chrysostom and His Time,* vol. I, *Antioch* and vol. II, *Constantinople,* Sister M. Gonzaga has performed a useful and long-awaited task.

    The first volume of Baur's study covers Chrysostom's Antiochene period and deals comprehensively, in a series of short chapters, with the various phases of his activity as monk, priest, liturgist, orator, classicist, polemicist, apologist, dogmatist, and moralist. Volume II follows Chrysostom to Constantinople and treats of the events of those theologically, ecclesiastically, and politically turbulent years.

The merits of this book have been familiar to students of ancient Christian life and thought for some thirty years. Although his scholarship is impeccable, Baur was not writing strictly for specialists but for a broader circle. For that reason he has woven generous excerpts from the works of Chrysostom himself into his text in an effort to bring the personality of his hero closer to the reader. That personality has always been a subject of controversy. Chrysostom was no "diplomat" in the modern sense of the word. He had none of the worldliness of his distinguished colleagues in the priesthood. Neither the glamour nor the frownings of authority had any hold on him. Among the Greek Fathers, he was practically alone in opposing the unholy alliance between the Church and the Empire. His generally unbending attitude caused his adversaries to refer to him as a man "without knees." When his noisy dispute with the Empress Eudoxia took a turn for the worse, he did not hesitate to begin a sermon for the feast day of John the Baptist with the pointed remark that Herodias was "once again" demanding John's head on a platter. It is not surprising that Chrysostom should have made many enemies in high ecclesiastical and political places. But, as Dom Baur wisely observes, what his critics regard as his clumsy and tactless ways may be just the reverse side of his moral greatness. One thing is sure: no shepherd of souls was ever more devoted to his flock or more revered by them.

Chrysostom has never lacked admirers in the Church. Augustine hailed him as a "priest of surpassing distinction," and Aquinas, who usually knew whereof he spoke, remarked that he would have traded the entire city of Paris for Chrysostom's *Homilies on St. Matthew*. Nor is his fate deprived of an ironic twist. The latest report is that Chrysostom has become a conversation piece among Greenwich Villagers. Of all the sermons that have come down to us from antiquity few are more likely than his to appeal to the modern Christian. It is also worthy of note that, in the privileged circles where Greek still claims the allegiance of lettered men, Chrysostom continues to be read as the best representative of Christian classicism.

In a statement that Baur endorses wholeheartedly, H. Leitzman described Chrysostom as "the most charming personality among all the Greek Christian Fathers." The verdict has never been challenged to my knowledge. Sister M. Gonzaga deserves every praise for having made this towering figure more readily accessible to the English reader. The only regret that scholars will wish to express is that no attempt was made to bring Baur's own exhaustive and extremely useful bibliography up to date.

Gerhart B. Ladner. *The Idea of Reform: Its Impact on Christian Thought and Action in the Age of the Fathers.* Harvard University Press, 1959.

Despite much current interest in such prominent Patristic themes as the return to Eden or the transformation of man in the image of God, no one as yet had attempted to deal *in recto* with the vast complex of Christian renewal ideas implied in, and best expressed by, the notion of reform. Gerhart B. Ladner's timely study, *The Idea of Reform: Its Impact on Christian Thought and Action in the Age of the Fathers,* which sets forth the results of some ten years of reflection and research, fills this lacuna in a singularly thorough and competent manner. The first part of the book distinguishes the idea of reform from the cosmological, vitalistic, and millennarian renewal ideas prevalent in the ancient world, as well as from the related concepts of conversion, baptismal regeneration, and penance, which are presupposed to it but contain it only in germ. The way is thus cleared for a definition of the notion of reform, which, as Ladner understands it, is "the free, intentional and ever perfectible, multiple, prolonged and ever repeated efforts by man to assert and augment values pre-existent in the spiritual-material compound of the world (p. 35)." Part II begins with a survey of the pre-Christian, biblical, and patristic terminology of renovation and reform and goes on to discuss the various expressions of that idea in the Letters of St. Paul, in whom the early Christian renewal ideology is all but entirely rooted. There follows a detailed analysis of reform ideas of the Greek Fathers in some of their most distinctive aspects: the return to Paradise, the recovery of man's likeness to God, and the theme of the Kingdom of God—three forces which, in the author's happy phrase, "molded the sacral culture of the Byzantine world (p. 82)." Ladner then proceeds to examine the reformative elements in the works of the Latin writers, in the liturgical texts, and in Canon Law. The investigation reveals, among other things, that Western thought is characterized from Tertullian forward by its emphasis on the idea of a renewal for the better (*renovatio in melius*), over and above the mere return to paradisiac innocence; by its profound and equally fruitful doctrine of the felicitous fault—the famous *felix culpa* of the liturgy— formulated explicitly for the first time by St. Ambrose; by its courageous and epochal efforts to dissociate the notion of the Kingdom of God from that of the earthly Basileia of Constantine and his followers; and, during the later period, by its marked preference for the theme of the *Civitas Dei* or Heavenly City, with its strong social and communal connotations, as opposed to that of kingly rule favored by the Greek tradition. Part III deals appropriately with monasticism as a vehicle for reform and with the presence of reform elements in the ideal pursued by monks, priests, and presence of reform elements in the ideal pursued by monks, priests, and pious laymen known to the ancient world as *conversi.*

These brief remarks do not begin to do justice to a book which moves with ease and clarity through an extraordinary variety of intricate and sometimes controversial problems such as Augustine's notion of time, his concept of the two cities, the reform ideas inherent in his educational program, the pre-eminence of the priestly office over that of the lay ruler, the notion of the soul as the mirror of God, the monasticization of the clergy in the West, the relation of innovation to tradition implied in Pope Stephen I's celebrated formula, *Nihil innovandum nisi quod traditum est,* and a host of other theologically and historically relevant doctrines around which large segments of patristic thought gravitate. Oppositions and subtle shades of meaning are indicated but never forced or distorted. Thus Ladner is careful to observe that the idea of renewal for the better is not totally foreign to Greek thought or, for that matter, that the deification theology of the Greeks is not altogether absent from the works of the Latin writers. What is even rarer among historians, he is fully aware of the philosophical implications of his method, as Appendices I and II on "The Definition of an Idea" and "Metahistorical Conceptions" clearly demonstrate.

The theme that Ladner has chosen to explore is not only coeval with Christianity; it lies at its very heart. The life of the soul, as the Church Fathers saw it, is not a state but a dynamic situation characterized by unceasing progress, indeed, not just an *extasis* or going out of oneself but an *epektasis* or perpetual going beyond oneself in the direction of an ever more perfect God-likeness. Such is the view which St. Paul advances in an often quoted passage of Phil. 3:12-14, and which Gregory of Nyssa expressed in a nutshell when he suggested that "to find God is to seek Him endlessly." Reform in this sense, Ladner reminds us, is above all personal an individual reform. The concept of Church reform with which it is so inextricably bound up in the modern mind is alien to Christian antiquity and does not make its appearance until the time of Gregory VII. It is not surprising, nevertheless, that in their efforts to promote a restoration within the precincts of the Faith, the medieval reformers should have drawn extensively upon the vast repertory of personal renewal ideas found in the works of the Fathers. It is not surprising either that the same ideas should already have played a prominent part in the rise of monasticism, which first comes into sight in the second half of the third century and at the beginning of the fourth century as a reaction against, and a compensation for, the dangers besetting a now officially recognized and increasingly worldly Christianity. Ladner's treatment of the leading principles and various facets of the monastic life is admirable, as usual. Oddly enough, however, his book contains but few allusions to the first great monastic document of the ancient world, Athanasius's *Life of St. Antony,* which is entirely governed by the notion of progressive reform, and which remained to the last one of its most vivid illustrations.

Ladner rightly insists that the ideal embodied in the concept of reform possesses a specifically Christian flavor and owes little or nothing to pagan thought. This is not to deny that the Christian writers were influenced in various ways by contemporary philosophy. Ladner himself detects certain terminological resemblances between Basil or Gregory of Nyssa, for example, and Plotinus. It may be interesting to note that in his treatise *On Virginity,* 12, Gregory has, in fact, not only stolen a few words or phrases from Plotinus but practically lifted a whole section out of *Enneads* I.6.5. Yet just how Christian a Christian remains even when he plagiarizes a pagan may be seen by comparing the two passages in question. Like Plotinus and in the very same terms, Gregory describes at length the purification of the soul and its ascent toward God. But whereas the pagan philosopher had asserted that "this attempt to win back his grace must be man's business," Gregory proclaims that it is most emphatically "not man's business but the great gift of God." It would be difficult to state more concisely and more effectively the vast distance that continues to separate the two ideals even when they appear to be most closely related to each other.

There can be little doubt that reform in the Ladnerian acceptation, although adumbrated in the Old Testament, is properly a Neo-Testamentary and more specifically Pauline notion. For that reason the author may be justified in restricting the investigation of its sources to the New Testament writers. Having gained this much, the present reviewer cannot help feeling that he would have added new depth to his study by examining systematically not only the typological or prophetic aspects of the Old Testament but certain key notions such as that of "return," with all its highly original implications. It is significant that there is no Hebrew word for progress in the Old Testament. The ideal preached by the prophets is defined almost invariably by the notion of restoration or return, as in Amos 4:8-11, Isaiah 1:24ff, and Jeremiah 30:20. The last of the three prophets just mentioned may not have hit upon the idea of reform in its strictest sense when, anticipating a state in which the youngest and most recent would coincide with the oldest and the best, he predicted nostalgically that the children of Israel would be as aforetime; but he came close to it and paved the way for its definitive formulation in New Testament times.

Experience has shown more than once that it is perilous to deal with a whole period through the instrumentality of a single category, however broad and comprehensive that category may be. Ladner makes no such claim for the idea of reform. Yet it could well be that he has found in that idea a kind of Archimedean point with which to lift the world of patristic thought. His solidly structured, superbly documented, and delicately balanced synthesis has all the earmarks of a great book.

Paul Aubin. *Le Problème de la "conversion": étude sur un thème commun à l'hellénisme et au christianisme des trois premiers siècles.* Paris: Beauchesne, 1963. 236 pp.

Paul Aubin's book, *Le Problème de la "conversion": étude sur un thème commun à l'hellénisme et au christianisme des trois premiers siècles,* inaugurates auspiciously a new series entitled "Théologie Historique," published by the Faculty of Theology of the Catholic Institute in Paris and directed by its dean, Père Jean Daniélou. The book belongs to the same category as those of Rahner and Grant in that it deals with a notion on which early Christian thought and pagan philosophy frequently intersect. Unlike the classic studies of the late A. D. Nock and G. Bardy on the same subject, Aubin has limited himself to the use of the word *epistrophê* ("conversion") in the philosophic and religious writings of the first three centuries. He has examined and classified some 1,300 texts in which the term occurs, with a wide variety of meanings. His repertory for that period comes as close to being exhaustive as anyone could possibly hope. To this list have been added some 200 samplings from the fourth and fifth centuries, which lay outside the scope of his study and are only intended as a useful complement to it. As regards these later texts, his conclusion is that in them the word *epistrophê* did not take on any radically new meanings but simply acquired a greater psychological depth.

Beneath the purely linguistic aspect of Aubin's study lies the deeper issue of the spiritual values proper to Christianity and their repercussions on human existence. The results of his painstaking analysis show that the word "conversion" and its content stem mainly from the Septuagint, where *epistrophê* translates *shûe,* the term used by the Hebrew Bible to express the notion of a return to God. To return in the biblical sense is not simply to revert to one's point of departure. It means to return in the emphatic sense, or to turn from the wrong way to the right way after having abandoned it. Such a return consists essentially in giving up one's attitude of rebellion against God in favor of an attitude of total dependence upon God. In the works of the Christian authors, as opposed to the pagan authors, "conversion" is closely allied to *metanoia* or repentance. It frequently assumes an ecclesial connotation: one converts in and to the Church, and the Church itself is converted or turned toward God. It also takes on an apostolic aspect, for Christians are those who cannot be indifferent to the plight of their fellow human beings and must therefore work for their "conversion." Whereas in the Old Testament the end of this conversion is the adherence to the Covenant and a renewed fidelity to the Mosaic Law, for the Christian the end is in the final analysis the new and eternal covenant, which finds its fulfillment in afterlife. Throughout his work, Aubin repeatedly stresses the vast distance that separates philosophic conversion from religious and Christian conversion. For a Christian, *epistrophê* is never, as it was for the pagan philosophers, a conversion toward oneself and toward what is highest in oneself (e.g., philosophic contemplation) but perfect union with God. More importantly, in the New Testament view, God himself converts or turns toward man and converts man toward himself. Both notions, needless to say, are totally foreign to pagan thought.

It was all the more important to be reminded of these ideas since the traditional notion of conversion, both in its biblical and in its philosophic acceptations, has ceased to play a significant role in modern thought, where it was replaced at an early date by the mere transition from unenlightened to enlightened self-interest. Unfortunately, by focusing his attention exclusively on the word *epistrophê*, Aubin has singularly limited the scope of his inquiry, especially since the Greek possesses a number of synonyms and derivatives often used to express this concept. He was thus led to minimize the importance of certain crucial texts, such as the allegory of the cave in Plato's *Republic*, in which the highest education (that of the philosopher) is described as a conversion or turning around of the soul (*peristrophê*) from the world of shadows or opinion to that of genuine knowledge. It is this famous analogy, one suspects, that underlies and in large measure explains all later philosophic disquisitions on the common theme of the tropisms of the soul.

Hugo Rahner. *Greek Myth and Christian Mystery*, trans. Brian Battershaw. New York: Harper and Row, 1963. 399 pp.

The long overdue translation of Hugo Rahner's book, *Greek Myth and Christian Mystery*, represents a major contribution to the timely subject of Christian humanism, as it is sometimes called. The Christian message was originally revealed to Semites and expressed in forms and modes proper to the Semitic mentality. In order to penetrate into the Greco-Roman world, it had to be cloaked in the distinctive speech and images of an altogether new category of hearers. Rahner's essay illustrates by a series of concrete examples the process by which the early Christian writers seized upon some of the most famous literary themes of classical antiquity and used them as a vehicle to convey the new and more sublime truths of Christianity. The first chapter, which lays the theoretical foundation for the rest of the book, assesses the different theories proposed by modern scholars to explain the relationship between the pagan and Christian mysteries and goes on to sketch the evolution of the pagan mystery cults throughout the pre-Christian and Christian periods. In accordance with the findings of recent scholarship, the author rejects the once popular thesis that Christianity was genetically derived from, and hence essentially dependent upon, these pagan cults. At the same time he is eager to show that, since the Christian message is addressed to human beings, it cannot be conceived as something purely eschatological or otherworldly but must bear some similarity to the world of human reality and values. It is precisely these similarities, often suggested by the Bible itself, that enabled the Church Fathers to forge definite links between the biblical message and pagan religion and to use the pagan myths as an effective *paideia* toward Christ.

The chapters that follow are devoted to an examination of specific themes and images originally belonging to the cultural apparatus of Greece and subsequently christianized by the Church Fathers. Thus, in the works of the latter, the cosmic cross of the pagan authors, with its arms extended in the four directions of the universe, becomes a prefiguration of the mystery of Christ recapitulating the work of creation. The mystery of the *ogdoad* or number eight, the old Pythagorean symbol of perfection and rest, serves to express the hidden realities of baptism. The sun and moon cults of the ancient civilizations are referred back respectively to the historical Jesus, the "sun of righteousness" (Mal. 4:2) or the "dayspring from on high" (Luke 1:78), and to Mary and the Church; the soulhealing moly of the god Hermes serves as a reminder that the soul can only be healed through obedience to a higher power. The mandrake, Circe's poison, an antitype of the moly, is promoted to the rank of a health-giving and beneficent flower which is compared to the virtues of the saints. The "fruit-destroying willow," which reproduces itself not through seeding and fruit but through the hidden power of its roots, is seen as a symbol of sexual continence, of death and life mysteriously united.

By far the most popular of the old Greek myths was the legend of Odysseus, and none seemed better suited to express the mystery of the Christian life. Accordingly, the last part of Rahner's book traces the various stages of the canonization both of Homer and of his hero, Odysseus, whose voyage back to Ithaca portrayed for the Hellenistic Christian the soul's long journey amid the perils of this world. The Sirens, who as the result of a gross mistranslation happened to be mentioned in the Septuagint, became the emblems both of deadly lust and of deadly knowledge. The mast to which Odysseus was tied typified the Cross with all its mystic power, and the ship that carried him and his companions across their tideless sea became an image of the Church. In time, Homer himself was transformed into a seer whose blind eyes were able to discern in advance the message of the Logos to come.

The use of these symbols was dictated in many cases not by purely practical or esthetic considerations but by "reasons" that lay hidden within the recesses of the human soul, a fact which accounts both for their extraordinary richness and for their limitations. To explain this peculiar logic, Rahner has made intelligent use of modern experimental (specifically Jungian) psychology. Each symbol could and usually did take on a variety of meanings from one author to another and very often in a single author. Odysseus journeying to Ithaca represented the Christian soul longing for the port of eternity; but he could just as well symbolize man's attachment to the things of this world, as he does for Clement of Alexandria. One need not add that this attempt to translate the realities of Christianity into a new medium was fraught with dangers. The Church Fathers were fully aware of these dangers, but for them the risk was, to use Plato's expression, a noble one and one well worth taking.

Not everything in Rahner's book is new, but even when the author touches upon well-known themes, he always manages to add to our knowledge of them or to cast them into a more vivid light. His essay brings out with remarkable lucidity and penetration the uniqueness and transcendence of Christianity fulfilling all that was of permanent value in the piety of Hellas. It puts us into immediate contact with the magnanimous gesture by which the Church claimed the noblest heritage of Greece as her own, and, without compromising her principles or lapsing into syncretism, attempted to fetch everything home to Christ. When the Christians turned to the works of the pagan writers, they did so not as seekers after a treasure but as possessors of a treasure that they were eager to share with others. Their ultimate purpose was to rescue from the world of pagan culture what they regarded as elements of unconscious Christianity imbedded in it.

The dust jacket quotes Mircea Eliade as saying that "this is without doubt one of the most important books published in the last ten years." We might add that it is also a beautiful book, written with grace and distinction, and betraying a knowledge bred of long and assiduous commerce with the authors of antiquity. Living as he does in a disenchanted and desacralized world, the modern reader may find these Christian interpretations of the old pagan myths remote from his daily concerns and foreign to his own universe of thought. Rahner's book may help him to catch a glimpse of the beauty that most of us have forgotten and for which we continue to long secretly. More importantly, it illustrates what the Church itself does when in its liturgical and sacramental catechesis it continues to clothe its teachings in symbols borrowed from the world of nature or from Old Testament history. Finally, the book enables us to understand how, by this intelligent adaptation to a new cultural milieu, Christianity succeeded in being both timely and timeless, how it was able to remain traditional without becoming traditionalist. By the same token, it suggests the type of effort that must be made today if Christianity is to become incarnate in the emergent civilization that it is once again called upon to redeem.

SELECT BIBLIOGRAPHY

1. Editions of Early Christian Writings in the Original Languages.
(A standard abbreviation follows each entry.)

Bibliothèque Augustinienne (Oeuvres de Saint Augustin). Paris: Etudes Augustiniennes, 1947ff. This edition has a French translation on the facing page. BA

Corpus Christianorum, Series Latina. Turnhaut, Belgium: Brepols, 1953ff. CCL

Corpus Scriptorum Christianorum Orientalium. Louvain, 1903ff. CSCO

Corpus Scriptorum Ecclesiasticorum Latinorum. Vienna, 1866ff. CSEL

Loeb Classical Library. London and Cambridge, MA: Harvard University Press, 1912ff. This edition has an English translation on the facing page. It only contains a few texts of early Christian writers. LCL

Patrologiae Cursus Completus, Series Latina. 222 volumes in-quarto. Edited by J.-P. Migne Paris, 1844-1855. PL

Patrologiae Cursus Completus, Series Graeca. 168 volumes in-quarto Edited by J.-P. Migne. Paris, 1857-1868. This edition has a Latin translation. PG

Patrologiae Latinae Supplementum, 5 volumes in-quarto. Edited by A. Hamman. Paris, 1958-1974. PLS

Sources chrétiennes. Paris, 1942ff. This edition has a French translation on the facing page. SC

2. English Editions of Early Christian Writings, in Series (A standard abbreviation follows each entry.)

Ancient Christian Writers. New York, NY and Mahwah, NJ: Paulist Press, 1946ff. ACW

The Ante-Nicene Fathers. Buffalo, NY, 1885-1896. Reprinted by William B. Eerdmanns Publishing Co. of Grand Rapids, MI, 1951-1956. ANF

The Catholic University of America Patristic Studies. Washington, DC: The Catholic University of America Press, 1922ff. CUA or PSt

The Fathers of the Church. Washington, DC: The Catholic University of America Press, 1947ff. FC

The Library of Christian Classics. Philadelphia: Westminster, 1953ff. LCC

A Library of the Fathers of the Holy Catholic Church. Oxford, 1838-1858. LF

A Select Library of Nicene and Post-Nicene Fathers of the Christian Church. First Series. Edited by Philip Schaff. Buffalo, NY, 1886ff. Reprinted by William B. Eerdmans Publishing Co. in 1956. NPN

A Select Library of Nicene and Post Nicene Fathers of the Christian Church. Second Series. Edited by Philip Schaff and Henry Wace. New York, 1890ff. Reprinted by William B. Eerdmans Publishing Co. in 1956. NPN, 2nd Ser.

The Works of Saint Augustine, A Translation for the 21st Century. Edited by John E. Rotelle. Hyde Park, NY: New City Press, 1990ff. This new series will eventually publish the complete works of Augustine in English. WSA

3. Editions of St. Augustine's Writings in Series

The following list is a complete record of St. Augustine's writings that are published as part of a series in the original Latin or in English translation. A few works are still not available in English. Augustine's works are listed alphabetically according to the Latin title. The English title in parentheses immediately follows the publication information on the Latin text. Standard abbreviations, as noted in sections 1 and 2, are used to identify the publisher of each work. *Patrology*, volume IV, edited by Angelo Berardino with an introduction by Johannes Quasten, is an invaluable source for publication details and other information on each of St. Augustine's works. With a few exceptions, the dates listed are those indicated in the Berardino volume. For more information on the dates of Augustine's works cf. S. Zarb, *Chronologia operum sancti Augustini* Rome, 1934; and A. M. Bonnardière, *Recherches de chronologie Augustinienne*, Paris: Etudes augustiniennes, 1965.

392 *Acta contra Fortunatum Manichaeum* BA 17; CSEL 25, 1; PL 42
    (*Proceedings against Fortunatus, the Manichean*) NPN 4
399 *Ad catechumenos de symbolo* CCL 46; PL 40
    (*To the Catechumens, on the Creed*) FC 27; NPN 3
415 *Ad Hieronymum presbyterum* or *Epistulae* 166-167 CSEL 44; PL 33
    (*To the Priest Jerome* or *Letters 166-167*) FC 30
c. 400 *Ad inquisitionem Januarii* or *Epistulae* 54-55 CSEL 34; PL 33
    (*In Answer to the Inquiries of Januarius*) FC 12
399 *Adnotationes in Iob* CSEL 28,3; PL 34
    (*Notes on Job*)
415 *Ad Orosium contra Priscillanistas et Origenistas* CCL 49; PL 42
    (*To Orosius, against the Priscillianists and the Origenists*)
c. 411 *Breviculus collationis cum Donatistas* CCL 149; CSEL 153;
    PL 43
    (*An abridgement of the Conference with the Donatists*)
c. 427 *Collatio cum Maximino Arianorum* PL 42
    (*A conference with Maximinus, Bishop of the Arians*)
397-400 *Confessiones* BA 13-14; CCL 27; CSEL 33; LCL (2 volumes);
    PL 32
    (*The Confessions*) FC 21; LCC 7; LCL (2 volumes); NPN 1
386-387 *Contra Academicos* or *De Academicis* BA 4; CCL 29;
    CSEL 63; PL 32
    (*Against the Academics* or *Answer to Sceptics* or *On the Academics*)
    ACW 12; FC 5
392 *Contra Adimantum Manichaei discipulum* BA 17; CSEL 25,1;
    PL 42
    (*Against Adimantus, a Disciple of Manicheus* or *Mani*)
c. 420 *Contra adversarium legis et prophetarum* CCL 49; PL 42
    (*Against an Adversary of the Law and the Prophets*)
c. 405-406 *Contra Cresconium grammaticum partis Donati* CSEL 52;
    PL 43
    (*Against Cresconius, a grammarian of the Donatist party*)
c. 420 *Contra duas epistulas Pelagianorum* BA 23; CSEL 60; PL 44
    (*Against Two Letters of the Pelagians*) NPN 5
400 *Contra epistulam Parmeniani* CSEL 51; PL 43
    (*Against a Letter of Parmenian*)
c. 396 *Contra epistulam Manichaei quam vocant fundamenti* CSEL 25,1;
    PL 42
    (*Against the letter of Mani which is called "the foundation"*) NPN 4
397-398 *Contra Faustum Manichaeum* BA 17; CSEL 25,1; PL 42
    (*Against Faustus, the Manichean*) NPN 4
397-98 *Contra Felicem Manichaeum* BA 17; CSEL 25,1; PL 42
    (*Against Felix, the Manichean*) NPN 4

?   *Contra Gaudentium donatistarum episcopum* BA 32; CSEL 53; PL 43
   (*Against Gaudentius, Bishop of the Donatists*)
c. 421 *Contra Iulianum* PL 44
   (*Against Julian*) FC 35
398-401 *Contra litteras Petiliani* BA 30; CSEL 52; PL 43
   (*Against a Letter of Petilian*) NPN 4
428 *Contra Maximinum Arianum* PL 42
   (*Against Maximinus the Arian*)
420-21 *Contra mendacium* BA 2; CSEL 41; PL 40
   (*Against Lying*) FC 16; NPN 3
428-430 *Contra secundam Iuliani responsionem opus imperfectum* CSEL 85; PL 45
   (*Unfinished Work against Julian's Second Response*)
399 *Contra Secundinum Manichaeum* BA 17; CSEL 25,2; PL 42
   (*Against Secundinus, the Manichean*)
418 *Contra sermonem Arianorum* PL 42
   (*Against a Sermon of the Arians*)
404 *De actis cum Felice Manichaeo* BA 17; CSEL 25; PL 42
   (*Concerning Proceedings with Felix the Manichean*)
c. 396 *De agone christiano* BA1; CSEL 41; PL40
   (*On Christian Combat*) FC 2
   ?   *De anima et eius origine* CSEL 60; PL 44
   (*On the Soul and Its Origins*) NPN 5
c. 400 *De baptismo, contra Donatistas* BA 29; CSEL 51; PL 43
   (*On Baptism, against the Donatists*) NPN 4
386-87 *De beata vita* BA 4 AND 4/1; CCL 29; CSEL 63; PL 32
   (*On the Happy Life*) FC 5; PSt 72
c. 401 *De bono conjugali* BA 2; CSEL 41; PL 40
   (*On the Good of Marriage*) FC 27; NPN 3
414 *De bono viduitatis* BA 3; CSEL 41; PL 40
   (*The Good* or *Excellence of Widowhood*) FC 16; NPN 3
399 *De catechizandis rudibus* BA 11; CCL 46; PL 40
   (*The First Catechetical Instruction* or *On Catechizing the Unlearned* or *Uninstructed*) ACW 2; NPN 3; PSt 8
413-426 *De civitate Dei* BA 33-37; CCL 47-48; CSEL 40; LCC (7 volumes; PL 41
   (*The City of God*) FC 8,14,24; LCC (7 volumes); NPN 2
c. 420 *De coniugiis adulterinis* BA 2; CSEL 41; PL 40
   (*Adulterous Marriages*) FC 27
c. 400 *De consensu evangelistarum* CSEL 43; PL 42
   (*On the Harmony of the Evangelists*) NPN 6
After 412 *De continentia* BA 3; CSEL 41; PL 40

(*On Continence*) FC 16; NPN 3

417 *De correptione Donatistarum* or *Epistula* 185 CSEL 57,2; PL 33
   (*On the Coercion of the Donatists* or *Letter 185*) FC 30; NPN 4

c. 426 *De correptione et gratia* BA 24; PL 44
   (*Admonition and Grace* or *On Rebuke and Grace*) FC 2; NPN 5

424-25 *De cura pro mortuis gerenda* BA 2; CSEL 41; PL 40
   (*On the Care to Be Taken for the Dead*) FC 27; NPN 3

After 4 April 397 *De diversis quaestionibus ad Simplicianum* BA 10;
   CCL 44; PL 40
   (*To Simplicianus on Various Questions*) LCC 6

388-396 *De diversis quaestionibus LXXXIII* BA 10; CCL 44A; PL 40
   (*On Eighty-three Different Questions*) FC 70

406-408 *De divinatione daemonum* BA 10; CSEL 41; PL 40
   (*On the Divination of the Demons*) FC 27

397, 426-27 *De doctrina christiana* CCL 32
   (*Christian Instruction* or *On Christian Doctrine*) FC 2; NPN 2

?   *De dono perseverantiae* BA 24; PL 45
   (*On the Gift of Perseverance*) FC 86; NPN 5; PSt 91

392 *De duabus animabus* BA 17; CSEL 25,1; PL 42
   (*On the Two Souls*) NPN 4

413 *De fide et operibus* BA 8; CSEL 41; PL 40
   (*On Faith and Works*) ACW 48; FC 27

393 *De fide et symbolo* BA 9; CSEL 41; PL 40
   (*On Faith and the Creed*) FC 27; LCC 6; NPN 3

After 399 *De fide rerum quae non videntur* BA 8; CCL 46; PL 40
   (*On Faith in Things Unseen*) FC 4; NPN 3; PSt 84

401-415 *De Genesi ad litteram* BA 48-49; CSEL 28, 1; PL 34
   (*On the Literal Meaning of Genesis*) ACW 41,42

393 *De Genesi ad litteram liber imperfectus* CSEL 28,1; PL 34
   (*An Unfinished Book on the Literal Meaning of Genesis*) FC 84

c. 389 *De Genesi adversus Manichaeos* PL 34
   (*On Genesis, against the Manicheans*) FC 84

417 *De gestis Pelagii* BA 21; CSEL 42; PL 44
   (*On the Proceedings of Pelagius*) FC 86; NPN 5

418 *De gratia Christi et peccato originale* BA 22; CSEL 42; PL 44
   (*On the Grace of Christ and Original Sin*) NPN 5

c. 425 *De gratia et libero arbitrio* BA 24; PL 44
   (*On Grace and Free Will*) FC 59; NPN 5

c. 412 *De gratia novi testamenti ad Honoratum* CSEL 44; PL 33
   (*To Honoratus on the Grace of the New Testament*) FC 20

428-429 *De Haeresibus* CCL 46; PL 42
   (*On Heresies*) PSt 90

387 *De immortalitate animae* BA 5; PL 32

(*On the Immortality of the Soul*) FC 4; PSt 90

388,391-395 *De libero arbitrio* BA 6; CCL 29; CSEL 74; PL 32
(*On Free Choice of the Will*) ACW 22; FC 59

388-391 *De magistro* BA 6; CCL 29; PL 32
(*On the Teacher*) ACW 9; FC 59; LCC 6

395 *De mendacio* BA 2; CSEL 41; PL 40
(*On lying*) FC 16

388-389 *De moribus ecclesiae catholicae, et de moribus Manichaeorum*
BA 1; PL 32
(*The Catholic and Manichean Ways of Life* or *On the Way of Life of
the Catholic Church and the Way of Life of the Manicheans*) FC 56;
NPN 4

388-89 *De musica* BA 7; PL 32
(*On Music*) FC 4

399 *De natura boni* BA 1; CSEL 25, 2; PL 42
(*On the Nature of the Good*) LCC 6; NPN 4; PSt 88

415 *De natura et gratia* BA 21; CSEL 60; PL 44
(*On Nature and Grace*) FC 86; NPN 5

Between 419-420 *De nuptiis et concupiscentia* BA 23; CSEL 42; PL 44
(*On Marriage and Concupiscence*) NPN 5

c. 415 *De natura et gratia* BA 21; CSEL 60; PL 44
(*On Nature and Grace*) FC 86; NPN 5

c. 426 *De octo Dulcitii questionibus* BA 10; CCL 44A; PL 40
(*On the Eight Questions of Dulcitius*) FC 16

? *De octo questionibus ex vetere testamento* CCL 33; PL 35
(*Eight Questions out of the Old Testament*)

401 *De opere monachorum* BA 3; CSEL 41; PL 40
(*On the the Work of Monks*) FC 16; NPN 3

386-387 *De ordine* BA 4; CCL 29; CSEL 63; PL 32
(*On Order*) FC 5

415 *De patientia* BA 2; CSEL 41; PL 40
(*On Patience)* FC 16; NPN 3

412 *De peccatorum meritis et remissione* CSEL 60; PL 44
(*On the Consequences and Forgiveness of Sins*) NPN 5

c. 415 *De perfectione iustitiae hominis* BA 21; CSEL 42; PL 44
(*On the Perfection of Human Righteousness*) NPN 5

429 *De praedestinatione sanctorum* BA 24; PL 44
(*On the Predestination of the Saints*) FC 86; NPN 5

417 *De praesentia Dei* or *Epistula* 187 CSEL 57; PL 33
(*On the Presence of God* or *Letter* 187) FC 30

387 or 388 *De quantitate animae* BA 5; PL 32
(*The Magnitude* or *Greatness* or *Quality of the Soul*) ACW 9; FC 4

c. 401 *De sancta virginitate*

(*On Holy Virginity*) FC 27; NPN 3

415 *De sententia Iacobi* or *Epistula* 167 PL33
(*Concerning Jacob*) FC 30

391-394 *De sermone Domini in monte* CCL; 35; PL 34
(*On the Lord's Sermon on the Mount*) ACW 5; FC 11; NPN 6

c. 412 *De spiritu et littera ad Marcellinum* CSEL 60; PL 44
(*On the Spirit and the Letter to Marcellinus*) LCC 8; NPN 5

399-420 *De trinitate* BA 15-16; CCL 50, 50A; PL 42
(*On the Trinity*) FC 45; LCC 8, WSA; NPN 3

c. 411 *De unico baptismo contra Petilianum* BA 31; CSEL 53; PL 43
(*On One Baptism, against Petilian*)

Between 398-401 *De unitate ecclesiae* or *Epistula ad catholicos de secta donatistarum* BA 28; CSEL 52; PL 43
(*Concerning the Unity of the Church*)

391 *De utilitate credendi* BA 2; CSEL 25,1; PL 42
(*On the Advantage* or *Usefulness of Believing*) FC 4; LCC 6; NPN 3

408-412 *De utilitate ieiunii* BA 2; CCL 46; PL 40
(*The Usefulness of Fasting*) FC 16; PSt 85

390 *De vera religione* BA 8; CCL 32; CSEL 77; PL 34
(*On the True Religion*) CC 6

413 *De videndo Deo* (*Epistula* 147) CSEL 57; PL 33
(*On the Vision of God*) FC 20

392-420 *Enarrationes in psalmos* CCL 38-40; PL 36-37
(*Expositions on the Psalms*) ACW 29,30; NPN 8

421 *Enchiridium ad Laurentium* or *De fide spe et caritate* BA 9; CCL 46; PL 40
(*Enchiridion* or *Faith, Hope and Charity*) LCC7; FC 2; ACW 3; NPN 3

386-430 *Epistulae* BA 46B; CSEL 34, 44, 57, 58; LCC (selected letters); PL 33
(*Letters*) 1-82 FC 12; NPN 1
(*Letters*) 83-130 FC 18; NPN 1
(*Letters*) 131-164 FC 20; NPN 1
(*Letters*) 165-203 FC 30; NPN 1
(*Letters*) 204-270 FC 32; NPN 1
(*Letters*) LCC
Select Letters LCC

? *Epistulae ad Romanos inchoata expositio* CSEL 84; PL 35
(*An Unfinished Exposition of the Epistle to the Romans*)

? *Expositio LXXXIV propositionum ex epistola ad Romanos* CSEL 84; PL 35
(*Exposition of 84 Propositions Concerning the Epistle to the Romans*)

? *Expositio epistulae ad Galatas* CSEL 84; PL 35

(*An Explanation of the Epistle to the Galatians*)

418 *Gesta cum Emerito Donatista* BA 32; CSEL 53; PL 43
These are minutes of meeting that took place between the Donatist Emeritus, and Augustine on September 20, 418.

? *Locutionum in Heptateuchum* CCL 33; CSEL 28,2; PL 34
(*Of Expressions in the First Seven Books of the Bible*)

c. 411 *Post collationem contra Donatistas* CSEL 53; PL43
(*Against the Donatists after the Conference of 411*)

? *Psalmus contra partem Donati* BA 28; CSEL 51; PL 43
(*A Psalm against the Donatist Party*)

? *Quaestiones Evangeliorum* CCL 44B; PL 35
(*Questions on the Gospels*)

Between 406-412 *Quaestiones expositae contra paganos* VI or *Epistula* 102 CSEL 34,2; PL 33
(*An Explanation of Six Questions against the Pagans*) FC 18

419 *Quaestionum in heptateuchum* CCL 33; CSEL 28,3; PL 34
(*Questions on the Heptateuch*)

? *Quaestionum septemdecim in Evangelium Matthaeum* CCL 44b; PL 34
(*Seventeen Questions in the Gospel of Matthew*)

? *Regula ad servos Dei* PL 32
(*The Rule of Saint Augustine*)

426-427 *Retractationes* BA 12; CCL 57; CSEL 36; PL 32
(*The Retractions*) FC 60

c. 418 *Sermo ad Caesariensis ecclesiae plebem* CSEL 53; PL 43
(*Sermon to the People of the Caesarean Church*)

? *Sermo ad catechumenos de symbolo* CCL 46; PL 40
(*Sermon to Catechumens on the Creed*) FC 27; NPN 3

398 *Sermo de disciplina christiana* CCL 46; PL 40
(*Sermon on the Christian Life*) FC 16

c. 410 *Sermo de urbis excidio* CCL 46; PL 40
(*Sermon on the Destruction of the City*) PSt 89

? *Sermo de utilitate ieiunii* BA 2; CCL 46; PL 40
(*Sermon on the Usefulness of Fasting*) FC 16; PSt 85

390-430 *Sermones* PL 38-39; CCL 41
(*Sermons*) FC 38; ACW 15; NPN 6; WSA (*Sermons 1-400* in 10 volumes)
Sermons for Christmas and Epiphany ACW 15

c. 386-387 *Soliloquiorum* BA5; PL 32
(*The Soliloquies*) LCC 6; FC 5; NPN 7

c. 427 *Speculum de Scriptura sacra* CSEL 12; PL 34
(This work is a collection of moral precepts from the Bible)

? *Tractatus adversus Iudaeos* PL 42

(*In Answer to the Jews*) FC 27
Between 413-418 *Tractatus in epistulam Joannis ad Parthos* PL 35
   (*Tracts on the First Epistle of John*) NPN 7; LCC 8
  ? *Tractatus in Joannis evangelium* CCL 36, 38, 39, 40; PL 35;
   BA 71, 72, 73A, 73B
   (*Tractates* or *Tracts on the Gospel of John*, 1-10) FC 78; NPN 7
   (*Tractates* or *Tracts on the Gospel of John*, 11-27) FC 79; NPN 7
   (*Tractates* or *Tracts on the Gospel of John*, 28-54) FC 88; NPN 7
   (*Tractates* or *Tracts on the Gospel of John*, 55-111) FC 90; NPN 7
   (*Tractates* or *Tracts on the Gospel of John*, 112-124) FC 92; NPN 7

4. Separate Editions of St. Augustine's Writings in Translation

The following list is a partial record of works published separately.

Against the Academics (*Contra Academicos*) and *The Teacher* (*De magistro*). Indianapolis, IN: Hackett Publishing Co., 1995

Augustine of Hippo, Selected Writings. Translated with an introduction by Mary T. Clark. New York and Mahwah, NJ: Paulist Press, 1984.

Basic Writings of Saint Augustine. 2 vols. Introduction and notes by Whitney J. Oates. New York and Toronto: Random House, 1948.

The City of God (*De civitate Dei*). Translated by M. Dodds. New York: Modern Library, 1950.

Confessions (*Confessiones*). Translated by Frank J. Sheed. Introduction by Peter Brown. Indianapolis, IN: Hackett Publishing Co., 1993.

Confessions (*Confessiones*). Translated with an Introduction and notes by Henry Chadwick. Oxford and New York: Oxford University Press, 1991.

Confessions (*Confessiones*). Volume I, Introduction and Text; Volume II, Commentary on Books 1-7; Volume III, Commentary on Books 8-13. Commentary by James J. O'Donnell. Oxford and New York: Clarendon Press, 1992.

The Confessions of St. Augustine (*Confessiones*). Translated with an introduction and notes by John K. Ryan. New York and London: Doubleday, 1960.

On Christian Doctrine (*De doctrina christiana*). Translated with an introduction by D. W. Robertson, Jr. Indianapolis and New York: The Bobbs-Merrill Company, Inc.,1958.

On Free Choice of the Will (*De libero arbitrio*). Translated by Anna S. Benjamin and L. H. Hackstaff. Introduction by L. H. Hackstaff. Indianapolis and New York: The Bobbs-Merrill Company, Inc., 1964.

On Free Choice of the Will (*De libero arbitrio*). Translated by Thomas Williams. Indianapolis, IN: Hackett Publishing Co., 1993.

Political Writings. Edited by Ernest L. Fortin and Douglas Kries.

Indianapolis, IN: Hackett Publishing Co., 1994. This is the most accurate, readable translation of well chosen selections from *De civitate Dei* (*The City of God*). It also contains selections from other writings on politics.

5. Bibliographical Tools

Bavel, T. Van. *Répertoire Bibliographique de saint Augustin,* 1950-1960. New York: Oxford University Press, 1963.

Di Berardino, Angelo, ed. *Patrology* Volume IV, The Golden Age of Latin Patristic Literature from the Council of Nicea to the Council of Chalcedon. Translated by Placid Solari, Westminster, MD: Christian Classics, Inc., 1988.

Donnelly, Dorothy F., and Mark A. Sherman. *Augustine's De civitate Dei: An Annotated Bibliography of Modern Criticism, 1960-1990.* New York: Peter Lang, 1991.

The *Revue des Etudes Augustiniennes* carries a critical bibliography of all the books and articles published each year on St. Augustine.

INDEX

ABOUT THE AUTHOR

A native of Rhode Island, Ernest L. Fortin, A.A., received his B.A. degree from Assumption College (Worcester, MA) in 1946, his Licentiate in Theology from the Angelicum (Rome) in 1950, and his Doctorate in Letters from the Sorbonne in 1955. He has also done post-doctoral work at the Ecole Pratique des Hautes Etudes (Paris) and the University of Chicago. He taught at Assumption College from 1955 to 1970, and as a part-time visiting professor of philosophy at Laval University from 1965 to 1972. Since 1971 he has been teaching theology and political theory at Boston College, where he also co-directs (with C. Bruell) the Institute for the Study of Politics and Religion. He has lectured widely to scholarly audiences both in America and in Europe. His publications include *Christianisme et culture philosophique au cinquième siècle: la querelle de l' âme humaine en Occident* (Paris, 1959); *Medieval Political Philosophy: a Sourcebook,* edited with M. Mahdi and R. Lerner (New York, 1963); *Dissidence et philosophie au moyen âge: Dante et ses antécédents* (Paris and Montreal, 1981); *Dantes Göttliche Komödie als Utopie* (Munich, 1991), and *Augustine: Political Writings,* edited with D. Kries (Indianapolis, 1994). His articles, review articles, and book reviews have appeared in a wide variety of professional journals and symposia. An English translation, with an introduction and notes, of Thomas Aquinas's *Commentary on the Politics of Aristotle* is scheduled to appear in 1997.

ABOUT THE EDITOR

J. Brian Benestad is professor of theology at the University of Scranton, a Jesuit University in Northeastern Pennsylvania. He has been teaching at Scranton since the fall of 1976. A native of New York City, he received his B.A. from Assumption College in 1963, a Licentiate in Theology from the Gregorian University (Rome) in 1968, and a Ph.D. in political science from Boston College in 1979. In 1981 he co-edited a collection of the U.S. bishop's policy statements issued between 1966 and 1980, and authored *The Pursuit of a Just Social Order* (1982). Most recently he completed an article entitled "Ordinary Virtue as Heroism," published in *Seedbeds of Virtue*, edited by Mary Ann Glendon and David Blankenhorn.